1999

THE EARLY ELIZABETHAN POLITY

Traditionally historians have argued that the court of Elizabeth I (1558–1603) was factional, divided between competing subjects who were manipulated by their Queen. This book provides a different account: of councillors who were united by two connected dangers, namely Catholic opposition to Protestant England and Elizabeth's refusal to marry or to settle England's succession.

This new account of the first decade of Elizabeth's reign investigates three main areas. It challenges the notion that Elizabeth I and her councillors agreed on policy, and that the Queen and her Secretary, William Cecil, formed an inseparable political partnership; it establishes the importance of rhetorical training and the relationship between education and Elizabethan debates on the issue of service to the Queen, balanced against service to the commonwealth; and it deals with the radical political conditions of the first decade, and argues that the origins of later Elizabethan crisis lay in the 1560s.

The book both represents an innovative blend of solid research in the Tudor archives, above all the papers of William Cecil, and demonstrates sensitivity to language and political culture and an awareness of the British and European dimensions of the period. It will become required reading for historians of Elizabethan England, shedding new light on the 'problem of Britain' in the latter half of the sixteenth century.

STEPHEN ALFORD is British Academy Postdoctoral Research Fellow and Research Fellow of Fitzwilliam College, Cambridge.

Cambridge Studies in Early Modern British History

Series editors

ANTHONY FLETCHER
Professor of History, University of Essex

JOHN GUY
Professor of Modern History, University of St Andrews

JOHN MORRILL
*Reader in Early Modern History, University of Cambridge,
and Vice Master of Selwyn College*

This is a series of monographs and studies covering many aspects of the history of the British Isles between the late fifteenth century and early eighteenth century. It includes the work of established scholars and pioneering work by a new generation of scholars. It includes both reviews and revisions of major topics and books which open up new historical terrain or which reveal startling new perspectives on familiar subjects. All the volumes set detailed research into broader perspectives and the books are intended for the use of students as well as of their teachers.

For a list of titles in the series, see end of book.

THE EARLY
ELIZABETHAN POLITY

*William Cecil and
the British Succession Crisis,
1558–1569*

STEPHEN ALFORD

CAMBRIDGE
UNIVERSITY PRESS

PUBLISHED BY THE PRESS SYNDICATE OF THE UNIVERSITY OF CAMBRIDGE
The Pitt Building, Trumpington Street, Cambridge CB2 1RP, United Kingdom

CAMBRIDGE UNIVERSITY PRESS
The Edinburgh Building, Cambridge CB2 2RU, United Kingdom
http://www.cup.cam.ac.uk
40 West 20th Street, New York, NY 10011–4211, USA   http://www.cup.org
10 Stamford Road, Oakleigh, Melbourne 3166, Australia

First published 1998

Printed in the United Kingdom at the University Press, Cambridge

Typeset in Sabon10/12pt [CE]

A catalogue record for this book is available from the British Library

Library of Congress cataloguing in publication data applied for

ISBN 0 521 62218 2 hardback

CONTENTS

ACKNOWLEDGEMENTS

In a book which, among other things, sets out to explore the difficulties of counsel, it is a pleasure to be able to thank friends and colleagues who have offered advice, encouragement, and support. John Guy supervised my doctoral dissertation: his energy and inspiration kept me and my project going for three years, and his commitment to turning the thesis into this book has been fantastic. I am equally grateful to my two examiners, John Morrill and Roger Mason, who gave me a stimulating viva in 1996 and have been happy to talk, advise, and read ever since. But there are others who have offered comments, thoughts, and references: Jane Dawson, Mark Goldie, Wallace MacCaffrey, Andrew Pettegree, Kevin Sharpe, and Jenny Wormald. John Cramsie and Jamie Hampson are great friends and critical and generous colleagues, and I would like to thank them also for giving me copies of their doctoral dissertations. John and I have talked about our projects – and a lot of other things – in pubs, coffee shops, restaurants, and offices from St Andrews to Finland, Minnesota. Alan Bryson, Chris Croly, Lisa Ford, and Natalie Mears have (often unwittingly) given me ideas, and I hope I have sent a couple back in return. William Davies of Cambridge University Press and Robin Harcourt Williams, Librarian and Archivist to the Marquess of Salisbury, also deserve thanks. All these people have heard far too much about William Cecil and I am extremely grateful.

So many members of my family have been incredibly supportive. Gwen and Alan Mills looked after me on a number of expeditions down to London. Joyce and David Scott have always been willing to act as base camp and supply centre. My parents made the fatal mistake of introducing me to Ladybird history books and they have valiantly dealt with the consequences since the late 1970s. Like my Nan, Mum and Dad have supported me at university for more years than they could reasonably have expected. Max has been superb: her encouragement over the past few years cannot easily be repaid. And thanks also to Albert, who has just about learned to tolerate the mounds of paper.

For help with – and permission to quote from – manuscript collections, I would like to thank the British Library; the Fitzwilliam (Milton) Estates; the Folger Shakespeare Library, Washington, D.C.; the House of Lords Record Office; the Huntington Library, San Marino, California; Lambeth Palace Library; the Earl of Moray; the Pepys Library, Magdalene College, Cambridge; the Public Record Office; the Marquess of Salisbury; the Syndics of Cambridge University Library; the Trustees of the National Library of Scotland. In the appendices, copyright material from the Lansdowne and Cotton collections is reproduced by permission of the British Library. The draft preamble to the subsidy bill of 1566 is in the custody of the House of Lords Record Office and is reproduced by permission of the Clerk of the Records. Some of the documents referred to in the text and reprinted in the appendices are Crown copyright material in the Public Record Office, reproduced by permission of the Controller of Her Majesty's Stationery Office.

ABBREVIATIONS

Additional	British Library, London, Additional MSS.
Cotton	British Library, London, Cotton MSS.
CJ	*Journals of the House of Commons.*
CP	Hatfield House Library, Hertfordshire, Cecil Papers.
Egerton	British Library, London, Egerton MSS.
Harley	British Library, London, Harley MSS.
Hartley	T. E. Hartley (ed.), *Proceedings in the parliaments of Elizabeth I. Volume I 1558–1581* (Leicester, 1981).
Hasler	*The history of parliament. The House of Commons 1558–1603*, ed. P. W. Hasler, 3 vols. (London, 1981).
Haynes	Samuel Haynes (ed.), *Collection of state papers . . . left by William Cecil, Lord Burghley* (London, 1740).
Journals, Commons	House of Lords Record Office, London, MS. Journals, House of Commons 1.
Journals, Lords	House of Lords Record Office, London, MS. Journals, House of Lords 4.
Lansdowne	British Library, London, Lansdowne MSS.
LJ	*Journals of the House of Lords.*
Murdin	William Murdin (ed.), *Collection of state papers relating to affairs in the reign of Queen Elizabeth from the year 1571 to 1596 . . .* (London, 1759).
PC 2	Public Record Office, London, Acts of the Privy Council, Elizabeth I.
SP 10	Public Record Office, London, State Papers, Domestic, Edward VI.
SP 12	Public Record Office, London, State Papers, Domestic, Elizabeth I.
SP 15	Public Record Office, London, State Papers, Addenda, Elizabeth I.

SP 46	Public Record Office, London, State Papers, Domestic, Supplementary.
SP 52	Public Record Office, London, State Papers, Scotland, Elizabeth I.
SP 63	Public Record Office, London, State Papers, Ireland, Elizabeth I.
SP 70	Public Record Office, London, State Papers, Foreign, Elizabeth I.
STC	*A short-title catalogue of books printed in England, Scotland, & Ireland and of English books printed abroad 1475–1640*, ed. A.W. Pollard and G.R. Redgrave (London, 1926); *STC*² refers to new references in the same work, ed. W.A. Jackson, F.S. Ferguson, and Katharine F. Pantzer, 3 vols. (London, 1986–91).

All quotations are in original spelling, but I have transcribed the thorn as 'th', silently extended contractions, and modernized the Elizabethan habit of using 'u' for 'v', 'v' for 'u', and 'i' for 'j'. In quotations from damaged or unclear sources, conjectural reconstructions are added in [brackets]. Words crossed out during editing are ~~scored~~ through. The same conventions apply to the documents transcribed in the appendices, where ^marks^ show textual additions above the line. All dates are New Style.

Introduction

The Quene of Scottes in dede is and shall allweise be a daungerooss person to your estate, yet there be degrees wherby the daunger may be more or less. If your M[ajesty] wold marry it shuld be less, and whylest yow doo not, it will incress. If hir person be restrayned ether here or at home in hir own C[ontrey] it will be less. If it be at liberty it will be gretar.[1]

I

Sir William Cecil, Principal Secretary to Elizabeth I, drafted this advice to the Queen on 6 October 1569, just a few weeks after she had found out about the secret marriage arrangements between Mary Stuart, Queen of Scots, and England's most senior peer, Thomas Howard, duke of Norfolk. Mary had been in protective custody in England since May 1568, and the Elizabethan regime was in the process of trying her for the murder of her second husband Henry, Lord Darnley, in 1567. The death of Darnley and opposition to Mary's government had led to the Queen of Scots' effective abdication – more in the style of Shakespeare's Richard II than a voluntary surrender of power in Scotland – followed by a spell of imprisonment between 1567 and 1568. But Mary and her cause represented more than a tricky legal problem for English and Scottish commissioners. The Queen of Scots was – or at least was perceived to be – a profound threat to the Elizabethan polity: a living connection between the ideological challenge of militant European Catholicism, the threat of Catholic subversion in England, Mary's claim to Elizabeth's crown, and Elizabeth's refusal to marry or to settle England's succession. How this sense of danger developed – and the part Cecil played in explaining and articulating it – is a major theme of this book.

But so too is the impact of this British crisis, in its European context, on the early Elizabethan polity. The politics of British emergency had serious

---

[1] Cotton Caligula C. 1, fo. 456r.

1

consequences for the regime – for the relationship between Elizabeth, her Privy Council, and her parliament; for the political culture and conciliar politics of the 1560s; and for the nature of 'ministerial service' in the middle of the sixteenth century. Perhaps the best way to explain the connection between the British impact of Mary Stuart and the domestic politics of Elizabethan England rests on the sort of counterfactual questions academic historians generally shy away from. What if Mary had been prepared to reign in Scotland in peaceful co-existence with her cousin? What if political circumstance had not allowed men like Cecil to develop a conspiratorial model of England's (and Britain's) political relationship with the Catholic powers of Europe? If Cateau-Cambrésis had not robbed England of its last Continental possession? If the Queen of Scots had been happy to ratify the Treaty of Edinburgh after 1560? Or – and perhaps the most significant – if Elizabeth had been willing to take the advice of her councillors and marry or, at least, settle the succession of the kingdom? Then, perhaps, men like William Cecil would not have had to cajole, press, and petition their Queen in the Council chamber and in parliament or – more radically – make provisions for the 'republican' and conciliar alternative they presented in 1563.

Patrick Collinson has called this reaction to political crisis – the 'readiness of the political nation', including William Cecil, 'to contemplate its own immediate political future' temporarily without the monarchy – a form of 'monarchical republicanism'.[2] He noticed two 'convulsive episodes' in Elizabethan political history: the parliament of 1572, with its call for a solution to the problem of Mary Stuart; and a parliamentary bill in 1584, which introduced a plan for a conciliar interregnum in the event of Elizabeth's sudden or violent death. For Professor Collinson, this was the 'Elizabethan exclusion crisis', in which England declared itself 'a republic which happened also to be a monarchy: or vice versa'.[3] In other words, political crisis forced Elizabethans to reconsider their relationship with their Queen: 'when it came to the crunch, the realm took precedence over the ruler. So citizens were concealed within subjects.'[4] Indeed, by 1583 Cecil could refer in print to the Queen 'and all her governours and magistrates of Justice', not just to councillors and servants.[5] Professor John

---

[2] Patrick Collinson, 'The monarchical republic of Queen Elizabeth I', in his *Elizabethan essays* (London and Rio Grande, 1994), p. 43.

[3] For the quotation, Collinson, 'Monarchical republic', p. 43; Patrick Collinson, 'The Elizabethan exclusion crisis and the Elizabethan polity', *Proceedings of the British Academy*, 84 (1995), 51–92.

[4] Patrick Collinson, '*De republica Anglorum*: or, history with the politics put back', in his *Elizabethan essays*, p. 19.

[5] William Cecil, *The execution of justice in England for maintenaunce of publique and Christian peace . . .* (STC 4902; London, 1583), sig. B1r.

Guy has argued that the political cultures of the periods 1558–85 and 1585–1603 were strikingly different, to such an extent that there were 'two reigns'. The distinction rests on the three elements of the early Privy Council's 'political creed': first, that England was a 'mixed polity'; second, that the 'prerogative of the ruler' was limited by the advice of the Council; and third, that 'the assent of the whole realm' in parliament was needed 'to effect significant political or religious change and in particular to resolve the issue of the succession to the throne'. The 'second reign' was different: the work of the Council was less collegial and less committed to conciliar policy-making. The 'watershed' was the execution of Mary, Queen of Scots – a dangerous woman but an important focus for collective effort.[6]

In recent years, other historians of the late medieval and Tudor periods have been willing to challenge old orthodoxies – court and Council faction and 'constitutional' parliamentary opposition to the 'government', for example – and more prepared to connect language to the political process and discuss serious subjects like counsel.[7] Institutional and administrative history is now less influential in Tudor studies than it was in the 1960s and the 1970s. Tudor specialists at the end of this century are perhaps more willing to accept the judgement of a historian of Henry VI: that the 'main business of political systems is to attend to the present need', and that political consensus 'usually rests on a series of less formal arrangements which have their own patterns and principles; patterns and principles which are all the more influential because they are shared and often unstated'.[8] Many of the most important sources in this study are personal

---

[6] John Guy, 'The 1590s: the second reign of Elizabeth I?', in John Guy (ed.), *The reign of Elizabeth I. Court and culture in the last decade* (Cambridge, 1995), pp. 13–14.

[7] Apart from Collinson, '*De republica Anglorum*', 'Exclusion crisis', and 'Monarchical republic', and Guy, 'The 1590s', see Simon Adams, 'Eliza enthroned? The court and its politics', in Christopher Haigh (ed.), *The reign of Elizabeth I* (London, 1984), pp. 55–77; Adams, 'Faction, clientage and party. English politics, 1550–1603', *History Today*, 32 (1982), 33–9; Adams, 'Favourites and factions at the Elizabethan court', in Ronald G. Asch and Adolf M. Birke (eds.), *Princes, patronage, and the nobility. The court at the beginning of the modern age c. 1450–1650* (Oxford, 1991), pp. 265–87; Terence Ball, James Farr, and Russell L. Hanson (eds.), *Political innovation and conceptual change* (Cambridge, 1989); Paul A. Fideler and T.F. Mayer (eds.), *Political thought and the Tudor commonwealth* (London, 1992); Dale Hoak (ed.), *Tudor political culture* (Cambridge, 1995); Lisa Jardine and Anthony Grafton, '"Studied for action": how Gabriel Harvey read his Livy', *Past and Present*, no. 129 (1990), 30–78; Markku Peltonen, *Classical humanism and republicanism in English political thought 1570–1640* (Cambridge, 1995); J.G.A. Pocock (ed.), *The varieties of British political thought, 1500–1800* (Cambridge, 1993); Quentin Skinner, *Reason and rhetoric in the philosophy of Hobbes* (Cambridge, 1996); David Starkey (ed.), *The English court: from the Wars of the Roses to the Civil War* (London and New York, 1987); Maurizio Viroli, *From politics to reason of state. The acquisition and transformation of the language of politics 1250–1600* (Cambridge, 1992); for important developments in Scotland, see Roger A. Mason (ed.), *Scots and Britons. Scottish political thought and the union of 1603* (Cambridge, 1994).

[8] John Watts, *Henry VI and the politics of kingship* (Cambridge, 1996), p. 13.

and not institutional – letters, diplomatic reports to the Queen and to her councillors, informal notes, rough drafts of minutes and petitions, and private memoranda, often prepared by Cecil. Early Elizabethan political culture was a complex blend of personality, of the practical needs of governance, of councillors' perception of themselves as classical governors, of a strong providential sense of England's relationship with Catholic Europe, and of the part Elizabeth I played in her polity.

II

New interpretations of the Elizabethan polity have important implications for individual councillors like William Cecil, and the relationship between subjects and their Queen. For too long, Cecil and Elizabeth have been viewed as an inseparable political partnership, bound together by a common interest in moderation and national safety. This relationship needs to be reassessed. But if Tudor political historians accept Collinson's belief that 'the Queen and Cecil' cannot be tacked together 'as if they were the front and rear legs of a pantomime horse' – or John Guy's argument that before 1585 Cecil and Elizabeth were 'virtually different species' when it came to 'intellectual genes', and that they 'subscribed to discordant political philosophies' – the effect is profoundly liberating.[9] Because historians accepted Cecil and the Queen as an inseparable partnership, it was tempting to endorse Sir Robert Naunton's view in the 1630s that, while Cecil obediently served his mistress, other privy councillors and courtiers engaged in factional pursuits.[10] The sources present a very different picture: of a Council working efficiently, often sharing a common interpretation of political events and policies; of a Queen effectively removed from the day-to-day operation of government, instinctively cautious and sometimes paralyzed by indecision; but, above all, of a Cecil far removed from the second-rate bureaucrat characterized by Thomas Babington Macaulay in the nineteenth century and Cecil's biographer in the twentieth, Conyers Read.

Cecil's modern political reputation can almost be dated precisely from April 1832, when *The Edinburgh Review* published Macaulay's biting (and anonymous) critique of the *Memoirs of the life and administration of the Right Honourable William Cecil, Lord Burghley* by Edward Nares, Regius Professor of Modern History at Oxford. Cecil, the *Memoirs* had contended, deserved to be put into a wide chronological context, and Nares understood the relationship between Elizabeth's throne, Continental threats,

---

[9] Collinson, 'Monarchical republic', p. 39; Guy, 'The 1590s', p. 13.
[10] Sir Robert Naunton, *Fragmenta regalia*, ed. Edward Arber (London, 1870), p. 20.

Mary Stuart, and Cecil's political position;[11] for Macaulay, on the other hand, Cecil was an average and uninspiring trimmer – luckily, it seems, because if 'he had been a man of original genius, and of a commanding mind, it would have been scarcely possible for him to keep his power, or even his head'.[12] And although Nares had at least some support from Burghley's contemporaries, who praised Cecil's commitment to the defence of England against the Catholic menace and his active patronage of learning,[13] Macaulay won the battle. In 1898 Martin Hume described Cecil as a born conservative, 'judicious, well-nigh incorruptible, prudent, patriotic, and clear-headed'.[14] Fifteen years later – and forty-two years before his standard biography of the early Cecil – Conyers Read called him a *politique*.[15] Wallace MacCaffrey once measured Cecil against the revolutionary Thomas Cromwell, whose 'talents had lain in his abilities to reshape and to modernize the structure of English administration, and to carry through with a steady hand the managed revolution of the Henrician Reformation'. Cecil was less imaginative and less creative, more conventional and cautious, a Protestant but his 'religious feelings were not deep'.[16]

Over the past few years, Cecil's reputation (like Cromwell's revolution in government) has been refined, readjusted, and challenged. The private Cecil – socially conservative, aristocratic, and obsessed with his family background – is now far more accessible.[17] His importance as a British politician was emphasized by Dr Jane Dawson in 1989,[18] and her work has made its mark on some recent and important studies.[19] But there are still some important deficiencies. Cecil's papers are some of the best sources on

---

[11] [Thomas Babington Macaulay,] 'Nares' *Memoirs of Lord Burghley*', *The Edinburgh Review*, 55 (1832), 271–96; Edward Nares, *Memoirs of the life and administration of the Right Honourable William Cecil, Lord Burghley . . .*, 3 vols. (London, 1828–31), I, pp. viii–ix; II, pp. 99–100.

[12] [Macaulay,] 'Nares' *Memoirs of Lord Burghley*', 276.

[13] For example, George Whetstone, *The English myrror. A regard wherein al estates may behold the conquests of envy . . .* (STC 25336; London, 1586), pp. 138–9; Hugh Broughton, *A treatise of Melchisedek, proving him to be Sem . . .* (STC 3890; London, 1591), sig. 2v–3r.

[14] Martin Hume, *The great Lord Burghley. A study in Elizabethan statecraft* (London, 1898), p. ix.

[15] Conyers Read, 'Factions in the English Privy Council under Elizabeth', *Annual Report of the American Historical Association*, 1 (1911), 115; Read, 'Walsingham and Burghley in Queen Elizabeth's Privy Council', *English Historical Review*, 28 (1913), 37; Read, *Mr Secretary Cecil and Queen Elizabeth* (London, 1955).

[16] Wallace MacCaffrey, *The shaping of the Elizabethan regime* (London, 1969), p. 302; for a reinterpretation, see MacCaffrey, *Elizabeth I* (London, 1993), pp. 63–9.

[17] G.R. Morrison, 'The land, family, and domestic following of William Cecil, Lord Burghley *c.* 1550–1598', DPhil thesis, University of Oxford (1990), pp. 5–8.

[18] Jane E.A. Dawson, 'William Cecil and the British dimension of early Elizabethan foreign policy', *History*, 74 (1989), 196–216.

[19] Roger A. Mason, 'The Scottish reformation and the origins of Anglo-British imperialism', in Mason (ed.), *Scots and Britons*, p. 181; Marcus Merriman, 'Stewarts and Tudors in the

early Elizabethan political culture, and yet Read thought that the Principal Secretary's notes 'are often tedious'.[20] He dismissed unfinished drafts,[21] and he had no real interest in the intellectual value of Cecil's work; Read looked at the memoranda empirically, but did not read them as exercises in political thought or policy. Sir Geoffrey Elton noted over forty years ago that Thomas Cromwell thought little of Plato but was aware of the 'sentence' of Aristotle and could talk on the subject of 'pollycy'.[22] A year earlier Read had mentioned that Cecil read Latin and Greek but 'took no interest in the unfolding glories of Elizabethan literature'.[23] Nevertheless, *Mr Secretary Cecil* is still the main, comprehensive, and basically unchallenged source on Cecil the political man. For over forty years, historians have had the dull and lifeless Cecil they deserve.

Perhaps the best way to characterize old Cecil historiography is the underuse of a significant and very rich reserve of historical material, coupled with a limited sense of the Principal Secretary's intellectual and political preoccupations, and aggravated by an obsession with Elizabethan court faction. Even in the 1990s, it is still possible to measure the 'factional intrigue' of Elizabeth's noblemen against a Cecil cast as the symbol of bureaucracy, meritocracy, and service.[24] But more questions have to be asked. The debate on faction has skewed any real sense of the policy-making process in early Elizabethan England. Who made policy? Was it Elizabeth, acting with Cecil as her 'chief minister'? Or is this interpretation as redundant for the 1560s as it is for the 1520s and 1530s?[25] What part did the Privy Council play in collating, debating, and (crucially) deciding policy? How did the sixteenth-century model of counsel – the duty of councillors to offer advice, and the freedom of a monarch either to accept or to reject it – work in political practice?[26] If the role of the Privy Council was significant, what was Cecil's part in it? Bureaucrat or political fixer?

mid-sixteenth century', in Alexander Grant and Keith J. Stringer (eds.), *Uniting the kingdom? The making of British history* (London and New York, 1995), pp. 120–1.

[20] Read, *Cecil*, p. 11.

[21] For example, Conyers Read, 'William Cecil and Elizabethan public relations', in S.T. Bindoff, J. Hurstfield, and C.H. Williams (eds.), *Elizabethan government and society* (London, 1961), p. 33, on 'A necessary consideration of the perillous state of this tyme', 7 June 1569; see below, pp. 182 n.3, 194–8.

[22] G.R. Elton, 'The political creed of Thomas Cromwell', in his *Studies in Tudor and Stuart politics and government*, 4 vols. (Cambridge, 1974–92), II, pp. 216–17.

[23] Read, *Cecil*, p. 11.

[24] Wallace MacCaffrey, 'Patronage and politics under the Tudors', in Linda Levy Peck (ed.), *The mental world of the Jacobean court* (Cambridge, 1991), pp. 28–9.

[25] John Guy, 'Thomas Wolsey, Thomas Cromwell and the reform of Henrician government', in Diarmaid MacCulloch (ed.), *The reign of Henry VIII. Politics, policy and piety* (Basingstoke and London, 1995), pp. 39–43.

[26] John Guy, 'The rhetoric of counsel in early modern England', in Hoak (ed.), *Tudor political culture*, p. 294.

How did Cecil approach, synthesize, and interpret information and intelligence? What was the relationship between his work as Principal Secretary and his own political and mental world? What were his influences? Purely Protestant, or something more to reinforce the perception he had of his own place in the early Elizabethan political scheme of things?

III

William Cecil had a political creed in the 1560s. It rested on the principle that both the Privy Council and parliament had a duty to counsel, guide, and direct Elizabeth, even in matters of 'state' like the Queen's marriage, the succession to the kingdom, and England's religion. In a British context, he extended this interpretation of the polity to the work of Council and parliament in Scotland and developed a strong sense of the political and ecclesiastical relationship between England, Ireland, and Scotland. Cecil understood and accepted the culture of Tudor imperialism but – like Sir Thomas Smith in *De republica Anglorum* and unlike Elizabeth – he believed that the Queen's *imperium* was limited by the advice of her councillors in Council and in parliament.

It is sometimes too easy for the historian to take theory and impose it on historical events; in this way, arguments can become circular and self-fulfilling. In the opening chapter of this book, I have tried to explore the mental world of Cecil: his education, training, and early political career. There are some important connections between the nature of the Cecil archive and the Principal Secretary's approach to policy: for example, his memoranda written *in utramque partem*, using the skills of a rhetorical training at Cambridge in the 1530s and Gray's Inn in the 1540s, and designed to explore the political issues of the 1560s. Professor Quentin Skinner and Dr Markku Peltonen have explored Tudor rhetorical training, classical models of behaviour for gentlemen in the sixteenth century, and expressions of Elizabethan republicanism;[27] what I wanted to do was to take these insights and use them to illuminate the archives, to move one step beyond the purely empirical approach of Conyers Read. The implications of this for a study of Cecil are important. Elizabethans made a connection between intellectual (and especially classical) pursuits, historical models of action and behaviour, and active policy. Contemporaries understood the importance of the *vir civilis*, the man who leads a productive public life, able to take part in the councils (and counsels) of his prince. Roger Ascham, Cecil's old teacher at Cambridge in the 1530s and Elizabeth

---

[27] Skinner, *Reason and rhetoric*, pp. 19–87; Peltonen, *Classical humanism and republicanism*, pp. 2–12.

I's Latin secretary in the 1560s, began *The scholemaster* by introducing readers to Cecil at dinner, keen to talk 'most gladlie of some matter of learning'. Debate and discussion in Cecil's chamber, even with 'the meanest at his Table', were important to a man whose head was 'so full of most weightie affaires of the Realme' – surely not as a diversion but as part of the public life of an active man, Cicero's man of *negotium*.[28]

Cecil's private notes written *in utramque partem* became part of the process of Elizabethan policy-making, crucial to his role as Principal Secretary, privy councillor, and governor. An important element in the making of policy at Council level was information, intelligence, and synthesis. Cecil received reports from ambassadors and representatives, analyzed their contents, and combined the presentation of evidence with his own notes on the problem. Cecil's influence on this process was reinforced by the nature of very sensitive meetings: he often wrote and edited the minutes for the Council and perhaps presented the findings to Elizabeth. These meetings on delicate subjects often dealt with the activities of Mary Stuart, and they were a crucial element in the development of British policy.[29] And Cecil's approach was genuinely British, or perhaps more accurately conceived in terms of England, Ireland, and Scotland. He was part of a defined Anglo-Scottish Protestant community. He understood the strategic and political implications of the interference of Scottish mercenaries in Ulster and the part sympathetic Scots could play in helping to pacify Ireland. Cecil was aware of the benefits of Protestant unity and of a 'league' and 'amity' between England and Scotland, reinforced by a peaceful Ireland. He explored alternatives to Stuart rule in Scotland, and managed to blend the principles of Protestant co-operation and ecclesiastical independence with the standard English claim of superiority over the northern kingdom. The way Cecil articulated this British political creed – the impact of England's political relationship with Scotland and Ireland and the vocabulary he used to explain his concept of Britain – is a central concern of this book.

---

[28] Roger Ascham, *The scholemaster* (STC 832; London, 1570), sig. B1r.
[29] Hiram Morgan, 'British policies before the British state', in Brendan Bradshaw and John Morrill (eds.), *The British problem, c. 1534–1707. State formation in the Atlantic archipelago* (Basingstoke and London, 1996), pp. 66–88.

1

William Cecil and early Elizabethan political culture

'The difference between politics and political culture', according to Professor Dale Hoak, 'is essentially the difference between political action and the codes of conduct, formal and informal, governing those actions'. Politics and political culture are not separate or independent, and, ideally, 'the two histories should be written as one: political "reality" is by definition a compound of both'.[1] This book deals with the politics of succession in the 1560s, the impact of British and European events on the early Elizabethan polity, and the political creed of William Cecil. The politics of the decade are crucial; but they are complemented – even reinforced – by the preoccupations of Elizabethan governors. This chapter will explore the political world and mentality of Cecil: his political papers and their value, his education and Edwardian experiences of government, his sense of place and purpose in Elizabethan government, and, above all, the impact that perhaps all of these had on Cecil's understanding of his own position in the polity and the relationship between the Queen, her Council, and the Lords and Commons in parliament.

I

According to Robert Beale in 1592, the 'practise of the place' of the Queen's Principal Secretary 'consisteth partlie in dealing with her Majestie and partlie with the rest of her highnes most honorable privie Councell'. For Beale, the Secretary had two main responsibilities: 'the manner of givinge councell and advise to a Prince or in the assemblie of Councellors'.[2] In one

---

[1] Dale Hoak, 'Introduction', in Dale Hoak (ed.), *Tudor political culture* (Cambridge, 1995), p. 1.

[2] R[obert].B[eale]., 'A Treatise of the Office of a Councellor and Principall Secretarie to her Majestie', in Conyers Read, *Mr Secretary Walsingham and the policy of Queen Elizabeth*, 3 vols. (Oxford, 1925), I, pp. 423–4. The standard account of the work of the Secretary in the sixteenth and seventeenth centuries is still Florence M. Greir Evans, *The Principal Secretary of State. A survey of the office from 1558 to 1680* (Manchester, London, and New York, 1923).

9

sense, the Principal Secretary and the staff of the Privy Council were very personal servants of the crown. Sir Nicholas Throckmorton advised Elizabeth in November 1558 'to call Master Cicill to exercise the rome of Secretarie *about your person*'. He also proposed William Honyng, a clerk of the signet, and Bernard Hampton, Clerk of the Privy Council during the 1560s, as 'clerkes of the councell, *to attend uppon your person for the dispatch of your lettres and orders*'.[3] At the beginning of the reign, Cecil swore two oaths: the one as a privy councillor and the other as Principal Secretary.[4] In 1563 and 1564 he described the office as 'secretary of the state' or 'secretory of estate', which, before the seventeenth century, generally meant a relationship with a royal state of majesty and power; but definitions were changing, certainly in 1563, when Cecil had to imagine England without a monarch and public power exercised by a 'council of estate'.[5]

But although there was a sense of close physical connection between the monarch and her Principal Secretary, the job was, above all, a political office. Cecil organized meetings of the Council; Elizabeth did not attend. Cecil read and assessed information and intelligence from the regime's agents and representatives, drafted notes for his colleagues, spoke in meetings of the Council, and acted as liaison between the Queen, her councillors, and ambassadors. He was a central figure in the (sometimes frustrating) political process of advising the monarch and he had the job of handling the Council in its administrative or institutional form. In 1564 Cecil described himself as 'a secretory of estate', 'an artificer of practisees and Co[u]nsuls' – a sense, perhaps, of the Secretary as a political fixer, advising, counselling, and organizing.[6] The political context of Cecil's work as Principal Secretary and as a policy-maker is one of the main underlying themes of this book.

Perhaps the most important source for the political historian of the Elizabethan regime is Cecil's archive, which is unmatched in quantity and quality by any other councillor or courtier in the 1560s. This was not the formal record of Council meetings during the first decade, printed in the nineteenth century as the *Acts of the Privy Council*. The *Acts* do not record

---

[3] J.E. Neale, 'Sir Nicholas Throckmorton's advice to Queen Elizabeth on her accession to the throne', *English Historical Review*, 65 (1950), 94, with my italics.

[4] SP 12/1, fo. 3v, in Cecil's holograph; SP 12/1, fo. 12r.

[5] 'A clause to have bene inserted in an act ment for the succession', 1563, SP 12/28, fos. 68r–69v, and printed below, pp. 225–8; Cecil to Sir Thomas Smith, 11 January 1564, Lansdowne 102, fo. 56r; cf. Smith's reference to the 'cloath of estate' as a symbol of the royal power of the monarch, *De republica Anglorum*, ed. Mary Dewar (Cambridge, 1982), Book II, chapter 3, p. 88. On the development of the modern term 'state', see Quentin Skinner, 'The state', in Terence Ball, James Farr, and Russell L. Hanson (eds.), *Political innovation and conceptual change* (Cambridge, 1989), pp. 90–131, especially pp. 90–101. See below, pp. 41–2.

[6] Lansdowne 102, fo. 56r.

debates and there are serious gaps in the record.[7] These late fair copies do not hold the key to Elizabethan policy-making or the nature of the relationship between councillors and their monarch. The same is true for the Jacobean Council.[8] The real sources are less bureaucratic and more informal, written for the politics of the moment: letters to and from ambassadors, councillors, and courtiers; private memoranda written by Cecil to work through political problems; Cecil's own records of sensitive meetings of the Council, sometimes turned into the form of petitions to the Queen; and parliamentary papers prepared for Elizabeth and drafted for MPs determined to present concerns and criticisms to their monarch. These sources help to blur some of the institutional boundaries. Sir Geoffrey Elton and Michael Pulman assumed that because clerks were sent out of the Council chamber during sensitive meetings, this is a limitation for historians.[9] In fact, the opposite is true for the 1560s: Cecil acted as the Council's clerk, and his holograph notes are far more valuable. This apart, the Clerk of the Council, Hampton, was trusted enough to produce fair copies. But Hampton's relationship with Cecil is even more important. He was involved in projects which would have had little to do with his duties as Clerk, unless Elizabethan historians are willing to reinterpret the nature of the polity. Hampton was a key draughtsman in the delicate relationship between Queen and Council in the parliamentary session of 1566, and he worked on some political papers which can only be described as private Cecil projects.[10]

These sources form part of Cecil's archive as Principal Secretary. This collection has to be reconstructed from at least four modern archives: the Public Record Office's State Papers collection, the Lansdowne manuscripts at the British Library, scattered volumes and papers in the collection owned in the seventeenth century by Sir Robert Cotton, and the Cecil Papers at Hatfield House in Hertfordshire. That these papers are where they are is pure accident, and there is no effective difference between, say, the official State Papers from the 1560s and the Hatfield archive. Both collections represent the work of Cecil as Principal Secretary. Elizabethan 'state' records were, in effect, private papers. After Cecil's death in 1598, his

---

[7] For the original Elizabethan acts, see PC 2/8–10, printed as *Acts of the Privy Council of England*, ed. J.R. Dasent *et al.*, New Series, 46 vols. (London, 1890–1964). On the nature and state of the registers, see E.R. Adair, 'The rough copies of the Privy Council Register', *English Historical Review*, 38 (1923), 410–22, particularly 418–19.

[8] John R. Cramsie, 'Crown finance and governance under James I: projects and fiscal policy 1603–1625', PhD thesis, University of St Andrews (1997), pp. 14–15, 17–18.

[9] G.R. Elton, 'Tudor government: the points of contact. II. The council', in his *Studies in Tudor and Stuart politics and government*, 4 vols. (Cambridge, 1974–92), III, pp. 21–2; Michael Barraclough Pulman, *The Elizabethan Privy Council in the fifteen-seventies* (Berkeley, Los Angeles, and London, 1971), p. 52.

[10] See below, pp. 149–50, 153–6, 182 n.3, 194, 207–8.

eldest son, Thomas, received his printed books; but the papers from his 'study over the porche' were bequeathed to Robert Cecil. In the classical tradition of a father's advice for his son in the affairs of the commonwealth, he left Robert his 'writinges concerning . . . causes, either for hir [the Queen's] Revenue, or for affaires of Counsell or state to be advisedly perused by him'. What are now the Cecil Papers at Hatfield would have been moved from Burghley House to Salisbury House, both on the Strand, in 1598; and probably from there to Hatfield when Salisbury House was demolished at the end of the seventeenth century.[11] The modern Lansdowne collection is separated from Cecil's other papers because his secretary in the 1580s and 1590s, Michael Hickes, spirited them away after his master's death. After a journey through the libraries of John Strype and the first marquis of Lansdowne, they arrived at the British Museum in 1807.[12] Cecil's notes on Anglo-Scottish affairs now in the Cotton collection were part of Sir Robert Cotton's library by 1632, but they seem also to have been used by William Camden in the research for his *Annals*. They were an appropriate part of the collection of an enthusiastic Briton who styled himself 'Bruceus' as a mark of his supposed descent from Robert the Bruce.[13] Victorian editors were responsible for the rather artificial division of Cecil's secretarial archive into categories like 'Domestic', 'Foreign', 'Ireland', and 'Scotland', but, with some work, his papers can be reintegrated quite well.

So, in spite of chance, time, and the poor archival practices of the sixteenth and seventeenth centuries, the sources for a study of Cecil are remarkably good. There are certainly gaps. Although some of Cecil's outgoing letters survive in the papers of Sir Thomas Smith (in France during the 1560s), the earl of Sussex (in Ireland), and Sir Nicholas Throckmorton (in France and Scotland), there should be more.[14] Even the

---

[11] Hatfield House Library, Hertfordshire, FP 2/93. Although Samuel Haynes published his edition of transcripts from the collection at Hatfield in 1740, unbound bundles of manuscripts were later catalogued by Dr Samuel Adee. Adee helped William Murdin to produce the second *Collection of state papers*, published in 1759, and both men seem to have been working from 'the Original papers of Lord Burghley & of his Son the Earl of Salisbury' in 1765. Charles James Stewart, a London bookseller, properly catalogued the collection in the nineteenth century and arranged the papers into their present volumes between 1831 and 1850. I am extremely grateful to Robin Harcourt Williams for providing me with this archival background to the Cecil Papers.

[12] *A catalogue of the Lansdowne manuscripts in the British Museum*, ed. Henry Ellis, 2 vols. (London, 1812–19), I, p. ix.

[13] Kevin Sharpe, *Sir Robert Cotton 1586–1631. History and politics in early modern England* (Oxford, 1979), pp. 69–70, 71–2; Jenny Wormald, 'The creation of Britain: multiple kingdoms or core and colonies?', *Transactions of the Royal Historical Society*, sixth series, 2 (1992), 178–9.

[14] The main collections are Lansdowne 102 (to Smith), Cotton Titus B. 13 (to Sussex), and Additional 35830 and 35831 (to Throckmorton).

scattered letters to the earl of Leicester, Sir Walter Mildmay, Sir William Petre, Thomas Randolph, Sir Ralph Sadler, the earl of Shrewsbury, and Sir Henry Sidney, and between Cecil and members of the Scottish Protestant congregation, cannot account for the shortfall. In June 1565 Cecil told Sir Thomas Smith that his was 'the twentyth lettre all redy wrytten this daye', which was a Sunday.[15] The day before, he had produced a long memorandum on the 'perills and troobles' posed by the marriage of Mary Stuart to Henry, Lord Darnley; a day later, he wrote over three thousand words in 'Summary' of a meeting of the Privy Council and corrected Bernard Hampton's fair copy of his original.[16] So even with gaps in the evidence, Cecil's output was truly prolific.

Cecil kept his own drafts on political issues. It is unclear how he organized his personal archive in the 1560s, but he was able later on in his career to compile extremely detailed chronologies of the reign, listing events by year, month, date, and subject.[17] When the prosecution case was being built against Norfolk in 1572, Cecil was able to find and to quote from a single letter sent by the duke of Norfolk, the earl of Sussex, and Sir Ralph Sadler to Elizabeth in 1568.[18] And at least two political proposals written in the 1560s re-emerged in the 1580s.[19] There is good reason to think that, like other Elizabethan courtiers, councillors, lawyers, and MPs, Cecil had an exceptionally organized study. Apart from letters, he kept drafts of 'official' documents (like minutes of Privy Council meetings) and private memoranda which he wrote to explore policies, options, and political dangers. These public and private papers met in documents prepared by Cecil for (and probably delivered to) the Privy Council. Some of these distinctions need to be explained. In this book, 'minute' is shorthand for what Cecil variously described as 'Thopinion of the Counsell', 'A Summary of the consultation and advise gyven by the Lordes and others of the Pryve Counsell', 'the determination of the Counsell', or 'A Consultation'. These notes have a place of meeting, a list of councillors in attendance, and a date. Occasionally, they were turned into 'petitions' to Elizabeth pressing for definite action and policy. More difficult to place are some of Cecil's notes prepared two or so days before a meeting, and which are structurally and textually similar to the minutes in draft form. Perhaps Cecil used his own text – prepared in advance to explore policy or synthesize intelligence from ambassadors, agents, and representatives – to fashion the account of what his colleagues had said during a meeting. As a (theoretically) junior councillor, Cecil would have spoken near the begin-

---

[15] Cecil to Smith, 3 June 1565, Lansdowne 102, fo. 111r.
[16] See below, pp. 127–9.   [17] CP 229, no. 4.
[18] Cotton Caligula C. 1, fo. 260v; SP 12/85, fos. 33v–34r.
[19] See below, pp. 111, 196–8.

ning of meetings. This procedure could have been used – perhaps like his interviews with the Queen – to establish an agenda and present basic facts and information to his colleagues. There was an oral dimension to debate, counsel, and policy-making but this, unlike Cecil's archive, cannot be reconstructed.

Cecil was an experienced man in Council and he understood the seniority of his position. In a tense moment with his brother-in-law, Lord Keeper of the Great Seal Sir Nicholas Bacon, in 1563, he made his point very clearly. He was 'unworthy hir majesties Secretary and unhable Councellor'; but he was 'no clerke to write your resolutions, nor lettres for yow or the Councell; there be Clerks for that purpose'.[20] In a sense, he had the best of both worlds: a clerk like Hampton, who was quite prepared to step in to draft private letters or collaborate on political projects; an ability to take issues to the Council and influence debate and the making of policy; and yet, at the same time, an executive independence, emphasized by his ability to act as a channel of communication between monarch, Council, and representatives abroad. It was not the first time he had experienced this basic political situation. But although he clearly dealt with the Council as the first duke of Northumberland's conciliar 'man of business' during the reign of Edward VI, the work he did before, during, and after important meetings on sensitive subjects in the 1560s was far more 'political'. In fact, some of Cecil's notes on 'matters' and 'causes' for the Council in the early 1550s match the day-to-day administrative business recorded by the Elizabethan clerks in the official acts.[21] The crisis of the 1560s must have been profoundly disconcerting for Cecil and his colleagues, but the evidence it left behind of serious political debate is extremely valuable.

II

The basic foundation for work on Cecil, and perhaps the key to his intellectual approach to political problems in the first Elizabethan decade, is the private memorandum (or 'memorial'), setting down a problem and possible solutions, often organized into sections *pro* and *contra*; carefully structured, usually edited, and sometimes completely rewritten and adjusted. Historians have reacted to the Cecil memoranda in different ways.

---

[20] Lansdowne 102, fo. 70v, 21 July 1563.
[21] For example, SP 10/14, fos. 147r–148r, 26 August 1552; SP 10/15, fo. 124r, November 1552; SP 10/15, fo. 107r, 24 November 1552; D.E. Hoak, *The King's Council in the reign of Edward VI* (Cambridge, 1976), p. 30; C.S. Knighton, 'The principal secretaries in the reign of Edward VI: reflections on their office and archive', in Claire Cross, David Loades, and J.J. Scarisbrick (eds.), *Law and government under the Tudors* (Cambridge, 1988), pp. 163–75.

Professor Wallace MacCaffrey called them 'a kind of scholastic *quaestio*',[22] and Professor Norman Jones made a connection between Cecil's notes in this form, his intellectual processes, and the response to the needs of governance.[23] Although Renaissance and Tudor research has begun to work out the links between education and its influence on governors and councillors – in effect, the classicization of politics in the sixteenth century – Sir Thomas Elyot made the connection in 1531. Elyot examined the 'education or fourme of bringing up of the childe of a gentilman, which is to have authoritie in a publike weale'.[24] He suggested a solid and early diet of Latin and Greek authors.[25] Editions of classical texts were clearly available in England from the middle of the fifteenth century, generally in Latin and imported from Europe, but English translations by printers like Caxton soon began to appear. Robert Whittington of Magdalen College, Oxford, edited Cicero's *De officiis*, which was printed in 1534. In 1547 the King's printer, Richard Grafton, published an English translation of *The ethiques of Aristotle*, partly in order to explore (the title page explained) Aristotle's 'preceptes of good behavoure and perfighte honestie'.[26] By the early part of the sixteenth century, an impressive corpus of known classical and Renaissance texts was available to read either in original languages or in translation, and they offered readers the chance to explore the nature of monarchy, the state of the commonwealth, and public behaviour, and to develop the skills of political persuasion. Authors took classical terms like *respublica* and turned them into English; in effect, they became part of a domestic debate which could be carried out in the vernacular. Humanist curricula became extremely popular: at St Andrews, for example, where George Buchanan planned an 'ordre of the College of Humanite' in the 1560s;[27] and at Cambridge, the university of one of Buchanan's admirers, Roger Ascham. Ascham was the author of *The scholemaster*, a book written during the last decade of his life, when he served as Elizabeth's Latin secretary. But he was also a member of a circle of classical scholars at Cambridge in the 1530s and 1540s, of whom William Cecil was one.

---

[22] Wallace MacCaffrey, *The shaping of the Elizabethan regime* (London, 1969), p. 303.

[23] Norman Jones, 'William Cecil and the making of economic policy in the 1560s and early 1570's', in Paul A. Fideler and T.F. Mayer (eds.), *Political thought and the Tudor commonwealth. Deep structure, discourse and disguise* (London and New York, 1992), p. 169.

[24] Sir Thomas Elyot, *The boke named the governour* (STC 7635), Book I, chapter 4, p. 15v; ed. S.E. Lehmberg (London and New York, 1962), p. 15.

[25] Elyot, *Governour*, Book I, chapter 10, pp. 29v–35v; ed. Lehmberg, pp. 28–33.

[26] John Guy, 'Introduction', in John Guy (ed.), *The Tudor monarchy* (London, 1997), pp. 2, 8 n. 8; Quentin Skinner, *Reason and rhetoric in the philosophy of Hobbes* (Cambridge, 1996), pp. 22, 68–9; *The ethiques of Aristotle* (STC 754; London, 1547).

[27] George Buchanan, *Vernacular writings*, ed. P. Hume Brown (Scottish Text Society, 26; Edinburgh and London, 1892), pp. 8–10.

Both Ascham and Cecil were part of what Professor Winthrop Hudson described in 1980 as the 'Cambridge connection': the men who, after university, worked in government between 1547 and 1553 and were transferred (almost wholesale) into office in 1558.[28] This 'Athenian' group is the key to Cecil's academic training. It was young and avant-garde. The two senior members of the group, John Cheke and Thomas Smith, were both twenty-one years of age when Cecil entered Cheke's college, St John's, in 1535. Both Cheke and Smith began to introduce the Erasmian pronunciation of Greek to their younger students, which involved them in an extremely serious power struggle with the Chancellor of the University and Master of Trinity Hall, Stephen Gardiner, in 1541. Cecil learned Greek and lectured in the subject for six years. It was this challenging intellectual environment, with its emphasis on rhetorical training and pure classical tradition, which helped to develop Cecil's skills in setting down and debating policy privately on paper.

The main texts of rhetorical study were practical in focus. Elyot argued that at fourteen (Cecil's age in 1535), Quintilian's *Institutio oratoria* should be read for 'instructyng diligently the childe in that parte of rhethorike, principally whiche concerneth persuation'.[29] Professor Lisa Jardine has argued that the *Institutio oratoria* is 'a self-contained scheme of education for the public servant as opposed to the professional academic'.[30] As a student, Cecil would have read Cicero's main works – *Rhetorica ad Herennium*, *De inventione*, *Topica*, *De oratore*, *De partitione oratoria* – which were often described as 'Cicero's rhetorical books';[31] he certainly seems to have owned 'Retorica tulli in 16' at the end of the decade.[32] Cicero's *De officiis* was published as *The thre bookes of Tullyes offyces* in London in 1534, and at least two students at Cambridge in the 1540s (Roger Soresby at Peterhouse and Peter Williamson of Corpus Christi) owned personal copies.[33] Rhetoric was a practical exercise which, through clear organization and arrangement, could explore issues and persuade and convince hearers. Erasmus emphasized the relationship between proposition, reasons, and proof; and classical authors explained the structure of

---

[28] Winthrop S. Hudson, *The Cambridge connection and the Elizabethan settlement of 1559* (Durham, North Carolina, 1980).

[29] Elyot, *Governour*, Book I, chapter 11, p. 36r; ed. Lehmberg, p. 34; Skinner, *Reason and rhetoric*, p. 34.

[30] L. Jardine, 'Humanism and dialectic in sixteenth-century Cambridge: a preliminary investigation', in R.R. Bolgar (ed.), *Classical influences on European culture A.D. 1500–1700* (Cambridge, 1976), p. 145.

[31] Skinner, *Reason and rhetoric*, pp. 33–4.

[32] Hatfield, Library catalogue (1568), fos. 1r–6v.

[33] *Books in Cambridge inventories. Book-lists from vice-chancellor's court probate inventories in the Tudor and Stuart periods*, ed. E.S. Leedham-Green, 2 vols. (Cambridge, 1986), I, pp. 70–5 (Soresby), 90–1 (Williamson); II, pp. 217.

orations.[34] But the connection between Cecil and this sort of training is even stronger. Two of his fellow students at Cambridge in the early 1540s, Richard Rainolde and Thomas Wilson, later translated ancient texts and classical principles into English. Rainolde published *A booke called the foundacion of rhetorike* in 1564; Wilson had discussed *The arte of rhetorique* a decade earlier.[35] For Rainolde, rhetoric was a practical exercise, because 'Nothyng can bee more excellently given of nature than Eloquence, by the which the florishyng state of commonweales doe consiste: kyngdomes universally are governed, the state of every one privatlie is maintained.'[36] As important was Rainolde's method. *A booke called the foundacion of rhetorike* was a translation of a set of rhetorical exercises by the Greek rhetorician Aphthonius, printed in the early sixteenth century, but more accessibly published in London *c.* 1520. Aphthonius' *Progymnasmata* was the central guide to structuring rhetorical exercises *in utramque partem*, based on a question and argued *pro* and *contra*.[37]

The language and structure of this form of debate were clear from marginal notes of the Latin translation of Aphthonius, and Rainolde included these technical terms in his translation. Wilson also explained and helped to define the method. For both men, rhetoric was practical. Wilson distinguished between a debate on 'a particuler matter,' and the interests of a logician 'who talketh of thynges universally, without respect of persone, time, or place'. He distinguished between two sorts of rhetorical question, 'Questions infinite' and 'Questions definite'. 'Every question, or demaunde in thynges, is of two sortes. Either it is an infinite question, and without ende, or els it is definite, and comprehended within some ende.' According to Wilson's model, Cecil's political memoranda were 'definite questions' which 'set furthe a matter, with the appoynctment, and namyng of place, time and persone'.[38] Rainolde called this sort of exercise a 'thesis' or 'a certain question in consultacion had, to bee declaimed upon uncertaine' an issue. It usually began with a question – for example, 'Is warre to be moved upon a juste cause?' – which was a '*Propositum*, that is to saie, a question, in determinacion'. A thesis was 'a reasonyng by question, upon a matter uncertaine'. The reasoning could be divided into two, questions 'Civill' and 'Contemplative'. Contemplative questions were 'comprehended in the

---

[34] Skinner, *Reason and rhetoric*, p. 41.
[35] Richard Rainolde, *A booke called the foundacion of rhetorike* . . . (STC 20604; London, 1564); Thomas Wilson, *The arte of rhetorique, for the use of all suche as are studious of eloquence* . . . (STC 25799; London, 1554); Skinner, *Reason and rhetoric*, pp. 29–30, 52–3.
[36] Rainolde, *Rhetorike*, p. 1r.
[37] Skinner, *Reason and rhetoric*, pp. 27–9.
[38] Wilson, *Rhetorique*, p. 1r–v.

minde, and in the intelligence of man'; civil questions were 'daily practised in the common wealthe'.[39] So Cecil's private 'memorials' can be described as civil theses or definite questions. He was certainly well out of Cambridge by the time Wilson and Rainolde put pen to paper, but the method was known at the university and associated with the St John's group in the 1530s and 1540s. *The arte of rhetorique* had a fairly late influence, but *Progymnasmata* was owned by at least three students or Fellows in the late 1530s and early 1540s. One Cambridge bookseller, Nicholas Pilgrim, also had a copy.[40]

The rhetorical method of arguing *in utramque partem* was perfectly suited to balanced political debate. Rainolde suggested an *exordium*, followed by a narration, considerations of whether the issue was lawful, just, profitable, or possible, and a conclusion.[41] At a simple level, notes written *in utramque partem* allowed Cecil to structure his thoughts on key issues. In October 1568, for example, Cecil drafted a plan of notes to be sent to the duke of Norfolk on Elizabeth's right to arbitrate in British affairs. The manuscript begins with a civil thesis, structured around a section *contra* to the argument and divided into A and B.[42] In 1562 Cecil presented a set of arguments against a proposed interview between Mary Stuart and Elizabeth and a short 'Replycat'.[43] In a 'discourse' on military aid for the Scottish lords of the congregation in 1559, he wrote one basically complete version and then redefined it in another. Both versions begin with a civil thesis.[44] Most of these written notes show signs of editing. Cecil often summarized issues in the margin, and went back through his text to correct words, arguments, and sentences. In a memorandum on the British implications of the Queen of Scots' marriage to Darnley in 1565, he seems to have worked through the same manuscript more than once; during the first attempt, Cecil left gaps to go back to, fill in, and rework.[45]

These were involved and important exercises, in which Cecil engaged himself in political dialogue. The memoranda are often sophisticated and highly structured pieces. In a note on Mary and Darnley from September 1565, Cecil split the discussion into six sections. He began with the 'state of the Controversy' in two sections (followed by a longer prose discussion),

[39] Rainolde, *Rhetorike*, pp. 53v–54r.
[40] *Cambridge inventories*, ed. Leedham-Green, I, pp. 36–7, 38–42, 61–70, 70–5; II, p. 803.
[41] Rainolde, *Rhetorike*, p. 54r.
[42] CP 155, fo. 124r, in Cecil's holograph, 16 October 1568, printed in Haynes, p. 482.
[43] 20 June 1562, Cotton Caligula B. 10, fos. 211r–212v; 30 June 1562, Cotton Caligula B. 10, fos. 209r–210v.
[44] For the first draft, August 1559, Cotton Caligula B. 10, fos. 86r–88v; for the second, Cotton Caligula B. 10, fos. 33r–37v.
[45] 24 September 1565, Cotton Caligula B. 10, fos. 350v–353r, 353v.

the arguments against Mary's position, and reasons for and against war. The 'Reasons to mak warr' were based on standard *sententiae* which argued, for example, that 'It is better to begyn with the ennemy a farr of than neare.' The 'Reasons' end with a note on 'Bellum: justum, necessarium, possibile'. The 'Consideration' moved from basic 'causees' for action to Cecil's own 'Causees to move me not to consent presently to warr'. Cecil had explored most of the options open to the regime.[46] He composed a more general discussion in 1569, which runs to over five thousand words and survives as 'A short memoryall' and the 'Extract out of the booke of the state of the Realme'. This was a policy exploration by subdivision. Cecil began with an outline summary of the 'Great', 'manny', and 'Imminent' perils facing Elizabeth and her kingdom. The 'Great' perils were broken down into 'persons' and 'Matters'; each, in turn, was subdivided again. Summary points became the foundation for longer prose discussions, which is a common feature of Cecil's memoranda. He was always able to move from basic evidence to proposed action, able to turn academic analysis into a central feature of the political and policy-making process.[47] It enabled him to spot dangers, alternatives, and options; it also meant that he actually thought through policy options.

Cecil's memoranda were not part of the closed form of political argument, in which the conclusion was reached before pen was set to paper. They forced Cecil to consider and reconsider arguments and philosophical or political points on both sides of an issue. The memoranda were usually genuine attempts to consider an issue or problem fully and fairly. In fact, it is often impossible to work out Cecil's position purely from the broken-down points *pro* and *contra*. And the method was important to him, both as an exploration of issues and options and as the link between the memoranda written in his study and the meetings of the Privy Council. This was the case in 1565, when Cecil was responsible for the minutes of debate on the Queen of Scots and Darnley. He began his notes with two questions, addressed the first (subdividing it into points) and then the second, developing the more important issues into discussions of their own. Bernard Hampton went through the rough draft and prepared a fair copy which Cecil read, edited, and broke down into numbered points. Hampton forgot to write in the heading for the 'Second Question' of the debate, and so Cecil did it for him.[48] Structured notes were an important part of Cecil's

---

[46] 24 September 1565, Cotton Caligula B. 10, fos. 350v–353v. The 'Consideration' was part of an intensive set of at least four meetings of the Privy Council between 24 and 29 September 1565. See below, pp. 133–8.

[47] *c.* July–August 1569, CP 157, fos. 2r–8v, printed in Haynes, pp. 579–88; see below, pp. 182–4.

[48] For Cecil's draft, 4 June 1565, SP 52/10, fos. 148r–151v; for Hampton's, Cotton Caligula B. 10, fos. 301r–308r.

private method of political dialogue and this transferred itself into debate in Council and, ultimately, the making of policy.

The relationship between exercises in rhetorical method and practical governance was made even more solid when Cecil entered Gray's Inn in 1540, after leaving Cambridge without taking a degree.[49] Cecil developed the skills of rhetorical argument and structure at St John's in the late 1530s, and his time at Gray's Inn should have focused and perfected his abilities. One of Cecil's teachers at St John's and a perfect bridge between academic and legal life, Thomas Smith, argued in his inaugural lecture as Regius Professor of Civil Law at Cambridge that law students' debates on philosophy and theology were clear, well argued, and eloquent.[50] Elyot called common law 'pleadynge used in courte and Chauncery[,] called motes', a 'shadowe or figure of the auncient rhetorike'. He reinforced the point by adding a marginal note on 'The arte of Retorycke in mooting'. The skills of a pleading lawyer were the talents of the orator. A law student could be asked to argue a question, which was a method he would have been familiar with from his school and university careers, and which Elyot defined in classical terms; 'that of Tulli', he told the kingdom's future governors, 'is called *constitutio*; & that of Quintilian *status causae*'. Even in a chancery case, a lawyer had to remember the parts of rhetoric – invention, disposition, and memory – and familiarize himself with a whole battery of 'certayne partes of an oration': narrations, partitions, confirmations, and confutations (which Elyot grouped together as 'reprehensions'); and declarations, bars, and replications (which he called 'rejoinders'). The lawyer had to rely on the rhetorical skills of elocution and pronunciation. It was a technical business, but 'they that have studied rhetorike, shal perceyve what I meane'. This was the lawyer as orator and, ideally, philosopher, poet, civil lawyer, and comic actor, 'whiche is all that Tulli in the person of the most eloquent man Marcus Antonius, coulde require to be in an oratour'.[51]

This was more than a technical or limited professional training: these were the skills and qualities of eloquence and method appropriate to governorship. Cecil the rhetorician, working out political arguments and developing the details of possible policy for debate in the Privy Council, is crucial. Cicero, Plato, Xenophon, and Aristotle were worth studying in themselves as good literature, but their work also described the nature 'of

---

[49] In his 'Memoriae nativitatum et aliarum rerum gestarum', Cecil recorded that he was admitted to Gray's Inn in 1541, CP 140, fo. 13r. The admissions register gives a slightly different date. Cecil was one of thirty-two admissions in 1540. He was called to the bar in 1541, became a pensioner in 1545, and an ancient in 1547. Harley 1912, fo. 167v.

[50] R.J. Schoeck, 'Rhetoric and law in sixteenth-century England', *Studies in Philology*, 50 (1953), 118.

[51] Elyot, *Governour*, Book I, chapter 14, pp. 56r–57v; ed. Lehmberg, pp. 53–5.

the diversities of lawes and publike weales'. They were models for public and private service, and, through moral philosophy, taught the two virtues of manners and civil policy. In this way, England would have 'a publike weale equivalent to the grekes or Romanes'.[52] Historical study, too, preserved and maintained the commonwealth, and the reader of history became a 'store of wisedoms for him selfe, and counsell for other'; by 'beholdyng' historians, 'as in a glasse', the reader 'discerneth and judgeth rightly of things present, and forseeth wisely of thinges to come'.[53] For Cicero and Quintilian, philosophy and history were central to public life. Cicero's *vir civilis* was a man who knew how to plead for justice in court and contribute to councils and public assemblies. History, philosophy, law, and rhetoric merged in the search for justice and public office; both Quintilian and Cicero preferred a life of public activity over one of leisure.[54] One man within Cecil's conciliar orbit, Thomas Norton, saw historical study as a foundation of ordered society and an enemy of idleness.[55]

Above all, this was a model for an active form of citizenship in which sixteenth-century Englishmen could act as *viri civiles* – governors, counsellors, and secretaries – and it involved a fairly lofty perception of one's role in government and governance.[56] Cecil and his colleagues were conscious of ancient behaviour and classical expectations. Sir Nicholas Bacon reminded himself of passages from Seneca and Cicero by having just under sixty *sententiae* lining his gallery at Gorhambury. The themes were friendship, moderation, fortune, the treachery of ambition, and the greatest good.[57] In 1553 Cecil prepared a defence of his part in the Jane Grey conspiracy, which included an account of his plan to leave England. John Cheke, the brother of Cecil's first wife Mary and one of his teachers at Cambridge, asked Cecil for his 'satisfaction to rede a dialogue of Plato where Socrates being in Prison was offred to escape and flee and yet he wold not'. According to Cecil's own account, he 'redd the Dialogue whose reasons in dede did stay me'.[58] The important point is not whether Cecil actually read Plato's *Phaedo* or even whether Plato kept him in England,

[52] Elyot, *Governour*, Book I, chapter 14, p. 59r–v; ed. Lehmberg, p. 56.
[53] Thomas Norton (ed.), *Orations, of Arsanes agaynst Philip the trecherous kyng of Macedone* . . . (STC 785; London, *c.* 1560), sig. *2v, *3r; cf. *The mirror for magistrates*, ed. Lily B. Campbell (Cambridge, 1938), pp. 65–6.
[54] Skinner, *Reason and rhetoric*, pp. 67–9.
[55] Norton (ed.), *Orations, of Arsanes*, sig. *2v.
[56] Skinner, *Reason and rhetoric*, pp. 67, 72.
[57] Patrick Collinson, 'Sir Nicholas Bacon and the Elizabethan *via media*', *Historical Journal*, 23 (1980), 260.
[58] Lansdowne 104, fos. 1v–2r, in Cecil's holograph, printed in Patrick Fraser Tytler (ed.), *England under the reigns of Edward VI and Mary*, 2 vols. (London, 1839), II, pp. 194–5.

but that he used this defence at all: for Cecil it was a cultural key, a natural and persuasive way of defending and defining behaviour.

This was not a strange or an archaic thing to do. For Elizabethan governors, classical values and situations were absolutely appropriate. An MP stood up in the Commons in 1566 and delivered a speech in which he justified discussing the royal succession by claiming the support of Cicero. His text closely mirrored a line from Nicholas Grimalde's 1556 English translation of *Marcus Tullius Ciceroes thre bokes of duties*. 'But if question, or comparison be made, to whome the greatest dutie ought to be yeelded: our countrie, and parents be the chief, by whose benefites we ar moste bounde: our children, and all our holle familie be the next.'[59] Grimalde introduced his text by hoping that 'a noble Counseler of England seemeth most meete to receive so noble a Senatour of Rome into a straunge region' but asked that, if he was welcomed, 'so famous a Romane may becomme familiar with our English men'.[60] Henry Peacham told his readers that although *De officiis* lay 'tossed and torne in every Schoole', it should be as precious to them as it was to Cecil 'who, to his dying day, would always carry it about him, either in his bosome or pocket, beeing sufficient (as one said of *Aristotles* Rhetoriques) to make both a Scholler and an honest man'.[61] Perhaps equally apocryphal, but just as important, were the *Certaine precepts, or directions* written by Cecil for his son (perhaps Robert and not the disappointing Thomas), and in circulation in the seventeenth century. These quite openly and consciously emulated Cicero's dedication of *De officiis* to Marcus, 'as *Tullie* sometime exacted from his Sonne, from the only hearing of *Cratippus* his Maister'. The commitment to public service and private virtue was clear. One of the 'foure-folde short remembrances' was, again echoing Cicero's commitment, 'To serve God and his Countrey, his Parents and his Friends'.[62]

Cicero's *De officiis* was central to the understanding Elizabethan governors had of their part in the political scheme of things. It not only established their importance in public affairs but also helped to reinforce a set of common and accepted political and personal values. *De officiis* emphasized the importance of the qualities of justice, fortitude, and

[59] SP 46/166, fo. 3r, printed in Hartley, p. 129; *Marcus Tullius Ciceroes thre bokes of duties, to Marcus his sonne, turned oute of latine into english, by Nicolas Grimalde*, ed. Gerald O'Gorman (Renaissance English Text Society, 12; Washington, London, and Toronto, 1990), p. 73; for other examples, see Markku Peltonen, *Classical humanism and republicanism in English political thought 1570–1640* (Cambridge, 1995), pp. 23–4.

[60] *Ciceroes thre bokes of duties*, ed. O'Gorman, p. 39.

[61] Henry Peachum, *The compleat gentleman. Fashioning him absolut, in the most necessary and commendable qualities concerning minde or body, that may be required in a noble gentleman . . .* (STC 19504; London, 1634), p. 44.

[62] William Cecil, *Certaine precepts, or directions, for the well ordering and carriage of a mans life . . .* (STC 4897; London, 1617), sig. A3r, pp. 25–6.

temperance.[63] The 1547 English translation of *The ethiques of Aristotle* is a far better guide than a modern edition, because it described these qualities and virtues as contemporaries accepted and understood them in the vernacular: 'temperaunce', 'Fortitude', 'Chastite', 'Liberalite', and 'equanimite'. *Sapientia* was a central virtue of the *vir civilis*; *The ethiques of Aristotle* had 'Sapience' as part of the first of two virtues, intellectual and moral.[64] The second book of *The governour* dealt with the qualities of 'mercy', 'placabilite', 'Humanyte', 'benevolence', 'beneficence', 'liberalitie', and 'amitie'.[65] These were just as relevant to late Tudor and early Stuart political life as they were in 1531. Cecil's close colleague Walter Mildmay gave some written advice to his eldest son Anthony in 1570, which Mildmay's granddaughter dutifully copied from another family version. Mildmay emphasized *patria* and parents, and he listed the qualities of *prudentia, justitia, amicitia, societas, liberalitas, fortitudo,* and *temperantia*.[66]

So the classical world, and ancient authors, affected sixteenth-century Englishmen in two, interconnected ways. First, they provided the skills of organization and a model for debate and eloquence; and second, they explained personal qualities and virtues, linked them to method – pleading in the courts for justice and using one's powers of reasoning in council, for example – and placed the *vir civilis* in his natural environment – the 'publike weale', according to Elyot, 'a body lyvyng, compacte or made of sondry astates and degrees of men, whiche is diposed by the ordre of equite, and governed by the rule and moderation of reason'.[67] For contemporaries, these were relevant and immediate concerns. On a wide political level, it was perfectly natural for Francis I of France, after his return from captivity in Spain in 1526, to hear counsel in the style of a Roman emperor.[68] More modestly, men like Cecil, Mildmay, and Bacon knew their classical texts, understood their significance, and applied (or at least thought they *should* apply) them to their political careers. The effect of this influence on a Council which had far more executive power than some of its Continental equivalents is crucially important, especially on 'state' issues like religion and succession; so, too, is the strain that this sense

---

[63] Skinner, *Reason and rhetoric*, pp. 76–7.
[64] Aristotle, *Ethiques*, sig. B3v, C1v–C2r.
[65] Elyot, *Governour*, Book II, chapters 6–11, pp. 119v–145v; ed. Lehmberg, pp. 111–36; Skinner, *Reason and rhetoric*, p. 79.
[66] Northamptonshire Record Office, Westmorland (Apethorpe) Miscellaneous 35, fos. 15v–20r; Northamptonshire Record Office, Westmorland (Apethorpe) Miscellaneous 28, fos. 313–22.
[67] Elyot, *Governour*, Book I, chapter 1, p. 1r; ed. Lehmberg, p. 1.
[68] J.A. Guy, 'The French king's council, 1483–1526', in Ralph A. Griffiths and James Sherborne (eds.), *Kings and nobles in the later middle ages* (Gloucester and New York, 1986), pp. 277–8.

of wider duty and personal propriety placed on a councillor's oath. These issues have not been at the centre of the debate on Elizabethan political culture and high politics, but they deserve to be.

III

The influence of Cecil's education and the 'Cambridge connection' are the keys to his career and his religion in the late 1540s and early 1550s. Even Cecil's personal life mixed, as perhaps only the sixteenth century could, career advancement, patronage, and religion. Mildred Cecil was the daughter of Sir Anthony Cooke, and the sister-in-law of Sir Nicholas Bacon. Mildred dedicated her English translation of *An homelie or sermon of Basile the Great* to the duchess of Suffolk, the principal Protestant court reformer in Edward VI's reign, and one of Cecil's main correspondents in Edward's reign. As patriarch, Cecil presided over a pious, reformed household; as Master of Requests and the duke of Somerset's personal secretary, he sat at the centre of a distinctly Protestant patronage network which benefited three of his old Cambridge friends, Thomas Smith, John Cheke, and Roger Ascham, the duchess of Suffolk, the then earl of Warwick, and William Turner. Although Cecil's own short accounts of his Edwardian and Marian years are at best sketchy – a less than complete note of events in his personal and professional lives and a short diary of the main religious events of Mary's reign[69] – the sense of his early career and religious commitments is based on two main themes: first, old contacts with the Cambridge group; and second, a deep sense of providence and duty, which began in his university days and marked his understanding of policy in the 1560s.

One of the best examples of the development of a reformed church in England and the Cambridge connection began at Cecil's house in November 1551 and continued, a week later, at the home of Richard Moryson. It was a debate on the sacrament in two parts. The two meetings prefigured the 1552 Second Book of Common Prayer, which was promoted in 1559. As an academic debate on transubstantiation, it involved men who connected the Edwardian political and religious settlement and the Elizabethan: Cecil, Cheke, Robert Horne (the dean of Durham), David Whitehead (the duchess of Suffolk's chaplain), and Edmund Grindal (eventually one of Edward's chaplains and bishop of London between 1559 and 1570); important Elizabethan councillors and ambassadors like Nicholas Throckmorton and Francis Knollys sat in on the debate and judged the proceedings. The two disputants on the Catholic side in the first meeting were John

---

[69] CP 140, fos. 13r–15v; CP 229, no. 2, printed in Murdin, pp. 746–7.

Feckenham and John Young, who were under arrest at the time; but at the second debate they were joined by Thomas Watson, a member of the old Cambridge group, with whom Ascham and Cheke discussed (according to Ascham) Aristotle and Horace's *De arte poetica*. Ascham compared Watson's play *Absalom* with George Buchanan's *Jephtha*, two plays which he thought were the only perfect blend of Aristotle and Euripides to be found in English, French, German, and Italian drama.[70] The 1551 meetings were serious contributions to a central theological issue, expressions of friendship, and examples of hard academic debate.

Cecil's Edwardian career rested on his talents of organization and experience. He was around thirty-seven years of age on the accession of Elizabeth, and twenty-nine at his appointment as a Secretary in September 1550. His secretarial colleagues, Sir William Petre and Sir Thomas Smith, were forty-five and thirty-seven, respectively. Nevertheless, Cecil was at the centre of Northumberland's move to rationalize and develop the Privy Council's executive, administrative, and judicial role in government.[71] But the part Cecil played in the politics of Edward's reign was more than institutional: Northumberland clearly worked through Cecil, and told him, in May 1553 and during an illness, that he wished him a good recovery 'bothe for your owne comforte as allso for the advauncement of the Kinges waightie affayres'.[72] Political responsibilities became opportunities. In August 1549, Somerset ordered printers to submit to Petre, Smith, or Cecil all English works; any one of the three men could stop publication and ban sales.[73] Along with the fact that in 1585 Cecil's chaplain, William Whitaker, defined the universal church as God's elect, this power makes it hard to accept Professor Patrick Collinson's argument that Cecil did not know what Calvinism was about until 1595.[74] Cecil and Cheke took an interest in the printer John Day, who was publishing translations of Calvin and the works of Thomas Becon in the late 1540s and, two years after Elizabeth's accession, kicked his press back into action with the *Sermons of John Calvin, upon the songe that Ezechias made*. Both Cecil and Matthew Parker kept a protective eye on Day into the 1570s. John Hooper, who

[70] John Strype, *The life of the learned Sir John Cheke, Kt. first instructor, afterwards Secretary of State, to King Edward VI* ... (Oxford, 1821), pp. 69–86; Roger Ascham, *The scholemaster* (STC 832; London, 1570), p. 57r; ed. Lawrence V. Ryan (Charlottesville, Virginia, 1974), p. 139.

[71] Hoak, *King's Council*, p. 63; Hoak, 'Rehabilitating the duke of Northumberland: politics and political control, 1549–53', in Jennifer Loach and Robert Tittler (eds.), *The mid-Tudor polity, c. 1540–1560* (London, 1980), pp. 40–1.

[72] Northumberland to Cecil, 7 May 1553, Lansdowne 103, fo. 46r.

[73] Hoak, *King's Council*, p. 195.

[74] Peter Lake, 'The significance of the Elizabethan identification of the pope as antichrist', *Journal of Ecclesiastical History*, 31 (1980), 161–78, particularly 163 n. 8; Collinson, 'Bacon', 267.

returned from Zurich a radical Zwinglian demanding the removal of images and music from churches, was a friendly and concerned correspondent of Cecil's in the early 1550s.

The general picture of Cecil's early political and religious work, then, is active, reforming, and moderately Calvinist. But most accounts of his religion in the 1550s have been established on a false premise and have, perhaps more significantly, missed the point. Cecil kept fairly quiet during Mary's reign, and probably for good reason. His servant, Francis Yaxley, kept him in touch with court affairs, and he seems to have divided his time between sitting for Lincolnshire in the 1555 parliament and concentrating on his estates. The crucial point is this: the principle that, for example, Francis Walsingham was a 'better' Protestant than Cecil because he was abroad between 1553 and 1558 must be flawed.[75] Walsingham was studying civil law at Padua rather than sitting at the feet of Calvin. More research needs to be done on Cecil's relationship with the theory and practice of 'Nicodemism' and underground support for Protestantism in the 1550s.[76] But the important focus for any study of Cecil a decade later is the general sense of his early Protestantism and the providential edge it gave to his Elizabethan political analysis. By condemning him out of hand as a *politique*, a man who steered his way between extremes, basically untouched by any deep religious feelings, historians have generally cut themselves off from Cecil's sharp and defined sense of the part solid religion and honest faith played in encouraging the stability of the commonwealth and the political security of England. There have been some moves to compensate for this by stressing Cecil's anti-Catholicism – which was genuine, but always part of a larger and more subtle political interpretation of Britain and Europe. His sense of providence and policy was often more sophisticated.[77]

In 1564, a slightly miserable Cecil told Sir Thomas Smith that although

---

[75] Conyers Read, 'Walsingham and Burghley in Queen Elizabeth's Privy Council', *English Historical Review*, 28 (1913), 35, 37, argued that Walsingham was 'radically protestant' and Cecil a '*Politique*', who in 'contrast with Walsingham . . . preferred national considerations before religious ones'. Cf. E.I. Kouri, who asked the profoundly misleading question: 'For true faith or national interest? Queen Elizabeth I and the Protestant powers', in E.I. Kouri and Tom Scott (eds.), *Politics and society in Reformation Europe* (Basingstoke and London, 1987), p. 413.

[76] For some important preliminary work, see Andrew Pettegree, *Marian Protestantism. Six studies* (Aldershot and Brookfield, Vermont, 1996), pp. 103–5; cf. Carlos M.N. Eire, 'Prelude to sedition? Calvin's attack on Nicodemism and religious compromise', *Archiv für Reformationsgeschichte*, 76 (1985), 120–45.

[77] Malcolm R. Thorp, 'William Cecil and the antichrist. A study in anti-Catholic ideology', in Malcolm R. Thorp and Arthur J. Slavin (eds.), *Politics, religion, and diplomacy* (Sixteenth Century Essays and Studies, 27; Kirksville, Missouri, 1994), pp. 289–304; Thorp, 'Catholic conspiracy in early Elizabethan foreign policy', *Sixteenth Century Journal*, 15 (1984), 431–48.

his 'owtward actions' were 'most comenly in publick thynges of the world, yet I thank God, I doo submytt all my conceptes and thoughtes as mere folly, to the wisedom and piete of the Gospell'.[78] For Elizabethans, there was a strong cultural connection between the physical health of the human body, the welfare of a commonwealth, and the crucial part governors and magistrates played in preserving the state of a kingdom. In his chapter on 'The Experience or practise necessary in the persone of a governor of a publike weale', Elyot compared 'the universall state of a contray or citie' to 'the body of man, wherfore the governours in the stede of phisitions attending on their cure, ought to knowe the causes of the decaye of their publike weale whiche is the helthe of their countraye or cytie'.[79] Cecil reversed the same metaphor to frightening effect in 1569: Elizabeth was the patient, being operated on by the Catholic powers of Europe using Mary Stuart as their scalpel.[80] Spiritually, national sin reflected the state of the kingdom. In 1568 Cecil edited 'A prayer for the Quene being sicke', which began with the line 'O most just god and mercyfull father which of thy justice doest punishe us with sicknes for our synnes'.[81] Probably during the outbreak of plague in 1563, he corrected a draft of 'The prayour or Collecte'. In health and prosperity, Elizabeth's subjects had 'cleane forgotten' God and themselves; they had deserved God's 'severe rodde of this terrible plage', because by the 'inwarde infection of our myndes, these outwarde diseases of our bodyes have *by the order of thy Justice o Lord issued and followed*'.[82] In April 1569 he explained to a correspondent how his daughter had had 'a dooble bastard tertiann' fever for ten days. 'God comfort me with her amendment', he continued, 'for I knolledg his wrath shall be very burdenooss if my synnes be avenged with loss of hir'.[83]

But there was more to the spiritual health of the polity than illness or distemper, and for Cecil this included the political security of the kingdom and the effectiveness of its governance. He was, in this sense, heavily providential: Cecil's notes often present an interpretation of the state of Britain and Europe in which the future of England depends on faith and true reformed worship in the kingdom. One of Cecil's early memoranda, 'A Memoryall of thynges to be reported to hir Majesty', not only pointed to the problem of 'papistes, Jesuittes and seminary prestes' in England but also connected religious life and discipline to foreign and domestic problems. Cecil explained that to 'remedy this mischeff', archbishops and

---

[78] 11 January 1564, Lansdowne 102, fo. 56r.
[79] Elyot, *Governour*, Book III, chapter 25, p. 248r; ed. Lehmberg, pp. 231–4.
[80] From 'A short memoryall', CP 157, fo. 2r, printed in Haynes, p. 579.
[81] Lansdowne 116, fo. 75r–v.
[82] Lansdowne 116, fo. 73r, with Cecil's holograph in *italics*.
[83] Cecil to Nicholas White, 15 April 1569, Lansdowne 102, fo. 141r.

bishops 'wold be charged to have more regard to ther charges': the defects were covetousness and 'loosnes of lyff'.[84] Privy councillors often put problems in an ecclesiastical or providential context. This meant, on one level, 'preserving the creditt and reputation' of a commonwealth by establishing a secure ecclesiastical settlement,[85] and defending the succession interests of Elizabeth by moving 'to avaunce, stablish and fortefy in dede the profession of relligion both in scotland and in England and to demynish, weaken and feble the contrary'.[86] On another, it involved Catholic powers acting as the instruments of God 'for the synnes of his people both here and ellswhere that do abuse the name of his Gospell'. The invasion of England by the French king in June 1569, and the 'conquest and spoyle of the small flock that are now with all extremity compelled by armes to defend them selves against only the Popes tyrannous bloody and poysoning persequutors', rested on God's will.[87] It is this key idea – that religious and ecclesiastical failure would incur the wrath of God – which underpinned and helps to explain the panic over justices of the peace opposed to the Elizabethan settlement in 1564, and Cecil's belief, four years later, that 'the service of God and the syncere profession of the Christian Relligion is much of late decayed'.[88]

IV

The politics of providence needed application, attention, and careful balancing. The problem with the 'Gloriana approach' to Elizabethan politics is that it assumes that the success of the regime was inevitable, when contemporaries felt that it was not. Reinforced by a tradition of 'factional' interpretations of the way in which court and Council operated – split into groups with different and conflicting interests, fighting for patronage and over policy – it is too easy to stress the disharmony of the regime at the expense of common interest.[89] It is also tempting to point to

---

[84] SP 12/4, fo. 135r.

[85] SP 12/7, fo. 186v, during the debate on military intervention in Scotland, 27 December 1559.

[86] SP 52/10, fo. 149v, and Cotton Caligula B. 10, fo. 304r, on the proposed marriage between Mary Stuart and Darnley, 4 June 1565.

[87] SP 12/51, fo. 10v.

[88] CP 157, fo. 4r, printed in Haynes, p. 582.

[89] J.E. Neale, 'The Elizabethan political scene', in his *Essays in Elizabethan history* (London, 1957), pp. 59–84; Conyers Read, 'Factions in the English Privy Council under Elizabeth', *American Historical Association Report*, 1 (1911), 109–19; Read, 'Walsingham and Burghley', 34–58. For some important reinterpretations by Patrick Collinson and Simon Adams, see Collinson, 'The monarchical republic of Queen Elizabeth I', in his *Elizabethan essays* (London and Rio Grande, 1994), pp. 31–57, especially pp. 40–1; Adams, 'Faction, clientage and party. English politics, 1550–1603', *History Today*, 32 (1982), 33–9; Adams, 'Eliza enthroned? The court and its politics', in Christopher Haigh (ed.), *The reign of*

incidents in, rather than patterns of, political life, and to find 'factions' when the rigorous demands of Council committed councillors to hard administrative work. For the 1560s, there is only one meeting of the Council where councillors presented clearly divided advice to Elizabeth, and even then it was split on the practical application of policy and not on principle.[90] The Elizabethan 'faction debate' was argued on a false premise, in the tradition of Sir Robert Naunton's wholly unreliable *Fragmenta regalia*. It made the mistake of assuming that Elizabethan political life was static when, in actual fact, it was conducted dynamically in a providential framework which forced councillors to take policy – and certainly policy on the succession and England's precarious place in Europe in the 1560s – extremely seriously. They were obliged to offer sometimes painful and unacceptable advice, reinforced and advised by classical models of political behaviour and private virtue. There *was* a basic tension in 'The othe of a Co[u]nsellor' between counsel 'as maye best seme in your conscience tend to the savety of hir Majesties person, and to the commen weale of this realme'. The difference was sometimes not one of formula or convention: in 1567, for example, Elizabeth openly contrasted 'pleasing perswations of comen good' and the authority of the prince as head of the body politic.[91]

This is not to say that Elizabeth's early privy councillors did not disagree, but collisions between colleagues were fairly natural parts of the political process. Cecil was unhappy with the behaviour of his brother-in-law and the Lord Keeper of the Great Seal, Bacon, at some point in the 1560s and he wrote him a note to ask for an explanation and, more importantly, for a reconciliation. Bacon replied on the same sheet, which was meant to be burned by Cecil but survived his fire. Determined to abide by the 'Rules of frendshypp', Bacon apologized.[92] They were also on awkward terms in July 1563, when Bacon objected to the dispatch of diplomatic letters. Cecil had followed the normal procedure for collecting councillors' signatures but he claimed that Bacon was out when he called in. Rather than following the 'first degre in frendship', which was 'to have broken with me privately', Bacon openly tackled Cecil in the Council chamber.[93] Cecil thought that Bacon had missed at least one stage in the process of reconciling a

---

Elizabeth I (Basingstoke and London, 1984), pp. 55–77; and Adams, 'Favourites and factions at the Elizabethan court', in Ronald G. Asch and Adolf M. Birke (eds.), *Princes, patronage, and the nobility. The court at the beginning of the modern age c. 1450–1650* (Oxford, 1991), pp. 265–87. For an attempt to put factionalism back on the early Elizabethan agenda, see Susan Doran, 'Religion and politics at the court of Elizabeth I: the Habsburg marriage negotiations of 1559–1567', *English Historical Review*, 104 (1989), 908–26.

[90] See below, pp. 66–7.
[91] Cotton Charter 4.38 (2), printed in Hartley, pp. 174–5.
[92] Lansdowne 94, fo. 195r.
[93] Cecil to Bacon, 21 July 1563, Lansdowne 102, fos. 69r–70v; see below, pp. 213–14.

disagreement. But disagreement, after all, was not faction. Even the great factional issue for historians like Camden and Read, the relationship between Cecil and Robert Dudley, earl of Leicester, has to be questioned. Differences in religion – between Cecil as a *politique* and Dudley as a 'hot gospeller' – are now no longer relevant. Although Cecil compiled a list of reasons against marriage between Leicester and Elizabeth in late 1566 or 1567, this is perhaps evidence more of honest analysis than it is of personal hatred. Even the 'particular frendes' of Leicester listed by Cecil were in no sense a 'faction'. Cecil seems to have been more concerned to preserve balance: to maintain the smooth running of Council and court by giving no cause for offence, and to protect the regime against the re-emergence of the 'slaunderooss speches of the Quene with the Erle' which had caused so many problems in the very early years of the reign. The memorandum had more to do with the danger of creating factions than with delineating them.[94] In fact, Cecil's relationship with Leicester seems to have been cordial and productive. Leicester took part in some of the most important meetings of the Privy Council in the 1560s. The two men worked together on Scottish policy in 1565; they were provided with reports on the situation in Scotland by Sir Nicholas Throckmorton, Leicester's 'political brain' in the middle of the decade and one of Cecil's regular correspondents.[95] Cecil told Sir Henry Sidney in 1568 that 'my Lord of Lecester is in my howss at dyce, and merry, wher', he added with false modesty, 'he hath taken paynes to be evill lodged these .2. nightes, and to morrow we retorn both to the Court'.[96] The evidence is too patchy to indulge in deep analysis, but the relationship between Cecil and Dudley seems to have been one of tolerant and earnest co-operation; at best, perhaps, friendship.

In fact, the early Elizabethan Privy Council was a remarkably stable and effective group of men. Continuity was the keynote. Cecil's notes from 18 November 1558 clearly point to the need for Marian councillors' advice and presence. The register noted the attendance of 'Lord Admyrall' Edward Clinton and 'Lord Chamberlain' William Howard of Effingham at the first meeting of the Privy Council on 20 November.[97] But even before the official meeting of the Council, Cecil planned a gathering of the archbishop of York, Nicholas Heath, the marquess of Winchester, the earls of Shrewsbury and Derby, Sir Thomas Cheyney, and Sir William Petre. Important security measures were tackled by Winchester and Sir Walter Mildmay (who took the jewels from the privy chamber into safe custody) and Howard of

---

[94] CP 155, fos. 28r–29v; Simon Adams, 'The Dudley clientele, 1553–1563', in G.W. Bernard (ed.), *The Tudor nobility* (Manchester and New York, 1992), pp. 241–3.

[95] Adams, 'Dudley clientele', p. 243.

[96] 5 November 1568, SP 63/26, fo. 61r.

[97] PC 2/8, fo. 195; *Acts of the Privy Council of England*, ed. Dasent *et al.*, VII, p. 3.

Effingham and Sir Edward Rogers (who helped to put the chamber in order).[98] Cecil, the other new Elizabethan candidates, and some old Marians sat as an unofficial core Council three days before the first meeting of the Privy Council. Patrick Collinson has called the early Elizabethan 'regime' a 'stable governing group', and it was.[99] Councillors who died during the 1560s were replaced by men who were well known to the Queen, the court, and the Council, some of whom had been unofficially tipped for office in November 1558: Lord Robert Dudley, Mildmay, and Sir Ralph Sadler.[100]

But what part did this stable, coherent, and experienced group of councillors play in the governance of the realm? Because historians have generally been happy to portray Elizabeth as the master puppeteer of the court, controlling, manipulating, and guiding, it has been difficult to ask a crucial question. It is, in some ways, more than a little subversive: who exercised public power in the early Elizabethan state? The Queen or her councillors? In one sense, it was very clearly Elizabeth. The Lords admitted as much in 1563 when they pointed out that their monarch was 'Anima Legis, and is reputed in lawe', and so when the prince died, the law died.[101] The whole political and legal system described by Sir Thomas Smith in 1565 rested on the authority and the life of one woman. This is why Elizabeth's position as an unmarried female monarch unwilling to settle the succession, Mary Stuart's claim to the English throne, and the perceived threat of European Catholicism triggered such a profound crisis in the 1560s. Elizabeth acted as a final (and often negative) check on policy. After a month of detailed negotiations with the Scottish lords of the congregation and intensive debate, with two-thirds of her councillors in support of active intervention in Scotland in 1559, the Queen vetoed the proposal. In 1564 Elizabeth personally pressed Lord Robert Dudley as a suitable match for the widowed Mary Stuart. She panicked after the deposition of Mary in 1567 because, on the one hand, she did not accept the principle that subjects could resist a monarch but, on the other, realized that the Queen of Scots' behaviour was unacceptable. Cecil and Leicester co-ordinated their attempts to persuade Elizabeth to act. Both men offered counsel by letter and in person, but she was not 'disposed to gyve any answer of moment'.[102]

---

[98] 18 November 1558, SP 12/1, fo. 4r–v, in Cecil's holograph.

[99] Collinson, 'Monarchical republic', p. 40.

[100] Dudley seems to have responsible for organizing the stables on 18 November 1558, SP 12/ 1, fo. 4v. Throckmorton proposed Mildmay as one of two principal secretaries on the Edwardian model: Neale (ed.), 'Throckmorton's advice', 96.

[101] SP 12/27, fo. 136v, printed in Hartley, p. 60.

[102] Cecil to Leicester, 15 May 1567, Magdalene College, Cambridge, PL 2502, fo. 737; Leicester to Cecil, 16 June 1567, SP 12/43, fo. 23r–v.

The exercise of public power depends upon at least two separate actions: the decision to introduce a policy and its execution. Historians generally accept that the Elizabethan Privy Council could order, change, and adjust administration, at the centre or in the counties, through its 'instruments', letters signed by a quorum of councillors. The first Elizabethan decade was clearly more conciliar than the last, when Cecil alone authorized warrants for payment on behalf of his colleagues.[103] In fact, Elizabeth was almost written out of daily business in the 1560s. In 1558 Cecil consciously de-politicized the privy chamber. Because it was staffed by women, the Henrician chamber's powers over the privy purse and the royal signature were restored to the secretaryship. It was Cecil who kept the stamp of Elizabeth's sign manual.[104] Although councillors clearly spoke to Elizabeth in person, the Council's opinion as a political, executive, and consultative group was transferred through Cecil's pen and, very probably, his audiences with the Queen. Petitions from the Privy Council, written and edited by Cecil, became an important form of access. Elizabeth signed diplomatic dispatches to her representatives in Europe, Scotland, and Ireland, but Cecil usually drafted them. Unless the Queen was willing to dictate instructions – and often correct two or perhaps three redrafts – then structure, language, and emphasis were Cecil's responsibility. The same was true of proclamations. Cecil drafted texts and corrected the secretarial fair copies which ended up as the final printed version. Even the two texts of the unpublished defence of the regime prepared after the northern rebellion were a collaborative effort between Bernard Hampton as clerk and Cecil as draughtsman.[105] If Elizabeth was particularly determined to tackle a serious problem – her authority over parliament in 1566, for example – then she was perfectly prepared to correct drafts or chair meetings of the Council.[106] Her involvement in the early stages of action was less enthusiastic.

But did Cecil and the Privy Council do more than execute policy made at a higher level? And what was the relationship between counsel and action? Elyot called consultation 'the generall denomination of the acte wher in men do devise to gether', but the final part of his sentence is crucial: the debate involved active decision-making, where the councillors 'do devise to

---

[103] Elton, 'Council', 23; John Guy, 'The 1590s: the second reign of Elizabeth I', in John Guy (ed.), *The reign of Elizabeth I. Court and culture in the last decade* (Cambridge, 1995), p. 14; see below, pp. 209–10.

[104] Pam Wright, 'A change in direction: the ramifications of a female household, 1558–1603', in David Starkey (ed.), *The English court: from the Wars of the Roses to the Civil War* (London and New York, 1987), pp. 152, 153 n. 26.

[105] CP 157, fos. 9r–12r; SP 12/66, fos. 147r–152v.

[106] See below, pp. 151–2.

gether & reason what *is to be done*'.[107] Although Elizabethan privy councillors clearly debated issues and influenced the daily business of government, counsel suggested action, and counsel on significant issues – like the Queen's marriage, the succession, and the kingdom's religion – suggested more than a passing concern with what today could be called 'national' policy. In 1563, when Cecil imagined England, Wales, and Ireland controlled by a 'council of estate', 'usually named a privee Counsell', he commented that this group of men had traditionally had 'authorite to govern, command, and direct the publick affayres of the realme' in 'the lyves of the kynges or Quenes of the realme'.[108] Six years later his colleague, Sir Francis Knollys, argued that it was not possible for the Queen's 'most faithfull cownsellors to governe' her state well unless she could 'Resolutelie followe theire opynions in waightie affairs'.[109] One standard humanist-classical thesis for debate was 'that action not based on knowledge was worthless and knowledge wasted without resulting action'.[110] This was a real issue for Elizabethan privy councillors in the 1560s. Preservation of the commonwealth was a duty, even if it involved upsetting the Queen, a point which the first decade of her reign made very clearly. At times, councillors were genuinely torn between personal obedience to the monarch and their commitment to something more public. Maurizio Viroli has drawn a distinction between the 'Ciceronian tradition of political virtues' and 'politics as the art of the state' in Italy between the thirteenth and the beginning of the seventeenth centuries.[111] But there was a tension even in the apparently less sophisticated 'Ciceronian tradition' of civil philosophy which had formed such an important part of Cecil's education. The model of counsel could – and did – suggest more to Elizabeth's councillors than it did to the Queen herself. They were, in a sense, *too* well trained for active governorship, office, and counsel.

V

The tone of Knollys' advice, and the verbs he used, seemed to leave little room for noncompliance. So Elyot's textbook for competent governors and Knollys' plea for active policy tested the boundaries of what Thomas

---

[107] Elyot, *Governour*, Book III, chapter 27, p. 252v, with my *italics*; ed. Lehmberg, p. 236–7.
[108] SP 12/28, fo. 68v, printed below, pp. 225–8.
[109] Knollys to Elizabeth, 17 January 1569, SP 12/49, fo. 57v.
[110] John Guy, 'The Henrician age', in J.G.A. Pocock (ed.), *The varieties of British political thought, 1500–1800* (Cambridge, 1993), p. 14.
[111] Maurizio Viroli, *From politics to reason of state. The acquisition and transformation of the language of politics 1250–1600* (Cambridge, 1992), pp. 2–3, 6.

Hobbes later called counsel and command.[112] This is a remarkably common theme in (and a significant comment on) the politics of the relationship between Queen and Council in the 1560s. This was probably all too near the bone for Elizabeth, but she was a woman and that was one of Knollys' main problems. She simply had to trust her councillors as a matter of course; the relationship was complicated by her sex. Women were the spiritual equals of men, but in the hierarchy of God's creation they were subordinate.[113] Knollys presented a practical example. 'A generall in the fielde seinge an enterprice to be taken', he told Elizabeth, could choose some of his captains to consider the feasibility of the plan: what was the point of the exercise if the general acted 'contrarie to theyre opynions'?[114] Knollys' metaphor was male and it was exclusive.

Female rule and the complexities of counsel were as much a comment on the *nature* of the Elizabethan polity as they were on its politics. There were a number of general issues. In 'A pollitique discoorse touchinge the governement of this Realme', Sir Nicholas Throckmorton told Elizabeth that in her 'parson' consisted 'the pollitique life of all your people and also the health of your owne state and others'. 'You must thearefore beware of womanish levitie', for 'wheare the Kinge governeth not in severitie and prudence theare dooth emulation and ambition sowe theire seedes'.[115] Elizabeth could adopt the same disabling form in parliamentary addresses. But there was a more significant issue, and it involved contemporary perceptions of the nature and source of political control in the kingdom. John Aylmer hinted at this in *An harborowe for faithfull and trewe subjectes*, which he published in 1559.[116] Aylmer had an agenda: the book was written to counter John Knox's *First blast of the trumpet*. His argument has also been compared to justifying the Thatcher government on the grounds that the prime minister could be restrained by her cabinet.[117] But the fact that Aylmer argued the points he did (and the resonance they have with the early Elizabethan polity) deserves to be explored.

Aylmer based his analysis on the familiar and conventional 'forms of government' from the third book of Aristotle's *Politics*. England was 'not a mere Monarchie, as some for lacke of consideracion thinke, nor a meere

---

[112] Thomas Hobbes, *Leviathan*, ed. Richard Tuck (Cambridge, 1991), part II, chapter 25, pp. 176–82.

[113] Constance Jordan, 'Woman's rule in sixteenth-century British political thought', *Renaissance Quarterly*, 40 (1987), 421–2.

[114] SP 12/49, fo. 57v.

[115] Northamptonshire Record Office, Fitzwilliam (Milton) Political 102, *c.* 1558, unfoliated.

[116] John Aylmer, *An harborowe for faithfull and trewe subjectes, agaynst the late blowne blaste, concerninge the government of wemen . . .* (STC 1005; London, 1559).

[117] Collinson, 'Monarchical republic', p. 35.

Oligarchie nor Democracie, but a rule mixte of all these, wherein ech one of these have or shoulde have like authoritie'.[118] In this, he agreed with his contemporary, Sir Thomas Smith, who argued six years later that 'any common wealthe or governement' was 'alwayes mixed with an other'.[119] This was a commonplace and its basic conservatism can be sensed from Aristotle as its source. But two of Aylmer's assumptions deserve closer attention. The first concerned the relationship between monarch and Council. English rulers 'have theyr counsel at their elbow' to advise on the choice of the 'executors' of the law, the judges.[120] In effect, Aylmer's defence against the 'regiment' of women in England seemed to rest on the argument that the kingdom was effectively governed by the Council. If this was a popular cultural assumption, then it had profound implications for the polity in the 1560s, governed by a female monarch who refused to play by the rules of her sex and the requirements of dynasty.

Aylmer also discussed parliament. For historians like A.F. Pollard and Sir John Neale, the Elizabethan House of Commons was developing a strong sense of its own 'corporate' identity which led, almost inevitably, to the clash between king and parliament in the 1640s.[121] But after the historiographical rise, parliament's reputation fell. In 1986 Sir Geoffrey Elton wondered 'whether the institution . . . ever really mattered all that much in the politics of the nation, except perhaps as a stage sometimes used by the real contenders over government and policy', but certainly not as a prelude to civil war. It was a closely fought and in some ways antagonistic debate.[122] In fact, the influence of Neale lives on in some of the main printed and biographical sources for the Elizabethan parliaments.[123] So although it is fairly easy to understand what historians have thought and still think about the role of parliament in the sixteenth century, it is harder

---

[118] Aylmer, *Harborowe*, sig. H2v–H3r.

[119] Smith, *De republica Anglorum*, ed. Dewar, book I, chapter 6, 'That common wealthes or governements are not commonly simple but mixt', p. 52; for a more detailed discussion of Aylmer, Smith, and 'mixed government', see Michael Mendle, *Dangerous positions. Mixed government, the estates of the realm, and the making of the Answer to the xix propositions* (Alabama, 1985), pp. 48–56; and below, pp. 116–17, 210–12.

[120] Aylmer, *Harborowe*, sig. H3v.

[121] A.F. Pollard, *The evolution of parliament* (London, 1920); J.E. Neale, 'The Commons' privilege of free speech in parliament', in R.W. Seton-Watson (ed.), *Tudor studies* (London, 1924), pp. 257–86; Neale, *Elizabeth I and her parliaments 1559–1601*, 2 vols. (London, 1953, 1957).

[122] G.R. Elton, *The parliament of England 1559–1581* (Cambridge, 1986), p. ix; Elton, 'Parliament', in Haigh (ed.), *Reign of Elizabeth I*, pp. 79–100.

[123] Principally Hartley, p. ix, which set out to print 'many of the raw materials' used by Neale in his 'life-long work on Elizabeth's Parliaments'. Neale and his research assistants and colleagues at the Institute of Historical Research also worked on the short biographical studies of MPs eventually published in 1981, and edited by Hasler; for a critical review, see John Guy, 'Law, faction, and parliament in the sixteenth century', *Historical Journal*, 28 (1985), 451.

to work out how Elizabethan councillors and MPs interpreted the nature, power, and authority of the Lords and Commons. Contemporary books are one source. For Aylmer, parliament was the 'image' and 'the thinge in dede' of the mixed polity, 'wherin you shal find these .3. estats': the king or queen as monarch, the nobility as aristocracy, and burgesses and knights as the democratic element.[124] But Cecil provided a few clues to his own sense of the part parliament played in the polity. Like Aylmer, he used the term 'the three estates' to describe parliament. In 1563 Cecil told Sir Thomas Smith that there had been 'ernest sutes made by the .3. estates to the Quenes Majesty ether for mariadg, or stab[lishing] of succession'. He had written 'sutes made by both', but scored out the last word: perhaps he inserted '.3. estates' as a more effective synonym for 'both houses'?[125] In 1566 Bernard Hampton wrote a summary of (or perhaps a plan for) Cecil's preamble to the Subsidy Bill, which referred to Elizabeth's 'assured declaration publickly made to a selecte number of her three estates'.[126] Cecil believed that parliament could debate the Queen's marriage and the succession to the kingdom, and establish ecclesiastical and religious laws. He could also imagine a session of parliament held without a living monarch, able to choose a successor to the crown. He drafted the plan in 1563 but it re-emerged in 1585. In an emergency a parliamentary statute would replace the royal writ to summon the Lords and Commons. Elizabeth, significantly, would have none of it.[127]

But parliament in the 1560s did not want to stand as a separate constitutional unit in its modern sense, and MPs did not want to challenge Elizabeth's authority. In the second parliament of the reign, Cecil and the Privy Council wanted to persuade the Queen to settle the succession for her own good and for the good of the kingdom.[128] Cecil and his colleagues in the Council believed that parliament had a part to play in the administration of the 'mixed polity' of England, acting with the Queen. But even this was a fairly controversial point for an imperial monarch: writing as a counter to Henry VIII's caesaropapism, in 1531, the common lawyer Christopher St German defined 'the kynge in his parlyament' as 'the hyghe soveraygne over the people'.[129] The presbyterian Thomas Cartwright used the Aristotelian model of the 'mixed polity' to explain the relationship between church and state. Archbishop Whitgift rejected the parallel:

[124] Aylmer, *Harborowe*, sig. H3r.
[125] 18 February 1563, Lansdowne 102, fo. 22r.
[126] SP 12/40, fo. 194r.
[127] See below, pp. 111–16, 225–8.
[128] See below, pp. 142–57.
[129] *St German's doctor and student*, ed. T.F.T. Plucknett and J.L. Barton (Selden Society, 91; London, 1974), p. 327; John Guy, *Christopher St German on chancery and statute* (Selden Society Supplementary Series, 6; London, 1985), p. 23.

England was 'but a "monarchy"', and the 'government of this kingdom is a right and true monarchy'.[130] Aristotle and a tradition of French conciliarism could merge to form an outwardly conservative but potentially radical model for the English polity. In *De republica Anglorum*, Smith argued that the authority of parliament 'abrogateth olde lawes, maketh newe, giveth orders for thinges past, and for thinges hereafter to be followed, changeth rightes, and possessions of private men, legittimateth bastards, establisheth formes of religion, altereth weightes and measures, giveth formes of succession to the crowne'. This mix of 'commonwealth' issues and 'matters of state', or high policy, is startling. Of course the prince was 'the head, life and governor of this common wealth', but parliament was 'the whole head and bodie of the realme of England' because it was 'the whole universall and generall consent and authoritie aswell of the prince as of the nobilitie and commons'.[131] Although the power of parliament clearly lay in the royal foundation of its authority, it had the ability to contribute to serious debate.

This was not an academic issue. Smith was in France at the time of the first session of the second parliament and Cecil corresponded with him on political and diplomatic issues. *De republica Anglorum* is a snapshot of one version of the Elizabethan polity in the early 1560s. It is also a clue to the very different political creeds of the Queen and Cecil. *Fragmenta regalia* had Cecil 'wholly intentive to the service of his Mistris' and, following Naunton, more recent commentators have interpreted the Queen and her Principal Secretary as an enduring but effective partnership.[132] But what was this difference and how did it manifest itself? First, it was not purely a matter of temperament. Elizabeth was her father's daughter but there was a more central question of interpretation. In parliament on the issue of succession, she tended to defend herself by pleading good government. In the *apologia* which Cecil drafted for her on 5 November 1566, Elizabeth 'made mention of hir Government from the begynning with what care she had used the same, without sekyng any particular benefitt by Injureng of others, without brekyng of law or Justice, without sekyng of the blood of any person, and such lyke'.[133] When the issue of the freedom of the Commons to debate her marriage and the succession of the kingdom was raised in 1566, Elizabeth countered by arguing that these were 'certain matters' which were 'very unmete for the tyme and place'.[134] But this was

---

[130] John Guy, 'The Elizabethan establishment and the ecclesiastical polity', in Guy (ed.), *Reign of Elizabeth I*, p. 127; Guy, 'Henrician age', pp. 43–4.
[131] Smith, *De republica Anglorum*, ed. Dewar, Book II, chapter 1, pp. 78–9; chapter 4, p. 88.
[132] Sir Robert Naunton, *Fragmenta regalia*, ed. Edward Arber (London, 1870), p. 20.
[133] SP 12/41, fo. 10r, printed in Hartley, p. 150.
[134] 24 November 1566, SP 12/41, fo. 61r, in Cecil's holograph with Elizabeth's corrections.

not just a question of short-term political sensitivity: the Queen consulted her senior law officers, who turned her disapproval of the debates into the general legal principle that 'the order and directions of all the proceedings' lay in the power of the monarch, 'as to the chiefe and head of that body'.[135] One MP argued that because the king, 'This head, with the consent of the whole bodie', had established parliament as a council to 'view & hearken out the benefittes or inconveniences', it was this council's duty to advise freely and without restraint.[136] Elizabeth emphasized the right of the head to 'commaund the fete not to stray' without question;[137] her MPs believed that the limbs, as part of the whole body, must help its head come to a decision. They were very different interpretations of their respective roles in the polity.

Elizabeth defined herself as an imperial monarch. In the first edition of *Actes and monumentes*, 'Elisabetha regina' was portrayed as a second Constantine, holding the symbolic instruments of imperial rule – the sceptre (a symbol of secular sovereignty) and the orb (an emblem of world-wide Christian dominion) – and able to break the keys of St Peter.[138] The title page of *A chronicle at large*, reprinted in 1569 by Richard Grafton, had Elizabeth holding Solomon's sceptre. Woodcuts of both David and Solomon, two of Henry VIII's favourite and 'imperial' Old Testament kings, were set to the right of Elizabeth. Like William the Conqueror, Solomon bore the orb and the sceptre.[139] Her position as 'supreme governor' of the English church paralleled the late Roman imperial practice and language of the emperor as *gubernator*, or governor. This was as true for the 1560s as it was in 1589, when Richard Cosin in his *Ecclesiae Anglicanae politeia* described Elizabeth as 'tanquam supremus secundum Deum gubernator'.[140] Although the religious settlement of 1559 combined Edwardian theology and the apparatus of the Henrician and Edwardian churches, for Elizabeth it was the imperial power of the English crown which was the important principle. In late 1569 or early 1570 she declared that she had used 'no other authority ether given or used by us as Quene

---

[135] *Reports from the lost notebooks of Sir James Dyer*, ed. J.H. Baker, 2 vols. (Selden Society, 109, 110; London, 1994), I, p. 125.

[136] SP 46/166, fo. 3v, printed in Hartley, pp. 129–30.

[137] 2 January 1567, Cotton Charter 4.38 (2), in Elizabeth's holograph, and printed in Hartley, p. 174.

[138] Dale Hoak, 'The iconography of the crown imperial', in Hoak (ed.), *Tudor political culture*, pp. 55, 94–5; cf. Frances A. Yates, *Astraea: the imperial theme in the sixteenth century* (Harmondsworth, 1977 edn), pp. 38–51.

[139] Richard Grafton, *A chronicle at large and meere history of the affayres of Englande and kinges of the same . . .* (STC 12147; London, 1569).

[140] Walter Ullmann, '"This realm of England is an empire"', *Journal of Ecclesiastical History*, 30 (1979), 200; James E. Hampson, 'Richard Cosin and the rehabilitation of the clerical estate in late Elizabethan England', PhD thesis, University of St Andrews (1997), p. 275.

and Governor of this realme than hath ben by the lawe of God & this Realme always due to our progenitors, soverayns and Kinges of the same'. This was proved by 'lawes and recordes and storyes'.[141] In the second draft prepared by Cecil, the claim became more solid: the authority was 'always annexed to the Crown of this realme' and due to the Queen's progenitors, and evidenced by 'good sufficient and auncient authoritees'.[142] In 1584 or 1585 Cecil wrote a defence of Elizabeth's position against the threat of Europe. In it, he argued that the English monarch wore a closed crown because Constantine as an emperor and as king of Britain wore 'the Crown Imperiall'.[143] The evidence had been gathered by Henry VIII's research group in the 1530s, but it was still as relevant thirty years later. Like her father, Elizabeth believed that the English crown enjoyed secular *imperium* and spiritual supremacy, and this was put to practical use. In 1565, for example, articles for church doctrine and preaching and for the administration of prayer and the sacraments were circulated 'by vertue of the Queenes majesties letters commaunding the same'.[144] Like Cawdrey's case in the 1590s, the debate over clerical dress in the first decade demonstrated Elizabeth's determination to stick rigidly to the royal supremacy and her own governorship of the church.[145]

Cecil's expressions of imperial power were more nuanced than they seem. In his plan for a short interregnum in the event of the Queen's death, Cecil developed a mechanism for allowing a 'council of estate' to direct the public affairs of the realm, to maintain friendship with England's neighbours, and to support the work of local spiritual and temporal officers and ministers. If the 'clause' had been put into a bill on the succession, then a statute would have given the Privy Council the right to exercise the power of the crown and parliament the responsibility to transfer and secure the 'Imperiall crowne of this realme'. In other words, Cecil was able to detach the quality of imperial power from the person of the monarch, and do so by statute. This was not an academic piece on the nature of imperial power and public authority, but a very practical examination of its location.[146] In 1566 Cecil argued that if the marriage of the Queen and the 'stablishyng of succession' were not solved, then parliament could 'procede to discussion of the right of the successor'.[147] Three years later, he posed a political question in the form of a civil thesis, and asked 'Whyther it wer not good to

---

[141] CP 157, fos. 10v–11r.
[142] SP 12/66, fo. 150r; Guy, 'Henrician age', p. 42.
[143] SP 12/75, fo. 142r.
[144] *Advertisements partly for due order in the publique administration of common prayers* . . . (STC 10026; London, 1565).
[145] Guy, 'Ecclesiastical polity', pp. 130–8; Hampson, 'Cosin', p. 27.
[146] SP 12/28, fos. 68r–69v; see below, pp. 111–16, 225–8.
[147] SP 12/40, fo. 195r.

prohibitt all persons to treate uppon the title of a successor, but by
parlement or by licenss of the Quenes Majesty'.[148] The issue was not
whether the succession could be discussed by parliament; it was whether
the subject could be taken outside the two fora.

VI

Cecil revealed his political creed in the working papers he prepared for
business in the Privy Council and, in 1563 and 1566, in drafts he wrote for
MPs. Even rough versions are important clues to the way he perceived and
(more importantly) felt able to articulate political issues. Cecil engaged
himself in a process of political definition and redefinition. In 1566, for
example, Bernard Hampton summarized the intention of the preamble to
the Subsidy Bill, which was the 'Repetition' of parliament's 'suite for
stablishing the succession, and her Majesties assurid declaration publickly
made to a selecte number of hir three estates of hir determination in
convenient time to have due regard to the same'.[149] As a political
statement, the sentence is important in itself. But Cecil was involved in
something more significant: the preamble forced him to define and explain
the relationship between the Queen and the three estates. In the first draft
of a separate petition to Elizabeth earlier in the session, Cecil altered
Bernard Hampton's fair copy to argue that 'our assembly' had 'a *leefull*
suffrance and *duetyfull* liberty' to tackle issues which were honourable for
Elizabeth and 'profitable' for the realm; this was an ancient and laudable
custom '*necessarely* annexed' to parliament.[150] The effect was stunning.
Read properly, without the need to spot civil war on the horizon or a group
of puritan 'left-wingers' itching to make trouble, even this small alteration
suggests something different to the model of the relationship between
Elizabeth and Cecil offered by so many historians. Cecil's two drafts of the
'declaration' of 1569 or 1570 are just as subtle. The first draft openly
acknowledged that the Elizabethan ecclesiastical settlement was an imperial one, but it was 'more clerely recognised by all the estates of the
Realme'.[151] The second draft introduced an interesting parliamentary
twist. English religion was 'more clerely recognized *to the Imperiall Crown
of this realme* by all the estates' not purely 'of the Realme', which he
crossed out, but 'of the *same in parlementes*'.[152] If Elizabeth had seen or

---

[148] October 1569, Cotton Caligula C. 1, fo. 458r, in Cecil's holograph.
[149] SP 12/40, fo. 194r.
[150] SP 12/41, fo. 39v, with Cecil's alterations in *italics*.
[151] CP 157, fo. 11r.
[152] SP 12/66, fo. 150r, with Cecil's holograph corrections in *italics*.

altered the draft – and there is no evidence that the Queen had any part in its composition – she would have been supremely unhappy.

If this difference in outlook between Cecil and his Queen was not a periodic clash of will or personality, then how can it be explained? Practically, Elizabeth was open to the same cultural influences as Cecil. She was good at Greek and Roger Ascham acted as her Latin secretary in the 1560s. Aristotle, Cicero, and Quintilian should have been familiar to her. But her mentality was different. She spoke the language of duty in the first and second parliaments of the reign, but her emphasis was on the power and word of the prince. Elizabeth accepted the difference between England and the rest of Europe – that 'in some thinges the Ecclesiasticall externall pollicy of our Realme differreth from somme other Contreys', as Cecil coyly put it in 'A declaration'[153] – but there is no sense in which she interpreted British and European politics in the providential terms offered by Cecil. Elizabeth's vocabulary of diplomacy included terms of 'amity' and 'love' between cousins and dynasties; Cecil's was based on conspiracy, the actions of the Guise, organized Continental Catholicism, and domestic subversion. But above all, Elizabeth's perception of her own role was royal and sovereign. She may well have agreed with Whitgift: estates could be mixed together, and they were represented in parliament, but England was a monarchy. For Cecil, the polity was more subtle and multilayered than Elizabeth was prepared to accept.

But Cecil also bore the burden of tradition and training. When young men have read laws and their history, the orations of Cicero, and the works of Plato, Xenophon, and Aristotle on 'the diversities of lawes and publike weales', wrote Elyot, they 'have wonne suche a treasure, wherby they shall alway be able to serve honourably theyr prince, and the publike weale of theyr countray'.[154] But were the two interests identical? How should duty be channelled? Through the personal service of the monarch or public service to the commonwealth or state? Elyot probably sensed no difference between the two. But by the 1560s concepts and definitions were changing, influenced by the development of legal theories about the *status* of monarchs in the fourteenth and fifteenth centuries, mirrors for magistrates, and Italian political writing. By 1563 it was possible for Lawrence Humphrey to argue that the vices of a ruler can 'spread the same into the whole state'.[155] Political crisis also made its mark. Privy councillors in the 1560s were supremely conscious that an unmarried Queen and an unsettled succession were military and ideological risks: they could not afford the luxury of imagining that public interest and personal service sat comfort-

---

[153] CP 157, fo. 10v.
[154] Elyot, *Governour*, Book II, chapter 14, p. 59r–v; ed. Lehmberg, p. 56.
[155] Skinner, 'State', pp. 96–101.

ably together. The combination of Elizabeth's determination to do nothing and her councillors' fears for the future in an ideologically unstable and dangerous Europe encouraged a low level of constant frustration and, more seriously, a practical political examination of the location of public power in the polity. For the same reason, but from a radically different point of view, the Catholic Edmund Plowden distinguished between the Queen's natural and mortal body and the body politic, involving policy and government, and concerned with the 'Management of the publick-weal'.[156]

Cecil's sense of his own position was fairly standard and traditional. When he used the word 'minister', he generally meant a servant of the crown.[157] But the political pressures of the 1560s meant that the decade was a bridge between the emphatically personal service of Thomas Wolsey and Thomas Cromwell and the civil lawyer Richard Cosin's use of the term 'the public interest' in 1593, well before its usual dating in the seventeenth century.[158] If the two 'philosophies' of governance in the sixteenth century were an established sense of politics 'as the art of preserving a *respublica*' in the classical sense and politics as the preservation of the state, then the mentality of privy councillors in the 1560s falls firmly into the first category.[159] But Cecil was prepared to push the limits of counsel and argue, with his colleagues on the Council and MPs in parliament in 1563 and 1566, that there was something more permanent than the life or the physical body of the Queen. 'Reason of state' came later, but classical civil philosophy, the ability of the Privy Council to operate as an effective executive board, and a keen sense of providence in international politics combined to make sure that the first Elizabethan decade was not the opening chapter of a glorious reign or the beginning of a great partnership historians and their readers have come to expect.

---

[156] Marie Axton, *The Queen's two bodies. Drama and the Elizabethan succession* (London, 1977), p. 17.

[157] For ten examples, see Stephen Alford, 'William Cecil and the British succession crisis of the 1560s', PhD thesis, University of St Andrews (1996), p. 39.

[158] John Guy, 'Thomas Wolsey, Thomas Cromwell and the reform of Henrician government', in Diarmaid MacCulloch (ed.), *The reign of Henry VIII. Politics, policy and piety* (Basingstoke and London, 1995), pp. 39–43; Hampson, 'Cosin', pp. 240–1; cf. J.A.W. Gunn, 'Public interest', in Ball, Farr, and Hanson (eds.), *Political innovation*, p. 196.

[159] For the distinction, see Viroli, *Reason of state*, pp. 2–3.

2

The politics of Britain and the development of the British succession crisis 1558–1559

The politics of Britain and Cecil's place in the Elizabethan polity were connected beyond separation. Had it not been for Cecil's strong sense of crisis in the 1560s – of the conspiratorial connections between the claim of Mary Stuart to the English crown, a Catholic international, and subversion in England, real or perceived – then the need to have Elizabeth married and the succession settled may well have been stripped of its radical urgency. Cecil established his own context for the actions of Council and parliament in the 1560s – in effect, what Dr Jane Dawson has called 'the British dimension' of Elizabethan policy.[1] This chapter sets out to do three things. First, it will explore Cecil's perception and understanding of the relationship between England, Scotland, and Ireland in the late 1550s and 1560s – how the three kingdoms co-existed and interacted. Second, it will look at the making of a British policy in Elizabeth's first decade, both conceptually and as a practical issue of policy-making. And finally, this chapter will examine the regime's first opportunity to put policy into action, in Scotland in 1559.

I

British policies were a reality in the 1560s.[2] Elizabethan governors were profoundly conscious of the kingdom's relationship with Scotland and the strategic and political importance of what Elizabeth, through Cecil's pen, referred to as 'hir land', Ireland.[3] Historians of the sixteenth century now realize that it is no longer acceptable to separate Anglo-Scottish relations from political developments in Ireland, or vice versa.[4] Although Victorian

---

[1] Jane E.A. Dawson, 'William Cecil and the British dimension of early Elizabethan foreign policy', *History*, 74 (1989), 196–216.
[2] For a discussion, see Hiram Morgan, 'British policies before the British state', in Brendan Bradshaw and John Morrill (eds.), *The British problem, c. 1534–1707. State formation in the Atlantic archipelago* (Basingstoke and London, 1996), pp. 76–80.
[3] Cecil to the earl of Sussex, 14 December 1561, Cotton Titus B. 13, fo. 71r
[4] Jane E.A. Dawson, 'Two kingdoms or three? Ireland in Anglo-Scottish relations in the

editors and archivists tried to put State Papers into neat categories like 'Domestic', 'Scotland', 'Ireland', and 'Foreign', it is hard to escape the fact that the Elizabethan Privy Council considered, debated, and proposed policy holistically. A meeting or a report could take Mary Stuart as its focus, but councillors often went on to explore the implications for England's ecclesiastical settlement, the pacification of Ireland, relations with the French and Spanish monarchies, and the (perceived) presence in England of a fifth column of politically and religiously dissatisfied subjects. The point is made very clearly in Cecil's collections of Anglo-British papers, which range from reports from ambassadors and representatives to the Privy Council's recommendations for action in Ireland, Scotland, and, significantly, England. There were two important elements. The first was the development of Cecil's 'master metaphor' for the 1560s, the provocative image of Elizabeth as 'pacient', the Pope and the Kings of Spain and France as 'authors and workars', and Mary Stuart as 'the Instrument'.[5] The second was perhaps more prosaic: the strategic connection between the effectiveness of English policy and the limitations that local and national political considerations – military instability in Ireland or the links between the French court and the regime in Scotland, for example – could place on the execution of London's orders.

The relationship between England and Scotland in the 1560s rested on two competing traditions. The first was a theory of English superiority over Scotland which, politically, could be traced back to the 'Great Cause' of Edward I and culturally to the myth of Brutus, established by Norman-Welsh clerics like Gerald of Wales and Geoffrey of Monmouth and promoted by Ranulph Higden in the fourteenth century, William Caxton in the late fifteenth, and Richard Grafton in the 1560s.[6] This interpretation of the relationship between Scotland and the English crown became politically important in the Scottish campaigns of Henry VIII and the duke of Somerset in the 1540s and it formed an important part of Cecil's reading of the British situation in the 1560s. The second tradition was, on the face of it, more enlightened. In the late 1540s, English writers began to explore expressions of common interest with the Scots – of an amity reinforced by

---

middle of the sixteenth century', in Roger A. Mason (ed.), *Scotland and England 1286–1815* (Edinburgh, 1987), pp. 113–14.
[5] 'A short memoryall', CP 157, fo. 2r, printed in Haynes, p. 579.
[6] Roger A. Mason, 'The Scottish reformation and the origins of Anglo-British imperialism', in Roger A. Mason (ed.), *Scots and Britons. Scottish political thought and the union of 1603* (Cambridge, 1994), pp. 161–6; Mason, 'Scotching the Brut: politics, history and national myth in sixteenth-century Britain', in Mason (ed.), *Scotland and England*, pp. 60–84; Richard Grafton, *A chronicle at large and meere history of the affayres of Englande and kinges of the same* (STC 12147; London, 1569). Grafton's sources included Caxton, Geoffrey of Monmouth, Gildas, Ranulph Higden, and John Mair (sig. A1v).

Protestant religion, and of profound similarities in culture and language. By the 1560s, there was not only an integrated Protestant culture in England and Scotland but a defined and active community of courtiers and councillors, north and south of the border, who corresponded regularly.[7] Cecil was perhaps the preeminent member of this group of Anglo-Scots, although the letters of Robert Dudley, earl of Leicester, Francis Russell, earl of Bedford, Sir Nicholas Throckmorton, Thomas Randolph, James Stuart, earl of Moray, and William Maitland of Lethington are extremely important.

But there was something curiously Orwellian about the relationship between England and Scotland, even in the 1560s. Although English Protestants were genuinely interested in expressions of amity and co-operation with their northern co-religionists, they still spoke the language of Edwardian and Henrician propaganda. Thomas Berthelet argued in 1542 that Scottish kings 'have always knowleged the kynges of Englande superior lordes of the realme of Scotlande, and have done homage and fealtie for the same'.[8] It was equally acceptable to claim that through the archbishop of York, an ecclesiastical appointment 'made' by King Coill, England had ecclesiastical authority in Scotland under the archbishop's 'dominion'.[9] Cecil was part of this rather odd Anglo-Scottish Protestant culture. He was in Scotland in 1547 as part of the duke of Somerset's expeditionary force, and later helped William Patten to produce *The expedicion into Scotlande* by lending him his campaign diary. Patten maintained that England and Scotland were 'separate by seas from all oother nacions, in customes and condicions littell differinge, in shape and langage nothynge at all'.[10] John Hooper, later one of Cecil's ecclesiastical correspondents, wrote of 'one Realme and Ilond devydyd from all the worold by imparkyng of the sea by naturall discent of parentayge and blud, one in langayge and speche, in form and proporcion of personayge one, one in maner and condicion of lyvyng'. And yet even Hooper maintained the division between England and Scotland was the work of the Devil's agents,

---

[7] Jane Dawson, 'Anglo-Scottish Protestant culture and integration in sixteenth-century Britain', in Steven G. Ellis and Sarah Barber (eds.), *Conquest and union. Fashioning a British state, 1485–1725* (London and New York, 1995), pp. 87–114; Simon Adams, 'The Lauderdale papers 1561–1570: the Maitland of Lethington state papers and the Leicester correspondence', *Scottish Historical Review*, 67 (1988), 51–5.

[8] Thomas Berthelet, *A declaration, conteynyng the just causes and consyderations, of this present warre with the Scottis, wherin alsoo appereth the trewe & right title, that the Kinges most royall majesty hath to the soveryntie of Scotlande* (STC 9179; London, 1542).

[9] Richard Grafton, *An epitome of the title that the kynges majestie of Englande, hath to the sovereigntie of Scotlande, continued upon the auncient writers . . .* (STC 3196; London, 1548), sig. C1r.

[10] William Patten, *The expedicion into Scotlande of the most woorthely fortunate prince Edward, duke of Soomerset . . .* (STC 19479; London, 1548), sig. B2r.

who had taught the northern kingdom 'disobedience unto here Naturall and Laufull prince and superiour powre the Kynges majestie of Englond'.[11] Cecil had access to a document referring to English superiority in Scotland which had formed part of Edward Foxe's text on the caesaropapism of Henry VIII, *De vera differentia*, and was reprinted in Henry, Lord Stafford's translation of Foxe in 1548.[12] The jottings in Cecil's papers at Hatfield House refer to 'the booke of nootes gathered owt of the Kinges majesties recordes for the Justyfycacion of his highnes propriety And superiority to the realme of Scotland'.[13] The book was in the 'kepinge' of Master Mason; Sir John Mason, Cecil's colleague and a privy councillor from 1550 until his death in 1566, owned a handwritten volume of medieval texts and precedents on Anglo-Scottish affairs.[14] But at the same time, James Henrisoun, an Edinburgh merchant and a proponent of British co-operation, submitted his second book to Cecil in 1548, 'The Godly and Golden Booke for concorde of England and Scotland'. 'Amitie', 'mutuall love', and a 'noble and wel agreyng Monarchie' were key themes.[15]

During the late 1540s, Cecil was part of an Anglo-Scottish culture which indulged in expressions of common political, religious, and cultural interest but happily restated the medieval claim of English superiority over the northern kingdom and reinvented it to suit the needs of the sixteenth century. So the message was rather muddled. In 1548 the King's printer, Richard Grafton, produced *An epistle or exhortacion, to unitie & peace* between England and Scotland; in the same year, Grafton printed *An epitome* of evidence of the English claim over the northern kingdom, which supported the efforts of 'diverse' to bring about the 'union of Scotlande unto youre highnes' but provided 'furder declaracion of your majesties title to the superioritie thereof'. Scots had fought 'against the mother of their awne nacion: I mean this realme now called Englande the onely supreme seat of thempire of greate Briteigne'.[16] Grafton's reference to 'empire' is intriguing. In one sense, England's relationship with Scotland during the reign of Edward VI was an extension of his father's belief in the imperial

[11] John Hooper, *A declaracion of Christe and of his offyce . . .* (STC 13745; London, 1547), sig. A3r.

[12] Edward Foxe, *De vera differentia regiae potestatis & ecclesiasticae . . .* (STC 11219; London, 1538), pp. 85v–87r; Edward Foxe, *The true dyfferens betwen the regall power and the ecclesiasticall power. . .*, trans. Henry, Lord Stafford (STC 11220; London, 1548), pp. 98v–99v; G.D. Nicholson, 'The nature and function of historical argument in the Henrician reformation', PhD thesis, University of Cambridge (1977), pp. 118, 177.

[13] CP 234, no. 1.

[14] For the volume, 'Collegit Joannes Masonius', and dated 1549, see Additional 6128.

[15] Dawson, 'Cecil', 198–9; Marcus Merriman, 'The assured Scots. Scottish collaborators with England during the Rough Wooing', *Scottish Historical Review*, 47 (1968), 22–3.

[16] Richard Grafton, *An epistle or exhortaction, to unitie & peace . . .* (STC2 22268; London, 1548); Grafton, *Epitome*, sig. A5v.

power of the English crown. In 1918 C.H. Firth argued that the word
'empire' – for Henry VIII an expression of sovereignty – 'came to signify a
composite state formed by the union of two or more states'. According to
Firth, the duke of Somerset proposed that England and Scotland should be
called an empire and its sovereign the Emperor of Great Britain.[17] In
'England Tryumphant', Cecil had the voice of England explain how 'my
people the britons' chose Constantine the Great as their ruler. Constantine
'enjoyed Joyntly the Crown Imperiall and my Crown as a kyng'. So the
Britons were ruled by a Romano-English monarch wearing the imperial
crown and, Cecil explained, 'all my kynges successyvely in all ages have
had the honor to weare a Crown cloos as no other kyngdom'.[18] In the first
edition of *Actes and monumentes*, John Foxe referred both to 'this realme
of England and Scotland' and to 'this my country of England and Scotland'.[19] But the core kingdom was England. Richard Grafton explained
how the English King Ambrosius Aurelianus killed Hengist; as a result,
'this Realme was delivered from the tyranny of Saxons, and restored to the
whole Empire & name of greate Briteigne'.[20] In 1531 the duke of Norfolk
described the inscription on the seal of Arthur, which read 'Patricius
Arcturus, Britanniae, Galliae, Daciae Imperator', and the claim for English
overlordship of Scotland merited a section in the 'Collectanea satis
copiosa'.[21] Even from the early 1530s, evidence in defence of Edward I's
suzerainty over Scotland could be used to show 'that the authority of the
English crown extended over other realms, and that the sum of the king's
feudal rights amounted to a right of empire'.[22] In 1604, this tradition
allowed John Thornborough to claim that 'many shires [make] one
kingdom; many kingdoms one imperial monarchy'.[23] In the same year,
James VI and I called to mind 'the blessed Union, or rather Reuniting of
these two mightie, famous and ancient Kingdomes of England and Scotland, under one Imperiall Crowne'.[24]

In a period of rather hazy definitions and meanings, this relationship

---

[17] C.H. Firth, '"The British empire"', *Scottish Historical Review*, 15 (1918), 185.
[18] SP 12/75, fo. 142r; for Cecil's related notes on 'Anglia Personata loquens, England shaped
into a person spekyng', see Lansdowne 103, fos. 52r–55v.
[19] Mason, 'Anglo-British imperialism', p. 185 and n. 102.
[20] Grafton, *Epitome*, sig. A3v.
[21] Graham Nicholson, 'The Act of Appeals and the English Reformation', in Claire Cross,
David Loades, and J.J. Scarisbrick (eds.), *Law and government under the Tudors* (Cambridge, 1988), pp. 23–4; Cotton Cleopatra E. 6, fos. 41v–42r.
[22] John Guy, 'Thomas Cromwell and the intellectual origins of the Henrician revolution', in
Alistair Fox and John Guy, *Reassessing the Henrician age. Humanism, politics and reform
1500–1550* (Oxford and New York, 1986), pp. 159–60.
[23] Brian P. Levack, *The formation of the British state* (Oxford, 1987), p. 2 n. 4.
[24] Jenny Wormald, 'The creation of Britain: multiple kingdoms or core and colonies?',
Transactions of the Royal Historical Society, sixth series, 2 (1992), 177.

could be extended to Ireland. In July 1568 Matthew Parker, the archbishop of Canterbury, sent a letter to Cecil. Parker had found evidence that in 1246 or 1247, Henry III 'caused al the chronicles to be searched concernyng the superiorytie in scotland'. Parker made a very dubious linguistic connection between his source and England's relationship with Scotland. 'In story it is reported that the prince of the realme bi right is not Dominus hibernie but rex hibernie.'[25] Precisely translated, this had the English monarch as king (rather than lord) of Ireland, which is exactly what Henry VIII had maintained in 1541. This statement was an extension of England's break with Rome in the 1530s. The argument had been made that Ireland's 'regal estate' rested in the papacy and that the role of the English king as *dominus* was 'but a governance under the obedience of the same'.[26] 1541 ended that, when Ireland was 'united and knit to the Imperial Crown of the realm of England'.[27] Either this meant that Ireland was an independent kingdom or – and perhaps this makes more sense in the light of English military efforts to pacify the island – it had become part of the imperial English state. Sir John Davies maintained that when he spoke 'of the monarchy of England', he included 'the Kingdom of Ireland within the circle of that imperial Crown'.[28] In 1583 Cecil wrote of the 'Realme of England and Ireland' and yet, later in the same book, he explained that the Queen was 'possessed of the two realmes of England & Ireland'. But it was possible to explore Elizabeth's 'kingship' in territorial terms, as 'a Prince soveraigne over divers kingdomes and nations'.[29]

The structure of government in Ireland mirrored that of England.[30] The Irish parliament was an important element in the kingdom's institutional structure. A royal council in Ireland was active in the sixteenth century. Nicholas White was (in Cecil's words) 'one of the Quenes Majesties counsell in Irland'. It was possible also to refer to the 'privy council' of Ireland.[31] There was some sense of equality and parity. Ireland's central courts were basically identical to their English counterparts. The Irish exchequer and chancery managed the crown's financial and legal business.

---

[25] 4 July 1568, SP 12/47, fo. 3r.

[26] John Guy, *Tudor England* (Oxford and New York, 1988), pp. 358–9.

[27] Ciaran Brady, 'England's defence and Ireland's reform: the dilemma of the Irish viceroys, 1541–1641', in Bradshaw and Morrill (eds.), *British problem*, p. 92.

[28] John Guy, 'The Tudor theory of "imperial" kingship', *History Review*, 17 (1993), 16.

[29] William Cecil, *The execution of justice in England for maintenaunce of publique and Christian peace* . . . (STC 4902; London, 1583), sig. A2r, D2v, D1r. The references to 'realm' and 'realms' were not typographical errors, because they were reprinted in the second, corrected edition published by Christopher Barker in January 1584 (STC 4903).

[30] Ciaran Brady, 'Court, castle and country: the framework of government in Tudor Ireland', in Ciaran Brady and Raymond Gillespie (eds.), *Natives and newcomers. Essays on the making of Irish colonial society 1534–1641* (Dublin, 1986), pp. 22–49.

[31] Cecil to White, 8 September 1569, Lansdowne 102, fo. 150v.

Even the points of contact between London and lowland England – justices of the peace, assize circuits, and sheriffs – were present on the Irish scene. But in reality, Irish institutions were not completely independent. Poynings' Law of 1494 ensured that the Irish parliament could not meet without the King's licence, and all proposed measures had to be submitted to the English Privy Council before they could be introduced. In legal cases, the Court of King's Bench in London tried Irish lawsuits on appeal. The Privy Council heard petitions and judged them directly from Ireland, bypassing the 'privy council' in Dublin. Furthermore, general political interest in Ireland and its problems was limited. Some early Elizabethans perceived Ireland as a territory which had to be tamed and controlled rather than positively and productively governed. The perceived political situation in Ireland – outside interest or domestic unrest – was a risk to English security. This was one of Cecil's concerns. His interest in Ireland (and Scotland) was by no means philanthropic, but Cecil did have a strong sense of the political state of Ireland and the relationship between its main players.

The Irish bewildered and frustrated the English, and the English seemed unable to control the kingdom or crucial political leaders like Shane O'Neill. But there were important channels of communication which became part of the development of British policy. Cecil was one of the main contacts between London, the council and Viceroy in Ireland, and Scotland. He advised the earl of Sussex (between 1558 and 1565) and drafted instructions which were sent out by Elizabeth to Sussex's successor, Sir Henry Sidney. When Cecil was in Edinburgh and away from the court and Council in June and July 1560, the Privy Council sent letters signed by between five and eight of its members. Bernard Hampton independently sent two letters, directly addressed to Sussex, in late June and early July.[32] When the Privy Council was waiting for detailed news of the Treaty of Edinburgh, it sent Sussex a brief description by letter and a summary 'scedule' drafted by Hampton. It was important for the Queen's representative in Ireland to have details of a treaty with British implications and to let him know of military preparations in Berwick and naval readiness at Portsmouth.[33] This was not 'English' policy-making. In return, he was expected to send regular reports back to England. Even during a military emergency in 1561, Cecil was shocked at a month's gap in Sussex's correspondence, 'so perplexed, with lack of intelligence from yowr Lord-

---

[32] Hampton to Sussex, 29 June 1560, Cotton Titus B. 13, fo. 10r; Hampton to Sussex, 6 July 1560, Cotton Titus B. 13, fo. 10v.

[33] Privy Council to Sussex, 12 July 1560, Cotton Titus B. 13, fo. 13r; for 'A note of theffect of the Principall matters concludyd', Cotton Titus B. 13, fo. 16r–v; for Hampton's drafts of the 'scedule', Harley 289, fo. 71r–v; and SP 52/4, fo. 88r–v; for the importance of the Treaty of Edinburgh, see below, pp. 83–5.

ship and that realme at any tyme sence I served in this Court'.[34] Later that
year, Cecil was clearly annoyed at not being able to act in his accepted role
as a channel of communication between Sussex, Elizabeth, and Ireland,
because 'the Quenes Majesty daylye noteth to me herin a great lack that
she can have no knoledg from hir land there'.[35]

Many connections between London and Ireland were personal and
individual. When Cecil drafted a set of 'pryvat instructions' for the new
Deputy, Sir Henry Sidney, in July 1565, it was 'to be used and communicated by hym with such of hir Majesties Counsell in Irland as he shall
thynk mete'. The paper outlined local political conditions, policy, explained sensitive issues like the handling of Tyrone, Shane O'Neill, and
explored some of the connections between the settlement of Ireland and
the influence of Scotland.[36] Between 1558 and 1565 some letters were
carried from Ireland to Cecil by Sir William Fitzwilliam, Mildred Cecil's
cousin and a relative of both Sussex and Sidney. Cecil often replied to
Sussex in his own hand and signed his letters 'W. Cecill'; sometimes, he
used the Clerk of the Privy Council, Hampton, as his private clerk. The
political and religious state of Scotland and events in Europe – the place
of William Maitland of Lethington and the earl of Moray at the Scottish
court, religion in Scotland, and the 'synod nationall at Poyssy', for
example[37] – were subjects of letters.

Cecil's grasp of the British context of Elizabethan policy should not come
as a surprise, and one of the members of his household, the cartographer
and Old English scholar Laurence Nowell, is an important connection here.
Nowell, like Cecil, knew the geography of Ireland. He produced a (now
lost) description of the island, 'Hiberniae Descriptio', which possibly
included a map. This may have been drawn in 1564, with a supplement in
1566.[38] In 1567 John Goghe drew a map of Ireland which bore the names
of principal local chieftains, reproduced the arms of noblemen, and was
personalized by Cecil with his manuscript notes. This project was very
closely related to a Cecil memorandum on the siting of garrisons in Ulster,
and perhaps connected to a map of the north of Ireland supplied by Sir
Henry Sidney.[39] In 1592 Robert Beale wrote that the principal secretary
'must likewise have the booke of Ortelius' Mapps, a booke of the Mappes
of England . . . and also a good descripcion of the Realm of Irelande', with

[34] Cecil to Sussex, 25 July 1561, Cotton Titus B. 13, fo. 48r.
[35] Cecil to Sussex, 14 December 1561, Cotton Titus B. 13, fo. 71r.
[36] 9 July 1565, SP 63/14, fos. 44r–47v.
[37] Cecil to Sussex, 7 October 1561, Cotton Titus B. 13, fo. 62r.
[38] Peter Barber, 'A Tudor mystery: Laurence Nowell's map of England and Ireland', *Map Collector*, 22 (1983), 18.
[39] 'Hibernia: Insula non procul ab Anglia Vulgare Hirlandia Vocata', Public Record Office, *Museum catalogue* (London, 1974), p. 57; Dawson, 'Cecil', 197.

names of Irish or English leaders and their followers.[40] Beale may well have been influenced by Cecil. As Principal Secretary, Cecil collected an impressive set of manuscript maps of Ireland, Berwick, Carlisle, and the northern Marches.[41] His main reference work, 'A general description of England & Ireland', produced by Laurence Nowell in the middle of the 1560s, was still in use in 1598. 'A general description' was far more strategically focused than the printed maps of England, Scotland, and Ireland produced during the 1540s, 1550s, and 1560s, especially its representation of the political and territorial state of Ireland. Nowell's map covered England and Ireland 'with the costes adjoyning'. It went as far north as the western islands of Isla and Jura and Argyll and Angus, south to parts of Brittany and Normandy, and east to Flanders. The map of Scotland had all the main centres of interest in a British context: Dunbar, Edinburgh, Glasgow, Perth, St Andrews, Stirling, and Galloway and Kintyre, the two main links between Ulster and Scotland. The representation of Ireland included main settlements, geographical features, and the names of political and territorial leaders within the pale and to the Gaelic west. On the back of 'A general description', Cecil listed routes, distances, and itineraries from London to York and to the borders with Scotland. These were practical issues in the 1560s, during a period when events in Edinburgh, Berwick, the Marches, and Ireland played an important part in policy-making.[42]

The key to this process was correspondence and local and national expertise. During sensitive negotiations with the French for 'the leage betwixt england and scotland' at Edinburgh in June 1560, Cecil sent Sir William Petre 'a lettre intercepted, sent from a french secretory in the Castle to the towne', and he asked Petre to hand it to Bernard Hampton. If Hampton could 'do nothyng to it', it could be sent to 'Master sommer'.[43] This was John Somers, one of Sir Nicholas Throckmorton's secretaries in France. Presumably the letter was in code, and Hampton may well have had access to what Robert Beale later described as the Principal Secretary's 'speciall Cabinett' of 'signetts, Ciphers and secrett Intelligences'.[44] Hampton was definitely handling Cecil's letters to other councillors,

[40] R[obert] B[eale], 'A Treatise of the Office of a Councellor and Principall Secretarie to her Majestie', printed in Conyers Read, *Mr Secretary Walsingham and the policy of Queen Elizabeth*, 3 vols. (Oxford, 1925), I, pp. 428–9.

[41] R.A. Skelton and John Summerson, *A description of maps and architectural drawings in the collection made by William Cecil First Baron Burghley now at Hatfield House* (Roxburghe Club; Oxford, 1971), pp. 58–9.

[42] Additional 62540; Peter Barber, 'The minister puts his mind on the map', *British Museum Society Bulletin*, 43 (1983), 18–19; Barber, 'Tudor mystery', 16–21; cf. the work of George Lily, in Rodney W. Shirley (ed.), *Early printed maps of the British Isles. A bibliography 1477–1650* (London and New York, 1980), plates 13, 15, 16, and 17.

[43] Cecil to Petre, 21 June 1560, CP 153, fo. 1r.   [44] Read, *Walsingham*, I, p. 428.

because Cecil asked Petre to instruct Hampton to send 'these lettres' to another expert on France and Scotland, Throckmorton.[45] The main point is this: British policy was discussed and executed by a team of men in England, Ireland, Scotland, and Europe, many of whom had had experience of British and Continental diplomacy. Although councillors', courtiers', and diplomats' aims may have been unashamedly anglocentric — the preservation of the Elizabethan regime – their sense of what had to be done to achieve stability was not. Success rested on peace and security in Ireland, a strict policy on Stuart government and French influence in Scotland, and a tight grip on the religious state of England.

II

So England was set in fairly defined relationship with Ireland and Scotland: one was a kingdom, governed on behalf of the English crown by a viceroy responsible for political and military stability, who received letters and orders from the Queen and the Privy Council; the other was a separate and independent kingdom, governed in the late 1550s by a regime with strong French connections, but open to two influences – the presence of a group of Protestant noblemen and, in English eyes, capable of being defined as the northern part of 'Great Britain', under the political and ecclesiastical authority of the English crown. Cecil's understanding of the relationship between Ireland and (particularly) England and Scotland became part of the Elizabethan policy-making process in June 1559, when the regime began to receive reports of the Protestant Scottish congregation's opposition to the mother of Mary Stuart, Mary of Guise. As a sphere of French influence, Scotland became strategically important to the security of England's northern border. It remained so until at least British union in 1707. Ireland had been a concern to the regime in London since the 1530s, open as it was to French and Spanish intrigue, domestic political instability, and mercenary involvement. The close connections between Ulster, Kintyre, and Galloway could limit the effectiveness of English or Protestant Anglo-Scottish policy in Scotland; but they were also a tried and tested way of supplying and reinforcing England's enemies in Ireland.

Domestic resistance to the French in Scotland in 1559 could be read in two ways: first, that it was a profound danger, opening up the threat of an attack from the north; or second, that it was the best opportunity the Elizabethan regime had had in a year to stifle French influence in Scotland. Both arguments were heard in the Council chamber, especially in a debate in December 1559 when Cecil pressed for a forward, military policy and

[45] CP 153, fo. 1r.

his brother-in-law and Lord Keeper of the Great Seal, Sir Nicholas Bacon, took a more cautious stand. Cecil was not immediately committed to full military intervention, but he was prepared to support co-religionists in Scotland. It was all the more positive because the congregation not only spoke as an ancient nobility committed to the protection of the common-weal, but marketed itself as a religious and ideological group, determined to preserve Protestantism and suppress idolatry.[46] For Cecil, this was the opportunity for England to co-ordinate a British stand against the military and ideological threat of Continental Catholicism. Why he believed that this was necessary lay in the European politics of the late 1550s. This was, in a very real sense, the origin of the British succession crisis.

In April 1559 France, England, and Spain signed the two treaties of the Peace of Cateau-Cambrésis to end conflict in western Europe. Apart from the practical consequences of the war between France and Spain – in England, malnutrition and starvation – Cateau-Cambrésis became a symbol of political failure: Elizabeth lost Calais to the French for eight years, after which the French could either return the town or pay an indemnity. This proposal was made by the French without Philip II's approval.[47] But the clause on Calais was based initially on a premise which would haunt and test the English regime for the first twelve years of Elizabeth's reign: that Mary Stuart, the daughter of Mary of Guise and granddaughter of James IV of Scotland and Margaret Tudor, had a better claim to the English crown than Elizabeth, and that Calais, as a result, did not have to be returned to a Tudor.[48] Dynasty was reinforced by ideology. In April 1559 Pope Paul IV decided to excommunicate Elizabeth, but Philip II protested. The issue was debated in the Curia in August 1559.[49] So from the very beginning of Elizabeth's reign there was an explosive mix of a competing claim to the same throne and a new and delicate Protestant regime under pressure from the Catholic powers.

After 1559 Cecil began to construct an interpretation of the operation of British and Continental politics which influenced debate in the Privy Council and policy-making in the 1560s. His notes and memoranda considered the implications of Mary Stuart's claim to the English crown,

---

[46] Roger Mason, 'Covenant and commonweal: the language of politics in Reformation Scotland', in Norman MacDougall (ed.), *Church, politics and society: Scotland 1408–1929* (Edinburgh, 1983), pp. 97–126; cf. 'The Effecte of the Agremente bitwyne the quene dowager of Scotland and the lordes of the Congregacion publyshed by proclamation at Edynborough', 10 July 1559, Harley 289, fo. 67r–v.

[47] M.J. Rodríguez-Salgado, *The changing face of empire. Charles V, Philip II and Habsburg authority 1551–1559* (Cambridge, 1988), p. 317.

[48] Julian Lock, '"Strange usurped potentates": Elizabeth I, the papacy and the Indian summer of the medieval deposing power', DPhil thesis, University of Oxford (1992), p. 269.

[49] Rodríguez-Salgado, *Changing face of empire*, pp. 330–1.

her connections with France and the papacy, and the influence of Continental Catholicism on religious and political subversion in England. The link between 'Daungers within the realme, or from forrayn partes, or from both' was close. With a 'lack of good government Ecclesiasticall', people were 'not duly tought to lyve in obedience to the laws established for matters of Relligion'. 'Contrary wise', Cecil wrote in summer 1559, 'papistes, Jesuittes, and seminary prestes do dayly increass, and do pervert the symple and wyn dayly manny to ther faction'.[50] He began to collect and to piece together the evidence for a conspiracy organized against the Protestant regime in England. His notes set European affairs in terms so providential and, for contemporaries, politically frightening, that for the rest of the reign it was impossible to separate the fact of international conspiracy from the fear of domestic subversion. If there was a strong sense of political crisis in the 1570s and 1580s, it was because the politics of the first decade had provided it with a language and vocabulary of emergency.

During the negotiations at Cateau, there had been a proposal for marriage between Philip II and the eldest daughter of Henry of France. It was also true that Henry had added a proposal to partition England to his request to Philip to restore Catholicism and French authority in Scotland. But Philip had protected Elizabeth against papal excommunication and the duke of Guise, Mary's uncle, seems to have been unhappy with the peace.[51] Cecil's interpretation was very different. On 20 May 1559 he explored the issue of how the French King 'caused' his son Francis and daughter-in-law Mary to 'publish' their title to Elizabeth's crown; according to Cecil, Charles Guise, cardinal of Lorraine maintained that the couple could be accepted as the only representatives of England at the negotiations. From Cecil's account of the talks, the Spanish commissioners refused to stand up to Lorraine for this claim. The only moderating influence at the French court was the constable of France, Montmorency. It was also clear that the Spanish representatives had agreed to the French demands for Calais.[52]

By June 1559 the pieces were beginning to fit into place. The Privy Council told Sir Nicholas Throckmorton in France that 'it is cume to our knowledge by suche advertisementes as have byn brought to me the Secretary, that *amongst other the triumphees there prepared in one of the same there is one made* for the king dolphyn hang in *it certen* Scuchions of armes *wherin is* in one parte the armes of Englande and Scotlande

---

[50] SP 12/4, fo. 135r; cf. Carol Z. Wiener, 'This beleaguered isle. A study of Elizabethan and early Jacobean anti-Catholicism', *Past and Present*, no. 51 (1971), 42.
[51] Rodríguez-Salgado, *Changing face of empire*, pp. 326–32.
[52] CP 152, fo. 35r, in Cecil's holograph.

quartered'.[53] Cecil collected two sketches of the offending heraldic quarter-ings,[54] and he wove the evidence into a wider interpretation of Europe and England's place in it. The 'usurpation of the armes of england' included the 'J[o]ustes, plate, hanginges, seales' in France, and evidence of the 'usurpa-tion of the stile of england and Irland' was sent 'in a grete seale to scotland' and a 'seale brought by sir Nicholas Throkmorton'. Cecil's interpretation was, in a sense, self-fulfilling. These 'Breff notes to prove the french evill meaning towardes england' were probably written in August 1559; Throckmorton, instructed to track down these offences in June, only confirmed and reinforced the regime's fears. But at the conspiratorial heart of the problem was the Treaty of Cateau-Cambrésis, at which the French, wrote Cecil, 'by there practise with the burgunnions' claimed the title to the throne of England.[55] This elementary thesis transferred itself into two versions of Cecil's private discussion of 'the weighty matter of Scotland' in August 1559, where, he pointed out in the final draft, it was clear how the French 'labored to have had the Burgunnions concluded a peace without england'.[56] The first version was slightly different:

And lykewise in the treaty of the peace at Chasteau in Cambresy it appered what they wold have compassed. when they [the French] pressed the Burgondions to conclude with them, and overpass the treaty with england. alledging that they cold not tell how to treate with england but to the prejudice of there right, the Dolphyns dowghter then having right to the Crown of england. how bold they wold have bene, if at that tyme she had bene quene of france and hir husband kyng as he now is. for then the wisedome of the Constable governed the rashnees of the Guisians.[57]

The 'peace concluded' meant that the 'rashnees of the Guisians' was in the ascendant, and this triggered a whole set of conspiracies and evidence: the French 'practise at Roome for bulles', actions in Ireland, military prepara-tions in Germany and Denmark, and, above all, 'The old hatred of the howse of Guise' with 'There authorite at this present' and 'There private respectes to avance' Mary Stuart's claim.[58]

But for Cecil the loss of Calais and the malice of the Guise were significant for another reason. They were evidence that, after the collusion at Cateau-Cambrésis and an obvious difference in religion, the Continental powers were determined to ally against England and prevent any sort of co-operation between Elizabeth and Scotland. The political manoeuvrings of summer and autumn 1559 were based on intelligence, evidence, and, for

---

[53] 13 June 1559, SP 70/5, fo. 31r–v, with Cecil's additions and corrections to the secretarial copy in *italic* script.
[54] Cotton Caligula B. 10, fos. 17v–18r; CP 201, fo. 131r–v.   [55] SP 12/6, fo. 74r.
[56] Cotton Caligula B. 10, fo. 34r, in Cecil's holograph.
[57] Cotton Caligula B. 10, fo. 87v, in Cecil's holograph.
[58] SP 12/6, fo. 74r; cf. Cotton Caligula B. 10, fos. 87v–88r, especially, fos. 34v–35r.

Cecil at least, some tentative and informal prodding. Two men were in Scotland by the summer – Sir Henry Percy and Thomas Randolph – but it was Percy who acted as Cecil's contact with Sir William Kirkcaldy of Grange, one representative of the lords of the congregation. Kirkcaldy wrote to Percy and Cecil, Percy and Kirkcaldy to Cecil, John Knox to Cecil, Percy, and Sir James Croft in Berwick.[59] Even the idea of the congregation restoring the liberty of the kingdom of Scotland came second, as a defining characteristic for Cecil, to the lords' religion. Grange gave Percy a note of 'The names of the erlles lordis with some principall barons and gentilmen of the congregatioun', Sir Henry sent it south, and Cecil endorsed it 'Protestantes of Scotland'; in August Cecil began his 'short discussion' of Scotland with 'Whither it be mete that England shuld helpe the Nobilite, and protestantes of Scotland to expell the french or no'. But religion, however crucial, had to be balanced against military power and the political situation.[60]

July and August 1559 were two months in which practical politics had to be measured against a commitment to the cause of British Protestantism and domestic security. In the first week of July Cecil knew the names of the main members of the congregation, and the nature of the forces under 'the quene and frenche'; he was also given a short list of neutrals including men who would 'subscrybe with them to keip owt the frenche men'.[61] Cecil and Sir Thomas Parry, his Privy Council colleague and Treasurer of the House-hold, worked together in the same month. Both men wrote to Percy on 4 July 1559 and, just over a fortnight later, collaborated on a 'Memoryall' of the political state of Scotland in which Cecil, at the bottom of the sheet, used Grange's intelligence to list the principal lords.[62] Between these dates 'The Effecte of the Agremente bitwyne the quene dowager of Scotland and the lordis of the congregacion' appeared, published, according to the note, on 10 July 1559 by proclamation.[63] If this is a contemporary copy, then London had an extra source to confirm the Scottish lords' political and religious position, because the first, second, and fourth articles dealt with the protection of 'the Religeon', the suppression of 'Idolatrye', and the departure of the French, who were 'not to come in withoute the consent of the hole nobylitie'.[64] Cecil had mixed these themes in a letter of instruction to Percy, to communicate with Grange, on 4 July; 'ye maye assure hym', Cecil wrote in his original draft of the letter sent out to Percy, 'that rather than that realme shuld be with a forren nation and power oppressed' and deprived of its ancient liberties, and the members of its nobility who sought

[59] SP 52/1, some of it printed in *The works of John Knox*, ed. David Laing, 6 vols. (Wodrow Society; Edinburgh, 1846–64), VI, pp. 1–77.
[60] Cotton Caligula B. 10, fo. 33r.   [61] SP 52/1, fo. 94r.   [62] SP 12/5, fos. 41r, 42v.
[63] Harley 289, fo. 67r–v.   [64] Harley 289, fo. 67r.

to maintain 'the truth of Christian relligion' – and at this point he had 'ageynst impyete', but scored it out – 'be expelled the authorite of England wold adventure with power and force to ayde that realme ageynst any such forren invasion'.[65]

The whole response seemed, at least on paper in early July, positive. Cecil wrote of the 'perpetuite of a brotherly and nationall frendshipp betwixt the ij realmes' of Scotland and England, and he apologized for using Percy as a go-between, but 'considering the place and office which I here hold', it was an unfortunate necessity. Although Cecil esteemed Grange 'both for his wisedome and his relligion', Kirkcaldy was still 'a private gentillman', and this was significant: names apart, the congregation was an unknown quantity and Cecil and the Privy Council had, first, to work out the Scots' reserves of military power and their commitment to a campaign against the French and, second, whether an offensive action would serve the interests of England. The Scots were being courted and questioned by the Privy Council, with Cecil handling the intelligence in a process which effectively bypassed the Queen; this is true for the archives and detectable in the tone of Cecil's correspondence. He wrote that 'the authorite of England' would protect the Scots against foreign invasion, and England 'in dede I dare also affirme wold be as sorry to see that auncient nation to be overthrowen and oppressed, as this our owne'.[66] This letter, as Parry and Cecil explained in another drafted on the same day, was written by Cecil in his office of principal secretary.[67] On 28 July 1559 Cecil and Bernard Hampton prepared a letter for the lords of the congregation. The letter was not sent but it demonstrates that at least four councillors (Northampton, Bedford, Pembroke, and Howard of Effingham) used Cecil's contacts with Percy and Grange as intelligence, and that the Council was prepared to express and articulate the regime's solidarity with the Scots' cause. Cecil drafted and corrected the original text of the letter, which was eventually taken seriously enough to be copied up and signed by four of his colleagues; it also suggests that in summer 1559 Cecil was the Council's main contact with Scotland, its principal source of intelligence on the congregation, and a draughtsman for his colleagues. The Council had 'conceved' in the congregation's 'good meaninges both towardes Godes glory, and the freedome of your Contrey', and the councillors wanted the lords to know 'that we shall not neglect such Godly and honorable enterprisees, upon hope that therby this famose Ile, maye be conjoyned at the last in hartes as it is in Contynent land with one sea, and in one uniformyte of language, manners and Conditions'.[68]

---

[65] SP 52/1, fo. 101r–v.   [66] SP 52/1, fo. 101v.   [67] SP 52/1, fo. 98r–v.
[68] SP 52/1, fo. 146r.

So what was the English policy in July 1559? Were Cecil, the Privy Council, and Elizabeth prepared to act, individually or jointly? Did sympathy for co-religionists in Britain override the strategic concerns of the English? The short answer is a qualified no. Once again, Cecil became the principal political intermediary between the congregation and its sympathizers in England. He drafted a letter to the earls of Argyle and Glencairn, James Stuart (the future earl of Moray), and the lords Boyd and Ochiltree on 28 July, in which he agreed with their aims and principles but questioned the wisdom of English military action. Elizabeth and England, he wrote, had 'abandoned Idolatry and brought our salvior Christ Jesus into this kingdom' and there was every hope that the same blessing would fall on the Scots, 'and therby this terrestryall kyngdom of Christ may be dilated thrugh this noble Ile, and so the old Great ennemyes of the trew Chirch of God, may be kept owt, and putt to confusion'. Cecil sympathized with the oppressive political state of Scotland. He explained how the congregation's enemy, 'the Popish kirkmen', had in England been challenged by the 'first reformation' of Henry VIII; he pointed to Denmark as a model for religious reform.[69] But the main point of the letter was clear: the lords had done little to help themselves, and Cecil told them that 'the difficultees of the tyme herin be such, as can not so well answer yow at this instant, as hereafter uppon furder understandyng of your procedinges I shall have better occasion'. After Mary Tudor's European war, and the 1559 peace with France, England could not afford to involve itself in Scotland: 'what a matter of weight it is to enter in warr, ether not provoked, or not forseene'.[70]

So was Cecil a British unionist? Did he share John Knox's vision of 'a perpetual concord betuix these two Realmes'?[71] Knox could afford to take a religiously purist line and his call for close co-operation was shaped by his experience of the 'Edwardian moment'. He told Cecil in July 1559 that these were 'the materis in which I have laubored ever sence the deathe of King Edward'.[72] He collaborated with Anthony Gilby in 1558 and Alexander Whitelaw of New Grange in 1559, both of whom had proven track records. Gilby had pressed for marriage between Edward VI and Mary Stuart and Whitelaw discussed a union between Elizabeth and James, Lord Hamilton in summer 1559. Religion and dynasty were complementary. Cecil's sense of the relationship between England and Scotland was perhaps more sophisticated. He was certainly conscious of the power of the call for religious union and he used the Edwardian vocabulary of 'one

[69] SP 52/1, fos. 147r–48r; Gordon Donaldson, '"The example of Denmark" in the Scottish Reformation', in his Scottish church history (Edinburgh, 1985), pp. 60–70.
[70] SP 52/1, fo. 148v.   [71] The works of John Knox, ed. Laing, VI, p. 31.
[72] The works of John Knox, ed. Laing, VI, p. 46.

island' Protestantism in his personal dealings with the congregation in 1559 and in drafts for the Privy Council. In the civil thesis 'Whither it be mete that England shuld helpe the Nobilite, and protestantes of Scotland to expell the french or no' in August 1559, Cecil's fourth reason *contra* was that 'the sea of Rome, the Emperor, the King Catholike, the Pope and Potentates in Italy, the Duke of Savoye, will rather conspyre with the french Kyng, than to suffer theis ij monarchies to be joyned in one manner of Religion'.[73] A central concern of Cecil's European thought was the concept of England and Scotland bound by a common 'amity', 'knitt in a lyke Religion'.[74] In this way, a British Isles united by co-operative Protestantism could stand alone against the aggressive powers of a Catholic Europe led by the French, who had engineered the Treaty of Cateau-Cambrésis to strip England of its last territorial possession on the Continent and claim the title of queen for Mary Stuart.

But could England intervene in the affairs of Scotland and help the lords of the congregation? And should it? Cecil asked three 'Questions' in August 1559: 'What is to be done to answer the french attemptes?' 'Whyther ayde shalbe gyven to scotland or no?' 'What manner of ayde, secrett or oppen?' He turned them into civil theses in 'A breeffe Consideration', with sections *pro* and *contra*.[75] Behind policy in 1559 lay the historical reasons for an English alliance with Scotland and this is strikingly clear in these two exercises *in utramque partem*. The main thrust of the argument *pro* help for the Scots was that the English crown had superior jurisdiction over Scotland as a junior kingdom and that the two countries were part of a single and independent Britain – in the same way that ''l'hemperor is bound to defend the state of Millane, or of Boheme, being held of the Empyre'.[76] Most of the recent studies of Cecil have argued that although he was perfectly familiar with the claim of English authority over Scotland he did not use it in negotiations with the lords of the congregation.[77] This is probably true, but it does underestimate the significance of arguments for imperial or territorial superiority in Cecil's idea of Britain and the way in which they were used to justify and sanction military intervention. 'The Crowne of england hath a just and unfeyned title, of longer contynuance, than the frendshipp, betwixt scotland and fraunce, unto the superioretye of Scotland' was for Cecil an historical statement;[78] but it was also a convenient political and intellectual way of side-stepping the tricky problem of aiding subjects (the lords of the congregation) against their

---

[73] Cotton Caligula B. 10, fo. 33r; Cotton Caligula B. 10, fo. 86r.
[74] Cotton Caligula B. 10, fo. 33r.
[75] Cotton Caligula B. 10, fos. 86r–88v, 33r–37v.   [76] Cotton Caligula B. 10, fo. 86v.
[77] Dawson, 'Cecil', 198–200; Mason, 'Anglo-British imperialism', pp. 181–2.
[78] Cotton Caligula B. 10, fo. 33v.

governor, absentee or not (Mary Stuart and the regent of Scotland, Mary of Guise). The same argument reappeared in 1568, when Cecil used these ideas to explain Elizabeth's right to try Mary, in the relationship of a senior British monarch to a junior one.[79] English superiority was a mechanism and justification for change and action. Historically, Cecil argued, by the 'title of Superiorety the Crowne of england hath uppon differencees, decided the Controversyes, and appoynted the Crowne of Scotland as to [whom] it was thought'; 'england is of duty and in honor bound to preserve the realme of Scotland from such an absolute Dominion of the french'. The way Cecil used the argument is important. The fact of England's superiority was not at issue: these arguments could be used to justify aid for the Scots only if it was found 'agreable to Godes lawe for every Prynce and Publyk state to defend it selfe', 'not disagreing to Godes lawe to use the same manner of defence that the ennemye useth in his offence'. There were reasons against intervention but the argument for territorial empire and superiority was not a point for rhetorical examination.[80]

So Cecil's concept of the relationship between England and Scotland had imperial, territorial, and religious implications. Although he used evidence of the supposed jurisdiction of the archbishop of York over Scotland – a commonplace in English polemical writing even in the early eighteenth century – this was part of a political and historical tradition and not a plan for action. There is no suggestion that an extension of English ecclesiastical power over Scotland was part of a *quid pro quo* for military support in 1559 and 1560. Cecil wanted a 'league' and 'amity' between the two kingdoms but this meant partnership rather than domination, and political and constitutional settlement rather than dynasty. Co-operation with Scotland predated the kingdom's alliance with France and English intervention in its internal affairs was clearly justified and sanctioned by history. In religion it meant an independent and Protestant ecclesiastical settlement modelled on England's 'first reformation': the issue of episcopacy in Scotland was not discussed but there is no sense in which English plans in summer 1559 were the first stage in a 'Canterburian plot' to subvert the Scottish Reformation.[81] Even before the Reformation Parliament in 1560 – the principles of which were tacitly accepted by the Elizabethan regime later in the decade and written into its negotiations with the Queen of Scots – Cecil wanted a Protestant Scotland bound into a political agreement with its southern neighbour.

---

[79] See below, pp. 163–4.   [80] Cotton Caligula B. 10, fos. 33r, 86r.

[81] For a discussion of the relationship between the English and Scottish churches in the second half of the sixteenth century, see John Morrill, 'A British patriarchy? Ecclesiastical imperialism under the early Stuarts', in Anthony Fletcher and Peter Roberts (eds.), *Religion, culture and society in early modern Britain* (Cambridge, 1994), pp. 210–12.

The details of this model for Scotland's political, constitutional, and ecclesiastical future were endorsed by Cecil on 31 August 1559. He called it 'Art. pro conjunctione Anglie Scotie' but its main title was 'A memoriall of certain pointes meete for restoring the Realme of Scotland to the Auncient Weale' – the internal settlement of Scotland was, in this sense, indistinguishable from 'perpetuall peace' or even for Scotland 'to be made one Monarchie with England'.[82] The settlement of Scotland was pressed as an antidote to French power, because the French 'seketh allways to make Scotland an Instrument to Exercise therby theyr malice upon England and to make a footestoole therof to looke over Ingland as they may'.[83] But the main theme of the text was effective, secure, and Protestant government for Scotland, supervised by the lords of the congregation. In his letter to Argyle, Glencairn, Stuart, Boyd, and Ochiltree a month earlier, Cecil had told the congregation that 'your doinges maye beare the unyversall name of the great Counsell of Scotland, for lack wherof your adversaryes maye rejoyse, and your frendes rest Perplexed': in other words, success and justified action meant, in part, adopting an accepted constitutional and political form. The role of this council was crucial. In the draft of Cecil's letter to the congregation, the indefinite article of 'a great Counsell of Scotland' was scored out in favour of the definite 'the great Counsell of Scotland'; 'such', he continued, 'is the valor and opinion of authorite, and such hath bene not onely in france but in other realmes the lawdable reformation of the Commen weales almost ruynated by insolency of Governors'.[84] In effect, Cecil advised the congregation to market itself as a great council of the realm.

The 'memoriall' developed the general theme. It proposed for Scotland a freedom from 'all Idolatry like as England is', to be 'provided by consent of the thre Estates of the land', and policed by a 'free generall counsell' without the Pope's interference. The three estates had to act as the guardians of any settlement between Mary Stuart, her French husband, and the kingdom of Scotland. The 'saide thre Estates' would deal with revenue and expenditure, including 'how much the Queene shall have for her portion and estate during her absence'. It was clear that 'a Counsell in Scotland' should be appointed in Mary's absence 'to governe the hole Realme, and in those cases not to be directed by the french'. The three estates of Scotland had to have the 'autoritie fourthwith to intimate' to Mary Stuart and her husband 'theyr humble requestes, and yf the same be not effectually graunted then finally they may committ the Govvernaunce' of Scotland to the next heir, 'binding the same also to observe the Lawes

---

[82] Lansdowne 4, fos. 26v–27r, printed below, pp. 223–4.   [83] Lansdowne 4, fo. 26r.
[84] SP 52/1, fo. 149r.

and Auncient rights of the Realme'. The 'nex heyres to the Croune' of
Scotland, as the 'memoriall' made clear, were 'the house of Hameltons'.
With the signature of James Hamilton, earl of Arran at the top of the list in
the congregation's call in August 1559 for the rejection of French interference and the restoration of ancient liberties, this fact was more than a
lucky coincidence. But the implications of this transfer of power, which, in
the proposal, would have fallen by due process to the three estates of
Scotland, were even more important.[85]

This statement of the estates' authority to grant the crown to the
Hamiltons preceded the final, and even more serious, proposed bridle on
Franco-Stuart power in Scotland. 'Fynally', the last paragraph of the
'memoriall' began, 'yf the Queene shalbe unwilling to this as it is likely she
will in respecte of the greedy and Tyrannouse affection of fraunce, then is it
apparant that Almightie god is pleased to transferr from her the Rule of
that Kingdom for the weale of it'. This was effective deposition; deposition
without Mary in the country, perhaps, but, intellectually and politically, a
commitment and statement of enormous proportions. The removal of
Mary was proposed as the first stage of an amity or union with England.
After the end of the Stuarts, and in a state of freedom, Scotland could
consider 'what meanes may be devised through godds goodnes to accord
the two realmes to endure for ever'. Although it was written as a 'last
resort' clause, the implication of the closing paragraph compared to the
opening section is clear: 'the best worldly felicitie' for Scotland was
'perpetuall peace' or union with England and, if this was Cecil's political
preference, it meant the end of Stuart rule in Scotland.[86] The proposed
settlement was so comprehensive and effectively policed, in fact, that it
would have been wholly unacceptable to Mary: Cecil developed, and the
York commissioners tried to negotiate, a similar settlement for Scotland in
1568 and it was too sensitive to be exposed to the Queen of Scots.[87]

The concluding section to 'A memoriall of certain pointes meete for
restoring the Realme of Scotland to the Auncient Weale' is strangely alien,
first, to the traditional picture of the early Elizabethan regime as a shy and
timid creature and, second, to Cecil's reputation as a politically unambi-
tious administrator. Cecil and his colleagues sensed conspiracy and danger
in the early years of the reign. England did seem to stand alone against the
main European Catholic powers. But the 'memoriall' (like Cecil's private
written notes from summer 1559) demonstrates the power of the language
of British Protestant imperialism and the providential terms in which early
Elizabethan governors interpreted and made sense of Continental and

[85] Lansdowne 4, fos. 26v–27r.   [86] Lansdowne 4, fo. 27r.
[87] See below, pp. 167–71, 175–6.

British political affairs. Edward Nares realized that the regime faced a crisis of policy in 1559 and that intervention against the French in Scotland was based on a 'double motive': first, the prospect of the establishment of Mary, 'thereby paving the way for an invasion of England, and the removal of Elizabeth'; and second, the dangerous threat of European Catholicism. Nares printed the 'memoriall', which was, in its own way, an act of intellectual courage; he was appointed to the Regius Professorship at Oxford in 1813, and was hardly in a position to endorse (as he put it) 'such disturbances in an hereditary monarchy'. But at least Nares dealt with the whole text of 'pro conjunctione Anglie Scotie', and he even tried to explain the 'doctrine here inculcated' of 'a regular though not voluntary, abdication of the throne'; this is more than Conyers Read was prepared to discuss in *Mr Secretary Cecil*. Read summarized or briefly quoted from thirty lines out of a total of sixty-nine in the 'memoriall', and he ignored the last paragraph. This has had the effect not only of distancing readers from the link between Cecil and detailed policy in 1559 but of underplaying the relationship between action, political thought, and the work of Protestants who had been out of favour under Mary Tudor and were either back in political and religious life or in print in the new regime. It misrepresents also the connection between policy-making and sensitive or dangerous political situations.[88]

To countenance the effective deposition of Mary Stuart, in or out of Scotland in 1559, was a bold move, especially in the light of the perceived threat from Europe; but it was precisely because France seemed determined to use Mary as a contender to the English throne in a wider invasion plan that 'pro conjunctione Anglie Scotie' was written as a proposal for the political realization of the British Protestant imperialist vision of an island united and defined by religion, standing against the Continent. It was part of a politics that was at once dynastic and providential. But it was also an important comment on the relationship between a governor and his or her governed. The 'memoriall' defined a queen like Mary by the idolatry of her reign, the Stuart abuse of ancient rights, and the presence of foreigners. It rejected them, and offered both an alternative and a mechanism for change: in 1559 a Hamilton succession engineered by the three estates of Scotland, all guaranteed by, and aimed at securing, a British Protestant settlement. Put in a wider context, the 'memoriall' is a stunning mix of religion as justifying ideology, dynasty in politics, and British Protestant vision. Cecil was at the centre of it.

But one issue remained open in late August 1559: the explosive request

---

[88] Edward Nares, *Memoirs of the life and administration of the Right Honourable William Cecil, Lord Burghley . . .*, 3 vols. (London, 1828–31), II, pp. 92–5, 99–100; Conyers Read, *Mr Secretary Cecil and Queen Elizabeth* (London, 1955), p. 145.

by the congregation for military support by England. At a time when, intellectually and ideologically, England was starting to commit itself to the Protestant Scots, Cecil's letters to their leaders took the form of a polite rejection letter: he supported the congregation's position but could not go further.[89] On 27 August, three days before the 'memoriall', Cecil told Sir Thomas Chaloner that 'ayde' in the form of two thousand men had been sent to reinforce the Regent.[90] But if the Elizabethan regime wanted the sort of settlement sketched in the 'memoriall', with its vision of a British Protestant bastion, then the Scots had to be given more help.

III

In the late autumn of 1559, more evidence of Franco-Stuart pretensions to Elizabeth's throne arrived in England in the form of commissions issued by Mary and her husband, Francis, and introduced by the text 'Franciscus et Maria Dei gratia Rex et Regina Franciae, Scotae, Angliae, et Hiberniae'.[91] This claim was more than a personal insult: it was a reminder that England was part of a wider pattern of European dynastic politics, that the person and the crown of Mary Stuart embodied this threat, and that there were serious reasons at least to consider some form of preemptive military action. If June, July, and August 1559 had been months of debate and theoretical planning, then it was becoming increasingly clear that pressure from the Scots (in the form of a diplomatic mission) and persuasion from within (in the person of Cecil) were going to try to turn rhetorical examination on paper into debate in Council and letters of support into practical policy. By early December 1559 at least, Cecil had been converted to an active policy of military intervention; where, precisely when, and how are less certain, but it definitely happened at some point between very early August 1559 and the diplomatic mission of William Maitland of Lethington, Sir Robert Melville, David Forrest, and John Willock to the English court in the first week of December; it was clear, certainly, that Cecil had been receiving strong and consistent intelligence from Croft and Sir Ralph Sadler throughout the autumn.

The embassy's political purpose in England was a rather conservative one. In November, 'the nobles, gentlemen and burgesses of Scotland' issued Maitland of Lethington with instructions on how to 'direct the sute and complainte', in their distress, to Elizabeth. French oppression and the ancient rights of Scotland usurped were the main themes of the text in a 'Sute that this violence & oppression of the frenshe myght be Removit';

---

[89] 28 July 1559, SP 52/1, fo. 148v.   [90] SP 70/6, fo. 132r.
[91] Cotton Caligula B. 10, fos. 63r–v, 64r–v; SP 52/1, fos. 279r–280r, 280v–282r, 283r–287r.

religion was not. Because the Protestant concerns Cecil had expressed throughout the summer of 1559 were not used by the Privy Council in their presentation to Elizabeth later in December, solidarity with co-religionists was probably not the key to the Queen's sympathy. Far more relevant for policy, in fact, were the practical dangers of French power in Scotland, and Lethington was instructed to play on the argument that 'this practise off the frenshe is not attempted onely against this kyngdome off Scotland bot also against the crown and kyngdomes of England and Irelande'. The French had devised 'to spred abroode (though maist falsly) that our quene is Ryght heyre to England & Ireland', and they demonstrated this in 'publick J[o]ustinges in france' and the use of Elizabeth's arms, style, and title.[92]

There is a strong feeling that there was more to Maitland of Lethington's message than the domestic concerns of the 'naturall blode' of Scotland.[93] Although the instructions were drafted in November 1559, they were clearly written to touch an English nerve which Cecil, for one, had spent some time exposing. Maitland of Lethington arrived in London in time for the first recoverable foreign policy debate of the reign; Cecil, as one of the privy councillors who supported active intervention rather than distant support, co-operated with his Scottish counterpart. Cecil endorsed and kept Lethington's own set of questions on the congregation's position in Scotland, which was probably a crib sheet for Maitland and began with a question on the 'probable Reasons' to demonstrate the French 'purposes' in the conquest of the kingdom. In seven points, it dealt with the questions and issues which were important to any debate on England's commitment: French provisions for governing the kingdom, the names of men who had 'declarit theymselfis opinly ag[ainst] the ffrensche', the supporters of the French, the military power of the congregation, the forces that could be taken to the borders and 'howsone yf succours off England shold Joyne with theym', the provision of supplies, and the state of the Scots' naval power. A set of instructions 'to be answered unto by master Secretarie touchynge the affayres of Scotlande' for Thomas Randolph's return north also provides a snapshot of England's position a day after Cecil's acknowledgement of Lethington's answers. Without hostages, 'no oppen ayde of entry of men' could be given, no less than twenty-eight days seemed reasonable for the campaign, and any Scottish soldiers would be entertained and paid 'as the lieutenant of england shall see cause'. So Randolph, armed with Cecil's notes and his own copy of Maitland of Lethington's crib sheet, was ready to state the English position: a package of tightly

---

[92] Additional 23108, fos. 11v–12v.   [93] Additional 23108, fo. 11r.

controlled military aid, English command, and the Scots' commitment to a month of campaigning action.[94]

The Privy Council met to debate Scotland on 27 December 1559 and presented its notes in the form of a petition to Elizabeth the next day. This rehearsed ideas of European (but mainly French) conspiracy which Cecil had been working on for months. Cecil wrote the minutes, which were extremely rough and heavily edited (both at the time of writing and later on, from some of the alterations); but whether they were a planned and reorganized version of the councillors' individual contributions or a basically verbatim set of notes from the meeting is unclear. From the structure of the 'Th'opinion of the Counsell' (which progresses from justifications to a detailed set of recommendations for action) and from Cecil's comment that it developed 'after long and carefull disputes and debates and at severall tymes collected and accorded uppon', it was a fairly ordered piece of work. 'Th'opinion', then, was not a written version of the only debate of its sort in the winter of 1559, but it at least provides a glimpse of the Council in action, the councillors' perception of their own role, and their earliest attempt to persuade the Queen on British policy. The councillors' duty to Elizabeth was 'to gyve yow our advise and Counsell', for the 'discharge of our duety and uppon our sure hope that your Majesty will accept in good parte, our good wills and indevors', because they were bound by 'othe and otherwise'. But the significant point is the degree to which they were divided on the issue of help for Scotland.[95]

From Cecil's drafts and Randolph's detailed diplomatic notes, the commitment to military intervention appears stronger than it actually was. The Privy Council was clearly and openly divided between men who, on the one hand, accepted the political interpretation of French posturings in Scotland but could not agree with a military policy and those, on the other, who were prepared to back a campaign. It was a Council split based on interpretation: not on religion (although only the conservative Arundel, the Lord Steward, was thoroughly 'ageynst the exploict and ageynst any oppen, or costly ayding') and certainly not on political experience. Five councillors 'stode dowtfull towchyng any exploict into scotland': Sir Nicholas Bacon (Lord Keeper of the Great Seal), the marquess of Winchester (Lord Treasurer), Sir William Petre, Sir John Mason, and Dr Nicholas Wotton (dean of Canterbury and York). Three of these men had been associated with Mary Tudor's regime, but so too had the earl of Pembroke, Lord Clinton (Lord Admiral), Lord Howard of Effingham (Lord Chamberlain), and Sir Richard Sackville, and these four joined the marquess of

---

[94] Harley 289, fos. 68r–69v; Egerton 1818, fos. 7r–8v.
[95] SP 12/7, fos. 185r–190v, 191v.

Northampton, Sir Thomas Parry (Treasurer of the Household), Sir Edward Rogers (Comptroller of the Household), Cecil, and Sir Ambrose Cave in supporting intervention. Cecil met Parry, Cave, and Sackville a day after the meeting; Bacon had spoken to the Council as an opponent of military intervention on 15 December. It seems that his Elizabethan reputation for eloquence ensured that a number of copies of the speech were made, but the original has not survived; these later versions are possibly flawed, probably expanded, but all basically the same. Using Cecil's edited notes for the Queen, his own minutes from what seems to have been a 'campaign meeting' for supporters of intervention, and the Bacon text, it is possible (with some care) to piece together the debate on Scotland, its arguments, and the nature of the divided Privy Council.[96]

This debate was a comment on the councillors' perception of England's position in Europe; it was not, generally, a call for imperial control or superiority and certainly not an expression of British Protestant unity. Like Maitland of Lethington's detailed crib sheet, and Thomas Randolph's 'memoriall' of Cecil's answers to specific military questions, the Privy Council divided itself on the practical issues of intervention; in other words, Cecil's colleagues (except Arundel) agreed with the *grounds* for action which Cecil developed at the beginning of his minutes on 27 December. Their justifications were clear enough. The French King and his wife had challenged 'in sondry poyntes derogatory' Elizabeth's 'most undowted right and title to this your Crowne of england', and the interconnected issues of the English arms, jousts and 'entrees into townes', tapestries, 'clothes of estate and such lyke', 'the usurpyng of your stile and title' of England and Ireland, and 'seales graven' were paraded as proof. The councillors agreed that although the French made peace with Elizabeth 'they mynd no longer to kepe it than they maye see tyme mete for there purpoose to breke it'; they would take every opportunity 'to avance there pretenced title ageynst your Majesty and your issue which we besche God shortly gyve yow'. It seemed clear that the French were going to take Scotland and then turn their attention to an invasion of England.[97]

Cecil's contention was that England ought to preempt a French attack by sending troops into Scotland and, as he put it to Parry, Cave, and Sackville in Parry's chamber, 'I can not for any reason that I yet have hard, thynk any otherwise than I have doone.' If France used its force of German mercenaries in the north of England, then it was likely that the English forces would lose. A lack of 'Captaynes and good men of warr', and the 'discomforture of the hartes' of the common people by 'a battell wonne by

<hr />

[96] For the meeting between Cecil, Parry, Cave, and Sackville, SP 52/1, fo. 318r; for one copy of Bacon's text, Harley 398, fos. 12v–21r.
[97] SP 12/7, fos. 185r–186r.

so strong an ennemy' forced him to think 'that it is the surest counsell for the Quenes Majesty to prevent this daunger of the french and to empech there conquest of Scotland'.[98] The strange irony of Cecil's and Bacon's different perspectives on policy is that they used basically the same evidence for opposite purposes. The councillors agreed as a group that the establishment of the church and 'the state ecclesiasticall' were central to the ordering of the commonwealth, and the fact that this had not been achieved by late 1559 was a cause for concern;[99] Cecil made the same instinctive reaction earlier in the year, because disobedience meant subversive mischief. But he used these concerns to press for action; Bacon, on the other hand, took a different view. England was short of 'monye, menn and freindes'. Elizabeth did not have enough money 'to upholde her owne estate as is beseeminge in tyme of peace, and to paye such Debtes as shee owethe within this Realme and withoute'. The kingdom's nobility, gentlemen, and commons were unable to bear the financial burden, and the spirituality was in a state of absolute poverty. Bacon's two groups of 'discontented personns' in religion and old Marian men who were out of favour with the new regime would have been accepted by Cecil as people who 'ar not duly tought to lyve in obedience to the laws established for matters of Relligion'.[100] To describe this sort of disagreement as faction would be extremely misleading.

But it was also an issue of interest and involvement. Back in August 1559, Cecil was concerned that even when the Scots had a king, they 'never cam to the feld with more than xvth dayes victell nother cold abyde longar to gythar'.[101] It was an issue in December when, even at his most positive to attract English support, Maitland of Lethington was 'not abill for the present to giff Resolut answer' to a question on the size of the force the congregation could put in the field, and how soon.[102] Thomas Randolph wondered what 'shalbe advised' if the Scots could 'mayke no lenger aboad in the feldes the xiiij or xviij dayes their purpose beinge not yet achived', but Cecil insisted on at least twenty-eight.[103] Bacon turned this sort of vagueness into an effective argument against military help for the congregation. He used Maitland of Lethington's round figure of three thousand men as proof of a potential bad investment by England, and made the same point by accepting that the Scots could not campaign for over thirty days. The congregation's weakness – based on reports that the Scots could not beat the French without the help of England – was used by Cecil and his sympathetic colleagues to press for military action; Bacon, on the other

---

[98] SP 52/1, fo. 318r.   [99] SP 12/7, fo. 186v.
[100] Harley 398, fos. 13r–14v; SP 12/4, fo. 135r.   [101] Cotton Caligula B. 10, fo. 35v.
[102] Harley 289, fo. 69r.   [103] SP 52/1, fo. 298r.

hand, recounted the frustrated efforts at taking Scotland by English kings from Edward I to Henry VIII.

The debate on intervention in December 1559 was a reminder that England was part of a wider pattern of European politics. The perceived conspiracies of the French were elements of Cecil's rationale. Bacon also accepted them but wondered whether 'the house of Guise, the chief upholders of this Quarrell, shall contynew theyr favour & governance about the Kinge or No'.[104] Even shifts of influence at the French court could be argued into a proposal for nonintervention, letting the French hamper their own operations and leaving time for Elizabeth to secure a marriage. The debate was also a measure of the fragile balance between a commitment to a policy which was beneficial in theory but difficult to pursue in practice. In December 1559 the Privy Council's push for an active policy of military intervention failed even with the full support of ten councillors, nearly two-thirds of the entire group. The debate did two things. First, it established a pattern of action by Council throughout the decade, with meetings held without the Queen, usually centred on a British problem in a European context, and closely related (textually and editorially) to Cecil's own interests and intelligence; and second, it challenged the theory of counsel with the practice of Council. Although the meeting on 27 December 1559 debated a crucial and sensitive issue, Cecil's draft notes were rejected by Elizabeth. But what was the relationship between the true model of counsel – the offer of advice to the monarch out of duty and not right, and the monarch's freedom to reject – and practical politics? Did councillors expect action on the advice they gave out of duty, oath, and conscience? Even Nicholas Bacon was one of the victims of the constant tension between his duty to Elizabeth and personal political conviction, when he had to go before the justices of the peace as Lord Keeper of the Great Seal to defend military action, probably in early 1560. 'When thie neighbours house is on fyre', he argued in terms he would have rejected in the Council debates, 'it is tyme for thee to take heede to thyne owne'.[105]

Cecil also found it hard to balance the competing forces of his own political commitments and obedience to the Queen's instructions. At some point after Elizabeth's first rejection of the Council's advice, although the note is undated, Cecil drafted the text of a letter to the Queen. It is usually assumed that this was a letter of resignation in the modern sense, and Conyers Read even went so far as to say that it 'is an interesting early example both of the recognition of ministerial responsibility and of the refusal of a minister to administer a policy with which he was in

[104] Harley 398, fo. 20v.
[105] Folger Shakespeare Library, Washington, D.C., V.a.143, fo. 44.

fundamental disagreement'. Professor Wallace MacCaffrey has marked it as an act of desperation. Read was perhaps nearer the mark: Cecil was profoundly unhappy with the decision not to intervene, and he did not want to administer the policy (or, rather, lack of it). In 'considering the proceding in this matter for removing of the french owt of Scotland', he could not with his 'conscience gyve any contrary advise' and so asked 'to be spared to entermedle therin, and this I am forced to doo of necessite'. The 'therin' is significant: the note was not a draft resignation letter but a request to be removed from policy on Scotland. Cecil explained his reason. He would never 'be a minister in any your Majesties service, wherunto your owne mynd shall not be agreable, for thereunto I am sworne, to be a minister of your Majestes determynations and not of myne owne, or of others though they be never so manny'.[106]

The politics of 1558 to 1560 help to reinforce two themes of this book: first, the British perspective of policy-making in the 1560s, which was so important to Cecil; and second, Cecil's perception of his place in the polity and the implications this had for his relationship with Queen, Privy Council, and parliament. The British succession crisis in Elizabeth's first complete decade had its roots in the interconnecting fears and realities of Mary Stuart's claim to the throne, the dangers of internal subversion, and the threat of Continental Catholic war against Protestants. The only real way to neutralize the danger was action in England: a husband and an heir for Elizabeth and a sure and declared succession to the throne. In Cecil's Council minutes in December 1559, the privy councillors registered their 'most inward and harty desyres and wish to your Majesty an honorable mariadge to your own contentation and agreable with the condition and state of thes your realme'. Nicholas Bacon argued independently that if the Queen would marry 'yt shall doe much to the endinge of that controversye' of Mary, her succession pretensions, and French influence in Scotland.[107] In Anglo-Scottish politics and diplomacy, 1558–60 established Cecil's approach to the British problem: an island united by Protestantism and committed to the limitation of Stuart power by treaty and religious alliance.

---

[106] Lansdowne 102, fo. 1r; Read, *Cecil*, p. 161; Wallace MacCaffrey, *Elizabeth I* (London, 1993), p. 64; Wallace MacCaffrey, *The shaping of the Elizabethan regime* (London, 1969), p. 64.

[107] SP 12/7, fo. 186v; Folger Shakespeare Library, Washington, D.C., V.a.143, fo. 40.

3

Anglo-British negotiations for a
settlement 1560–1563

In December 1559 Henry Killigrew was worried that Mary Stuart 'dothe carrye her selfe so honorably, advisedlye and discrythelye, as I can not but feare hir progresse'. 'Me thinkethe', he continued in a letter to Lord Robert Dudley, 'it were to be wisshed of all wyse men, and her Majestes good subjectes, that the one of these two Quenes of the Ile of Bryttaine were transfformed into the shape of a man, to make so happie a mariage, as therby ther might be an unitie of the holl Ile, and their appendances'. Men who were 'conversant in [hi]Storyes' knew that marriage was the key to security.[1] If Killigrew had read his chronicle histories, he may have made the connection between a king like the mythical Gorboduc, an insecure succession, civil war, the divided empire of Britain, and England's position a year into Elizabeth's reign.[2] In 1560 there was a serious and apparently irreconcilable problem: Elizabeth and Mary were two monarchs in the same island, with claims and counter claims to the English throne, either supported or opposed by Catholic Europe, and justified by two competing ideologies. The pretensions of Mary Stuart and all that they seemed to stand for – England's isolation, a possible invasion, Continental Catholic tyranny – were too serious and too immediate for cosy reflections on an idealized marriage and a peaceful settlement of the problem by dynasty and hope alone.

I

Cecil's arguments from December 1559 were just as relevant a month later. 'There be manny argumentes', he wrote in late January 1560, 'to prove that the french meane to seke the conquest of this realme, by pretence of the

---

[1] 31 December 1559, Harley 6990, fo. 5r, printed in Joseph Stevenson (ed.), *Selections from unpublished manuscripts in the College of Arms and the British Museum illustrating the reign of Mary Queen of Scotland 1543–1568* (Maitland Club, 41; Glasgow, 1837), pp. 84–5.
[2] See below, pp. 100–1.

title which they make therto'. The Treaty of Cateau-Cambrésis, Mary Stuart's use of the arms, style, and title of England, and the French recruitment of German mercenaries were individual but composite parts of a single threat. To 'provide for the defence of the realme', Cecil listed the need to send the duke of Norfolk to the Borders with a substantial military force, to dispatch Sir Nicholas Throckmorton back to the French court, and to 'send to Kyng Philipp to understand his mynd, and to obteyne his frendshipp'. Anthony, Lord Montague and Sir Thomas Chamberlain were ordered to Spain; the set of instructions the two men received before they left is one of the keys to England's intricate foreign and succession policy.[3] For England, Spain was an important counterbalance against French aggression. Although it was really only in 1569 that England's fear of Catholic conspiracy turned into an open conflict with the Spanish, Cecil did not entirely trust the motives or the policies of Philip even in the early days of Elizabeth's reign, especially in the Spanish King's relationship with the French at Cateau-Cambrésis.[4] But one principle of action was clear for the English in 1560: intervention in Scotland and firm action against the Queen of Scots had to be justified to Spain. If London overstepped its mark and turned a defensive military action into an offensive one, then there was every possibility that Philip's fragile support would collapse. So Montague and Chamberlain had the sensitive task of selling English policy to the Spanish: the reason, the justifications, and the military proposal itself. According to Cecil's draft instructions, the French had clearly worked with Pope Paul IV 'ageynst hir Majestes right to the Crowne of england'; pushed by the Guise, Mary Stuart had 'attempted new thynges very derogatory' to Elizabeth and her kingdom. To restore Scotland to its 'auncient lyberty, and freedome' and to 'save both the realmes from the Dominion of the french', England wanted to support the nobility of Scotland and avoid 'the calamite of that realme'.[5]

English policy was under pressure in 1560. It was not debated or decided in isolation, but carefully and by a regime painfully conscious of the danger of testing the patience of Spain and losing the 'ernest frendshipp' – or, as Cecil emphasized in his draft of Montague's and Chamberlain's instructions, 'ernest and *very brotherly* frendshipp' – of Philip.[6] So in 1560, at a time when most of the Privy Council wanted the kingdom to enter Scotland with a military force and Cecil's supporters were able unashamedly to

---

[3] Lansdowne 103, fos. 3r–4r; for Throckmorton's instructions, CP 232, fos. 224r–228v; for Cecil's drafts of the instructions for Montague and Chamberlain, Cotton Vespasian C. 7, fos. 109r–118v.

[4] 20 May 1559, CP 152, fos. 34r–35r.

[5] Cotton Vespasian C. 7, fos. 109v–110r, 112r.

[6] Cotton Vespasian C. 7, fo. 110r.

defend and define the policy in confessional terms, England had to tread carefully and sensitively. This short period of intense diplomatic and military action, in which English policy was decided and executed under the extremely watchful eye of Catholic Europe, should stand as a small case study of the very early Elizabethan polity in foreign policy action: how it approached the developing succession crisis and its implications, the way in which Cecil gathered and dealt with intelligence, the relationship between the Privy Council and the Queen, the regime's sense of how a settled Britain could be structured in England's interests, and the significance of the Continental political situation.

At some point between early January and February 1560, the Privy Council managed to convince Elizabeth that military action in Scotland was central to the protection of England's interests. The duke of Norfolk was sent to Berwick to defend the border in January. It was also clear that Cecil and his small 'campaign group' had finally won a practical victory: Montague and Chamberlain were instructed to tell Philip that 'many wise men be in dout the loss of a small tyme past shall be to hir gretar chargees by the dooble'.[7] This had been the principle behind the interventionists' argument a month earlier; in fact, the provisions for military action and England's defence in January were written almost verbatim from the 'opinion of the Counsel' in December: the soothing message to Philip, an approach to the Protestant princes of Germany, and a defensive strategy for the north.[8]

But there was still the significant problem of political language. To sell the policy to Elizabeth the Scots, like the English Privy Council, argued for the strategic benefits of intervention. This meant that the lords of the congregation had to define and explain themselves in terms of an ancient nobility being repressed by the usurping French. This was different to the confessional way in which the congregation had explained itself to Mary of Guise in May 1559, and it sat awkwardly with the tentative approach Cecil made to the Scottish lords in June and July. Elizabeth's personal instructions to the duke of Norfolk, on the other hand, dealt with the threats to England and the needs of the nobility – and not the religious congregation – of Scotland.[9] But although Elizabeth refused to accept the purely religious and revolutionary declarations of the Scottish congregation, there is some evidence to suggest that the Privy Council was pushing (or at least trying to push) the Queen towards a more ideological declaration of English policy. One of the earliest expressions of this confessional approach – and the

[7] Cotton Vespasian C. 7, fo. 114v.
[8] Lansdowne 103, fo. 4r.
[9] CP 152, fos. 48r–49r, printed in Haynes, pp. 217–18.

agreement of English military aid for the Scots – was the final text of the Treaty of Berwick in February 1560.

Cecil did not attend the Berwick negotiations, but he collaborated with the Scottish lords and helped to draft the text of the treaty. Cecil's alterations to the document are interesting. They reinforced an emphasis on the *'auncient rightes and* libertye' of Scotland and the right of the king-dom's nobility to act 'in *the name of the whole realme'* and in the *'liberty of there contrey'*, but they also declared a commitment to 'this cause for meyntenance of *Christian* religion'.[10] So the importance of Berwick lay not only in the firm commitment England made to sending troops into Scot-land, but also for the way in which it explained and expressed support for the lords of the congregation. Lord James Stuart, Lord Ruthven, Sir John Maxwell, William Maitland of Lethington, John Wishart of Pitarrow, and Henry Balnaves of Halhill represented the duke of Châtelherault 'and the remanent of the Lordes of his partie Joyned with him this cause for meyntenance of Christian religion and defence of the auncient rightes and libertie of their Country', and Cecil played a large part in describing and defining the lords in this way.[11] This protection of 'a Christian realme in profession of Christes true religion' by its nobility was echoed in Elizabeth's ratification of the Berwick agreement in March 1560, based on the Queen's imperial power to act for the 'Juste and due preservation of bothe these Kingdoms, thus conteynid in one Ile as in a little worlde by it selfe'. Both England and Scotland were 'knytt in one continent Ilonde to gether at the creation of the worlde, and severed notoriously from all the reste of the same worlde'.[12] The sentence could quite easily have come from John Hooper, Richard Grafton, and William Patten in 1548 or Cecil and the Privy Council in July 1559: it was one significant element of a British Protestant imperial argument which justified itself by appealing to national liberty and common religion. The themes of Protestantism, freedom from tyranny, and the French attack on England's interests and Elizabeth's crown moulded themselves into the same argument. In a letter to the earl of Huntly on 18 March 1560 Cecil managed to reinforce a call for the preservation of 'a naturall governance' in Scotland against the French and 'honorable service for your natyve Contrey' with 'the concord of theis ij realmes being at the Creation knitt in one Ile and with one language, and one sort of people having no difference but name'.[13]

The Privy Council still had to persuade Elizabeth to express policy in confessional or ideological terms. In late March 1560, determined to keep

---

[10] Cotton Caligula B. 9, fo. 35r.
[11] CP 152, fo. 56r; Cotton Caligula B. 9, fo. 35r.
[12] Egerton 1818, fo. 9v.
[13] CP 152, fo. 68r–v.

pressing the Queen on the merits of forward policy in Scotland, Cecil drafted a statement of the Privy Council's opinion. On the face of it, the note was a clear presentation of advice written 'for the avoyding of long speche to declare the accord and consent of our simple opinions'. But Cecil's corrections to the draft reveal a more subtle relationship between the intention of the piece and the political influence it was meant to have on Elizabeth. The councillors based their 'short rehersall' on a number of arguments 'wheruppon we have from the begynning of this consultation layd the fundation of our counsells'; still, Cecil's original sentence was more forthright, centring on the councillors' 'argument'. The introduction was written in the language of humble counsel, but the more direct expressions of agreed and corporate opinion – 'for discharge of our allegiance and of our othes, thynketh most expedient and necessary', 'we doo all certenly affirme in our consciencees we thynk' – were barely changed. The privy councillors offered advice which they thought had to be taken. Cecil's text was blunt: 'we thynk it mete that your Majesty shuld follow your former determynations without delaye'. The privy councillors were even prepared to argue that if an active British policy did not continue to be followed 'we then doo wish that these our Counsells had not bene gyven'. Elizabeth had the power to refuse the advice but she faced a united and remarkably decisive Privy Council.[14]

The strategic implications of the Treaty of Berwick were also profoundly important. For the first time in the decade, Cecil explicitly linked the concerns of the regime in Scotland and policy in Ireland. In a *quid pro quo* for English military aid for the congregation, the Scots agreed to help in Ireland by agreeing to 'a mutuall and reciproke contracte' between Lord Lieutenant Sussex and the earl of Argyle. The principle was simple: Argyle would use his power in the north-west of Scotland and his seasoned troops (many of whom had already fought as mercenaries in Ireland) to counter trouble in Ulster. This was part of a coherent and radically new strategy. In April 1560 Cecil produced a set of 'Articles declaring both the state of the North part of Irlande, and what is requyred of the part of Scotlande to help that the same be set in good order'. Friendship and comprehension were major aims of the project – Elizabeth's 'boantefull goodnes' and protection, willing to act as 'a good and gracious sovverayn Lady and Quene' – but compulsion and the power of Argyle lay in the background. So, in effect, Cecil was able to make a strong connection between aid for the Scots, Protestant solidarity, and policy in Ireland. And the principle was still solid in April 1561, when Cecil wrote to Argyle asking him to support

---

[14] Cotton Caligula B. 10, fos. 89r–92v.

Elizabeth's lord lieutenant in Ireland and complimenting him on his constancy in the Gospel.[15]

Cecil played an important part in transforming intelligence from Scotland and Europe into forceful and compelling counsel. As Principal Secretary, he handled the letters sent by Norfolk and his Council to London and from Elizabeth and the Privy Council to Scotland. The Privy Council's evidence was old Cecil territory: proof of Spanish complicity at Cateau-Cambrésis, the pretence of Mary Stuart's claim to the throne of England, French military preparations, and the repression of the Scots. It was also the subject of new information which had been sent south four days before the Council's meeting and its petition on 23 March 1560. Thomas Randolph had seen a copy of 'the begynnynge and endinge' of a patent which proved the French and Stuart use of the title and arms of England; Norfolk wrote to Cecil with the news.[16] But the force of the Privy Council's argument lay in the frank coherence of Cecil's carefully marshalled argument: the kingdom was in extreme danger and it was 'honorable' to relieve Scotland and a worthwhile financial investment. Back in August 1559, the first argument *pro* support for the lords of the congregation had been the right of defence in the law of nature. It followed in spring 1560 that England could '. . . remove that which was so lykely by there owne procedinges and demonstrations to hurt and dammage this your Majestes estate'.[17]

The Privy Council's statement had two immediate effects. A proclamation was issued on 24 March which rehearsed the substance of the Council's notes; it also used a language of conspiracy and subversion perfected by Cecil. But more significantly, the proclamation demonstrated that the Privy Council was committed to the public definition of England as a kingdom fighting for British Protestant concerns and prepared to defend itself against the threat of Continental military action, for which Cecil had helped to shape and define both the image and the language. This defensive England understood the connection between the Stuart claim to the English throne, the preparations in France, the machinations of the Guise, and the assault on the ancient and Protestant nobility of Scotland. For Cecil, it

---

[15] Jane E.A. Dawson, 'Two kingdoms or three? Ireland in Anglo-Scottish relations in the middle of the sixteenth century', in Roger A. Mason (ed.), *Scotland and England 1286–1815* (Edinburgh, 1987), p. 119; Dawson, 'The fifth earl of Argyle, Gaelic lordship and political power in sixteenth-century Scotland', *Scottish Historical Review*, 67 (1988), 3; Dawson, 'William Cecil and the British dimension of early Elizabethan foreign policy', *History*, 74 (1989), 207–9; CP 152, fo. 57v; for Cecil's 'Articles', National Library of Scotland, Edinburgh, Advocates 33.1.1, vol. 1 no. 2; Cecil to Argyle, 2 April 1561, SP 63/3, fo. 138r.

[16] 19 March 1560, CP 138, fo. 25r, printed in Haynes, pp. 265–6.

[17] Cotton Caligula B. 10, fos. 89v–92r; for Cecil's notes from August 1559, Cotton Caligula B. 10, fos. 33v, 86r.

meant a certain type of policy and a new emphasis on the kingdom's domestic state, two themes which he continued to develop over the decade and refined in 1569. In 'A memoryall of certen matters to be Considered by hir Majesty' on 25 March 1560, Cecil listed an alliance with the German princes, the 'mustryng, arming, and trayning of the people', naval preparations, an assessment of the royal army in the south of England, the defence of Portsmouth, the Isle of Wight, Jersey, Guernsey, and Portland, the building up of treasure, and the government of Wales as elements of a single policy to secure the kingdom. There was also a link between the religious state of England, punishment by God, and success in policy; this providential connection between national sin and salvation had been a concern in early summer 1559.[18]

In spring 1560 'the Ire of God' was more likely to manifest itself in a French invasion or in the severe displeasure of Philip of Spain. The military campaign in Scotland and the new sense of focused and ideological English policy was putting a heavy strain on the relationship between Elizabeth and Philip. Chamberlain and Montague reached Toledo with England's policy *apologia* only a few days before the resolute Privy Council presentation and exactly a week before Cecil's 'memoryall' of action of 25 March. The Council was united in March: Cecil did not have to append a list of his colleagues who either supported or did not support the Council's general line on continued intervention; in this sense at least, he had made progress since the divided (and rejected) opinion of the councillors in December 1559. But there were signs that the common and agreed commitment to military action was starting to strain in early April 1560.

Opposition to what was clearly turning into a serious test of Spanish friendship and patience, according to Cecil's relative, Lord John Grey of Pirgo, came from a group of 'pagetyans'.[19] Conyers Read called them 'a Spanish faction', unhappy with the direction of English policy and keen to press the merits of a Tudor–Habsburg marriage. In fact, there was little support for the Habsburg plan in 1560; even when it became a real issue in the middle years of the decade, support for Archduke Charles of Austria's marriage suit was not a mark of religious affiliation.[20] Grey's letters are an odd mixture of hyperbole and political assessment from a distance. In the opening letter he called Sir John Mason 'and all his fellowes suche arche

---

[18] *A proclamacion declaryng the quenes majesties purpose, to kepe peace with Fraunce and Scotlande, and to provyde for the suretie of hir kyngdomes* (STC 7910; London, 1560), reprinted in Paul L. Hughes and James F. Larkin (eds.), *Tudor royal proclamations*, 3 vols. (New Haven and London, 1964–9), II, pp. 141–4; for 'A memoryall', SP 12/11, fo. 84r–v.

[19] Grey to Cecil, 1 April 1560, SP 12/12, fo. 1r.

[20] Conyers Read, *Mr Secretary Cecil and Queen Elizabeth* (London, 1955), p. 168; Susan Doran, 'Religion and politics at the court of Elizabeth I: the Habsburg marriage negotiations of 1559–1567', *English Historical Review*, 104 (1989), 910–11.

practesers agaynst god'; in the second he mentioned the earl of Arundel, Sir William Petre, and Sir Thomas Parry. Cecil, by contrast, was held up as the maintainer of God's cause, the defender of England, and the protector of the Queen.[21] But the issue between Cecil and the 'pagetyans' was a difference of opinion. Cecil knew that Paget had supported Mary Tudor's Spanish war against France but he was not a privy councillor in 1560. Arundel had opposed the principle of any help for the Scots in December 1559, and Mason and Petre shared his doubts. But Parry, the other old Marian on the Privy Council, had been a supporter of intervention and a member of Cecil's 'campaign group'. These men were conservative, but they disagreed with Cecil in spring 1560 on grounds of experience, temperament, and age and not from factional interest.

Grey's 'pagetyans' had every reason to feel uncomfortable in early April 1560. These men seem to have been the only critics of a policy in Britain expressed in Protestant terms; significantly, the rest of the privy councillors were not. The Spanish ambassador also felt this sense of aggressive Protestant vitality; in March 1560 he had described the frightening prospect of English support for the Scots destroying neighbouring countries on the Continent.[22] Philip II sent a special envoy, de Glajon, who dictated a message to Sir Francis Knollys. The King wanted Elizabeth to 'have hyr realme in saffetye owte of the dawnger of the frenche, & that the matters myght be so composed in skotland, that the rebelles myght be chastened, & yet this realme owte of alle dawnger', and so de Glajon had been sent 'to be a mediator' between Elizabeth and the French 'for a good conclusyon of peaxe & for reformation of all injuries'. But because a force was already in place, Philip expected Elizabeth to 'revoke hyr armye or to abstayne from force .40. or .50. dayes'. The whole purpose of the English expedition was to preempt a full French attack; Spain's request was unacceptable. Knollys argued on paper that because the French King had 'gone the onely waye abowte to accomplyshe his wycked desyr of the Conqwest of this hyr realme of ynglond, unles the frenche aforesayd eyther by fayre meanes do remove theyr force, or els that by force they may be removed from skotlond'.[23]

The regime tried to play a diplomatic delaying move but it was still prepared to defend military intervention even under pressure from the Spanish. Knollys probably met de Glajon before 8 April; he had time to copy up the ambassador's answer and add his own long postcript. Knollys

---

[21] SP 12/12, fo. 1r; Grey to Cecil, 20 April 1560, CP 152, fo. 137r, printed in Haynes, pp. 295–6.

[22] Julian Lock, '"Strange usurped potentates": Elizabeth I, the papacy and the Indian summer of the medieval deposing power', DPhil thesis, University of Oxford (1992), p. 292.

[23] CP 152, fos. 112r–113r, printed in Haynes, p. 280.

gave the transcript to Cecil, who endorsed it and wrote his own diplomatic answer based on Knollys' report of the interview. Cecil offered a defence of Elizabeth's policy in the face of French aggression since June 1559.[24] His *apologia* was based on 'A memoryall of Injuryes Committed sence the treaty of the last peace', which Cecil drafted on 5 April 1560, a catalogue of the offences of the French King and the Queen of Scots, an account of Throckmorton's discussions at the French court, and a short chronology of Anglo–French relations between June and August 1559.[25] In one sense, Cecil's reply worked: English forces carried on fighting in Scotland, and the first assault on Leith took place a month after the presentation of de Glajon's message. But Philip's embassy succeeded in one crucial area: under general pressure from Spain, England had to consider a timetable for a settlement of the British problem.

II

At the end of May 1560 Cecil and Dr Nicholas Wotton were sent north to negotiate a diplomatic settlement between the lords of the congregation, the French, and Elizabeth. Cecil had been abroad with Reginald Pole in 1554 and 1555. Wotton was a privy councillor and the dean of Canterbury and York but he was an experienced French diplomat. These two men negotiated a remarkable settlement for the early Elizabethan regime: a treaty which seemed to invite the end of hostility in Britain, concluded (as Cecil pointedly maintained in 1569) under the great seals of France and Scotland and entirely valid. The negotiations in June and July 1560 are important for two reasons: first, they are examples of Cecil at work, trying to deal with French ambassadors who represented everything he had written and debated against in the council chamber; and second, the end result of the negotiations – the Treaty of Edinburgh, concluded in July 1560 – was a model for a settlement of Britain which influenced nine more years of diplomacy and shaped Cecil's British political creed in the first decade.

May 1560 was not a good month for the English campaign in Scotland. It seemed progressively to be running out of steam. One court correspondent at Greenwich was amazed that Calais could have fallen more quickly than Leith, and he reported to the earl of Shrewsbury that 'my Lordes here are in a marvelous perplexitie that there is no more don'. He hinted, too, at the depressing situation in Europe. Montague had been recalled from Spain and Chamberlain left as resident ambassador; more ominously, the substance of Philip's reply to the two men was 'reserved [for the] King of

---

[24] CP 152, fos. 113r–115v, printed in Haynes, pp. 280–3.
[25] CP 198, fo. 111r–v.

Spaines Embassadours here who [have] dayly conference with the frenche Embassadour'.[26] This was a dangerous combination. A few days before, Lord Admiral Clinton had sent an urgent note to Cecil. The letter was written out of 'very dewty and love to the quenes majeste and my contrey' but he urged Cecil to 'kepe this Lettar to your sellff and thenk to hyd my ffoly'. According to Clinton, the northern campaign was running out of supplies and energy. But the expedition was central to England's protection: 'ffor lett the ffrench prosper in skotland and be yow then assurid that her hynes shall never be in quyet bot shall have contyneall attemptys agenste her majestie', based on their 'insaseat longing' for England.[27] From the secrecy of Clinton's depressing report, and the fact that the Queen had to be reminded of the Franco-Stuart offences against her in early May, Elizabeth's resolve seems to have been flagging.[28]

It was with this sense of depressed urgency that Cecil and Wotton were sent into Scotland. Their mission was explained in a set of diplomatic instructions signed by Elizabeth on 26 May 1560; Cecil went through the text and summarized the main points in marginal notes.[29] They began the journey four days later. Letters were exchanged daily between Cecil and Wotton and Elizabeth; these passed from Edinburgh to London through Berwick and back again. The two men kept in touch with the Privy Council, which sent instructions north. Cecil had two personal correspondents to whom he sent letters in his own holograph, without the interference of a clerk: Petre and Norfolk in Berwick. Petre – one of Cecil's factional opponents in *Mr Secretary Cecil* – received some remarkably honest assessments of the state of the negotiations. The aim of the mission was to satisfy Elizabeth's desire for peace and 'to gyve eare unto any communicacion or matter of treatie that may conduce to good agrement, and reasonable satisfaction of our Honnour and suretie of our Realme'. This was planned in two stages: first, at Newcastle by 5 June to meet Randan and Valence, the French ambassadors; and, second, at a meeting in Leith. The agenda was straightforward. From Cecil's marginal summaries, England wanted a French 'surceauce of armes', the 'perswasion to the scottes' that France wanted to 'dissever the frendeship and amitie betwixt these two kingdomes', the removal of French forces from Scotland, and the return of Calais. More than this, the negotiations were meant to settle Britain in the form that Cecil and the Privy Council had been working

---

[26] 16 May 1560, Lambeth Palace Library, 3196, fo. 95, with the signature removed and badly damaged, printed in Edmund Lodge (ed.), *Illustrations of British history, biography, and manners, in the reigns of Henry VIII, Edward VI, Mary, Elizabeth, and James I, exhibited in a series of original papers . . .*, 3 vols. (London, 1791), I, pp. 312–13.

[27] 12 May 1560, SP 12/12, fos. 50r–51v.

[28] Endorsed by Cecil as 'a memoriall for the Quenes Majesty', SP 12/12, fo. 43r–v.

[29] Cotton Caligula B. 9, fos. 121r–124r, 124v.

towards since 1559: autonomy for the Scots and the preservation of 'scottish relligion', based on a 'league' and 'agreed by contract' between Elizabeth, the French King and the Queen of Scots, and the nobility of Scotland. This was one of the earliest expressions of what would become, in 1568 and 1569, the proposal for a tripartite political agreement between Mary, Elizabeth, and James VI.[30]

One of the important themes of the negotiations for Mary Stuart's future in 1568 was the sense of alliance between the interests of the Queen of Scots' Protestant opponents and the English regime. The same was true, in a slightly different way, in June 1560. At Newcastle, Cecil, Wotton, Valence, and Randon settled the procedural details of the Edinburgh talks. In private, Cecil prepared a 'memoryall' of principles and demands for the English and Scottish parties. This was a unilateral exercise: only Wotton and Cecil talked to the French at Newcastle; the two men were four days away from Berwick where Sadler, Carew, and Percy could have given them the latest intelligence from the lords of the congregation. Cecil established some demands for the Scottish representatives to negotiate for themselves. These included the claim for 'Governance of scotland' to be granted to 'the nation of the land', the protection of liberty, a peace between England and (in Mary's absence) the kingdom's nobility, and the confirmation of the right of the duke of Châtelherault 'as second person of the realme'. The 'Thynges to be demanded of the french' by 'us onlye' were the removal of French troops from Scotland and the complete rejection of all references to the arms, style, and title of England by the Queen of Scots.[31] These terms came straight from the May instructions.[32] It was an important strategy: Cecil planned to co-ordinate the Scottish representatives and use the common interests of the British Protestant community, organized into two groups, to pressure the French into accepting a purely English proposal.

The shape of Cecil's diplomatic campaign was clear from the beginning of the Edinburgh negotiations. Only four days after the second preliminary meeting at Berwick, Cecil was extremely impressed by the work of William Maitland of Lethington; Maitland was prepared – significantly, from Cecil's Newcastle note – 'to work all the myndes of the nobilite to allow any thyng' Elizabeth determined.[33] Cecil said the same thing to Norfolk; the other Scottish lords, with the clear exceptions of Lord James Stuart and the earl of Arran, were too zealous for Cecil's liking. Nothing could persuade them of anything that appeared 'to hynder' religion. Maitland of

[30] Cotton Caligula B. 9, fos. 121r–123v; see below, pp. 164, 168, 193.
[31] 10 June 1560, SP 52/4, fos. 14r–v.
[32] Cotton Caligula B. 9, fos. 122r–v, 123v.
[33] Cecil to Elizabeth, 19 June 1560, SP 52/4, fo. 29v; Mark Loughlin, 'The career of Maitland of Lethington *c*. 1526–1573', PhD thesis, University of Edinburgh (1991), p. 55.

Lethington had helped Cecil to make sure that 'the whole' would not be sacrificed to less significant concerns.[34] On their first day in Edinburgh, Cecil and Wotton pressed Randan and Valence on the French use of the arms and style of England. Elizabeth's commissioners wanted a 'recompense'; the French representatives maintained that they had 'no power to talke of any recompense' but they did agree to the condition that 'the King and Quene our Sovveraine shall from hensforth forbeare to use and beare the said title'.[35]

In their first letter back to the Privy Council, Cecil and Wotton reported that 'we can get nothing but with racking and streyning, and we have it in woordes, they allways will steale yt away in penning and wryting'.[36] Support from the Scots was not the problem: despite the organizational intricacies of setting the congregation on the right path, it was clear to Cecil that 'all this nobilite of Scotland hate the french, and be devoted to england' and 'that the Nobilitie and gentlemen with the common people doo well conceive the frute of amitie betwexte these two Realmes and be utterly bent against the frenche'.[37] The formal expression of this amity – the contract between Elizabeth, the Scottish nobility, and the French – was going to be the 'hardest knott'. 'We perceave', Cecil told Petre, 'the french can nowise digest it'. He was also convinced that the conditions for a British treaty in its present form would 'allweise trooble there stomakes' and he doubted whether it could be maintained.[38] The Privy Council sent a more detailed proposal to Cecil and Wotton on 24 June 1560, and this concentrated on the removal of all references to the arms and style of England in France. One clause even suggested that the influence of Philip II could be used to put pressure on the French if they were unwilling to agree to an article linking the pretensions of Mary Stuart to compensation for the loss of Calais.[39]

The negotiations at Edinburgh lasted for nearly three weeks, and they seem to have put Cecil under a good deal of strain. He asked Petre 'to consider the burthen, and putt your fyngar to ease us'.[40] Cecil felt that the Queen's instructions were not clear enough. He would have been prepared to agree with the French on slightly more limited terms than lose the whole treaty but Wotton was too cautious.[41] Cecil arranged a private meeting with Valence to press 'him thus muche that there might be a mutuall

---

[34] 25 June 1560, CP 153, fo. 7r, printed in Haynes, p. 333.
[35] CP 2, fo. 34r.
[36] 19 June 1560, CP 152, fo. 177r, printed in Haynes, p. 327.
[37] SP 52/4, fo. 29r; CP 152, fo. 177r.
[38] 21 June 1560, CP 153, fo. 1r, printed in Haynes, p. 329.
[39] CP 2, fo. 48r–v.
[40] 21 June 1560, CP 153, fo. 1r, printed in Haynes, p. 330.
[41] Cecil to Petre, 27 June 1560, CP 153, fo. 8r, printed in Haynes, p. 334.

defence' between the two British realms 'and the same confirmed by acte of parlement bothe of Englande and Scotlande'. This was crucial: without it the congregation 'being left in dispayre shall the sooner be alienated' from Elizabeth. The problem was that a settlement was in danger of being smothered by paper; for the British 'contract' alone, the French produced seven proposed clauses lettered A to G.[42]

By early July the general shape of the final treaty was clear enough for Lord Admiral Clinton to write to Cecil with congratulations and the message that 'all your frendes ar her mery'.[43] One of the reasons for Clinton's optimism was the fact that communicating over long distance was slow: Cecil's letters in the last week of June were far more positive than the report of his depressing and tense meetings with Valence at the beginning of July, and Clinton wrote before Cecil's and Wotton's letter arrived at court. But on 5 July Cecil and Wotton wrote to tell Petre that the articles of a treaty were on parchment and ready to be signed the next day.[44] The crucial date was 2 July, when Cecil personally drafted the proposed clauses and sent them south.[45] Some of the basic principles had been agreed before this final burst of activity. On 26 June, for example, the French accepted the need to demolish Leith, to respect Protestantism in Scotland, to remove their forces, and to establish a governing council jointly chosen by the Queen of Scots and the congregation.[46] But there was a more British edge to the final agreement, an important sense in which the Scots (as Cecil and Wotton told Petre by letter) 'doo so well perceave as they doo acknowledge themselves perpetually bounde to Quenes Majestie for this inestimable benefite'.[47] Both the 'libertie of Scotlande' and Elizabeth's 'owne causes' – her 'undoubted right' to the English crown – were secured in 'open treaty'.[48] Cecil had achieved more, on his own admission, by 'bragges' than by eloquence, but the final treaty was a considerable and rather unexpected success.[49]

Cecil's explanation of the terms of the Treaty is perhaps more interesting than the final official text agreed at Edinburgh. Cecil and Wotton sent down an account to Elizabeth from Leith before the 'little ceremonie' to celebrate the end of the negotiations on 6 July 1560.[50] This was followed

---

[42] Cecil and Wotton to Elizabeth, 1 July 1560, CP 153, fos. 15r–16r, printed in Haynes, pp. 335–8; for Cecil's draft, SP 52/4, fos. 69r–71v.

[43] 3 July 1560, CP 153, fo. 22r, printed in Haynes, p. 344.

[44] CP 153, fo. 27r.

[45] Cotton Caligula B. 9, fo. 141r; SP 52/4, fos. 132r–148v.

[46] SP 52/4, fos. 54r–55r.

[47] 5 July 1560, CP 153, fo. 27r, printed in Haynes, p. 349.

[48] Cecil and Wotton to Elizabeth, 6 July 1560, CP 153, fo. 34r, printed in Haynes, pp. 351–3; for Cecil's original draft, CP 153, fo. 32r.

[49] Cecil to Norfolk, 26 June 1560, SP 52/4, fo. 54r.

[50] CP 153, fo. 35r, printed in Haynes, pp. 351–3.

two days later by a second and more detailed description of the Treaty, drafted by Cecil.[51] The Clerk of the Privy Council, Bernard Hampton, wrote a 'note of theffect of the Principall Matters' of the Treaty, and this was sent to the earl of Sussex in Ireland on 12 July – the Treaty was an important piece in the jigsaw of British and Irish policy.[52] These summaries are nearer to Cecil's own interpretation of the Treaty and the language he used to describe its implications than the final folios of Latin text. Although some of the Treaty's clauses dealt with French troops and supplies in Scotland and the demolition of Leith and Dunbar, the text was clearly not a military document. The main thrust of the Treaty was British: the rejection of Mary Stuart's pretensions to Elizabeth's throne and the internal government and religion of a Scotland united with England in Protestantism and alliance. Religion and the accord between the two kingdoms as principles were not altered by the French and would 'muche offende' them; or as Cecil put it to Norfolk 'The scottes remayn in there relligion, as a thyng that the french dare not medle withall'.[53]

The whole structure of the Treaty was everything Cecil had considered in 'A memoriall of certain pointes meete for restoring the Realme of Scotland to the Auncient Weale' in August 1559. The new British settlement rested on a Scottish council, the restoration of noblemen to their places, the rejection of French officeholders, the endorsement of the house of Hamilton as successor to the Scottish crown, and the binding of Mary by an agreement with England. According to Hampton's 'scedule', Scotland would be governed 'by a counsell of twelve of the noblemen of that countrie'; out of these councillors, the Queen of Scots would choose seven and 'the lordes of Parliament' five. Mary's seven, to put an extra institutional check on her selection, would be chosen out of twenty-four 'to be fyrst named in parliament by the three estates there'.[54] Cecil and Wotton told Elizabeth the same thing on 6 July. The Queen of Scots entered the arrangement only in the second stage of a naming process started by parliament. Cecil explained the relationship between parliament and council: that 'for Governance of the pollicy' of Scotland 'the three estates' would choose both the twenty-five candidates and the five definite councillors. Also, the council would be 'mayntened by the revennue of this Crowne'.[55] This was a meeting of two principles from the August 1559 'memoriall': rule by council, underwritten in Scotland by the three estates,

[51] Cecil and Wotton to Elizabeth, 8 July 1560, SP 52/4, fos. 162r–164r.
[52] Harley 289, fo. 71r–v; SP 52/4, fo. 88r–v; Cotton Titus B. 13, fo. 16r–v.
[53] Cecil and Wotton to Elizabeth, 6 July 1560, CP 153, fo. 34v; 26 June 1560, SP 52/4, fo. 54r.
[54] Harley 289, fo. 71r; SP 52/4, fo. 88r; Cotton Titus B. 13, fo. 16v.
[55] CP 153, fo. 34r.

and funded by revenue of the crown supervised by parliament. Cecil developed this idea of internal and self-regulating national government. Only 'subjectes of the land' would be able to hold 'ordynary officees of the realme ether for Justice cyvile or crimynall, or [the offices of] chancellor, tresoror, controllor'. This clause was written as a long-term guarantee of the control of the Scottish nobility. Parliament would be responsible for declaring men who attempted 'any force contrary to the order of the Contrey, or without the consent of the Counsell of the land' as rebels; there was no need, as Cecil put it, for the Queen of Scots and her husband 'to send any strange force to subdue the same'.[56]

This domestic settlement for Scotland would be policed, clearly and with implications for Cecil's proposals in 1568 and 1569, by England: with a 'league' between Elizabeth and the Protestant congregation and by a 'speciall clause', which bound the English Queen 'to performe and kepe the sayd covvenauntes' between Mary and 'the Realme and subjectes of Scotland'. Cecil knew that the French would do their best to break this British relationship and that 'our gretest difficultee at this present will stand upon contynuance of the leage betwixt your Majesty and this realme'; but he found 'the scottes, so peremptory, as they all stand fast therto that they will never accord to breake it of there part'.[57] There are two themes in Cecil's assessment of the Treaty: first, that it was a British settlement; and second, that it was an unprecedented and remarkable opportunity for peace based on parliament and council in Scotland under English supervision. It was a 'conquest' of Scotland that none of Elizabeth's progenitors 'with all there battells ever obteyned, that is in a manner the whole hartes and good wills of the nobilite and people' of the northern kingdom. But Edinburgh was also the Anglo-British solution to the succession which secured Elizabeth's 'undowted right to the Crowne of england and Irland'.[58]

III

Cecil's Treaty of Edinburgh was accepted gratefully and enthusiastically by both English courtiers and Scottish governors. Five days after the signing, Lord Robert Dudley wrote to tell the earl of Sussex that 'The newes of the north ar now growen to perfectyon, for ther is a peace concluded and agreed uppon.' Dudley did not have a text to send – Hampton and the Privy Council did that a day later – but he knew that the Treaty was honourable for Elizabeth, that it would settle the problems between France and Scotland, that it would involve a restoration in the kingdom, and that

---

[56] SP 52/4, fo. 163v.
[57] Cotton Caligula B. 10, fo. 105r.
[58] Cecil and Wotton to Elizabeth, 8 July 1560, SP 52/4, fos. 162v, 164r.

it meant government by a noble council.[59] The Scots were also impressed. After the Reformation Parliament in August 1560, they told Elizabeth that they had found 'them selfes delivered off that crewill scourge off strangearis' which had hung over their heads, and acknowledged a 'moste Juste caus to prayse and honour your majesty whome his [God's] providence hath apoynted to be the meane Instrument and onely workar off our deliverance'. There was a new faith, so it seemed, in the 'good Intellegence betuix both realmes' and the special relationship between the two Protestant powers of Britain.[60]

But the political facts did not quite measure up to councillors' and courtiers' optimism. The Treaty began a pattern of frustrated diplomatic effort in which the early Elizabethan regime tried to persuade Mary to ratify Edinburgh and drop her claim to the English throne; at the same time, it had to find some way of expressing in concrete terms the idea of a united and Protestant Britain. The negotiation of the Treaty was a measure of the diplomatic powers of Cecil – but Edinburgh was useless as a solution to the British crisis if the Queen of Scots refused to ratify it. Sir Nicholas Throckmorton spoke to Mary in August 1561 and she was in no mood to concede. She claimed that any reference to Cateau-Cambrésis, negotiated between France and England, had nothing to do with her, and that any article based jointly on her marriage to Francis II 'can not be as yt ys ratyfied untyll yt be cheangyd unto my name only bycause the king my lord and husbond is namyd yn yt'. Mary maintained that French troops and fortifications were no longer an issue in 1561 and that she had not used the arms and style of England since the death of her husband. As a general principle, there was little point in agreeing to a treaty she would not abide by: 'thowghe I do ratifie the treatie yff I have no wyll to kepe yt: me thynkythe . . . yt ys better to do well then to promyse well'. Throckmorton assured her that it was better to do both but to no effect.[61]

The spring and summer of 1561 was a crucial point of change in the relationship between British Protestants north and south of the border and the ability of the Elizabethan regime to deal with political and military problems. Some of England's natural allies changed their allegiance when Mary Stuart returned to Scotland in late August 1561. Although there was a strong sense of common interest between English and Scottish courtiers and councillors, national affiliations and the nature of royal service meant that the relationship between Protestantism and politics – the Protestantism of the lords of the congregation and the Catholicism of their political opponents – challenged the traditional relationship between religion and

[59] 11 July 1560, Cotton Caligula B. 9, fo. 135r. [60] Additional 23109, fos. 4r, 6r.
[61] Throckmorton to Elizabeth, 11 August 1561, Additional 35830, fos. 175v–176v.

partisan allegiance. Maitland of Lethington was in an awkward situation. He was a strong Protestant, committed to steering Scotland's religious settlement through the parliament of August 1560, and a man with solid reformed contacts with the English regime.[62] But as Cecil's counterpart in Scotland between December 1558 and May 1571 he was both a diplomatic representative of the congregation and after 1561 a servant of the crown. A purist like John Knox could afford to press the cause of religion in Scotland at the expense of political harmony but Maitland could not;[63] this tension began slowly to strain the relationship between members of the British Protestant community and undermine the language of common interest it used to express and define itself. The Treaty of Edinburgh failed in two ways: first, to quieten Mary and end her pretensions to the succession; and second, to establish Protestant conciliar government for Scotland as part of a wider reformed Britain.

Edinburgh had British political and military implications. For the Privy Council, it was important to send a summary of the Treaty to the earl of Sussex as Lord Lieutenant of Ireland, along with notes on preparations at Berwick and Portsmouth. But for the regime, Sussex became a symbol of British failure in the early 1560s: of the inability of the regime to cope with the situation in Ireland, of the breakdown of Anglo–Scottish links made at the Treaty of Berwick, and of the dangerous connections between England's enemies in Ireland and the Scottish court. By early summer the regime was fighting an expensive and depressing campaign in Ireland. In April Cecil reminded Argyle of his commitment to assist Sussex; by August Cecil told the Lord Lieutenant that 'The erle of Argile hath remayned in redyness all this yere to herken whan yow wold send to hym for ayde.' Cecil perceived that Argyle 'imagyneth that Lordship alloweth not his offer of frendshipp'. So the innovative principle behind Berwick was a dead letter.[64] In July 1561 Cecil reprimanded Sussex for the irregularity of his correspondence. There had been 'fowle rumors' of military disaster in Ireland in which the English forces 'hath had a greate overthrow'. By September the rumours were spreading into Scotland. Cecil was relying on reports sent out of Edinburgh by Thomas Randolph.[65] There were two main themes in Cecil's

---

[62] Loughlin, 'Maitland of Lethington', pp. 56–7; Simon Adams, 'The Lauderdale Papers 1561–1570: the Maitland of Lethington state papers and the Leicester correspondence', *Scottish Historical Review*, 67 (1988), 50–5.

[63] John Knox, *On rebellion*, ed. Roger A. Mason (Cambridge, 1994), pp. 182–209.

[64] Cecil to Argyle, 2 April 1561, SP 63/3, fo. 138r; Cecil to Sussex, 21 August 1561, Cotton Titus B. 13, fo. 54v; Dawson, 'Ireland', pp. 122–3; Ciaran Brady, *The chief governors. The rise and fall of reform government in Tudor Ireland 1536–1588* (Cambridge, 1994), pp. 93–4, 97–101.

[65] Cecil to Sussex, 25 July 1561, Titus B. 13, fo. 48r; Cecil to Sussex, 17 September 1561, Titus B. 13, fo. 60r–v.

letters to Ireland in 1561: the sense of frustrated failure in Irish military policy – and, for Cecil, long gaps in intelligence – and the importance of every aspect of governance. The affairs of the Queen of Scots, Maitland of Lethington's and the earl of Moray's influence at court, Scottish diplomacy in England, the state of Protestantism in France, and Elizabeth's persistent refusal to marry – 'wherin God alter hir mynd', Cecil added in October – were interconnected issues.[66]

The sense of distance between England and Scotland expressed itself in a developing and more formal diplomatic relationship between the two kingdoms. Thomas Randolph was sent north in March 1561 to tell the lords that England and Scotland had to unite in religion (on the model of the German princes) against the Pope and his allies. The key themes were amity, goodwill, and true religion; it was crucial for Mary to marry the right man.[67] But from this point on, Randolph's work as ambassador in Scotland became more formal. Although he worked with Maitland of Lethington before Mary's return from France and showed Cecil's correspondence to the Scottish secretary, Cecil knew that the political situation was about to change. He told Randolph in June 1561 that 'ye see our opinion here is that it shall do much hurt in scotland if the Quene shuld come thither before thynges be better established'. Cecil thought that even an hour's conference with Maitland of Lethington could have had some effect.[68] In early August Maitland asked Cecil to 'let lettres Ronne frequently betwixt ws that we may comunicat our Judgmentes' but he had already started to refer to the 'Quene my Soveraygne'. He had begun almost to reinvent his identity.[69]

The effect of Mary Stuart's presence in Scotland was stunning. In October 1561, just over a year after the Reformation Parliament, Maitland of Lethington wrote personally to Cecil to press the Queen of Scots' claim to the throne and her place in the English succession. This raised the controversial issue of the authenticity of Henry VIII's will.[70] Before her return to Scotland, Mary had symbolized an enemy; after 1561 her claim to Elizabeth's throne became an internal issue, complicated by Mary's undisputed sovereignty in Scotland and the realities of her subjects' service to the crown. The Queen of Scots became a diplomatic and practical problem in Britain rather than a theoretical and distant rallying point. Her absence had always been just as important; it had allowed Cecil to develop a model for

---

[66] Cecil to Sussex, 7 October 1561, Titus B. 13, fo. 62v, for the quotation.
[67] 20 March 1561, CP 152, fos. 108r–111v.
[68] Cecil to Randolph, 30 June 1561, Harley 6990, fo. 13r, printed in Stevenson (ed.), *Selections*, pp. 89–90.
[69] CP 153, fo. 86r.
[70] 7 October 1561, CP 201, fos. 139r–140v, printed in Haynes, pp. 373–4.

a Protestant Britain. As an element in future debate, especially during Mary's imprisonment in England, these concerns were central. But the new reality from 1561 was persistent diplomatic pressure for a settlement between the two British monarchs. The principles of the Treaty of Edinburgh did not leave the British political debate in the 1560s but they were sidestepped by the more gentle language of amity and friendship between Elizabeth and Mary.

Maitland of Lethington became the sponsor of a new British policy in early 1562 but he told Cecil that it was Mary who thought 'it convenient that the maters betuix theyr majesties for the more secret and better conveyance theroff shold first be digested be our familiar Lettres one to ane other'.[71] The new amity was based on a proposed meeting of the two queens to resolve their differences. Cecil was not immediately keen on the idea. He was frustrated in December 1561 by the way in which his efforts on behalf of Elizabeth seemed to have no effect.[72] But Cecil was still the focus of Maitland of Lethington's attention. 'I truste', wrote Randolph, 'that the lord of liddingeton at this tyme hathe playnlye dyscovered unto your honour, what he thynkethe, and what dysposition he fyndethe in his sovereigne'.[73] One of Maitland's other regular correspondents, Lord Robert Dudley, received a letter soon after 27 February, which complimented Dudley as the 'principall' of 'soche ministers as shall most ernestly traveil' for the benefit of England and Scotland. On the same day, Maitland wrote to Cecil to explain detailed policy and the issue of Mary's claim to the English succession.[74] Dudley was a 'principall' in general terms; Cecil clearly more significant as a political fixer.

The proposal began to take shape in spring 1562. In early March Randolph told Throckmorton that he found Mary and Elizabeth 'resolved in their hartes to meete thone with thother'. He was convinced that the meeting was going to happen: Mary's court was 'so farre resolved' that Maitland of Lethington was going to 'tayke his yornaye to the Quenes majestie to declare this Quene his mestres good wyll' for the interview. It was already being sold in Edinburgh as a deeply symbolic and humanist expression of unity and friendship, based on the female qualities of Elizabeth and Mary and 'paste the malice of men to chaynge the purpose'. They were 'women bothe', Randolph told Throckmorton, 'of the nature of all the reste, and desyer well to have that performed that their hartes

---

[71] Maitland to Cecil, 27 February 1562, CP 153, fo. 76r, printed in Haynes, p. 379.

[72] Cecil [to Throckmorton], 22 December 1561, Additional 35830, fo. 228v.

[73] 28 February 1562, SP 52/7, fo. 41v; cf. Maitland to Cecil, 28 February 1562, SP 52/7, fo. 46r–v.

[74] Maitland to Dudley, 27 February 1562, National Library of Scotland, Edinburgh, 9931, fo. 1r; Maitland to Cecil, CP 153, fos. 76r–78v, printed in Haynes, pp. 379–81.

desyer'. The interview was proposed as a symbolic marriage of the two queens. Mary was prepared to send 'her picture a ringe with a diemounde framed lyke a harte a precius Jouell' as a token of love and friendship.[75] George Buchanan wrote some verse to accompany the gift, three years before his poem on the birth of James VI and I with its vision of a British golden age.[76] Buchanan was certainly at Mary's court in spring 1562, instructing the Queen 'somewhat of Lyvie'.[77] As one of the most prominent humanist Latin poets of the period, Buchanan was perfectly suited to expressing faith in a new age of peace. This was dynastic union without marriage: the female equivalent of Elizabeth's subsequent plan to marry the earl of Leicester to Mary in 1564 and the duke of Norfolk's scheme in 1569 to unite England and Scotland by a Howard–Stuart union. More politically, the prospects for British and Irish peace looked good. The situation in Ireland had stabilized by the beginning of 1562. In early January Lord Keeper Bacon, the marquess of Northampton, the earl of Pembroke, Sir Francis Knollys, and Cecil indulged in a slightly different piece of symbolic theatre: Shane O'Neill on his knees and 'prostrat uppon his face', submitting himself in English and Irish, humbly requiring 'that we wold be meanes for hym to come to hir Majesties presence to acknoledg his obedience'.[78]

This new hope and optimism expressed itself in England in a proposal for 'Devices to be shewed before the quenes Majestie by waye of maskinge', composed in May 1562.[79] Its value as a political document has been underestimated. Joseph Robertson suggested that the masque was 'conceived in that spirit of dull pedantic allegory which disfigured the literature, and tainted the art of the age'. Professor Michael Lynch has unfavourably compared the masque to a festival given by the Queen of Scots in 1566. But the two events were very different. The Stirling triumph included a large mock battle, feasts, pageants, and fireworks: in effect, it was a show of political resilience and military strength.[80] The masque proposed for 1562 was something different. It was a representation of the British dynastic ideal of two queens ruling separately, but in peace, harmony, and love. It

[75] Randolph to Throckmorton, 4 March 1562, Additional 35831, fo. 17r–v.
[76] Philip J. Ford, *George Buchanan. Prince of poets* (Aberdeen, 1982), pp. 103, 105–7.
[77] George Buchanan, *Vernacular writings*, ed. P. Hume Brown (Scottish Text Society, 26; Edinburgh, 1892), p. 55.
[78] Cecil to Sussex, 7 January 1562, Cotton Titus B. 13, fo. 75r.
[79] Lansdowne 5, fos. 126r–127v, printed in E.K. Chambers and W.W. Greg (eds.), 'Dramatic records from the Lansdowne manuscripts', *Malone Society Collections*, 1 (1911), 144–8.
[80] Joseph Robertson (ed.), *Inventaires de la royne Descosse douairiere de France. Catalogues of the jewels, dresses, furniture, books, and paintings of Mary Queen of Scots. 1556–1569* (Bannatyne Club, 111; Edinburgh, 1863), pp. lxxx–lxxxii; Michael Lynch, 'Queen Mary's triumph: the baptismal celebrations at Stirling in December 1566', *Scottish Historical Review*, 69 (1990), 21.

was planned as a symbolic celebration of the effective 'marriage' of Mary and Elizabeth and their realms. The masque was written to be taken seriously and politically.

The 'Devices' were prepared for the 'haule' of 'Nottingham castell', and a delivery of silks was arranged at the beginning of May 1562 by John Fortescue, the Master of the Great Wardrobe, and Sir Thomas Benger, the Master of the Revels.[81] The writer planned three evenings of entertainment, set in the prison of 'Extreme Oblyvioun' on the first and 'a Castell' called 'the Courte of plentye' on the second; the prison and the court both became the scene of the third and final act. There were at least eight 'Ladyes maskers'. Elizabeth was read to on her own on the first night and at the beginning of the third, and her cousin was included in the final scene of unity and peace. The masque is not an understated piece. On the first night, Pallas enters the hall of the castle 'rydinge uppon an unycorne, havinge in her handes a Standarde, in which is to be paynted ij Ladyes handes one faste within thother', and over the hands, written in gold, the word 'ffides'. Pallas is followed by two ladies riding a golden lion and a red lion, both wearing crowns 'signifyinge ij vertues' of 'Prudentia' (for the lady on the golden lion) and 'Temperantia' (for the rider of the red lion). These two virtues have 'made greate and longe sute unto Jupiter' to take 'captive discorde, and false Reporte' (bound by the neck with golden ropes and brought in by six or eight 'Ladyes maskers') and punish them 'as they thinke goode'. Discord and False Report are thrown into the 'pryson of Extreme Oblyvioun', to be held by two locks – 'ineternum', from Prudentia; and 'nunquam', from Temperantia – and kept by the gaoler Argus, or Cirumspection. The two prisoners will be 'locked there everlastinglie', only to be let out 'nunquam'. At this point, the trumpets blow and the English ladies take 'the nobilitie of the straunger' and dance.

The next evening becomes the second stage of the healing process between the two kingdoms. 'Peace rydinge uppon a Chariott' drawn by an elephant, on which sits Friendship, enters the 'Courte of Plentye', followed by six or eight female maskers. After a procession around the hall, Friendship tells Elizabeth in verse that Pallas has made 'a declaracion before all the goddes, howe worthilie the night precedent theis ij vertues, Prudentia, and Temperantia, behaved them selves in Judginge, and condempninge' False Report and Discord. Because of this, Peace has been sent to live with the two virtues forever, supported by two porters; to Prudentia, 'Ardent desyer', and to Temperantia, 'perpetuitie', 'Signifyinge that by ardent desyer, and perpetuitie, perpetuall peace, and tranquillitie maye be hadd & kept throughe the hole worlde'. The Court of Plenty then becomes a spring

[81] Lansdowne 5, fo. 131r; Chambers and Greg (eds.), 'Dramatic records', 144.

of all sorts of wines from 'Condittes', and the English lords masque with the Scottish ladies.

The third night of entertainment is different. Peace is challenged by 'prepencyd Malyce, in the similitude of a greate serpent' and Disdain, riding a wild boar. In an orchard with golden apples, Disdain tells Elizabeth that Pluto, his master, is unhappy with Jupiter for allowing Prudentia and Temperantia to punish Discord and False Report, 'beinge ij of his chefe servauntes'. Malice has been sent to force Argus to release Discord and False Report or Ardent Desire and Perpetuity. Hercules as Valiant Courage, riding the horse Boldness and led by Discretion, are sent by Jupiter to 'confounde all plutos devices'. Disdain and Malice are 'mervailous warryours', so it is important for Valiant Courage to 'repaier unto the cowrte, of plentie, and there firste to demaunde of Prudentia, howe longe her plesure is of her honour, that peace shall dwell betwene her, and Temperantia'. In a dramatic mirror of Mary's ring-giving, Prudentia takes a 'bande of gold, A grandgarde of Assure, whereuppon shalbe wrytten, in letters of gold /Ever/' to Discretion. Temperantia, too, gives 'a girdell of Assure, studded with gold, and a Sworde of stile, whereuppon shalbe written /Never/'. After a few words to Elizabeth and Mary, Discretion arms Hercules with the 'grandgard of Ever' and the 'sworde, of Never', 'Signifyinge that those ij Ladies have professed that peace shall ever dwell with them, and Never departe from them'. Valiant Courage fights Disdain and Malice, 'in the myddeste of which fight, disdaine shall runne his wayes and escape with life, but the monster prepenced mallyce shalbe slaine for ever'. Some ungodly men may well still disdain the perpetual peace made between the two queens, but Malice was 'easye troden undere theis Ladyes fete'. The masque ends with a song 'that shalbe made heruppon, as full of Armony, as maye be devised'.[82]

So in the 'Devices', prudence, temperance, circumspection, peace, friendship, ardent desire, courage, and discretion are able to overcome discord, false report, malice, and disdain. In a cosmic setting, underscored by the power of Jupiter and Pluto, the masque merges the physical reality of horses, an elephant, and British dancing with the mythological symbolism of a unicorn and a golden lion. For the writer, it was the perfect expression of ideal peace: a universal and final punishment and banishment of evil, and a triumph of the innocence of friendship over the experience of division. The 'Devices' were planned as an expression of reconciliation between Mary and Elizabeth, sealed by Prudentia's and Temperantia's gift-giving. This is exactly what the two queens publicly and formally aspired to and believed in. Their relationship as cousins and the qualities of frankness, fairness, and friendship were woven into Mary's letters south; this sort of

[82] Lansdowne 5, fos. 126r–127v; Chambers and Greg (eds.), 'Dramatic records', 144–8.

language was also an important part of Elizabeth's own diplomatic contact with the Queen of Scots.[83] The premise was simple: peace in Britain depended on royal position and dynasty. But unfortunately for Prudentia and Temperantia, the work of Malice and Disdain in Europe meant that this approach to the succession crisis had to be challenged by political reality. In the end, Pluto had his victory.

IV

Even before the preparation of the Nottingham masque in early May 1562, the opening round of the religious wars in France was beginning to cast a shadow over the proposed interview. In March Cecil told Sir Nicholas Throckmorton that the French ambassador was convinced Elizabeth backed the Protestants.[84] There were few political constants: Sir Thomas Smith in France was consistently instructed 'to prosequute no other end but restitution of Callis', while Cecil made it clear that in London 'is a full determination made to kepe Newhaven' and defend it with force. Policy reacted to the fluid situation in Europe, 'for our determinations contynew allweise in one estate, and those there, never consist in one state 24 howres, but change with the tydes'.[85] Even Mary Stuart realized that the French civil war was going to have an effect. Randolph reported that she was still positive about the interview in late May but lamented the 'unadvised enterprice' of the Guise 'which shall not onlye brynge them selves in daynger of their owne persones, but also in hatred and dysdayne of maynie princes of the worlde'.[86] Maitland of Lethington travelled to Greenwich in early June 1562 to campaign for the meeting, but his efforts were wasted on the Privy Council. Cecil told Throckmorton quite openly that the Council was opposed.[87]

The Privy Council discussed the interview in May and late June 1562. There had been a 'resolution in counsell in Maye last', Cecil noted, 'that if thynges wer compounded in france, by the last of June, without prejudice to the state of this realme than hir Majesty might goo'.[88] Cecil prepared some private notes on the meeting *in utramque partem* on 20 June 1562, reproduced the same arguments ten days later, and wrote a 'Memoryall for the Progress' on 1 July.[89] There was a debate in Council on 20 June which

---

[83] For example, Mary to Elizabeth, 5 January 1562, CP 147, fo. 18r, printed in Haynes, pp. 376–8; Cotton Caligula B. 10, fos. 218r–219v, 228r–229v
[84] 24 March 1562, Additional 35831, fo. 22v.
[85] Cecil to Smith, 29 March 1562, Lansdowne 102, fo. 29r–v.
[86] Randolph to Cecil, 29 May 1562, SP 52/7, fo. 91r.
[87] Cecil to Throckmorton, 7 June 1562, Additional 35831, fo. 37r.
[88] Cecil's notes, 30 June 1562, Cotton Caligula B. 10, fo. 209r.
[89] Cotton Caligula B. 10, fos. 211r–212v; Cotton Caligula B. 10, fos. 209r–210v; Lansdowne 103, fo. 6r–v.

dealt with the subject of the proposed meeting. From Cecil's letters six days later, Randolph realized 'howe uncertayne yt ys yet whether the enterveue shall tayke place thys yere or not'.[90] Lord Keeper Bacon also made a contribution to the debate at Greenwich in July 1562.[91] The Council was united on the basic dangers of the meeting in its European context. Cecil read (and continued to read) the affairs of the Continent in a providential and conspiratorial context.

Cecil did not question the motives of Elizabeth and Mary. The Queen of Scots made the offer of a meeting 'that by that meanes she will enter into a firmor amytye with the Quene, and ther by to make a perpetuall leage betwixt both the realmes'; Elizabeth was also guided by a 'naturall inclynation' and the desire to make a 'firme leage' between 'them both and there realmes and Posteritees'. Cecil realized that there would be 'great Proffittes' for England if the two queens could settle their differences, including the 'utter dissolucion of the auncient leage betwixt france and scotland'. But the dangers outweighed the benefits. Once again, the complicated connection between England's domestic state, the military power of France, and the united efforts of the Catholic states played a significant part in Cecil's analysis. He argued that 'The affayres in fraunce remayne not onely uncompounded, but by bloodshed on both, lykely to increase in troobles.' For Cecil, this was a sign that the Guise were once again in the ascendant at the French court. On 20 June he listed the furtherance of Mary's title to Elizabeth's crown, the 'avancement of the Guisians creditt in france', and 'comefort to papistes' in England as some of the 'Reasons' against the interview. Ten days later he turned this into a more fluent discussion of the influence of the Guise and the implications of Mary's journey, and the fact that 'it may be thought that by hir Jornaye she will insinuat hir self to some sortes of people of this realme, to furder hir clayme', encouraging 'such people as love change, and speci[ally] the papistes, to confirme them in there opinion'.[92]

Cecil's central preoccupation was ideological and, like his brother-in-law, Bacon also made the connection between 'the affeccions and disposycions of the Queene of Scottes and the house of Guise' and the overthrow of Protestantism in Europe and (eventually) England.[93] The significant point is that this providential reading of European politics not only marked the intellectual approach of men like Cecil and Bacon and their Privy Council colleagues, but that it became the central principle of policy and a foil to

---

[90] Randolph to Cecil, 5 July 1562, SP 52/7, fo. 109r.
[91] For example, Harley 398, fos. 21r–24v.
[92] 20 June 1562, Cotton Caligula B. 10, fos. 211r–212r; 30 June 1562, Cotton Caligula B. 10, fo. 209r–v.
[93] Harley 398, fos. 21r, 23v.

the 'amity' preoccupations of Elizabeth. At the end of July 1562 Cecil argued that 'The Perills growing uppon the overthrow of the Prynce of Condees cause' involved the attempt by the Guise to control the 'whole regyment of the Crowne of fraunce', to please Philip of Spain, and to 'promote there nece the Quene of scottes to the crown of england'. He sensed wider Catholic involvement with an impressive degree of organization. The first part of the conspiracy would be based on a proposed marriage between Elizabeth and Philip, with Ireland given to the Spanish King. 'Whylest this is in work and that the protestantes rest as beholders onely', Cecil continued, 'the Generall counsell shall condemne all the Protestantes, and gyve the kyngdoms the Dominions therof, to any other Prynce that shall invade them'. At the same time, English Catholics would keep quiet, gather money, 'and to be redy to styrr at one instant' when a foreign military force attacked England or Ireland. When it got to this stage, Cecil argued, 'than will it be to late to seke to withstand it'. He likened the Catholic campaign to a rock falling from a mountain 'which whan it is comming no force can stey'. In this the Guisans could not be assuaged because they wanted two things: first, 'the desyre to have a kyngdom' – and note the singular – 'as england and scotland'; and second, 'the cruell appetite of a pope and his adherentes to have his authorite restablished fully without any new daunger of attempt', which presumably meant a final victory without any chance of defeat.[94]

It is this conflict of interpretation and interest between 1560 and 1563 – the language of amity, friendship, and dynasty measured against the defensive fears of British Protestants – which influenced and marked Anglo–Scottish diplomacy for the final seven years of Elizabeth's first full decade. From May 1568, when the Queen of Scots landed in England, she became the subject of British political proposals which had their roots in Cecil's private notes in 1559 and the Treaty of Edinburgh in 1560. But 1562, 1563, 1564, and even 1565 were different: royal marriage and love between cousins presented themselves as the solution to the succession crisis. In July 1562 Sir Henry Sidney was sent to Edinburgh to defend Elizabeth's position. The message was heard with 'great greefe' by Mary, 'as well apered by dyvers manyfest demonstratyonys not only in woordys but in contenars & watery eyes'.[95] Dudley received the same sort of account. The expression of love and amity between the two queens and their kingdoms was still very much part of diplomatic instructions and more plans were made for a meeting between August and September 1563 at York. But 1562 meant more than the failure of a single diplomatic

---

[94] 20 July 1562, SP 70/39, fo. 106v.
[95] Sidney to Cecil, 25 July 1562, SP 52/7, fo. 127r; cf. Maitland of Lethington to Dudley, 29 July 1562, National Library of Scotland, Edinburgh, 3278, fo. 1r.

proposal: it was a measure of the difference in world-view between Cecil and Elizabeth. Symbolic peace between two queens was a reality for Elizabeth; for Cecil, on the other hand, the nature of European politics meant that Mary Stuart could be more genuinely understood as part of a French Catholic conspiracy.

For the first four years of the reign Cecil mentally linked Mary's succession pretensions to the general threat of the Catholic kingdoms and provinces and the military power of France. In November 1562 Maitland of Lethington defended his 'perplexed' mistress, torn in her affections between France and Spain, but Cecil must have had very little sympathy.[96] Religious war apparently orchestrated by the Guise only confirmed intelligence he had received and interpreted since the early days of 1559. A week after Maitland's letter Cecil told Thomas Randolph that there were 'ij daungers, ye maye make accompt that we will to our uttermost Pursew': Catholic victory in France putting 'us here in daunger for our relligion', and attempts by the Guise to build 'there castells so high, as to overlooke the Quenes Majesty for hir estate in this Crowne'.[97] Because of the 'trobles' in France, the proposal for the 'entierview was disapointed'; but more than this, the 'varieties of thaffaires in ffrance' had 'so burned both our selves & our counsell here into so many shapes from time to time'.[98] It was under this sort of pressure, and with this view of European politics, that British policy was made.

Most of these themes and situations reappeared in some form during the middle and final years of the decade. Cecil's interpretation of political events was one constant; so, too, was the Privy Council's basic sense of unity and the part this played in trying to influence a Queen who placed so much faith in the power of royalty and the political wisdom of dynasty. This became a crucial issue in 1559 and 1560. It also tested the political priorities of Elizabeth, and the power of the Privy Council to challenge them, during the Darnley crisis. But an alternative to a dynastic solution had been clearly worked out by 1560. It rested on a political settlement secured by treaty, underwritten by the imperial power of the English Queen as a British monarch, bound together by Protestantism, and linked to a strong council and parliament in Scotland. In this sense, it was more appropriate to Britain when Mary was either outside her kingdom or inside an English castle. Between 1563 and 1568, however, English diplomacy had to deal with the more immediate problem of Mary in Scotland and the implications of Stuart rule.

---

[96] Maitland of Lethington to Cecil, 14 November 1562, Cotton Caligula B. 10, fo. 220v.
[97] 21 November 1562, Harley 6990, fo. 15r.
[98] Cecil [to Thomas Chaloner], 11 October 1562, Cotton Vespasian C. 7, fos. 224r, 225r.

⸎ 4 ⸎

New Tudor politics and the domestic impact of the succession issue 1560–1563

When Cecil and the Privy Council campaigned and petitioned for action on the succession in 1559 and 1560, the focus was on Scotland. After military intervention, the Treaty of Edinburgh was negotiated to solve the problem of Mary Stuart's claims to the English crown, and its diplomatic consequences were played out between 1560 and 1569; in the first three years (from 1560 to 1563) the regime began a short experiment – a policy of inclusion, trying to weave Mary into a British settlement by stressing friendship and amity between the two British queens. But between 1560 and 1563 the succession became a powerful domestic issue in England. This has been the conventional focus of Elizabethan historians. In 1966 Mortimer Levine explored the development of *The early Elizabethan succession question*; more recently, Dr Susan Doran has re-examined the relationship between religion, politics, and the courtships of the Queen.[1]

Council and parliament tried to persuade Elizabeth to marry by stressing her moral and monarchical duties. They experimented with this approach in 1559, 1563, and 1566. But one of the main problems of the traditional emphasis on the Queen's marriage is that this has encouraged a partisan approach to Elizabethan politics. This in turn relies on the false premise of court and Council faction. Dr Doran explored this issue in 1989 because she spotted groups and parties fighting for and against the marriage candidacy of Charles of Austria. She has reinforced this sense of partisan action by arguing that between 1561 and 1578 courtiers like the earls of Leicester and Sussex used court dramas and entertainments to press individual marriage suits.[2] But this model of political culture owes more to the insights of Naunton than it does to a more recent debate on the nature

---

[1] Mortimer Levine, *The early Elizabethan succession question 1558–1568* (Stanford, 1966); Susan Doran, *Monarchy and matrimony. The courtships of Elizabeth I* (London and New York, 1996).

[2] Susan Doran, 'Religion and politics at the court of Elizabeth I: the Habsburg marriage negotiations of 1559–1567', *English Historical Review*, 104 (1989), 908–26; Doran, 'Juno versus Diana: the treatment of Elizabeth I's marriage in plays and entertainments, 1561–1581', *Historical Journal*, 38 (1995), 257–74.

of the Elizabethan polity which emphasizes unity and cohesion and not division or faction – a form of politics which was collegial, focused, and galvanized into action by Elizabeth's refusal to marry or settle the kingdom's succession. In 1558 John Knox began a debate on the nature of the English polity: the promotion of a woman 'to bear rule, superiority, dominion or empire' was 'repugnant to nature, contumely to God, a thing most contrarious to His revealed will and approved ordinance, and finally it is the subversion of good order, of all equity and justice'.[3] John Aylmer replied in 1559 but his response, *An harborowe for faithfull and trewe subjectes*, reopened the wound it had sought to heal: a female monarch in England was acceptable because she was advised by a council which administered the execution of law and government.[4] The power of this interpretation to bind the Council and force it to consider alternatives to direct royal government has only recently been explored but its impact on political life in the 1560s was real and important.

I

The Queen's marriage and the succession to her crown were strongly connected in the early Elizabethan mind: parliamentary petitions considered them as two halves of a whole. But even by the middle of the decade, action on the succession seemed the best way to deal with the crisis facing the English polity. Elizabeth consistently promised to marry – in 1559, when the Queen declared that 'I happelie chose this kynde of life in which I yet lyve',[5] and in 1563 and 1566, when she accepted the Commons' and Lords' petitions with less grace – but she expected to be able to do it in her own time. When Cecil began to work on 'an act ment for the succession' in 1563 it was a tacit acknowledgement that the polity had to explore an alternative to royal matrimony. More important is the fact that succession united Council and parliament: there was no distinction between 'frontbenchers' and 'backbenchers' and no sense of factional struggle in Council; even when councillors disagreed on strategic issues, they accepted the wider interpretation which usually lay behind proposed policy – the hand of God encouraging the French to punish England's sins or the dangerous reality of Mary Stuart, supported by the combined powers of Catholic Europe. This providential reading of politics energized the issues of marriage in general and succession in particular.

There are two good examples of the way in which the traditional preoccupations and interpretations of the English marriage and succession

---

[3] John Knox, *On rebellion*, ed. Roger Mason (Cambridge, 1994), p. 8.
[4] See above, pp. 34–5.   [5] Lansdowne 94, fo. 29r, printed in Hartley, p. 44.

issues can be refocused. In 1561 Sir Thomas Smith composed a dialogue on the Queen's marriage, in which he explored the issue using three characters: Spitewed, who argued against marriage for Elizabeth; Lovealien, who proposed a foreign match; and Homefriend, who maintained that an English nobleman would be the best candidate.[6] The same question was introduced by Arostus, one of King Gorboduc's counsellors, in the final scene of Thomas Norton's and Thomas Sackville's *The tragedie of Gorboduc*. Arostus argued, like Homefriend, that a royal candidate should be a Briton, because the kingdom could not bear 'The heavie yoke of forreine governaunce' and 'forreine Titles' had to yield to 'Publike wealthe'.[7] Smith's dialogue and *Gorboduc* have often been used as starting points for the discussion of Elizabeth's marriage and succession, and they have generally been claimed by historians arguing for the importance of individual suits. Mortimer Levine sensed that Norton and Sackville supported the Grey claim to the English throne. Marie Axton, Susan Doran, and Norman Jones have pointed to the Dudley implications of the play.[8] But these partisan readings need to be re-evaluated and placed in what was clearly a more collegial political system. Elizabethan governors had a common sense of how the different elements in the English polity should have worked.

Smith was working on a more substantial project in the early 1560s. He completed *De republica Anglorum* in March 1565, which, in the sixth chapter of the first book, described England as a mixed polity and emphasized the part parliament played in securing the kingdom's succession. The first session of Elizabeth's second parliament sat between January and April 1563, and MPs pressed the Queen to name a successor. The marriage dialogue was an interesting academic exercise but as a theoretical model of the English polity and as a mirror of the session of parliament in 1563, *De republica Anglorum* reinforced the implications of the succession as a political issue. *Gorboduc* also has a more sophisticated message. It deserves to be read as a succession play and a comment on the central high political concern of the 1560s. One sixteenth-century chronicler argued

---

[6] Smith's dialogue survives in a number of manuscript copies but it was printed by John Strype, *The life of the learned Sir Thomas Smith, Kt. D.C.L. Principal Secretary of State to King Edward the Sixth, and Queen Elizabeth* (Oxford, 1820), pp. 184–259.

[7] Thomas Norton and Thomas Sackville, *The tragedie of Gorboduc, whereof three actes were wrytten by Thomas Nortone, and the two laste by Thomas Sackvyle* . . . (STC 18684; London, 1565), sig. E2r–v.

[8] Mortimer Levine, *Tudor dynastic problems 1460–1571* (London and New York, 1973), pp. 105–6; Marie Axton, *The Queen's two bodies. Drama and the Elizabethan succession* (London, 1977), p. 46; Axton, 'Robert Dudley and the Inner Temple revels', *Historical Journal*, 13 (1970), 365–78; Doran, *Monarchy and matrimony*, pp. 55–6; Norman Jones, *The birth of the Elizabethan age* (Oxford and Cambridge, Massachusetts, 1993), pp. 133–5.

that the golden cup of flattery in the second dumb show in *Gorboduc* represented the 'uncerten' Eric of Sweden as a potential husband for Elizabeth.[9] But this was an extremely selective reaction to the performance. The scene was a metaphor of counsel, designed to emphasize the destructive power of the 'parasites', Hermon and Tyndar, attached to Gorboduc's sons. Their 'dyvision and discention' led to an early British succession crisis and the miserable wasting of the kingdom.[10] The drama was performed before Elizabeth in January 1562 and was published by one William Griffith, apparently without the authors' permission, in September 1565.[11] So the text became more widely available at a point in the decade when Mary Stuart could effectively do and claim what she wanted and when Robert Dudley's suit to marry the Queen (and even the Grey claim) were irrelevant. The political situation in Britain and in England was completely different from the state of the marriage issue in 1561 but *Gorboduc* was still supremely relevant as a political document. In other words, the play had a more universal significance as a *succession* text than historians and literary critics have given it credit for.

Gorboduc explores the relationship between monarch, councillors, and counsel, and places it in the context of the British succession. Historically, Norton and Sackville developed the drama out of what was, at least in the 1528 edition of Wynkyn de Worde's *The cronycles of Englonde*, a basic and rather bland story. The chronicle concentrates more on Ferrex and Porrex than it does on Gorboduc (and this was perhaps reflected by Norton's and Sackville's choice of *The tragidie of Ferrex and Porrex* as the title for John Day's 'official' edition in 1570) and Wynkyn de Worde explained how the King's two sons 'became stoute & proude & ever warred togider for the londe'. Gorboduc reigned for fifteen years, died, and was buried at York.[12] These were the bare bones of the story. Norton and Sackville fleshed them out by turning it in into a tale of bad counsel, decisions poorly thought out, and British civil war. In 'Thargument of the Tragedie', they explained how 'for want of Issue of the Prince' the 'Succession of the Crowne became uncertayne'.[13] In fact, *Gorboduc* stands far more easily in the tradition of *The mirror for magistrates* than it does in the history of 'party political' pamphlets. In the preface to the edition of

---

[9] Norton and Sackville, *Gorboduc*, sig. B3r; Additional 48023, fo. 359v; Doran, 'Juno versus Diana', 263.

[10] John Guy, 'The rhetoric of counsel in early modern England', in Dale Hoak (ed.), *Tudor political culture* (Cambridge, 1995), p. 292; Norton and Sackville, *Gorboduc*, sig. A1v.

[11] Thomas Norton and Thomas Sackville, *The tragidie of Ferrex and Porrex, set forth without addition or alteration . . .* (STC 18685; London, 1570), sig. A2r.

[12] *The cronycles of Englonde with the dedes of popes and emperours and also the descripcyon of Englonde* (STC 10002; London, 1528), p. 16r–v.

[13] Norton and Sackville, *Gorboduc*, sig. A1v.

1559, *The mirror* held up the past as a 'loking glas', in which 'you shall see (if any vice be in you) howe the like hath bene punished in other heretofore'.[14] The text was wholly familiar to Norton, who had used the metaphor almost verbatim in the preface to his translation of the *Orations, of Arsanes* in 1560.[15]

The action of *Gorboduc* is based on history with a strongly moral and didactic purpose. Based on a humanist-classical reading of the past as guide to the present, reinforced by the metaphor of good counsel, the play represents an early Elizabethan attempt intellectually and politically to comprehend the problem which faced the English polity in the 1560s. At least one of the messages in *Gorboduc* must have been strikingly clear to an audience of courtiers and councillors. Both the King and his councillors had responsibilities to a kingdom and this is a point Gorboduc himself makes at the beginning of the second scene of the first act. The 'cause' was 'The Lyneall course of kinges inheritaunce' for the monarch, for his councillors, and for 'the state', 'Wherof both I *and you* have charge and care'.[16] The irony of Gorboduc's position is that he invites good counsel, accepts and understands it, but decides to split the kingdom between his sons; as a 'Myrrour' for all princes, this stood as a tale 'To learne to shunne the cause of suche a fall'.[17] But it was a measure, too, of the part that the King's Council and counsellors had to play in settling the matter of the kingdom's succession. In *De republica Anglorum*, Smith argued that as an element in the mixed polity, parliament had a duty to consider England's succession and its religion;[18] like Arostus, in the final act of *Gorboduc*, he would have accepted that as the 'commen counsell' of the kingdom, parliament could help to settle fairly Britain's future. For Arostus parliament is an effective conciliar partner with the crown – in his enthusiastically monarchical metaphor, the kingdom's 'Regall Diademe'.[19] Gorboduc's secretary, Eubulus, argues that it is too late for parliament to help to settle a kingdom being consumed (in the words of the chorus) by 'the cruell flames of Civyll fier';[20] he also rules out a popular solution to the problem caused by a monarch's flaws – '. . . not in secrete thoughte/ The Subject maye rebell against his Lorde/ Or Judge of him that sittes in *Ceasars* Seate'[21] – and his

---

[14] *The mirror for magistrates*, ed. Lily B. Campbell (Cambridge, 1938), p. 65.
[15] Thomas Norton (ed.), *Orations, of Arsanes agaynst Philip the trecherous kyng of Macedone* . . . (STC 785; London, *c.* 1560), sig. *3r.
[16] Norton and Sackville, *Gorboduc*, sig. A4v-A5r, with my emphasis.
[17] Norton and Sackville, *Gorboduc*, sig. B3r.
[18] Sir Thomas Smith, *De republica Anglorum*, ed. Mary Dewar (Cambridge, 1982), Book II, chapter 1, p. 78.
[19] Norton and Sackville, *Gorboduc*, sig. E2r.
[20] Norton and Sackville, *Gorboduc*, sig. C5r.
[21] Norton and Sackville, *Gorboduc*, sig. D5r.

preferred option would have been for the King's counsellors (Gorboduc's councillors and parliament as council) to have settled the matter before the final crisis:

> No, no: then Parliament should have ben holden
> And certaine Heires appoyncted to the Crowne
> To staie their title of established righte:
> And plant the people in obedience
> While yet the Prince did live, whose name and power
> By lawfull Sommons and auctorytie
> Might make a Parliament to be of force,
> And might have set the state in quiet staye:[22]

This would surely have had a more powerful and immediate impact on the play's first audience than historians and critics, in their desperate search for marriage candidates and secret meanings, have been able to admit.

For an Elizabethan audience in the early 1560s, the settlement rested on counsel and firm action by the three elements of the mixed polity: monarch, Council, and parliament. The councillors who had given the King 'grave advise & faithfull aide' were called on to ensure that, on Gorboduc's death, the succession would carry on an 'unbroken course' by 'undoubted right'.[23] MPs, as councillors, had called on Elizabeth to keep her part of this monarchical bargain in 1559 and would do so again in 1563; they were counsels which she politely (and not so politely) declined to follow. In this way, *Gorboduc* examined one of the central problems of the domestic succession issue in these early years. But the play also concentrated on the sixteenth-century model of a councillor as *vir civilis*, a man fitted for deliberation in councils and assemblies, committed to pleading for justice in the courts, dedicated to advancing and preserving his commonwealth.

Because of the crucial decision on the succession, Gorboduc's councillors are presented as men of *negotium*, or public activity; the action of the play does not allow a life of contemplative or academic leisure. In the second scene of the first act, Arostus makes it clear that counsel should and would be offered 'Of rightfull reason, and of heedefull care,/ Not for our selves, but for our common state'.[24] The duty of councillors is to offer 'playne & open' counsel and in the course of the play Ferrex and Porrex refuse 'the holsome advise of grave Counsellours', give credit to 'these yonge Paracites', Hermon and Tyndar, and suffer 'death and destruction therby'.[25] Philander, the frustrated and rejected councillor assigned by the King to Porrex, laments the 'most unhappy state of Counsellours' when their good

---

[22] Norton and Sackville, *Gorboduc*, sig. E3v–E4r.
[23] Norton and Sackville, *Gorboduc*, sig. A4v.
[24] Norton and Sackville, *Gorboduc*, sig. A6r.
[25] Norton and Sackville, *Gorboduc*, sig. B3v.

advice cannot be heard, 'Yet must thei beare the blames of yll successe'.[26] Cecil said almost the same thing to Sir Nicholas Throckmorton just under a month before the presentation of *Gorboduc* at court.[27] The King understands and accepts the counsel of Eubulus on the division of Britain by Brutus, but he still decides to separate his land because he trusts that 'mynyng fraude shall finde no way to crepe/ Into their fensed eares with grave advise'.[28] Like Elizabeth, Gorboduc is an admired, respected, and loved monarch, but the destruction of his kingdom lies in a failure of counsel. In the same way that Christopher Marlowe's *Edward II* deals with the strained relationship between a favourite and an ancient nobility, and Shakespeare's *Richard II* explores the themes of youth and temperament in the downfall of a morally and poetically self-absorbed king, *Gorboduc* (albeit in a wholly less sophisticated way) does at least three things: first, the play places counsel in the context of succession; second, it holds up an historical mirror to the Queen to remind her of the need to hear good advice; and third, the drama deals with the controversial issue of the location of power in the English polity in the 1560s.

II

In 1561 *Gorboduc* was performed by and for lawyers of the Inner Temple and, in January 1562, the play was taken to court. So by the time parliament met in January 1563, the Queen, her Council, courtiers, and common lawyers had experienced Norton's and Sackville's mirror for magistrates. But the fictional King Gorboduc had done something that by the winter of 1562 and 1563 Elizabeth had not: he had planned a pattern of succession. The Queen developed smallpox in December 1562, and her court and Council faced the serious prospect of the death of the last Tudor candidate to the English crown. The succession to the throne was still an open, unresolved, and probably unmentionable issue. Elizabethans knew what this meant and they understood the consequences. At the end of the second scene of the first act of *Gorboduc*, Norton's chorus supported a 'settled staie' in 'stedfast place by knowen and doubtles right' and argued that each 'chaunge of course unjoynts the whole estate'.[29] Later on it maintained, with the sort of providentialism so familiar to Cecil, that when kings neglect good advise 'Succeding heapes of plagues shall teache to late/ To learne the mischiefes of misguydinge the state'.[30] Cecil would not have

---

[26] Norton and Sackville, *Gorboduc*, sig. B8v.
[27] 22 December 1561, Additional 35830, fo. 228v.
[28] Norton and Sackville, *Gorboduc*, sig. B1r, B2v.
[29] Norton and Sackville, *Gorboduc*, sig. B2v.
[30] Norton and Sackville, *Gorboduc*, sig. C1r.

claimed anything so dangerously unsubtle in 1562 but he did correct a prayer connecting the Queen's life and the sins of the kingdom in 1563. Europe was being turned upside down by religious conflict in France, which had begun that spring; the proposed meeting between Mary Stuart and Elizabeth, as an Anglo-British attempt to negotiate an end to the succession crisis, had floundered in summer; and Elizabeth was beginning to come to terms with the expense of the Newhaven expedition. By the end of 1562 the four central domestic issues facing the polity were money, religious war, succession, and the Queen's health.

So when the first session of Elizabeth's second parliament met in January 1563, the MPs were drawn into a wider and more complex debate on the Queen's marriage, the succession, and the state of their polity. The royal reasons for calling parliament were very different, and as a privy councillor and Principal Secretary Cecil explained them to the Commons on 20 January 1563. Its Clerk, John Seymour, recorded that in an 'excellent declaracion', Cecil explained the cost of England's war in France: the charges at Berwick and Newhaven, the 'provision of Armour', the cost of the navy, and 'the cavillacion of the ffrenche for Calleys', concluding 'to consider for the Ayde'.[31] But on the second day of the session, 16 January, an anonymous 'burges' had already set the tone and introduced one of the central themes of 1563 by introducing a 'mocyon . . . at length for the succession'.[32] This began a pattern of debates and legislative proposals consistently covering January, February, March, and the beginning of April, and which involved a succession committee appointed by the Speaker of the Commons, Thomas Williams, a petition read by Williams himself, a declaration presented by the Lords, active contributions by the Privy Council, and a firm rejection by Elizabeth. But was this a short-term and panicked reaction to Elizabeth's illness in December 1562 or something more politically substantial?

The hint of a key to the first session of the second parliament, and indeed the whole problem of its MPs' commitment to what A.F. Pollard and Sir John Neale may have termed 'constitutional opposition' to Elizabeth, lies in an unlikely and copied source. On 11 January 1563, the dean of St Paul's, Alexander Nowell, delivered a sermon before the Queen. He introduced it with a biblical example which was strongly reminiscent of the relationship between Norton's and Sackville's characters of Gorboduc, Dordan, Ferrex, Philander, and Porrex. King David, 'being troubled with the insurrection of his own son Absolom', assigned one of his 'old sage counsellors', Achithophel, to guide the young man. Achithophel's advice

---

[31] Journals, Commons, fo. 219r; *CJ*, I, p. 63.
[32] Journals, Commons, fo. 217v; *CJ*, I, p. 62.

had no effect, the results were as unsavoury as David had sensed, and the counsellor hanged himself. There were two other main themes to Nowell's sermon: first, the English parliament was called in 1563 to make laws for 'service of God and the realm'; and second, the succession to the crown of the kingdom was an appropriate and necessary matter for parliamentary attention, along with the profanation of the sabbath, economic and social reform, and other 'commonwealth' issues familiar to the reader of *De republica Anglorum*. Nowell used a fragment of the sort of conversation he had heard during Elizabeth's illness, mixing concern for the Queen's health and the fears of religious war in Europe spilling over into England. 'Alas what trouble shall we be in', he repeated, 'even as great or greater then France ffor the succession is so uncerten and such division for religion'.[33]

For historians of the early Elizabethan polity, Nowell's sermon helps to uncover one strand of political language and thought in the first decade: parliament as a royal council, offering advice in humanist-classical terms, with its MPs as counsellors. One MP in 1566 made the connection even more explicitly.[34] Even if Nowell's purpose was not 'political' in the sense of consciously starting a campaign for action on the succession, he explained and defended parliament's duty to counsel and act. In this sense, the main themes of the sermon are perhaps closer to the concerns of Elizabeth's subjects in 1562 and 1563 than some of the later arguments for developing parliamentary liberty in the sixteenth century and 'corporate' action by the Commons presented by Pollard and Neale. Neale thought that he had found a 'choir' of 'left-wing protestants' and 'independents' in the early Elizabethan Commons. There have been other interpretations. G.R. Elton, for example, pointed to a 'temporary Dudley faction' in 1563, organized to press Lord Robert's marriage suit. Both Neale and Elton have been comprehensively and effectively challenged.[35] But the focus should be moved away from choirs and factions to the relationship between Lords, Commons, privy councillors, and the Queen. The first session of the second parliament can be read in the context of the debate on the succession in the very early 1560s and an attempt to press Elizabeth for the good of her kingdom.

The Commons' and Council's campaign to debate and legislate on the succession stands out clearly from the parliamentary sources. The early

---

[33] Cotton Titus F. 1, fos. 61r–64v; Alexander Nowell, *A catechism written in Latin*, ed. G.E. Corrie (Parker Society; Cambridge, 1853), pp. 223–8.

[34] See above, p. 38.

[35] J.E. Neale, *Elizabeth I and her parliaments 1559–1601*, 2 vols. (London, 1953, 1957), I, pp. 101, 103–5; G.R. Elton, *The parliament of England 1559–1581* (Cambridge, 1986), pp. 358–62; cf. Norman L. Jones, *Faith by statute. Parliament and the settlement of religion 1559* (London, 1982); and Simon Adams, 'The Dudley clientele and the House of Commons, 1559–1586', *Parliamentary History*, 8 (1989), 224–5.

debates on 16 and 18 January persuaded Thomas Williams to meet the privy councillors in the Commons (Sir Ambrose Cave, Cecil, Sir Francis Knollys, Sir John Mason, Sir William Petre, Sir Edward Rogers, Sir Richard Sackville, and Sir Ralph Sadler) and twenty-four chosen MPs during the afternoon of 19 January 'to drawe artycles of peticion for the Quenes mariage and Succession'. Rogers, Comptroller of the Household, was appointed as chair but John Seymour did not list the committee in his journal.[36] A week later, on 26 January, Thomas Norton read to the house 'A peticion devysed by the commyttyes [sic] to be made to the Quenes majestie'. The privy councillors in the Commons were 'requyred' to approach Elizabeth 'to move the Quenes majestie that master Speker with the hole howse may exhibyte to her highnes that peticion'.[37] Rogers liaised with the Upper House 'to furder the peticion of this house', which 'was well allowed of the Lords'. The final arrangements were made a day later, on 27 January, when Rogers and the rest of the Privy Council in the Commons announced that Williams would read the petition the next day.[38] In other words, the context of the campaign (organized by the Speaker of the Commons and the Privy Council, in close touch with the Lords) and its content (the speech itself in two versions, one endorsed and privately read by Cecil) are substantially clear.

Williams and the Commons' petition relied on an interesting reading of Lord Keeper Nicholas Bacon's first speech to the Parliament, in the Queen's name, on 12 January. In the short copy of Bacon's text, the Lord Keeper distinguished between parliamentary matters 'devyded into two partes': one, he explained, concerned church and religion; the other was based on 'pollicie for the common wealth, as well for provision at home as to provide for the forreine enemye abroade'. The two main issues of 'policy for the common wealth' were law reform and money.[39] Even in a longer version of the speech, Bacon concentrated on the same issues: succession was not part of the Queen's agenda at the beginning of 1563. The petition accepted that Elizabeth had called parliament 'for supplieng & redressing the gretest wantes & defaultes in this your commen weale, and for thestablishing the suerty of the same', but Williams consciously went beyond Bacon's call (as the Speaker put it) 'to have consideration of the gretest matters, that nerest touched the estate of our realme, & the preservation therof'. The petition took the next logical step and argued that there was 'nothing in this wholl estate of so great importance' to the Queen '& the wholl realme, nor so necessary at this time to be reduced into a

[36] Journals, Commons, fo. 218v; *CJ*, I, p. 63.
[37] Journals, Commons, fo . 221r; *CJ*, I, p. 63.
[38] Journals, Commons, fo. 221v; *CJ*, I, pp. 63–4.   [39] Hartley, pp. 70–2.

certenty, as the sure continuance of the governance & thimperiall crowne therof in your Majesties person'.[40]

This was part of a wholly conscious misunderstanding, engineered by the privy councillors in the Commons, the Speaker, and his committee of twenty-four. Two days after Bacon's opening speech and four before the first 'mocyon', Cecil coyly told Sir Thomas Smith that 'I thynk somewhat will be attempted to acertayne the realme of successor to this Crowne' but he feared that 'the unwillyngnes of hir Majesty to have such a person knowen will stey that matter'.[41] But the Commons' petition even went so far as to claim that Elizabeth had 'summoned this parliament, principally for thestablisheing some certen limitacion of thimperiall crowne', some-thing which was wholly against her political instincts and a perversion of the truth.[42] What followed was a set of short historical mirrors from 'forein nations' and English and Scottish monarchs, held up to Elizabeth to reinforce the danger of leaving an open succession. Cecil noted in the margin of his copy of the speech that Alexander the Great had 'dyed without children'. Before the union of Henry VII and Elizabeth of York the English crown was 'tossed in question betwene two royall howses', but it had been restored to 'setled unity'. Williams rehearsed the 'miserable estate' of Scotland after the death of Alexander III, and he pointed out that James V had limited the Scottish crown. This had worked in France and Elizabeth herself had been mentioned in Henry VIII's own limitation statute. Because in 1563 the only protection from the actions of a 'faccioun of heretickes' and 'contentious and malicious papistes' was Elizabeth's life, parliament pressed for a similar statute.[43]

On 1 February, the Lords presented a separate petition which was longer and, in terms of detail, more explicit than the Lower House's contribu-tion.[44] Williams' speech had relied on a few historical examples and Elizabethan fears of 'the great mallice' of the Queen's foreign enemies, 'which even in your life time have sought to transferr the right & dignity of your crowne to a stranger'.[45] The Lords' petition was more organized; it used classical and historical parallels to reinforce the practical arguments for a settlement of the succession. In this sense, it was more effective. The Commons' petition had been written as a collaborative effort between 20 and 28 January; the Lords' equivalent is more difficult to source, but it was an articulate, compelling, and united plea for royal action. The petition

---

[40] SP 12/27, fo. 139r.   [41] 14 January 1563, Lansdowne 102, fo. 18r.

[42] SP 12/27, fo. 139v.

[43] SP 12/27, fos. 139v–140v; cf. another version of the speech, Northamptonshire Record Office, Fitzwilliam (Milton) Political 169.

[44] Drafted by Bernard Hampton, SP 12/27, fos. 135r–138v, printed in Hartley, pp. 58–62.

[45] SP 12/27, fo. 140r.

listed eight 'causes' for a settlement of the succession, prefaced by a humble explanation of the Lords' concerns for Elizabeth, her imperial crown, and 'thuniversall weale' of the kingdom. The 'suerty & preservation' of these three things, the Queen's 'person crowne and realme', depended on a secure marriage and (echoing the Commons' proposal) 'somme certen limitacion might be made how thimperiall crowne shuld remain if god call your highnes without any heire of your body'. Cecil summarized the two calls as 'a petition to marry wher, with whom and as soone as shall pleas' and 'for the succession'. There were examples to demonstrate that 'it appeareth by histories, how in times past persons inheritable to crownes being votaries & relligious' had married for a secure succession. The nun Constantia married the Emperor Henry VI and gave birth to Frederick II. Peter of Aragon 'maried the better to establish & pacify that kingdome'. Antoninus Pius was worthy of credit but Pyrrhus 'is of all godly men detested for sayeng, he wold leave his realme to him that had the sharpest sword'. The scriptural evidence was also impressive. Sarah and Elizabeth were given children. God gave the kingdom of Judea 'lineall succession by descent of kinges'. Because there was 'no ordinary succession' during the time of the Judges, 'the people were often times over runne and caried to Captivity'. Through St Paul the spirit pronounced that 'whosoever maketh not due provision for his family is in danger to Godward' but the Lords emphasized that 'the places of the scriptures conteyning the said threateninges be sett furth with much more sharp woordes, then be here expressed'.[46]

The petition's classical examples were part of the fifth 'cause' for action; the biblical texts and parallels formed an epilogue. But the practical reasons for action were just as compelling as the moral and historical mirrors held up to the Queen by the Lords. Elizabeth's illness had clearly panicked her nobility and Council and so parliament became the opportunity to offer 'advise, consideration and consent, as is requisite in so great & weighty a cause'. A statute would 'brede terrour' in the Queen's enemies and protect her from danger. It was a method which had been used by Elizabeth's progenitors and other monarchs in Europe. In addition, a statute would encourage 'an universall and inward contentacion' in England. The alternative was 'factious, sedicious & intestine warre, that will grow through want of understanding to whom they shuld yeld their allegiances'. But the Lords' central concern (and the eighth of their reasons, working from the short term to the long term) was the effect of an unsettled succession on the governance of the kingdom in the event of Elizabeth's death.

The petition argued that the greatest danger in a kingdom was when the law died with a monarch. Every prince is 'Anima Legis, and so reputed in

---

[46] SP 12/27, fos. 135r–138r.

lawe, And therfore upoun the death of the prince, the lawe dieth, all the officers of justice wherby lawes are to be executed do cease, all writtes & commandementes to all partes for the execution of justice do hang in suspence'. All commissions for the preservation of common peace and the punishment of offenders lost their force; 'strength & will must rule, and nether lawe nor reason' and the realm would 'becomme a praye to strangers'. So an unsettled succession and the death of the monarch as *lex animata*, the living law, would lead to conflict and confusion. This issue also raised the awkward but crucial question of political control in a period of English 'vacation and interreigne'. Medieval political theory explained that in the government of a theocratic king it was the monarch who created the law and lay behind the execution of justice. In *De republica Anglorum* Smith described how the English 'prince giveth all the chiefe and highest offices or magistracies of the realme, be it of judgement or dignitie, temporall or spirituall', and that 'All writtes, executions and commaundementes be done in the princes name'. This was given a more controversial slant by Aylmer in 1559, who argued that effective government by an English queen rested on the laws of the kingdom, 'the executors whereof be her judges, appoynted bi her, her justices of peace and such other officers'. In this, she was guided by her Council 'which by travail abrod, know men howe fit or unfit they be for suche offices'.[47] The Elizabethan polity had to find an effective balance between what seemed to be two competing and contradictory traditions: first, that the power of the law and its officers died with the Queen but, second, that the execution of justice could operate under the supervision of the monarch's Council.

III

In February and early March 1563 Cecil became involved in the drafting of a comprehensive statute on the succession to tackle the potential problem of England without a monarch. Exactly when is not clear. Elizabeth replied to the Commons' petition on 28 January; John Seymour, the Clerk, recorded that she accepted it 'with an excellent oration differring the answer to furder tyme for the gravytye of the cases'.[48] But even after the Lords' petition on 1 February, the Queen clearly began to stall. The Lower House reminded her 'to have in remembraunce their peticion' on 12

---

[47] SP 12/27, fos. 136v–137r; Walter Ullmann, *Principles of government and politics in the middle ages* (London, 1961), pp. 157, 159; Ernst H. Kantorowicz, *The king's two bodies. A study in medieval political theology* (Princeton, 1957), pp. 8 n. 4, 92 n. 18, 100, n. 38; Smith, *De republica Anglorum*, ed. Dewar, Book II, chapter 3, p. 87; John Aylmer, *An harborowe for faithfull and trewe subiectes, agaynst the late blowne blaste, concerninge the government of wemen . . .* (STC 1005; London, 1559), sig. H3v.

[48] Journals, Commons, fo. 222r; *CJ*, I, p. 64.

February.[49] Four days later Sir Edward Rogers and Cecil told the Commons that the Queen 'dyd right well consyder that she forgot not the sute' but she wanted restraint.[50] Apart from a short reference to Sir Nicholas Bacon's reading of Elizabeth's 'devyse' on the succession on the closing day of the session, 10 April 1563, that was the last mention of the matter in Seymour's journal.[51]

But there was more going on in parliament after the Lords' petition than the official record of the Lower House reveals. In Cecil's archive as Principal Secretary there is an undated draft bill 'ffor restrayning of all persones from attemptes or hopes to the Quenes majesties perill'. It was drafted by a clerk in a court hand, the title scored out but apparently rewritten by Thomas Norton, the spokesman of the group of twenty-four, in January 1563.[52] The bill may well have been part of what Lord Keeper Bacon referred to in one speech as 'a readinge of a bill exhibited last wensday before my Lordes conteininge matter concerninge the succession of the Crowne of this Realme'.[53] Bacon's 'oracion' is in turn dated by the bill and a report by the Spanish ambassador. On 3 April 1563 Bishop de Quadra reported the appearance of (in Martin Hume's translation) 'an Act providing that in case the Queen dies no office, either judicial or in the household, shall become vacant'.[54] This puts the bill in late March – probably on the twenty-fourth – and Bacon at the end of the month, on the twenty-eighth. But de Quadra's comments are more interesting for another reason. The bill presented in March seems to have been drawn up as an insurance against what the Lords had, at the beginning of February, called a 'vacation and interreigne' in English government after Elizabeth's death. Bacon also hinted at this: the bill was based on 'matter concerninge the succession' but 'nether by that bill nor by any other acte alredy made any open and certaine declaracion or limitacion is made to whome the crowne shoulde remaine'.[55] Norton's copy of the succession clause fits. It would have prevented any person 'of what degree condition place or estate' from attempting in any way to 'clayme or pretende or utter declare affirme or publishe them selves' to 'have right or title to have or enjoy the crowne of England' during the Queen's life or from challenging Elizabeth's rights to the throne. But it made no attempt to declare a successor.[56] Cecil called the

[49] Journals, Commons, fo. 226v; *CJ*, I, p. 65.
[50] Journals, Commons, fo. 227v; *CJ*, I, p. 65.
[51] Journals, Commons, fo. 252v; *CJ*, I, p. 72.
[52] SP 12/28, fos. 73v–74r, 75v–76r, 77v–78r.
[53] Folger Shakespeare Library, Washington, D.C., V.a.197, fo. 4r.
[54] *Calendar of letters and state papers relating to English affairs, preserved principally in the archives of Simancas*, ed. Martin A.S. Hume, 4 vols. (London, 1892–9), I, p. 317.
[55] Folger Shakespeare Library, Washington, D.C., V.a.197, fo. 4r–v.
[56] SP 12/28, fos. 73v–74r.

whole attempt merely 'an act ment for the succession but not passed'. But he was personally and solely responsible for the inclusion of a 'clause to have bene inserted' in the statute.[57]

Cecil's 'clause' is perhaps one of the most significant drafts he completed in the first decade of Elizabeth's reign, for reasons which demonstrate his breathtaking ability to deal with political problems by applying a subtle form of radical conservatism. As a political and constitutional document, the 'clause' introduces at least three issues: the language of council and conciliar action, the power of a named council in the event of Elizabeth's death, and the ministerial status of councillors and governors in the 1560s. Its basic argument was simple. If the Queen died it would be 'very necessary beside the ordynary government of the Realme by the Pryncipall or ordynary officers' of the kingdom to have a 'Counsell of estate usually named a privee Counsell' to consider and direct the 'publick affayres' of England. These included relations with foreign princes and countries and matters of defence and justice.[58] Again, it fits Bacon's model: if the rest of the bill to which Cecil added his 'clause' had established the rights of a named successor to the crown, there would have been no real need for provisions for a period of interregnum.

Although the 'clause' was an effective endorsement of the tradition of conciliar involvement in the running of the military, legal, and financial affairs of the kingdom, there was still a real sense in which the death of the Queen – either by violence or through illness – would have exposed England to the dangers of religious war on the Continent. Both situations were equally serious but it was an assassination plot against Elizabeth which forced Cecil to revive and revise the 1563 plan for interregnum in 1585. Cecil knew in 1563 that control of the kingdom's reserves of armed force was crucial. In the 'clause', the whole mechanism of commanding and controlling military power in England, Wales, and Ireland rests with the Privy Council or its quorum of ten, who would have had the authority to give orders to treasurers, chamberlains, receivers, tellers, or any other officer, and, through money, control of the garrison towns and fortifications of England, Wales, and Ireland, their soldiers, naval personnel, ordnance, and even the jewels, money, plate, robes, silks, and bedding of the crown.[59]

The central argument of the 'clause' was that England should be practically governed in the short term by a council endorsed by a parliamentary statute, able to operate until parliament could declare a successor. The nature of this council, and the language Cecil used to describe it, is one of the keys to the way in which privy councillors

---

[57] SP 12/28, fos. 68r–69v; see below, pp. 225–8.
[58] SP 12/28, fo. 68r; see below, p. 225.   [59] SP 12/28, fo. 69r; see below, pp. 226–7.

understood and could conceptualize the location of power in the early Elizabethan polity. Cecil referred to the interregnum body as a 'privy council', a transitional 'privy council of estate', and a 'council of estate'; its members were 'councillors' and 'councillors of estate'. In all its forms, the council represented effective royal power. Cecil could describe it as a privy council, which was in all senses a group of councillors bound by oath to the Queen, and a council of estate; in *De republica Anglorum* Smith used the image of the 'cloath of estate' in the Queen's presence chamber to reinforce the personal power of the English monarch.[60] But there were also conciliar precedents. After the coronation of Richard II a great council of lay magnates and prelates appointed twelve councillors to act as an 'interim council of regency' before the king's first parliament, and a council of 'magnates and principal officials' summoned the first parliament of Henry VI. In 1546 Henry VIII planned a council by which his son Edward could be *'ordered and ruled* both in his mariage and also in orderinge of th'affaiers of the Realme aswell outward as inward . . . by the advise and councell of our right intirely beloved councellours'. This was a 'council of regency' as much as a privy council.[61] But the proposal in 1563 was more than an endorsement of a council's ability to run day-to-day government centrally and locally. The clear implication of the 'clause' was that a parliamentary statute could effectively transfer the imperial power of the Queen's person to a small executive board. In this sense, the privy council of estate planned in 1563 was close to the spirit of the provisions of Henry VIII's will before their usurpation by Protector Somerset. Henry envisaged the establishment of Edward 'in the crowne imperiall of this Realme after our decease' but combined this with the reality of a council managing the kingdom.[62]

In 1563 Cecil proposed English government by a privy council possessing the prerogative power of the crown. Even the use of the term 'council of estate' does not quite succeed in disguising the fact that in the event of Elizabeth's death, England would be governed by the small group of men who had served the Queen as privy councillors and officers of state. Between the death of the Queen and the parliamentary declaration of her successor, men 'knowen to be of the privee Counsell' would 'remayne and contynew counsellors with lyke interest, authorite, place, and degree'. The Council would meet as it had usually done during the reign. One of the

[60] Smith, *De republica Anglorum*, ed. Dewar, Book II, chapter 3, p. 88.
[61] J.S. Roskell, *Parliament and politics in late medieval England*, 3 vols. (London, 1981–3), I, pp. 196–7, 211; Ralph A. Griffiths, *The reign of King Henry VI. The exercise of royal authority, 1422–1461* (London and Tonbridge, 1981), pp. 22–8; SP 1/227, fo. 221v, printed in *Foedera, conventiones, litterae* . . ., ed. Thomas Rymer and Robert Sanderson, 20 vols. (London, 1704–35), XV, p. 115, with my emphasis; E.W. Ives, 'Henry VIII's will – a forensic conundrum', *Historical Journal*, 35 (1992), 801.
[62] SP 1/227, fo. 221v, printed in *Foedera*, ed. Rymer and Sanderson, XV, p. 115.

distinctions between Elizabeth's Privy Council and its posthumous successor was that new members could have been added by the Queen in her will, supported by the great seal, and that the councillors of estate had to take a new oath. Unfortunately, Cecil did not add a text of it to the 'clause'. From the relationship between the quorum of the new privy council and its members, it is clear that the 'clause' was a working draft. As Cecil edited the named members down from twelve to seven, he raised the quorum from six to ten, so there was room for expansion and development. After these corrections, the council's membership stood at the Chancellor or Lord Keeper of the Great Seal, the Lord Treasurer, the Lord President of the Council 'if any than shall be', the Earl Marshal of England, the Lord Steward 'of the howshold', the Lord Admiral, and the Lord Chamberlain. These were some of the 'great offices of the Realme' listed in the 'Acte concerninge placing of the Lordes in the Parliament Chamber & other Assemblies and conferences of Counsell' of 1539. A marquess, an earl, a viscount, a baron, and 'one secretary of the state' were originally part of the draft in 1563, but they were edited out. From the inclusion of the office of lord president, the main aim of Cecil's exercise was to establish the institutional shape of the council of estate (rather than name individual men for the jobs), to define and explain the mechanism of setting up unhindered council control, and to set down in law 'by awthorite of this parlement' the right of the council to operate as an executive board.[63]

So in 1563 the institutional offices of an English council of estate would have been filled by Bacon as Lord Keeper, the marquess of Winchester as Lord Treasurer, the duke of Norfolk as Earl Marshal, the earl of Arundel as Steward, Lord Howard of Effingham as Lord Chamberlain, and Lord Admiral Clinton. But, presumably from the process of involving men 'knowen' to be of the Privy Council, the senior officers' colleagues – Cave, Cecil, Bedford, Derby, Knollys, Mason, Northampton, Pembroke, Petre, and Sackville – would also have sat on the council. This makes more sense of Cecil's final quorum of ten, but it establishes one of two things: either first, that he had not finished editing the clause; or second, that this was, from the beginning, an institutionalized way of preserving the power of Elizabeth's existing councillors. So in this sense the 'clause' blended the baronial tradition of great officers of the kingdom claiming their right to take a full part in royal government with the early Elizabethan reality of a compact and competent Privy Council. In addition, the Lord Steward – although the 'clause' clearly points to the Steward of the Household and not the High Steward – and the Earl Marshal had substantial powers in the

[63] SP 12/28, fos. 68r–69v; see below, pp. 225–6; 31 Henry VIII, c. 10, *Statutes of the realm*, ed. A. Luders, T.E. Tomlins, J. Raithby *et al.*, 11 vols. (London, 1810–28), III, pp. 729–30.

event of a crisis in royal government. The office of constable had been dormant since the claim made by Edward Stafford, duke of Buckingham, at the beginning of Henry VIII's reign but two members of the Constable's Council (according to Thomas Starkey) were the 'lord marschal' and the 'chamburleyn of englond'. Starkey called this group a 'lytyl parlyament'. So the 'clause' of 1563 represented a powerful conciliar alternative to royal government without the Queen in the event of her death.[64]

Cecil's proposal to try Mary Stuart in 1568 was based more on the institution of great council than on privy council. But in January 1585 Cecil corrected two versions of a clause 'to be added to a Bil for the Quenes savetye' which, 'to the intent that this noble Realme' in a period of 'Interregn shall not lack a present Govvernement by direccion of such officers as in the lief time of her majestie', pressed for similar conciliar action endorsed by parliament.[65] Although the principle of the proposal was basically the same in 1585, the complexion of its council was not. In the alternative version of the plan drafted by Sir John Popham, Cecil explained that in place of the Queen's 'name and style' the council would use the style 'Magnum consilium coronae Angliae'. He went through the same copy and altered every reference to council from 'Grand' to 'Gret'.[66] The draft made it clear that the council would in part consist of 'all other persons that shall be of hir Majesties privy counsell at the time of her deathe', but the implication was obvious: the 1585 great or grand council was going to be based on a large group of the senior officers of the kingdom, temporal, spiritual, and legal. These officers were the Archbishops of Canterbury and York, the Lord Chancellor, the Lord Treasurer, the Lord Privy Seal, the Lord Great Chamberlain, the Earl Marshal, the Lord Admiral, the Master of Ordnance, the Chief Justice of the King's

---

[64] L.W. Vernon Harcourt, *His Grace the Steward and trial of peers. A novel inquiry into a special branch of constitutional government* (London, 1907), pp. 144, 148–51, 164–7; Thomas Hearne (ed.), *A collection of curious discourses written by eminent antiquaries upon several heads in our English antiquities*, 2 vols. (London, 1771), II, pp. 1–12, 90–154; Nicholas Pronay and John Taylor (eds.), *Parliamentary texts of the later middle ages* (Oxford, 1980), pp. 74–5, 87–8; John Guy, 'The king's council and political participation', in Alistair Fox and John Guy, *Reassessing the Henrician age. Humanism, politics and reform 1500–1550* (Oxford and New York, 1986), p. 141; David Starkey, 'Stewart serendipity: a missing text of the *Modus tenendi parliamentum*', *Fenway Court* (1986), 38–51; Linda Levy Peck, 'Peers, patronage and the politics of history', in John Guy (ed.), *The reign of Elizabeth I. Court and culture in the last decade* (Cambridge, 1995), pp. 98–106; Thomas Starkey, *A dialogue between Pole and Lupset*, ed. T.F. Mayer (Camden Society, fourth series, 37; London, 1989), p. 121.

[65] SP 12/176, fos. 40r–47v; Huntington Library, San Marino, California, Ellesmere 1192, fos. 1r–4r; for the quotation, SP 12/176, fo. 42v; cf. Patrick Collinson, 'The Elizabethan exclusion crisis and the Elizabethan polity', *Proceedings of the British Academy*, 84 (1995), 87–92.

[66] Huntington Library, San Marino, California, Ellesmere 1192, fos. 1v, 2r, 2v, 3r, 3v, 4r.

Bench, the Lords President of Wales and the North, and the Wardens of the Cinque Ports and the Northern Marches.[67] There are also similarities between 1585 and the plan in 1568 to consult the archbishop of Canterbury and the bishop of London, along with the nobility of the kingdom. The regime knew the men at court and in the localities and seemed prepared to use them.[68] Even in December 1688, when the lords spiritual and temporal sat in the council chamber, the peers of the realm soon started sending out letters from a larger group of peers and the lords of the Privy Council.[69] Broad representation was a more secure political option in 1585 and 1568. It was going to be a smaller operation in 1563.

The implications of Cecil's 'clause' were profound. In effect, he explored the same distinction made by the recusant lawyer Edmund Plowden: between a monarch's natural body – 'a Body mortal, subject to all Infirmities that come by Nature or Accident, to the Imbecillity of Infancy or old Age' – and the body politic, 'a Body that cannot be seen or handled, consisting of Policy and Government, and constituted for the Direction of the People, and the Management of the publick-weal'.[70] The 'clause' was based on the premise that royal and imperial power could, temporarily at least, be separated from the physical person of the Queen; it also endorsed the power of parliament to sanction a conciliar interregnum and find a successor. In other words, to prevent England from becoming a dangerously unstable kingdom in the event of the Queen's death, Cecil blended social and political conservatism – the involvement of the great officers of state and the continuation of the Privy Council in the cause of law, peace, and order – and a radical conciliarism. Professor Collinson has called this a form of 'monarchical republicanism'. Along with the bond of association of 1584, which was a 'quasi-republican statement' because the 'circumstance it envisaged was the extinction of the Queen', the late Elizabethan interregnum schemes point to the fact (in Collinson's eyes) that England 'was a republic which happened also to be a monarchy: or vice versa'.[71]

IV

So how does Cecil's 'clause', and the parliamentary campaign it was part of, fit into the pattern of early Elizabethan politics? Practically, it was a statement of 'monarchical republicanism' written twenty-two years before

---

[67] SP 12/176, fo. 42v.   [68] See below, pp. 177–8.
[69] Robert Beddard (ed.), *A kingdom without a king. The journal of the provisional government in the revolution of 1688* (Oxford, 1988), pp. 74–122.
[70] Axton, *Queen's two bodies*, p. 17.
[71] Patrick Collinson, 'The monarchical republic of Queen Elizabeth I', in his *Elizabethan essays* (London and Rio Grande, 1994), pp. 43, 50; Collinson, '*De republica Anglorum*: or, history with the politics put back', in his *Elizabethan essays*, pp. 18–19.

Professor Collinson's assessment begins. Cecil's mind perhaps looks un-radical in 1585 from the perspective of 1585, but it seems less so from that of 1563. Intellectually and philosophically, Cecil's creed in the 1560s is a good deal subtler. But was it republican or is this too modern a description for it? Or was Cecil's political instinct a purely practical response to Elizabeth's failure to declare a successor? If he was a republican, it was not by choice. A seal engraved 'Magnum consilium coronae Angliae' was not an alternative to effective royal government under Elizabeth; it was a necessary inconvenience, a short-term guarantee of peace and law. But the significant fact is that Cecil could *imagine* England without a monarch and effectively plan for a period of interregnum. It is increasingly clear that England did experience republicanism in the middle of the sixteenth century – a republicanism on a classical model, in which Cicero's and Quintilian's *vir civilis* could not only lead a *vita activa* by offering counsel and submitting advice but also involve himself in the legislative functions of parliament. Dr Markku Peltonen has argued that this form of repub-licanism was not a 'constitutional goal', but 'a theory of citizenship, public virtue and true nobility based essentially on the classical humanist and republican traditions'.[72]

Both Professor Collinson and Dr Peltonen have demonstrated that republicanism affected both the localities and the centre of power in Elizabethan England. Citizens were 'concealed within subjects': under pressure and in an emergency, Elizabethan governors realized that there was something more permanent than the physical life of the monarch. The classicization of politics in England in the sixteenth century allowed councillors and courtiers to express and understand political priorities in classical terms, reinforced by an ideal of service and political life. Reading Cicero and Quintilian and experiencing classical texts absorbed into vernacular studies like *The boke named the governour* must have had a profound impact. The first parallel edition of Cicero's *De officiis* was published in England in 1534, followed by other translations; Elyot reinforced this emphasis on text, culture, and training. Classical parallels and examples were becoming increasingly accessible, even in the 1530s. An English edition of *The golden boke of Marcus Aurelius emperour and eloquent oratour* had the emperor desiring 'the welth of his people, and the people his welthe', supported by fifty 'gentylmen knyghtes'. The last page of *The thre bookes of Tullyes offyces* had the translator saluting an oddly Renaissance-looking Cicero. The classical world, with its emphasis on active public service, was culturally accessible to Elizabethans.[73]

---

[72] Markku Peltonen, *Classical humanism and republicanism in English political thought 1570–1640* (Cambridge, 1995), pp. 10, 12.

[73] Collinson, '*De republica Anglorum*', p. 19; Antonio de Guevara, *The golden boke of*

This meant that a writer like John Barston could compare an urban political community to a classical *polis* or an Italian Renaissance city. But in his *Safegarde of societie* of 1576 Barston linked the microcosm to the macrocosm, and the macrocosm was England and its governance. For Barston the kingdom was a mixed polity, a 'triple regiment', in which laws were established by 'the free consent and agreement of all three, the prince of all, the noble and universall commons, in common parliament and councel togyther assembled'. Philip Sidney seems to have praised the 'well-mixed and balanced aristocracy' of Poland, Arthur Hall agreed in 1579, and Richard Beacon in 1594 had Solon declare that Romulus wanted to establish a mixed constitution in Rome. This was the position of Aylmer and Smith. Cecil was prepared to call parliament the three estates and define the power of the estates in relation to the position of the monarch. At least part of Cecil's republicanism lay in his belief that the lords and commons could and should play an important role in the governance of the realm.[74]

Cecil's 'clause' represented the early Elizabethan mixed polity and classical republicanism – defined as a commitment to the kingdom or the common weal – in action. In the plan for an emergency interregnum and in its vision of a parliament capable of authorizing a privy council of estate and choosing a successor, the project was a bold one. It was an admission also that public or national good could sometimes be defined in isolation from – even in direct opposition to – the will of an individual monarch. Cecil managed even to separate the person of the Queen from her imperial power. He applied the word 'minister' to 'all ordynary officers . . . as well spirituall as temporall'. Because these men would have to act as officers of the council and parliament this reference was, in some ways, a departure from his usual use of the term in the context of personal service to the prince. And what is more, it was the succession as a practical political issue which was responsible for this commitment to 'ordynary government' and the conservation of peace in the kingdom without the Queen.[75]

Politics in the 1550s and 1560s, like political language in the sixteenth century, was multilayered. Political ideas were discussed in what has been described as a 'polyglot form'.[76] Thomas Starkey's Pole, for example, explained the need for a permanent council in London to 'remedy al such causys & represse sedycyons' when the king and his council 'tendyd to

---

Marcus Aurelius emperour and eloquent oratour, trans. J. Bourchier (*STC* 12436; London, 1535), chapter 33, p. 56r; chapter 44, p. 85v; Cicero, *The thre bookes of Tullyes offyces/ bothe in latyne tonge & in englysshe*, trans. Robert Whittinton (*STC* 5278; London, 1534).
[74] Peltonen, *Classical humanism and republicanism*, pp. 48, 54–5, 68–9, 93–4; see above, p. 36.
[75] SP 12/28, fo. 68r; see below, p. 225.   [76] Guy, 'Rhetoric of counsel', p. 299.

any thyng hurtful & prejudycyal' to the liberty of 'the hole body of the pepul'. Writing at about the same time, Elyot expressed the political process of counsel in more classical terms.[77] So although the Queen's refusal to act on her marriage or the kingdom's succession could be – and was – expressed in the humanist-classical idiom of counsel it was possible also to define the political crisis of the 1560s in feudal-baronial terms of the *negotia regni*, or 'great affairs', of the realm which demanded the involvement of its senior officers.[78] There was not a baronial reaction against Elizabeth in 1563 but there was a conciliar response.

Cecil's experience of Tudor politics helps to put this into clearer focus. The provisions of Henry VIII's will rested on the constant supervision of Edward VI by the Lord Chancellor, the 'great master' of the King's household, the Lord Privy Seal, the earl of Hertford as Great Chamberlain, and the Admiral.[79] Richard Cecil, William's father, was a yeoman of the robes at the time of Henry's death, and should have witnessed the politicking of men like Sir Anthony Denny and Sir William Paget. Cecil was familiar enough with the controversial issue of the will's authenticity to counter William Maitland of Lethington's detailed and persistent questioning in the 1560s.[80] More substantially, Cecil signed the text of the duke of Northumberland's version of Edward VI's will. This clearly established a supervisory council for the young King's Grey successors and argued that, in the event of a break in the succession, 'the said imperialle Croune and other the premesses shalbe governed by the Counsell'. The will also required the support of Lords and Commons and the ratification of 'this our saide declaracion and lymytacion' by 'authoretye of Parleamente'.[81] The MP William Fleetwood owned 'an old booke of Parchmine' on the powers of the High Steward, and as Earl Marshal the fourth duke of Norfolk commissioned a copy of the *Modus tenendi parliamentum*.[82] Cecil was perfectly able in 1568 to plan a traditional Tudor great council. The early regime was anything but baronial – the rebellion of the northern earls in 1569 was in part a reaction to the new men set up around Elizabeth – but it is clear that Cecil and his colleagues in parliament and

---

[77] Starkey, *Pole and Lupset*, ed. Mayer, p. 112; Guy, 'Rhetoric of counsel', pp. 293–4; Guy, 'King's council', pp. 138–9.

[78] Guy, 'Rhetoric of counsel', p. 297.

[79] *Foedera*, ed. Rymer and Sanderson, XV, p. 115.

[80] Maitland of Lethington to Cecil, 4 January 1567, Harley 444, fos. 24r–25r.

[81] Harley 35, fo. 369r, printed in John Gough Nichols (ed.), *The chronicle of Queen Jane, and of two years of Queen Mary, and especially of the rebellion of Sir Thomas Wyat* (Camden Society, 48; London, 1850), pp. 91–100.

[82] J.S.A. Adamson, 'The baronial context of the English civil war', *Transactions of the Royal Historical Society*, fifth series, 40 (1990), 99; Starkey, 'Stewart serendipity', 38–51; Peck, 'Peers, patronage and the politics of history', p. 99.

in Council were attuned to the practice and culture of English conciliarism.[83]

So it is possible to find in the political creed of William Cecil in the 1560s a subtle and nuanced blend of the concerns of the humanist-classical *vir civilis*, the priorities of a feudal-baronial response to crisis in royal government, and a recognition that the day-to-day governance of Elizabethan England and Ireland needed stability and continuity. These three elements, more to the point, can be found on paper in 1563. The MPs in the first session of the second parliament did not indulge in a 'constitutional' campaign against Elizabeth; they wanted to present advice to the Queen and make the point that debate and decision on the succession were within their remit. 1563 was a call for partnership: parliament as the 'Regall Diademe', 'the whole realme both the head and the bodie', given life by the prince.[84] Cecil's 'clause' fits into the pattern of domestic succession politics between 1560 and 1563: the persistence of the 'political nation' of councillors and MPs turning gradually into insistence, the moral pressure put on Elizabeth to marry and to plan the kingdom's future, reinforced by historical and classical examples. The early debate on marriage and succession led to *Gorboduc*, which dealt with the issues of counsel and parliament. Elizabeth's illness and the financial needs of war in Europe encouraged the event of parliament and the question of succession to meet. But above all, Cecil's part in drafting a bill designed to deal with the succession allowed him to experiment with a significant conciliar alternative to direct royal government.

---

[83] See below, pp. 176–9; also, pp. 206–7.
[84] Norton and Sackville, *Gorboduc*, sig. E2r; Smith, *De republica Anglorum*, ed. Dewar, Book II, chapter 1, p. 79.

5

The Darnley marriage and weaknesses in the Elizabethan polity 1564–1566

Elizabeth I did not like political revolution or challenges to royal authority. She made this clear in May 1567 when, after the murder of Henry, Lord Darnley, the Scot Lord Grange approached her to ask for English support. Elizabeth was torn. She told Thomas Randolph of her 'greate myslykinge' of the Queen of Scots' actions, 'which nowe she dothe so myche deteste that she is a shamed of her'. But Elizabeth could still not support the opponents of her cousin. She did not like the idea that Mary's 'Subjectes sholde by anye force withstonde that which theie do see her bente unto'. Grange had written 'dyspytefullye' against his Queen; Elizabeth was furious that he could make her 'worce then anye commen woman'. But more ominously, Cecil could get no decision on policy because the Queen was not 'disposed' to give one.[1]

Elizabeth, Grange, Randolph, and Cecil acted out this cautionary tale for Elizabethan governors in 1567, but it was the final act of a process of political disintegration in Scotland which had begun with the marriage of Mary Stuart and Henry, Lord Darnley two years earlier, in 1565. Mary and Darnley were perceived as a threat because the Queen of Scots was a Catholic, and apparently supported by France and the Catholic powers of Europe. During the crisis, John Tamworth, Elizabeth's representative, was instructed in draft to confront the Queen of Scots with a simple argument: Mary and Darnley were in the process of suppressing Protestantism in Scotland because 'the favorors therof' had 'manifestly shewed them selves to favor' the Elizabethan regime, and 'have receaved help and comfort in ther necessitees of us'. The King and Queen of Scots wanted the help of English Catholics 'to practise troobles' in England, 'so as with the aydes that they will hope to have of some Pryncees abrode and from Roome also uppon pretence of reformation of Relligion'. The English clearly believed that the Scottish government wanted to renew its 'auncient leage' with

[1] Cecil to Leicester, 15 May 1567, Magdalene College, Cambridge, PL 2502, fo. 737; Randolph to Leicester, 10 May 1567, National Library of Scotland, Edinburgh, 3657, fo. 32r.

France against England.[2] This was a grimly compelling political interpretation of Mary Stuart's influence on British and European politics, which later allowed Cecil to compare her to a scalpel being used by the Catholic powers to operate on Elizabeth and her kingdom. Darnley only aggravated an existing problem. As the son of the exiled Matthew and Margaret Lennox, he could claim descent back to Henry VII. Elizabethans made the connection. In Cecil's papers there were two pedigrees which traced the royal line from Richard, duke of York to Elizabeth and from Margaret Tudor to Darnley.[3] In 1563 one of John Hales' arguments against Mary Stuart's claim to the English crown was that she was an alien and unable to inherit in England. Darnley did not have that problem.[4]

Most studies of Darnley have concentrated on his 'release' from England into Scotland. Dr Simon Adams interpreted Darnley's journey north as an unusually rash and reckless foreign policy exercise on the part of the English government. Like Dr Mark Loughlin, Dr Adams spotted a failure in the relationship between England and Scotland. Dr Jane Dawson reassessed the Darnley issue as a 'revolution in Anglo-Scottish relations in 1565' which was aggravated and made more embarrassing for the English government by serious trouble in Ireland.[5] This British and Irish context is crucial. The apparent failure of the earl of Sussex as Lord Lieutenant coupled with the support of 'all such as ar devoted to papacy ether in England, Scotland, Irland or els where' panicked the regime.[6] The expulsion of Scots from Ulster and the willingness of Irish political leaders to support Elizabeth and the new Viceroy, Sir Henry Sidney, were central issues.[7] In addition Shane O'Neill, the King of Tyrone who had apparently promised loyalty to Elizabeth three years earlier, established disturbing connections with the Pope and the Queen of Scots. In Scotland the marriage of Darnley and Mary encouraged political instability, and the match profoundly affected the operation of domestic politics in England. It challenged the preferred policy of Elizabeth, based on the proposal of a

---

[2] Drafted by Cecil on 1 August 1565 'but not sent', SP 52/11, fo. 3v.

[3] 15 August 1565, SP 12/37, fos. 11r, 12v, 13r; 19 August 1565, SP 12/37, fos. 17r, 18v, 20r.

[4] Folger Shakespeare Library, Washington, D.C., X.d.19; Jenny Wormald, *Mary Queen of Scots. A study in failure* (London, 1991 edn), pp. 148–9.

[5] Simon Adams, 'The release of Lord Darnley and the failure of the amity', *Innes Review*, 38 (1987), 123–53; Mark Loughlin, 'The career of Maitland of Lethington *c.* 1526–1573', PhD thesis, University of Edinburgh (1991), pp. 180–236; Jane E.A. Dawson, 'Mary Queen of Scots, Lord Darnley, and Anglo-Scottish relations in 1565', *International History Review*, 8 (1986), 1–24; Dawson, 'Two kingdoms or three? Ireland in Anglo-Scottish relations in the middle of the sixteenth century', in Roger A. Mason (ed.), *Scotland and England 1286–1815* (Edinburgh, 1987), pp. 124–5.

[6] Cecil memorandum, 2 June 1565, Cotton Caligula B. 10, fo. 299v.

[7] On Sidney in 1566 and 1567, see Ciaran Brady, *The chief governors. The rise and fall of reform government in Tudor Ireland 1536–1588* (Cambridge, 1994), pp. 113–25.

suitable match for Mary, tried the patience of English diplomats and representatives in Scotland, and pushed the Privy Council to the limits of debate, testing the important but fine line between counsel and political action. Between 1565 and 1567 Mary Stuart triggered a British and Irish political crisis in a European context. Although her own nobility eventually divided itself and shattered Stuart power in Scotland, the Queen of Scots' actions also revealed and tested the weaknesses of the Elizabethan polity in the 1560s.

I

By 1564 Elizabeth had a new proposal with which to settle the dispute between the two British monarchs. A year earlier parliament had put pressure on Elizabeth to solve the problem herself by marrying and settling the form of the English succession. The efforts of the Lords and Commons, offered as compelling counsel, had failed. The Queen had naturally seen the solution elsewhere. In 1562 and 1563 it lay in a meeting between Elizabeth and her cousin; a year later marriage became the new key to unlock the British problem – the marriage of Mary to an English Protestant in order to comprehend and to neutralize her political effect as the single and sovereign power in Scotland. Robert Dudley was Elizabeth's candidate for the match. Once Dudley's noble rank had been made suitably enticing in September 1564, Thomas Randolph and the earl of Bedford were issued with instructions to negotiate the marriage.

But support for the proposal was not as clear or as obvious in Scotland as Dudley's Protestant credentials implied. First, there was a distinct difference between the position of Mary and the relationship between the Privy Council and sympathetic Scottish Protestants. The nature and pattern of Anglo-Scottish court correspondence in the 1560s helps to establish beyond all reasonable doubt that there *was* a British Protestant culture, but the relationship between England and Scotland was in danger precisely because there was a Catholic challenge to Protestantism in Scotland. So support for Dudley as a candidate was not that simple. Bedford and Randolph reported to Elizabeth on 23 November that Moray and Maitland of Lethington were nominal supporters; they praised Dudley's virtues but he was no match for the Queen of Scots 'as onlie Earle of Leicester'. To make matters worse, Bedford and Randolph were told that in offering Dudley as a candidate for marriage 'you offer us ever one man and tayke from us our libertie and choyce'.[8] Once again, the Elizabethan regime felt

---

[8] Cotton Caligula B. 10, fos. 279v–280r, 282r.

the impact of Mary Stuart's presence in Scotland and the bond between a monarch and her personal servants.

So by autumn and early winter 1564 there were two problems facing Anglo-British diplomacy: first, the nature of royal service, which forced Protestants like Moray and Maitland of Lethington to balance service to the crown against the language and practice of religious unity in Britain; and second, developing rumours of Darnley's pretensions after December 1564. Cecil mentioned to Sir Thomas Smith that the earl of Lennox's friends wanted Darnley to marry Mary, and Cecil saw 'some devise to bryng the Quenes Majesty not only to allow therof, but also to move it to the Quene hir sistar'.[9] The idea had been mooted in 1562 and 1563 but it only began to take shape a year later.[10] Nevertheless Elizabeth was absolutely and firmly committed to Dudley's candidacy and 'very desyrooss to have my Lord of Lecester placed in this high degree to be the scottish Quenes husband'. But when it came to conditions 'which ar demanded', Cecil remarked in a telling comment, he saw Elizabeth 'than remiss of hir ernestnes'.[11] There was a large gap between intention and practical reality, and Elizabeth was not prepared to sacrifice the virtues of the first to the difficulties of the second.

Elizabeth seriously underestimated Mary. Diplomatic reports from Scotland were not the problem: intelligence was detailed and accurate and correspondence between a powerful group of councillors, courtiers, and diplomats crossed the border almost daily. Randolph was Elizabeth's permanent representative in Edinburgh, and he was sometimes joined by Throckmorton. Randolph wrote separate letters to the Queen, Cecil, and Leicester; he also kept in regular touch with Maitland of Lethington and the earl of Moray. Letters were passing regularly by courier and they were assessed and assimilated by individual privy councillors. But intelligence was only as good as the use to which it was put, and Elizabeth's privy councillors and diplomats seem to have been under pressure to press the Leicester proposal for all it was worth without being able to counter effectively the rise of Darnley and his influence on Mary and the Scottish court. Personality certainly played a part. Cecil was wary of Elizabeth's commitment to a Dudley–Stuart match; Randolph and Throckmorton were more trusting. Randolph told Leicester on 6 February 1565 to 'tayke yt as resolved' that he would 'travaile the beste I cane to bringe yt to effecte,

---

[9] 30 December 1564, Lansdowne 102, fo. 108r.
[10] Peter Osborne to Sir Thomas Chaloner, 22 February 1562, SP 12/21, fo. 105r–v; see the articles by Thomas Bishop, Margaret Lennox's servant, implicating her in a conspiracy to marry her son to Mary, SP 12/23, fos. 10r–15r; cf. R. Pollitt, 'An "old practizer" at bay: Thomas Bishop and the northern rebellion', *Northern History*, 16 (1980), 59–84.
[11] Cecil to Smith, 30 December 1564, Lansdowne 102, fo. 108r.

whearin god sende me suche prosperus succes'. He had sent an equally positive letter to Elizabeth the day before.[12]

In March 1565 Randolph wrote to Cecil and mentioned the match with Leicester, who 'beinge hym self a protestante sholde easlye inoughe bringe her to be of the same religion, or at the leaste cawse her to deale more moderatlye in those matters then yet she dothe'. He knew that if the marriage did not work out there would be 'inconveniences that maye arryse betwene the two Realmes', especially if Mary tried to re-establish a relationship with either France or Spain.[13] But he was still amazed when, only eleven days later, the proposal died because Leicester apparently no longer wanted to be part of Elizabeth's equation. He told Sir Henry Sidney 'that nowe that I have gotten thys Quenes good will to marrie whear I wolde have her, I cane not gette the man to tayke her, for whome I was sutor'.[14] By May 1565 Darnley was a significant player in Anglo-British politics. But in Randolph's reports in March he was not a prominent figure. Randolph only began to realize that there was something more to the Queen of Scots' attentions than innocent courtly respect in the middle of April. Cecil received the reports directly from Randolph and indirectly from Randolph's letters to Bedford.[15] The Council realized the seriousness of the situation and debated the problem on 1 May 1565. Throckmorton went into Scotland with a briefing from the Council.[16]

The Privy Council meeting on 1 May was the final consultation after a week of intensive Anglo-Scottish debate. The regime had 'playnly discovered' that Mary would 'have' Darnley on 15 April.[17] Maitland of Lethington arrived in London three days later to meet Elizabeth and to try to work with and influence the Privy Council. The similarity with the co-ordinated debate of December 1559 ends there, because Maitland spoke as the secretary of a Catholic Queen flirting with a dangerous marriage, not as the representative of the Protestant congregation. His aim was to secure Elizabeth's permission for the Lennox–Stuart union and obtain parliamentary recognition of Mary's claim to the English throne. The Privy Council met for a 'Consultation' on 23 April and spent a week in 'sundry conferences, long deliberations, & many argumentes'. According to the

---

[12] National Library of Scotland, Edinburgh, 3657, fo. 11v; SP 52/10, fo. 26r–v.

[13] 20 March 1565, Cotton Caligula B. 10, fo. 287r; cf. National Library of Scotland, Edinburgh, 3657, fos. 18r–20r, printed in part by Katharine P. Frescoln (ed.), 'A letter from Thomas Randolph to the earl of Leicester', *Huntington Library Quarterly*, 37 (1973–4), 86–8.

[14] 31 March 1565, National Library of Scotland, Edinburgh, Advocates 1.2.2, fo. 24r.

[15] Randolph to Bedford, 7 April 1565, SP 52/10, fos. 69r–70v; Randolph to Cecil, 15 April 1565, SP 52/10, fos. 75r–76r; Randolph to Cecil, 18 April 1565; SP 52/10, fos. 79r–80r.

[16] For the Council minute, Harley 6990, fos. 68r–69v, and SP 52/10, fos. 91r–92v; for Throckmorton's instructions, 24 April 1565, SP 52/10, fos. 83r–86r, 86v.

[17] CP 140, fos. 1r–2v.

'determination of the Pryve Counsell', Elizabeth found the Lennox–Stuart proposal 'very strang and unlikly on the part aswell of hir Sister as of the parentes of the Lord Darnley and him self being her Majesties subjectes, and so much bound to hir and the Crowne of England as none could be more'. Because of this the matter was passed to her councillors 'to understand their advises in the same'. Cave, Cecil, Clinton, Derby, Howard of Effingham, Knollys, Mason, Norfolk, Pembroke, Petre, Rogers, Sackville, and Winchester – nearly the whole Council – signed the text, but they were trapped by the political situation. The proposed marriage was clearly 'unmete, unprofitable, and directly prejudiciall to the sincere amity betwixt both the Quenes', but it was obvious that Mary would follow her own course; if – and it was an uncertain if – Elizabeth had anything to do with her cousin's decision, she 'shuld do well not taccord therunto' and 'move hir to forbeare from this as a thing playnly prejudiciall to them both'.[18] The Council thought that Mary would be better 'with somme other meter mariadg, being agreable to the honor of God, & to Justice, and convenient to maynteyne the concord & amity alredy begon betwixt the two realmes'. The first draft had 'fructfully begon', but not even diplomatic hyperbole could stretch the facts that far.[19]

This was the substance of Throckmorton's mission north: he could protest and persuade, but there was nothing the regime could effectively do to prevent the marriage from going ahead. Cecil and Bernard Hampton prepared a text which was a restatement of the Council's decision on 1 May. Elizabeth did 'simply mislike' the proposed marriage and found it 'for many just causes unmete to procede any furder as a matter dangerous to the commen amity that is presently betwixt these our two kingdomes'. Throckmorton was instructed to tell Mary that Elizabeth was 'content to permitt to hir a full Liberty that such whose advise she shall please to use, may consider of all the rest of our nobility within our realm or ether where being sortable for that purpose, and excepting the Lord Darnly, we shall be well content with the choyse of any'. This bore the stamp of old and failed policy but it also had an equally disturbing note of desperate pleading. But 'the principall scope' of Throckmorton's 'errand' was 'furst to understand how farr this matter is passed, and next therunto finding it not without hope to breake or to suspend it' and he made absolutely no headway.[20] He was too late to act. Mary was preparing to make Darnley a knight and a baron, and there was a plan to promote him to the ranks of earl of Ross and duke of Albany. The gates of Stirling were locked against Throckmorton and the Queen of Scots was determined to take an equally defensive

---

[18] CP 140, fo. 2r; SP 52/10, fo. 91v; Harley 6990, fo. 68r; Cotton Caligula B. 10, fo. 290r.
[19] For the first draft, see SP 52/10, fo. 92r.
[20] 2 May 1565, SP 52/10, fos. 95r–101v.

diplomatic stand.[21] On 21 May, just over a month after alarm bells had started ringing with Randolph, Throckmorton wrote to tell Leicester that the matter was too far gone to be broken and that the union was indissoluble without violence.[22] He told Cecil on the same day that although the marriage was postponed for three months and Mary had suspended Darnley's elevation to the dukedom, it was 'indissoluble'.[23]

April and May 1565 were depressing months for the Elizabethan regime but its failure to keep Mary and Darnley apart allows historians an intriguing insight into the operation of the Council and its members. For one thing, the earl of Leicester and Cecil were clearly working together. Throckmorton prepared 'A memoryall for my Lord of Leycestre and Master Secretorye', sent it to Cecil, and mentioned the document to Leicester. He wanted it to be passed to Elizabeth through the two councillors.[24] Exactly two years later, Cecil and Leicester co-ordinated their efforts to counsel Elizabeth by letter and in person; this was a similar exercise.[25] Throckmorton briefed Cecil when he returned to London at the beginning of June 1565; Cecil then prepared his own set of notes on 'The perills and troobles that may presently ensue, and in tyme to come follow uppon to the Quenes Majesty and state of this realm' if the marriage between Darnley and Mary went ahead.[26]

Cecil clearly sensed that it was the Protestant state of England that was in danger. Throckmorton's 'memoryall' had suggested practical solutions; Cecil's note on 'The perills and troobles' intellectually underpinned it. If the need for security was Throckmorton's main concern – military preparations in the northern Marches, the observation of potential troublemakers like the earl of Northumberland and Darnley's mother, Margaret Lennox – the reasons for insecurity were Cecil's central themes. According to Cecil, Mary and Darnley had a wide constituency of support. The marriage was supported by 'ther kynred on both sydes and all such as ar devoted to papacy ether in England, Scotland, Irland or els where'.[27] In Ireland the earl of Sussex had been recalled in April 1564 after his disastrous campaigns against Shane O'Neill but more failures meant that policy

---

[21] Throckmorton to Elizabeth, 21 May 1565, Cotton Caligula B. 10, fo. 291r–v.
[22] Magdalene College, Cambridge, PL 2502, fo. 396.
[23] SP 52/10, fo. 128r.
[24] 'A memoryall', 21 May 1565, SP 52/10, fo. 129r; Throckmorton to Leicester, 21 May 1565, Magdalene College, Cambridge, PL 2502, fo. 396.
[25] See below, p. 214.
[26] Throckmorton returned to London on 1 June 1565 and Cecil had definitely heard his news by 3 June, when he mentioned it in a letter to Sir Thomas Smith, Lansdowne 102, fo. 110r; Cecil had written his analysis of 'The perills' the day before, Cotton Caligula B. 10, fos. 299r–300v.
[27] Cotton Caligula B. 10, fo. 299v.

against Shane was in a state of confusion.[28] In England, by the end of 1564, the Council was beginning to realize that the Elizabethan settlement had barely touched Catholic or hostile justices of the peace. The archbishops' and bishops' returns of religiously trustworthy and untrustworthy justices of the peace were shocking: in the words of the Cornish report, a substantial group of magistrates were 'enemies, or at the Leaste, no favoreres of thecclesiasticall policie of this Realme'.[29] The unsettled succession, Darnley's family claim, the religion of Mary, Catholic sedition in England, tension in Ireland, and the influence of the Lorraine and the Guise blended into a seamless and compelling argument for preventing the marriage. Cecil argued that some subjects were 'affected to the Quene of scottes ether for hir self, or for the opinion of hir pretence to the crowne, or for the desyre to have a chaunge of the forme of Relligion in this realme, or for the discontentation they have, of the Quenes Majesty or hir succession'. But whatever their individual affiliations, 'the Generall scope and mark of all ther desyres is and allweise shall be to bryng the Quene of scottes, to have the royall crowne of this realme'.[30]

The second part of Cecil's discussion was meant to deal with 'The remedyes ageynst these perills, first accordyng to the consideration of the Perills and daungers' but it was left blank.[31] The second section was completed two days later, when thirteen councillors – Bacon, Bedford, Cave, Cecil, Clinton, Derby, Howard of Effingham, Knollys, Leicester, Mason, Petre, Rogers, and Winchester – met to discuss the crisis in a 'Generall Consultation and advise gyven by the Prive Counsell'.[32] Structured around Cecil's notes from 2 June, this was counsel with a strong purpose: to emphasize the dangerous position the regime was in.[33] Not only were the Council's sentiments 'consented by all persons, as a thyng of most moment and efficacy to remedy all these perills' – after Cecil's crucial corrections to the text the proposed solution was 'thought necessary by all persons, as the only thyng of most moment and efficacy to remedy all these perills and manny others'. It proceeded from the Privy Council's desire to 'advise and Counsell'.[34] But this was also policy thought out and debated holistically: not separated into boxes like domestic, ecclesiastical, or

---

[28] Brady, *Chief governors*, pp. 106, 110–11.
[29] CP 235, fo. 70av.
[30] Cotton Caligula B. 10, fo. 299r–v.
[31] Cotton Caligula B. 10, fo. 300v.
[32] For Cecil's original minutes, see SP 52/10, fos. 148r–151v; for Bernard Hampton's copy, corrected by Cecil, see Cotton Caligula B. 10, fos. 301r–308r, 308v.
[33] For the precise textual relationship between Cecil's notes on 2 June and the Council minutes of 4 June, see Stephen Alford, 'William Cecil and the British succession crisis of the 1560s', PhD thesis, University of St Andrews (1997), pp. 150–1.
[34] SP 52/10, fo. 149r–v.

foreign, but a comprehensive analysis of 'what perills might insew to the Quenes Majesty or this realme of the mariadg betwixt the Quene of scottes and the Lord Darly' and a set of recommendations 'mete to be doone to avoyde or remedy the same'. Cecil and his colleagues reduced the dangers facing the regime 'into onely twoo'. First, because Elizabeth was unmarried, a 'grete nombre' in England might 'be alienated in ther myndes from ther naturall duetyes' to the Queen. The marriage between Mary and Darnley could act as 'a meane to stablish the succession of both the Crownes in the issew of the same mariadg'. Second, Catholic support for the marriage meant that religious enemies would 'for furderance of ther faction in Relligion, devise all meanes and practisees that cold be within this realme to disturbe the estate of the Quenes Majesty and the peace of the realme'.[35]

So the marriage meant not only the threat of a Stuart succession after Elizabeth's death: it was part of the Queen of Scots' campaign 'to occupy the Quenes estate', reinforced by the 'furderyng of the relligion of Rome within this realme'. This had been Mary's intention, from the days when she had tried 'to impeche and dispossess the Quenes Majesty first wryting and publishyng hir self in all contrees Quene of england'. But there was more supporting evidence. Only providence and Elizabeth's 'contrary power' had prevented a military assault prepared in 'forren contrees' after the 'shamfull peace' made between France and Spain. And, although Mary's commissioners had negotiated the 'accord' at Edinburgh, she had still not ratified the Treaty.[36] By marrying Darnley, the Queen of Scots would harness the support of 'the faction of the papistes and other discontented persons' in England and 'have a portion of our owne power to serve'. Cecil and the Council predicted support for the marriage: 'in every cornar of the realm the faction that most favoreth the scottish title is growen stowt and bold'. Like Throckmorton, the Council argued that there were supporters of the Stuart option 'in this Court, both in hall & chambre'. Without action, this group would 'shortly increass and grow so great and dangerooss, as the redress therof wold be almost desperat'. This was the significance of the failure of the regime to penetrate and reform the commissions of the peace; the Council 'remembred how of late in perusing of the substance of the Justicees of the Peace in all the Countyes of the realme, scantly a thyrd part was found fully assured to be trusted in the matter of relligion'. This was the 'only stryng' upon which Mary's title 'doth hang'.[37]

The Privy Council's response was a comprehensive plan of action. The

---

[35] SP 52/10, fo. 148r.   [36] SP 52/10, fo. 148v.
[37] SP 52/10, fo. 149r; for Throckmorton's 'memoriall', see Cotton Caligula B. 10, fo. 297v.

solutions were grouped 'by some into three heades'. The first was Elizabeth's marriage, the only sufficient solution, accompanied by 'an ernest and
unfayned desyre and sute with all humbleness by prayer to Almighty God,
and advise and Counselles'. The second, very clearly, was 'to avaunce,
stablish, and fortefy in dede the profession of relligion in scotland and in
England, and to demynish, weaken, and feble the contrary'. Only the third
proposed course of action tackled Mary and Darnley directly: 'sondry
thynges ether to disappoynt and break this entended mariadg' or take the
sting out of the union.[38] Both 'truth and pollycy wer joyned togither' by
religion and its preservation was crucial. There had been a rumour that the
bishops, by Elizabeth's commandment, had dealt 'straightly' with 'some
persons of good relligion' because 'they had forboren to weare certen
apparrell & such lyke'; this had strengthened the Catholic 'faction' in
England and Scotland. But Elizabeth's intention had been 'only to maynteane an uniformyte aswell in thynges externall, as in the substance'.[39]
Other problems had weakened the polity. The 'quondam Bishoppes and
others' who had refused 'to acknoledg the Quenes majesties power over
them accordyng to the law' needed to be returned to prison. Bishops
complained that they 'dare not execute the ecclesiasticall lawes to the
furderance of relligion' because of threats by judges and lawyers 'not best
affected in relligion'. Lewd, seditious, and unlawful books in English were
coming in from abroad and were particularly popular in the north of
England, written against the Queen's authority and 'mayntening a forreyn
power'. Scottish monks and friars were serving as curates in English
churches, especially in the north, and men with 'ecclesiasticall lyvinges' in
the kingdom were abroad 'and from thence maynteane sedition in the
realme'.[40]

This was a polity in crisis: unable (at least according to the Council) to
maintain religious discipline and uniformity, aware of the extremely weak
link between the centre of power and the counties, and conscious of a
'faction' of pro-Stuart conservatives encouraged by the political strength of
the Queen of Scots and the inability of the Elizabethan regime to impose
ecclesiastical uniformity, and actively propagandized by foreign Catholic
powers. Europe was polarized; Spain and France had clearly conspired
against Elizabeth; and Mary was strongly supported in England (especially
the north) and Ireland and at court. Even the judges, 'having no small
authorite in this realm, in Governance of all partes of the realm', were a
weak link: the Council argued that they 'might' be sworn 'to the Quenes
majesty' – the clear implication was that their allegiance was uncertain,
nearly seven years after Mary Tudor had died. The execution of justice and

---

[38] SP 52/10, fo. 149v.   [39] SP 52/10, fo. 150r.   [40] SP 52/10, fo. 150v.

the ecclesiastical state of the realm were British issues. They complemented planned military preparations at Berwick, on the northern frontiers, the appointment of a lieutenant-general in the north, and nomination of a new Viceroy for Ireland after the failures of the earl of Sussex, Sir Nicholas Arnold, and Sir Thomas Cusake.[41]

II

Ecclesiastical and political stability and British security were the key themes of the Privy Council's meeting in early June and, eight days after the session, Cecil restated the arguments to Smith in France. The marriage in Scotland was a 'rash intention' which was dangerous 'principally for twoo respectes, for hurt of relligion and for fortefyeng of the Quene of Scottes title to this Crowne'.[42] Nevertheless, over the next couple of months the regime acted to secure the north of England and Ireland. At the end of July Cecil wrote to the earl of Shrewsbury on behalf of the Queen with a commission 'to be hir Lieutenant Generall in yorkshyre'.[43] In early July Sir Henry Sidney, the new Viceroy, was briefed by Cecil in a set of 'pryvat instructions'. Wide discretionary powers were 'gyven by the Quenes Majesty . . . to be used and communicated by hym with such of hir Majesties Counsell in Irland as he shall thynk mete'.[44] As the regime's troubleshooter in Ireland, Sidney had a massive responsibility to stabilize the political and military situation in the country.

The English Privy Council discussed Sidney's appointment on 4 June, but a day earlier Cecil had told Smith in France that 'Sir Henry sydney shall be Lord deputy in Irland'. Smith also received an analysis of the local political situation. Shane O'Neill had captured James MacDonnell, his brother Sorley Boy, and some English soldiers. Cecil explained that unless Elizabeth 'may have the possession of theis prisonors, it shall be proffitable; otherwise Shanes victory will be daungerooss for Irland'. By early summer 1565 O'Neill controlled the north of Ireland; he was able to extend his power south of Ulster and he was a danger to the government in Dublin.[45] The issue was this: would Shane 'convert his service therin to the contentation of hir Majesty by expelling of the scottes [from Ulster], and restoryng the Contrees possessed by them, to the trew ownors hir Majesties subjectes, or will otherwise, seke to reteyn the possession therof to his owne use'? In the handling of this, Sidney had to use his own skills. The central danger was

---

[41] SP 52/10, fo. 151r–v.
[42] 12 June 1565, Lansdowne 102, fo. 112r.
[43] 30 July 1565, Lambeth Palace Library, 3196, fo. 149.
[44] SP 63/14, fos. 44r–47v.
[45] Cecil to Smith, 3 June 1565, Lansdowne 102, fo. 110v; Dawson, 'Ireland', p. 125.

that Shane O'Neill would threaten English government in Ireland and make an extremely dangerous strategic connection with the Queen of Scots; in this it was important not to provoke him into forgetting 'his naturall duety and seke help owt of Scotland'.[46]

But Scotland itself was beginning to fragment. Thomas Randolph told Cecil in early July 1565 that it was a 'verie harde case'. The issues were the 'overthrowe of Religion and breache of Amytie'. At court, Darnley's behaviour was 'so strange'. Mary and her future husband kept to their own chambers, joined by a secret passage.[47] The earls of Moray, Argyle, Morton, and Glencairn met at Perth at the end of June and there were rumours on 4 July that they planned to seize the Queen of Scots and Darnley. According to Randolph's account, the earls 'do see their Sovereigne determened to overthrowe Religion' and they were equally keen to protect the amity between the two realms.[48] On 16 July 1565 Randolph reported Mary's and Darnley's marriage ceremony, conducted 'secretlie in her owne Palace' exactly a week before.[49] The Queen's opponents signed 'the band of the nobilitie' at Stirling on 19 July.[50] It was a strange reversal of Anglo-British politics: in late 1564 Moray and Maitland of Lethington had rejected Leicester as a suitable candidate for their mistress; less than a year later, Moray wrote to the earl of Bedford to discuss 'the intertenement of ane mutual amyte' between England and Scotland.[51] Mary's opponents once again became, in the words of the introduction to the Stirling band, the 'proffessors of godes word'.[52] This was a language of politics in Scotland which had not been heard since 1561: the preservation of the kingdom and its estates and the protection of 'the Innocentes, professoris of the gospell' against the 'poweris of the warld'.[53]

The Elizabethan regime concentrated all the diplomatic resources it had on controlling the situation. Randolph was already in place, and he was joined by Bedford on or just before 21 July 1565. Francis Walsingham's brother-in-law, John Tamworth, arrived in Scotland in August with instructions to meet Randolph and the Queen of Scots, deliver Elizabeth's letters, and explain how Mary's 'procedinges now of late' were 'very straung, not onely in hir actions towardes hir owne subjectes, but also towardes us'. Tamworth's mission was an expression of profound irritation: in a second

---

[46] SP 63/14, fos. 44v–45r.
[47] 7 July 1565, SP 52/10, fo. 172r; Randolph to Cecil, 2 July 1565, Cotton Caligula B. 10, fo. 312v.
[48] Randolph to Cecil, 4 July 1565, Cotton Caligula B. 10, fo. 316r; Randolph to Cecil, 4 July 1565, SP 52/10, fo. 318r.
[49] Randolph to Elizabeth, SP 52/10, fo. 180r.
[50] Lansdowne 8, fos. 91r–92r.
[51] 22 July 1565, Cotton Caligula B. 10, fo. 337r.
[52] Lansdowne 8, fo. 91r. [53] Cotton Caligula B. 10, fo. 337r.

set of instructions, 'but not sent', Mary was told that 'she knew very well wherin our offence did rest'. In her 'actions and procedinges' the Queen of Scots was 'counselled and advised to follow that waye, that is most lykly to dissolve the amyty betwixt us and hir'.[54] The earl of Bedford reported in mid-August that Mary 'getteth as many to her Masse, and never was there so many as now there were at it on Sondaye last', which was the twelfth. He had told the earl of Glencairn that 'I thought Religion there was quite overthrowen, excepte it were now holpen'.[55] The day after Bedford's letter, John Knox gave a sermon at Edinburgh for which he was 'inhibite preaching for a season'. In the introduction to the printed edition he explained how at 'that sermon were auditours unto me not onely professors of the truth and such as favor me, but rancke papistes, dissembled Hipocrites, & no small number of covetous clawbaks of the new court'. The title page bore a text from the First Letter to Timothy: 'The time is come that men can not abyde the Sermon of veritie nor holsome doctrine.'[56]

Criticisms by Knox were one thing – and he had, after all, consistently opposed the 'courtiers' who had argued that Mary's 'subjectis mycht not lauchfullie tack hir Messe frome hir' since her return to Scotland in 1561[57] – but political polarization was a more important and serious issue. At the end of August 1565 Cecil told Smith that 'troobles arrise . . . betwixt hir [Mary] and the Erle of Murraye and others being frendly to the comen amyty of both the realmes'. The Queen of Scots had sent for Moray but 'the mistrust is so farr entred on both sydes, that I thynk it will fall to an evill end'. By September Cecil thought that Mary had 'much less nombre of hertes [i.e., hearts] than hir subjectes'.[58] His fears were confirmed nine days later when the Queen of Scots and 'henry King of Scottis hir husband' issued a proclamation at St Andrews.[59] But Randolph in Edinburgh still suggested that there was a positive side to the problem: although he thought that without help the sympathetic Scottish nobility would be 'undone', Elizabeth had supporters in the kingdom.[60]

---

[54] For Tamworth's instructions, SP 52/10, fo. 201r; for the text 'not sent', drafted by Cecil, SP 52/11, fos. 1r–4v.
[55] Bedford to Cecil, 18 August, Cotton Caligula B. 10, fos. 344r–345r.
[56] John Knox, *A sermon preached by John Knox minister of Christ Jesus in the publique audience of the church of Edenbrough* . . . (STC 15075; n.p., 1566), sig. A4v.
[57] *The works of John Knox*, ed. David Laing, 6 vols. (Wodrow Society; Edinburgh, 1846–64), II, p. 291.
[58] Cecil to Smith, 21 August, Lansdowne 102, fo. 114r–v; Cecil to Smith, 1 September 1565, Lansdowne 102, fo. 117r.
[59] Annie I. Cameron (ed.), *The Warrender papers*, 2 vols. (Publications of the Scottish History Society, third series, 18–19; Edinburgh, 1931–2), I, pp. 44–5.
[60] Randolph to Leicester, 19 September 1565, National Library of Scotland, Edinburgh, Advocates 1.2.2, fo. 27r.

So what could or would the regime do? By September 1565 Cecil thought that there was a powerful domestic opposition to Mary; Randolph was sending out the same sort of signals to the earl of Leicester and Elizabeth. The Queen of Scots' relationship to England was developing into sharper focus: she was openly parading her Catholicism in Edinburgh, dividing the political elite in Scotland, and marginalizing the men most sympathetic to Protestant amity. Mary had treated Tamworth badly, and seemed absolutely set on dissolving the last elements of an Anglo-Scottish 'amity' which had long ceased to work as effective policy. She was also responsible for funding Shane O'Neill's campaign against the regime in Ireland. These facts were clear enough to Elizabeth and the Privy Council in autumn 1565. Policy was a more difficult issue: was the regime prepared to translate its irritation into military action? The answer lies somewhere in between the two extremes of inaction and invasion. In September 1565 the Privy Council debated a military option for England which would put an end, once and for all, to Mary's pretensions to the succession and to Elizabeth's crown, the dangers of a fragmented Scotland, the subversion of English policy in Ireland, and Stuart links with the Catholic powers of Europe. As part of this consultation exercise, the Council used an unlikely expert to help them to discuss the implications of a second Elizabethan expedition into Scotland.

Edmund Guest, bishop of Rochester from 1560 and Elizabeth's Chief Almoner until 1572, answered 'a Question demanded uppon the matter of Scotland' which Cecil endorsed 'Pro defensione Relligionis' in September 1565.[61] Guest was an odd choice for the commission but in some ways his clerical career paralleled Cecil's administrative rise to the principal secretaryship. He began his university studies at King's College, Cambridge in 1536 and became part of the Athenian group; four years after graduating MA in 1544, he dedicated *A treatise against the privy mass* to Cecil's first brother-in-law, John Cheke. Like Cecil he remained in England between 1555 and 1558; in 1559 he became the domestic chaplain to the household of Cecil's friend and correspondent, Matthew Parker. Guest conformed to the Elizabethan settlement: he took part in the disputation of March 1559, preached at Paul's Cross at Easter 1565, and wrote a manuscript contribution to the vestiarian controversy (perhaps the text of the sermon) which supported the regime's position.[62] He was not a Knox or a Buchanan; in his Marian career he did not even mirror his radical predecessor at Rochester, John Ponet. And yet the four points of Guest's 'Pro defensione Relligionis'

---

[61] Lansdowne 8, fos. 83r, 84r–85v; for a later, flawed copy, see Cotton Caligula B. 10, fos. 362r–365r.

[62] December 1564, Lansdowne 7, fos. 220r–224r, 225v.

are reminiscent of the arguments and the substance of *A shorte treatise of politike power.*

Guest's 'Pro defensione Relligionis' was part of an intensive period of Privy Council debate which, like so many important meetings in the 1560s, has to be reconstructed from Cecil's notes and minutes. Fourteen councillors met at Westminster on 24, 26, and 29 September 1565,[63] and Guest's text fits into some of Cecil's brief jottings on 28 and 29 September: 'To amass an army, to put them in redyness with spede so as they may be uppon the frontyre at the tyme of the Treaty'.[64] So 'Pro defensione Relligionis' was the justification for a military enforcement of a proposed treaty, based on a ratification of the Treaty of Edinburgh.[65] But the moral justifications for an armed response were crucial: in a private 'Consideration of the whole cause of Scotland', Cecil explored the civil thesis 'In what sort shall the Quenes Majesty redress the Injuryes'? The options progressively revealed themselves. 'If by warr, what thynges ar to be thought of befor the warr be taken?' First, it had to be 'a Just quarrell'.[66] By working through the problem *in utramque partem*, Cecil considered every angle. But war, first and foremost, had to be justified to God and to a reluctant Queen.

Guest's thesis rested on four arguments: first, that every prince 'ought to defende Christis religion', 'not onely in his owne countrye, but also in the next by him'; second, that 'every prince maye fight with an other prince that oppresseth godds religion'; third, that 'everye prince may fight against those princes wich Labour to overthrowe goddes religion'; and fourth, 'If inferioure magistrates maye fight against there prince for the defence of goddes religion . . . Therfore mich more one prince maye fight against an other prince for the defence of goddes religion.' So for Guest, Elizabeth could exercise *jus gladii*, the 'right of the sword': he accepted St Paul's argument that the prince should punish 'idolatrye & all wronge', and argued from the example of King Antiochus that a prince had a duty above and beyond the rights of inferior magistrates. John Ponet had used the same text to demonstrate his point in a chapter 'wether it be laufull to depose an evil governour, and kill a tyranne'. This was not quite Christopher Goodman's principle of 'doing the contrary' – interpreting commands phrased in a negative way as positive injunctions to act – but it does suggest that Guest was prepared to use a tradition of justified political opposition which had developed from Justinian's Code, through twelfth-century legal debate,

---

[63] Cotton Caligula B. 10, fo. 358r; the councillors were Arundel, Bacon, Cecil, Clinton, Howard of Effingham, Knollys, Leicester, Norfolk, Northampton, Pembroke, Petre, Rogers, Sackville, and Winchester.
[64] SP 52/11, fo. 105v.
[65] SP 52/11, fo. 105r.
[66] Cotton Caligula B. 10, fo. 350v.

Lutheran theology, and Protestant thought in the 1550s, and apply it to Elizabethan England. And given the state of Scotland in 1565 and the reports of Mary's 'idolatry', Guest's argument was compelling.[67]

For its part, the Privy Council worked through the evidence and tried, first, to establish the pattern of England's relationship with Scotland between 1564 and 1565 and, second, to propose policy. At the beginning of the meeting on 24 September 1565 Cecil 'declared at length all the procedinges from the first of Aprill past untill this present'. He had prepared two chronologies of Anglo-Scottish relations between June 1564 and September 1565:[68] from 'The principall Poyntes to be remembred and Considered in the matter of Scotland', prepared on the twenty-fourth, the Council would have heard a catalogue of Scottish and Anglo-British failure – how Moray had left the court on 7 April to 'avoyde the superstitiooss ceremonyes of that Quene in relligion', how the Darnley marriage meant the 'ruyn of that Contree', and how religion, mistrust, and military preparation threatened to throw Scotland into civil conflict.[69] The Council was determined to respond to the practical implications of the situation in Scotland and after Cecil read his chronology on 24 September it discussed the 'heades' of the issue; the 'determination' was continued two days later.[70] On 28 September the Council dealt with preparations for war: a letter to Randolph, the appointment of commissioners to meet Mary's representatives at the border, and the construction of an army. On the twenty-ninth it discussed the 'Matters to chardg the Quene of Scottes', which included 'a nombre of injuryes dayly doone' to English subjects, Mary's marriage without Elizabeth's consent, and the Queen of Scots' contact with Shane O'Neill in Ireland.[71]

But these were responses to a more fundamental crisis in British affairs. Although the Council's debates and discussions help to plot the development of England's reaction to the events in Scotland in September 1565, only Cecil's 'Consideration of the whole cause of Scotland' tried to work

---

[67] Lansdowne 8, fos. 84r–85v; John Ponet, *A shorte treatise of politike power, and of the true obedience which subjectes owe to kynges and other civile governours, with an exhortacion to all true naturall Englishe men* . . . (STC 20178; Strasburg, 1556), sig. H6v. On Goodman and the political background to resistance, see Jane E.A. Dawson, 'Resistance and revolution in sixteenth-century thought: the case of Christopher Goodman', in J. Van den Berg and P.G. Hoftijzer (eds.), *Church, change and revolution. Transactions of the fourth Anglo-Dutch church history colloquium* (Publications of the Sir Thomas Browne Institute, new series, 12; Leiden, 1991), pp. 70–1; and Quentin Skinner, *The foundations of modern political thought*, 2 vols. (Cambridge, 1978), II, pp. 127–8, 195–6, 204.

[68] Cotton Caligula B. 10, fo. 358r; for the chronology of 4 June 1564–13 September 1565, CP 140, fos. 1r–2v; for the chronology covering 18 November 1564–19 September 1565, Cotton Caligula B. 10, fos. 354r–357v.

[69] Cotton Caligula B. 10, fos. 354v, 355r; CP 140, fo. 2r–v.

[70] Cotton Caligula B. 10, fo. 358r.

[71] SP 52/11, fo. 105r–v.

through 'The state of the Controversy' and the arguments *pro* and *contra* intervention.[72] Structurally and rhetorically, it is a fascinating memorandum in which Cecil systematically dealt with the issues and reworked his private arguments. The 'Cause and matter', clearly, were for 'relligion' and 'title to the Crown, presently or to come'. Cecil may or may not have read Guest's 'Pro defensione Relligionis' by 24 September, but he still realized that England was treading on extremely sensitive ground: 'for Relligion, it is very doutfull, how to medle therin in an other Princes Contry'. This had been an issue in 1559 and 1560 but at best a theoretical one because Mary was out of her kingdom. The 'title' was a different issue: 'consideryng it is styrred upp by a forayn prince, who will never be quiet therin, without some satisfaction', the best counter to Mary's pretensions would be Elizabeth's marriage, so that the Queen of Scots 'beholdyng the state of this Crown to depend only uppon the breath of on[e] person our sovereign Lady, wold be so uncertayn in ther devisees having hope of issew of hir Majesties mariage'.[73] This was the core issue: a British crisis triggered by Elizabeth's refusal to marry, set in a European context, and put into perspective by the Queen of Scots' connections with Ireland.

Cecil's 'Reasons to mak warr' or to aid Mary's opponents were ideologically and practically convincing but the issue which stood as 'The Greatest matter justly to provok the Quenes Majesty' was Shane O'Neill and his communication with the Pope and the Queen of Scots. Back in July 1565 the Council realized that O'Neill could have jumped one of two ways: either used his forces to put pressure on the English pale and the government in Dublin, or made peace with Elizabeth. On 24 and 26 September the councillors heard that he had chosen the first option, and how Mary 'had receaved shan Oneyle into hir protection', with O'Neill intending 'to proclayme the Quene of Scottes Quene of Irland etc'. One of the 'Matters to chardg the Quene of Scottes' discussed on 29 September was 'The receaving of messadges out of Irland from shan Oneyle'. In fact, this issue – military pressure on the regime in Ireland and the discussion of a campaign in Scotland – was so serious that it became the sixth of Cecil's nine 'Causees to move me not to consent presently to warr'. 'The matters of Irland requyre presently to be seene to, for if the warr shuld be in scotland, it is sure that Irland will not be free.' This was a threat of war in three kingdoms and it dissuaded the Council from turning defensive preparations into an offensive campaign. This strategic situation also became the justification for the policy on Ireland adopted by the regime in 1567: 'a just

---

[72] Cotton Caligula B. 10, fos. 350v–353r; see above, pp. 18–19.
[73] Cotton Caligula B. 10, fo. 350v.

army' and 'some nombre of well ordrid people to plant in those parts of the northe'.[74]

Failure in Scotland was just as dangerous. One of the 'Reasons to mak warr' or 'ayde with force the Lords of scotland' was that if Moray and his allies, in a cause 'so joyned with the Quenes Majesty', were overthrown it would mean the alteration of 'relligion'. There would be a renewal of the alliance with France, followed by 'troobles in England, by practise to chang relligion here'. If Mary was not 'reduced by force to lyve quyetly and in amyty' she would 'never cess to be a trooblesom neighbor, ether by force, or by practisees consideryng she pretendeth title to this Crowne'. War was justified (*justum*), necessary (*necessarium*), and possible (*possibile*).[75] But the argument *contra* was just as solid: Elizabeth 'ought not first to judg ageynst the soverayn for the subject without dew hearyng of both partes'. That 'Pryncess must doo as they wold be doone unto' was a general principle; more ideologically, Mary could 'have ayde of monny from the pope, and hir unclees, wherwith she may be strongar in scotland than ever any hir progenitors'. The influence of Spain (working through Ireland) and France ('by releasing all titles of Calliss') were strong reasons to reconsider intervention. The 'meane waye' struck a balance between the two. This policy included military preparations, 'comefort' for the Scottish lords 'to stand upon ther gard', and a diplomatic mission to 'advertise the french kyng, and spanish of the Quenes Majesties intention to be none but to procure accord and peace in scotland'.[76]

The risk of British, Irish, and European war was too great, even after Guest had outlined the moral justifications and the Council had worked through both political options and practical responses. For Cecil there were nine 'Causees to move me not to consent presently to warr'; the eighth, significantly, was 'The lack of disposition in the Quenes Majesty to allow of warr, or of the charges therof', especially after Newhaven. 1562 and 1563 had burned her fingers and she was unwilling to spend money or set a precedent. This was one limitation but there were others: the 'uncertenty of the matters' charged against Mary, the dangerous example of setting subjects against their prince, the 'uncertenty of the warr once entred', cost, danger in Ireland, and the potential for subversion in England.[77] The issue had been easier for the Privy Council to deal with in 1559 and 1560, with

---

[74] Cotton Caligula B. 10, fo. 352r; 24 and 26 September 1565, Cotton Caligula B. 10, fo. 359v; 29 September 1565, SP 52/11, fo. 105r; Dawson, 'Ireland', p. 125. On O'Neill, military preparations, and the plantations, see Tomás Ó Laidhin (ed.), *Sidney state papers 1565–70* (Irish Manuscripts Commission; Dublin, 1962), pp. 47–8.

[75] Cotton Caligula B. 10, fo. 351v.

[76] Cotton Caligula B. 10, fo. 352r–v.

[77] Cotton Caligula B. 10, fo. 353r; Wallace T. MacCaffrey, 'The Newhaven expedition, 1562–1563', *Historical Journal*, 40 (1997), 1–21.

Mary in France, but it had still caused problems for Elizabeth. Then Cecil had been able to blend the practical benefits of a preemptive military strike and natural law to help a Protestant nobility stand against an absentee monarch.[78] But the lines were more blurred in 1565, especially at a point in the decade when rumours of the Bayonne conference and organized Catholic conspiracy started to appear in diplomatic reports.[79]

The Privy Council's debates in September 1565 determined the shape of England's relationship with Scotland and Ireland, even if the regime was not prepared to go to war. This, according to one Wyllyam Reed, writing to Lord Wharton on 5 October 1565, was still an open question.[80] Three days later Cecil told the earl of Shrewsbury that 'it is ment by hir Majesty to kepe peace with scotland, and not to make warr but whan she shall be provoked by invasion'. But although it was an approach to which 'all Counsellors here ar inclyning', Cecil admitted that 'ruyne' of the Protestant lords 'our frendes in scotland' would 'hynder the intelligence and amyty betwixt the realmes'. Still, in the ideologically polarized Europe of the 1560s there was 'no suerty to enter into warr without just cause'.[81] Protestant military action by the Elizabethan regime was too dangerous; but if 1565 proved anything at all it was that English policy was debated and executed in a British context and in a European arena.

III

During the meetings of the Privy Council on 28 and 29 September Cecil minuted the need to write to Thomas Randolph and to consider a 'treaty' between Elizabeth and Mary. He wrote Randolph's instructions right at the end of the month.[82] The draft for the mission outlined the text of a political settlement for Scotland. But the diplomatic thrust of the regime's stand on the government of the Queen of Scots and her unhealthy relationship with large sections of her nobility had something more to say about the diplomatic position England was in at the end of 1565. Part of Randolph's mission included a discussion of the way in which 'the sayd Quene may best be counselled, to accept hir Nobilite into hir grace, and in what manner assurance may be made to them, that they may lyve in obedyence and enjoye the liberty which they had before the mariadg'.[83] But Randolph was expected to discuss these issues with Malvesyr, the French representa-

---

[78] See above, pp. 67–8.
[79] Malcolm R. Thorp, 'Catholic conspiracy in early Elizabethan foreign policy', *Sixteenth Century Journal*, 15 (1984), 432, 442.
[80] Lambeth Palace Library, 3196, fo. 169.
[81] 8 October 1565, Lambeth Palace Library, 3196, fo. 187.
[82] SP 52/11, fo. 105v; for Randolph's instructions, SP 52/11, fos. 112r–113v.
[83] SP 52/11, fo. 112v.

tive who had been at Windsor at the end of August 1565 for ten days.[84] Under the watchful eye of the French, the proposal carried by Randolph called for 'a Generall & free pardon' (supervised by the English and French monarchs), a restoration of offices, no innovations in religion, and the observation of the law, all 'conteyned in one proclamation and duely warranted by the Quene and hir husband, and subscribed by all hir Counsell, and sworne by them all, and published'.[85]

But England was less in control of the diplomatic and political situation in autumn 1565 than the bullying tone of Randolph's message suggests. Cecil and the Privy Council were in an extremely difficult position: their interest in Scotland was Protestant and it was centred on the earl of Moray; but when England was under close investigation by the Catholic powers of Europe – especially the French, with their traditional concern (in Elizabethan eyes at least) for Mary Stuart – the regime had to offer an olive branch to the Queen of Scots and soothe the Protestant lords with fair words. This was not a problem for a Queen who did not like ideological declarations of policy (especially when they cost money), but the sensitivity of the issue for Cecil reveals itself in his letter to Shrewsbury on 5 October. When the earl of Moray travelled into England later in the month, Randolph reported from Edinburgh that 'ther is greate dyspleasure taken here that the noble men are receaved in Englande, and myche more dowted then is spoken of for their supporte'.[86] One of Cecil's diplomatic drafts for Robert Melville, the representative of the Queen of Scots' opponents, was not given to him; but it would have committed England to negotiating an 'accord' between Mary and 'the sayd Lordes in all ther reasonable causees'.[87] Cecil's final version explained the need for a just cause before war against Mary; nevertheless, it assured the lords 'that nothyng hath happened to hir [Elizabeth], sence hir comming to hir Crowne, more grevooss than to understand the estate of the same Lordes, to be so daungerooss as it is reported'.[88] On 23 October, in contrast, Elizabeth 'spake very roundly' to a Moray on his knees before the Queen, the Privy Council, and Malvesyr. The earl defended his stand. For the benefit of the French – and perhaps herself – Elizabeth argued the orthodox line 'that what soever, the world sayd or reported of hir, she wold by hir actions lett it appeare, she wold not to be a prince of a world, mayntean any subject in any disobedienc[e] ageynst the Prince'. It was an offence both to her conscience and to God.[89]

---

[84] CP 140, fo. 2v; Cotton Caligula B. 10, fo. 357v.   [85] SP 52/11, fos. 112v–113v.
[86] Randolph to Cecil, 24 October 1565, Egerton 1818, fo. 35r.
[87] Drafted by Cecil on 30 September 1565, SP 52/11, fo. 111r.
[88] Drafted by Cecil on 1 October 1565, SP 52/11, fo. 114r.
[89] SP 52/11, fo. 153r–v.

So was this hypocrisy or a fundamental crisis of policy? Guest turned upside down or the triumph of a moderate and careful diplomacy in an unavoidably awkward situation? The politics of 1564 and 1565 were difficult. The plan to unite Mary and Dudley was probably badly thought out by Elizabeth and certainly poorly executed. It also rested on the principle of peace and political settlement through dynastic union. 1564 foreshadowed Norfolk's proposal to marry Mary in 1569. The only difference between the two plans was that the first was supported by Elizabeth and the second did not have her permission; they were not different strategies.[90] Anglo-British diplomacy did not end in October 1565: Sir Walter Mildmay and Lord Lumley were instructed to visit the Queen of Scots in November 1565 in an effort to 'restablish a perfect amity and accord' between the two British monarchs, Moray still tried to canvass support in England, and Randolph continued to send reports south until June 1566.[91] But between 1566 and 1568 the relationship between England, Scotland, and Ireland fell into a predictable pattern. In Scotland Protestant and noble opposition to Mary Stuart focused on the murders of David Rizzio in March 1566 and Darnley in February 1567; and, as a consequence, appeals to Elizabeth to arbitrate between the parties of Moray and Mary, made more difficult by issues of justice, the right of a prince to support subjects against their monarch, and the keen interest of the Catholic powers of Europe.

Ireland was just as unstable as Scotland. Shane O'Neill's contact with the Scottish court became at least one of the reasons for the provocative strategy of coercion and plantation offered by the regime in 1566. In March 1566 Cecil told Sir Thomas Smith that 'we have cause to feare that Oneyles boldnes is fedd out of Scotland'. Sidney had to deal with the country 'for he hath found all out of joynt ther'.[92] A month later he changed his metaphor: Ireland was 'out of Tune', and vicechamberlain Sir Francis Knollys was sent over 'to conferr with the Deputy'.[93] After years of military failure and the shock of an alliance between O'Neill and the Queen of Scots security was a major concern in Ireland, even without physical intervention in Scotland. In July 1565 Shane had seemed capable of conformity to the regime. Less than a year later, he was purely a 'pernitious rebell' to be 'rooted out or chastisid'.[94] Knollys' visit was part of 'this intended enterprise' for Ulster. After 'debat' with Elizabeth on 24

---

[90] See below, pp. 199–203.
[91] For Mildmay's and Lumley's instructions, Cotton Caligula B. 10, fo. 367r; Moray to Cecil, 15 January 1566, Cotton Caligula B. 10, fo. 383r–v; Bedford and Randolph to Leicester and Cecil, 27 March 1566, Cotton Caligula B. 10, fo. 393r.
[92] 26 March 1566, Lansdowne 102, fo. 132v.
[93] Cecil to Smith, 11 April 1566, Harley 6990, fo. 72r.
[94] Elizabeth to Sir Henry Sidney, 28 March 1566, Ó Laidhin (ed.), *Sidney state papers*, p. 18.

June 1566 – and Sidney's reports to London – the regime began to mobilize defensive forces in Berwick and Bristol, and on the Isle of Man.[95]

These policies and preparations were not decided or executed in a vacuum: they were part of an Anglo-British strategy – reactive perhaps and ultimately ineffective, but conscious nevertheless of the subtle connection between problems in Ireland, the political situation in Scotland, and the impact on the English polity. The military preparation of June and July 1566 was not only a reaction to the internal political state of Ireland – and the need for Sidney to control O'Neill – but a response to the Queen of Scots' claim to the English crown. This questioned England's ability to control a fragmenting Scotland, raised the issue of perceived subversion and disobedience in England, and highlighted the foreign threat of organized Catholicism funded by the Pope and the kings of France and Spain. In one sense, the Elizabethan regime failed. It did not take advantage of the Treaty of Berwick's provision for military support from the earl of Argyle – Scots in Ireland and fears of Spanish 'practise' in the kingdom were still issues in 1569. Shane O'Neill's death in 1567 was not the end of the problem. But, nevertheless, Cecil and the Council were beginning to make some important and sophisticated connections, able (generally) to rely on common interest. The regime had 'fully discovered shans practisees with scotland', Cecil told Sidney in June 1566, but London had 'hope by promiss from our frendes ther, that although the same wer far past yet they shall stey'.[96]

The politics of Anglo-British diplomacy in the 1560s was a consistent and persistent theme in the relationship between the Elizabethan regime, organized Protestantism in Scotland, and Mary Stuart. But the diplomatic reality of the decade – the constant concerns over Elizabeth's marriage and her kingdom's succession, the claims of the Queen of Scots, and the Privy Council's fear of Catholic conspiracy – impacted upon domestic politics in England. The Darnley crisis and the progressive fragmentation of political life in Scotland energized debate south of the border, especially in 1566 when the second session of Elizabeth's second parliament met at Westminster. The parliament did not debate the shape of Anglo-British policy: that was done at the council table and in correspondence between London, Berwick, Edinburgh, and Ireland, with Elizabeth in the background. But what the Lords and Commons *did* want to do was to limit the power of the Queen of Scots to cause trouble. The only way to do this in England was to persuade Elizabeth to marry and to declare a successor. The implications for the polity, and in particular for the relationship between Queen, Privy Council, and parliament, were spectacular.

[95] Cecil to Sidney, 24 June 1566, SP 63/18, fo. 62r; Elizabeth to Sidney, 5 July 1566, Ó Laidhin (ed.), *Sidney state papers*, p. 30.
[96] 24 June 1566, SP 63/18, fo. 62r.

6

Cecil, parliament, and the succession 1566–1567

On 24 June 1566 William Cecil began a letter to Lord Deputy Sidney with the news that Sir Francis Knollys had arrived back from Ireland and was locked in 'debat' with Elizabeth, that the Queen of Scots was funding Shane O'Neill, and that the regime's 'frendes' in Scotland would do their best to counter any problems. He also told Sidney that 'The Quene of scottes is as I presently here delyvered of a child', but 'whyther it be a knave child or lass, we know not'. The messenger arrived before Cecil had finished the letter. Mary Stuart had a male heir.[1]

In 1565 the crisis over the Queen of Scots' marriage to Lord Darnley had shocked the Privy Council and questioned the ability of the regime to deal successfully with Scotland and control the political and military difficulties presented by Ireland. The failure of the Leicester proposal in 1564 had demonstrated that a dynastic solution to the British succession offered by the English was flawed. The irony of the Anglo-British politics of 1566 is that although Mary Stuart presided over a slowly fragmenting political elite alienated by her promotion of Darnley and apparently intimidated by her religion, she had at least produced a male heir; Elizabeth had not. In addition to the worry about the situation in Scotland and Ireland, conscious of European involvement in the two kingdoms and in England, short of money, and aware of Mary's claim to the English throne (which had not been resolved after the debates of 1563), the birth of James reopened the issue of the realm's succession. The politics of Britain and Ireland in Europe once again focused domestic political debate. And in what better place to discuss marriage for Elizabeth and succession in England, to paraphrase one MP in 1566, than 'this honourable Counsell . . . which is termed a parlament'?[2]

---

[1] SP 63/18, fo. 62r–v.   [2] SP 46/166, fo. 3v, printed in Hartley, p. 130.

I

The second session of Elizabeth's second parliament began in September 1566. It was, in some ways, an English reaction to the British crisis of 1565. Law, order, and religion – main themes from the Privy Council's debates in June 1565 – were also key issues a year later. The Commons debated bills to counter seditious books, tackle the poverty of church livings, reform religion and law, and deal with informers on penal statutes. The last bill was introduced by Sir Nicholas Throckmorton, who had done such an effective job of highlighting the subversive dangers of Catholicism in the counties and at court in 1565.[3] But parliament was called primarily to raise money for the crown, because of the cost of campaigning against Shane O'Neill, maintaining the navy, and funding the Newhaven effort to protect coreligionists in France. After Comptroller Sir Edward Rogers 'requyred the house' on 17 October 1566 'to have consideracion of the Quenes majestie['s] meanyng for somme ayde', Cecil explained the reasons in an 'excellent declaracion'. Along with Sir William Cordell, the Master of the Rolls, and the Privy Council in the Commons (Cave, Cecil, Knollys, Mildmay, Petre, Rogers, and Sadler), forty MPs were appointed to a committee 'to consider of the Rate and payment'. They met at two o'clock the next day in the Star Chamber; a clerk listed the members and Cecil noted down the financial details.[4]

But the session's business was not as simple as the efficiency of this meeting perhaps suggests. On the same day, one 'master Molyneux' made a 'mocion' for 'the Revyvyng of the sute for Succession', and this began a pattern of speeches, debates, and petitions which lasted well into November. Parliament was almost too convenient not to explore the succession, but the way in which this was done, and by whom, are issues which have dominated the historiography of the session. This rests in part on the relationship between money and succession in 1566. The entry in the Commons' Journal seems to suggest that Molyneux's 'mocion' included both 'the sute for Succession' and a call 'to procede with the Subsidie'.[5] This may well have been the result of John Seymour's short and compressed Commons' minutes but it affected Sir John Neale's analysis of the session in 1953, Sir Geoffrey Elton's challenge to Neale in 1986, and J.D. Alsop's reinterpretation in 1990. For Neale, Molyneux was a member of his 'choir' of 'left-wing' Protestants and 'independents'; his speech was 'surely the pre-arranged move in the succession campaign', linked to supply. Elton's

[3] 4 October 1566, Journals, Commons, fo. 256r; *CJ*, I, p. 73.
[4] 17 October 1566, Journals, Commons, fo. 259r; *CJ*, I, p. 74; 18 October 1566, SP 12/40, fo. 190r–v.
[5] 18 October 1566, Journals, Commons, fo. 259v; *CJ*, I, p. 74.

Molyneux turned Neale's interpretation on its head and spoke for Cecil as part of a 'conciliar manoeuvre'. Professor Michael Graves has argued that one of the keys to the Elizabethan parliaments was conciliar planning through the Council's 'men of business'. Although Alsop agreed with the general principle that the Privy Council planted speeches in 1566, he argued that a threat to withhold taxation was not part of the Commons' campaign of persuasion. So 1566 carries the historiographical baggage of nearly a century: from A.F. Pollard's belief in a developing sense of parliament's institutional identity, which Neale turned into 'an apprentice-ship to corporate action' for 1566, to Elton's assault on Neale.[6]

The Neale–Elton debate has made it difficult for Elizabethan historians to escape the influence of the Protestant choir and campaigns planned by the Privy Council. That councillors used MPs to further their own interests in 1566 is now generally accepted, but references to Neale's choir, even revisionist ones, are no longer relevant. Any analysis of the session is made more complicated by the nature of parliamentary evidence for the 1560s. The only consistent account of the session is John Seymour's. This is accurate even in the printed *Commons Journal* but exceptionally limited in content. Masters Molyneux, Monson, Bell, Kingsmill, Lambert, and Went-worth – the 'troublemakers' of 1566 – were mentioned by Seymour, but only four out of these six men are precisely identifiable. Molyneux could be John Molyneux, the MP for Nottinghamshire; but there was another Molyneux in the Commons in 1566, Richard, who sat for Liverpool. Elton argued that the MP Lambert was not William Lambarde the antiquary but the evidence is at best ambivalent. In other Commons debates the reader is presented with long arguments 'by dyverse Lawyers' or agreements in the House without divisions. Seymour's economy complements the fact that even from the seventeenth century parliamentary records were kept hap-hazardly and often poorly. Evidence from early nineteenth-century select committees suggests that before the Westminster fire in 1833, the parlia-mentary archive included draft and rejected bills and papers presented to the Houses.[7]

---

[6] J.E. Neale, *Elizabeth I and her parliaments 1559–1601*, 2 vols. (London, 1953, 1957), I, pp. 137, 139; G.R. Elton, *The parliament of England 1559–1581* (Cambridge, 1986), pp. 366–7; Michael Graves, 'The management of the Elizabethan House of Commons: the Council's "men-of-business"', *Parliamentary History*, 2 (1983), 11–38; Graves, 'Thomas Norton the parliament man: an Elizabethan MP, 1559–1581', *Historical Journal*, 23 (1980), 17–35; J.D. Alsop, 'Reinterpreting the Elizabethan Commons: the parliamentary session of 1566', *Journal of British Studies*, 29 (1990), 216–40; cf. A.F. Pollard, 'The authenticity of the "Lords' Journals" in the sixteenth century', *Transactions of the Royal Historical Society*, third series, 8 (1914), 35.

[7] On the contributions made by Bell, Monson, and Kingsmill, 23 October 1566, see Journals, Commons, fo. 262r (*CJ*, I, p. 75); for individual biographies, see Hasler, I, pp. 421–2 (Bell); II, pp. 400–1 (Kingsmill), 429–30 (Lambarde); III, p. 66 (Monson); for the debate by

But there are still some sources for 1566 and they raise important and sometimes controversial issues for Elizabethan historians. In fact, the confusion of the parliamentary collection before 1833 was responsible for the survival of one of the most significant documents for 1566: a text of the preamble to the Subsidy Bill, drafted by the Clerk of the Privy Council, Bernard Hampton, edited by Cecil and another member of the small team of lawyers working on the tax bill. The draft probably survived the fire when it was overlooked in a separation of Commons' and Lords' manuscripts in January 1658 but it was read by Neale in 1921.[8] This document is part of the most important source for the session: the archive of Cecil as Principal Secretary, working in collaboration with other privy councillors, Bernard Hampton, a large committee of MPs, and a small group of draughtsmen handling the Subsidy Bill. Most of the main sources for the session of 1566 – drafts of petitions to Elizabeth, memoranda, accounts of the Queen's addresses to parliament, and notes for privy councillors to deliver to the Commons on behalf of Elizabeth – are either in Cecil's hand or in his archive.[9] These papers have some important implications for the part Cecil played in the session and the nature of his service to the Queen and to the commonwealth.

For Cecil, parliament could and should have been the partner of both the Privy Council and the Queen; the session of 1566 was a practical demonstration of the fact. One of his better-known political notes from the 1560s had Elizabeth's marriage and the establishment of the succession as 'the uttermost that can be desyred' in 1566. Marriage was the easier issue to tackle, 'most naturall, most easy, most plausible to the Quenes Majesty'; succession was more difficult, 'both for the difficulte to discuss the right, and for the lothsomnes in the Quenes Majesty to consent therto'. His corollary was breathtakingly simple: for Elizabeth 'to determyne effectually to marry, and if it succede not, than procede to discussion of the right of the successor'.[10] But even this memorandum is not the best guide to Cecil's relationship with Queen, Privy Council, and parliament. Conyers Read suggested that it may have been written for the Council in September 1566, but there is no definite evidence to prove that this was the case.[11] More

'dyverse Lawyers', 19 October 1566, see Journals, Commons, fo. 260r (*CJ*, I, p. 75). On the parliamentary archive, see G.R. Elton, *England 1200–1640* (London, 1969), pp. 86–7.

[8] House of Lords Record Office, London, Main Papers (17 May 1499–2 March 1581), fos. 43r–44r, printed below, pp. 231–2; J.E. Neale, 'Parliament and the succession question in 1562/3 and 1566', *English Historical Review*, 36 (1921), 517; Neale, 'The Commons Journals of the Tudor period', *Transactions of the Royal Historical Society*, fourth series, 3 (1920), 153–6, 159–60.

[9] For the textual details, see Stephen Alford, 'William Cecil and the British succession crisis of the 1560s', PhD thesis, University of St Andrews (1996), pp. 168–9.

[10] SP 12/40, fo. 195r.

[11] Conyers Read, *Mr Secretary Cecil and Queen Elizabeth* (London, 1955), pp. 356–7.

compelling is the fact that Cecil worked on drafts prepared by the Clerk of the Privy Council to petition Elizabeth to act on her marriage and the succession to the crown and to use (as the Queen put it in a furious holograph comment) 'ony my privat answers to the realme' as the 'prologe to a subsides boke'.[12]

Cecil's political role in 1566 has been obscured, in part, by the traditional emphasis on 'government' privy councillors and 'backbenchers' in the Elizabethan parliaments. This distinction is misleading: councillors' official work in parliament was the result of an oath which bound them to 'beare trew fayth and allegiance' personally to Elizabeth.[13] Cecil, Comptroller Rogers, and Vicechamberlain Knollys all presented Elizabeth's views to the Commons in 1566. But this was not the work of the Elizabethan 'government'. In fact, there are good reasons to argue that the Privy Council was far from happy with the Queen's stand on marriage and succession and that obedience to the personal will of Elizabeth was beginning to feel the strain of political frustration.

According to two late Cecil diaries, the first written in 1571 and the other composed in 1579, the Queen was 'displesed' with the earls of Pembroke and Leicester 'and others' for 'furtheryng of the matter of succession in parlement without hir consent' on 27 October 1566. The two earls were excluded from the 'prive chambre' for their offence.[14] The Lords debated the succession on 26 October, exactly a week after the 'long argumentes by dyverse Lawyers' in the Commons.[15] Rogers, the Privy Council, and a committee of forty-four debated the succession on 23 October. By that date, the Lords had heard the committee's 'peticion by the severall declaracions of master Bell, master mounson, and master Kyngsmylle'; this suggests either that the three men acted as liaison between the two Houses or that they spoke on behalf of their colleagues in a full meeting of the Lords, Rogers, and the committee. Bell, Monson, and Kingsmill were formally named as members of the group of commoners on 31 October.[16] According to Neale, the three men were puritan agitators in an independent campaign which the Privy Council was trying desperately to counter;[17] in fact, Bell, Monson, and Kingsmill seem to have been doing

---

[12] Lansdowne 1236, fo. 42r, printed by Neale, 'Succession question', 519–20.
[13] 'The othe of a Co[u]nsellor', 17 November 1558, SP 12/1, fo. 3v.
[14] CP 140, fo. 3v; SP 12/83, fo. 129r.
[15] 26 October, Journals, Lords, fo. 162 (*LJ*, I, p. 638); 19 October 1566, Journals, Commons, fo. 260r (*CJ*, I, p. 75).
[16] 23 October 1566, Journals, Commons, fo. 262r (*CJ*, I, p. 75); for the members of the committee, see Journals, Lords, fos. 164–5 (*LJ*, I, p. 640), printed in Sir Simonds D'Ewes, *The journals of all the parliaments during the reign of Queen Elizabeth, both of the House of Lords and House of Commons*, ed. Paul Bowes (London, 1682), pp. 126–7.
[17] Neale, *Elizabeth I and her parliaments*, I, pp. 142–4.

everything but that. If Elizabeth was offended on 27 October, it was because the Comptroller of the Household, the privy councillors in the Commons, and the Lords were determined to debate her marriage and the future of the kingdom.

This was not 'government' versus 'opposition' in the Commons. From mid-October until November 1566, the Privy Council and parliament applied persistent pressure to Elizabeth to act. The relationship was complementary: the identifiable MPs who spoke in succession and marriage debates in the Commons were genuinely interested in the issues. There is no evidence to suggest that they were either constitutional radicals – and the intervention of Paul Wentworth on the 'Lybertyes' of the Commons rang important bells for historians like Neale[18] – or Council stooges. Elton claimed that Cecil's memorandum 'To require both mariadg and sta-blishyng of succession' leads to the 'most probable conjecture' that Molyneux was acting 'on behalf of a councillor – indeed, the councillor most concerned to see policy accomplished'. Similarly, Elton traced the MP Lambert through his seat for Aldborough in Yorkshire, a duchy of Lancaster borough under the patronage control of Sir Ambrose Cave, through Cave as a privy councillor.[19] This is an idiosyncratic reading of limited and circumstantial evidence. Cecil was important in 1566 but not in the way that Elton tried to prove.

The relationship between Council and MPs was more subtle. Cecil played a crucial part in bringing together the interests of his colleagues, the Commons, and the Lords. At the end of October there were two clear stages of action: the preliminary moves made by Rogers and the Commons' 'comyttyes' between 19 and 25 October and two meetings of thirty lords, forty commoners, and the Privy Council held on 31 October and 2 November. From this point on, the chronology becomes important. When the Commons returned from a brief adjournment between Thursday 31 October and Tuesday 5 November – only the committees from the two Houses met on Saturday 2 November in the 'utter chamber of the parliament'[20] – the Lords 'requyred that xxx of this house shulde be before the Quene at the palace this afte[r] noone'; the MPs were chosen by the Speaker, Richard Onslow.[21] Elizabeth rejected parliament's suit. A day later, Cecil and Rogers 'redde in writing notes of the Quenes majestes saying before the Lords and commyttyes'. The main argument was all too

---

[18]   11 November 1566, Journals, Commons, fo. 267v (*CJ*, I, p. 76); Neale, *Elizabeth I and her parliaments*, I, pp. 152–3; J.E. Neale, 'The Commons' privilege of free speech in parliament', in R.W. Seton-Watson (ed.), *Tudor studies* (London, 1924), pp. 277–8.

[19]   Elton, *Parliament of England*, pp. 366, 371.

[20]   31 October 1566, Journals, Commons, fo. 264v; *CJ*, I, p. 76.

[21]   5 November 1566, Journals, Commons, fo. 265v; *CJ*, I, p. 76.

clear: 'and touching lymytacion for Succession the perilles be so grete to her persone' that 'tyme will not yet suffer to treate of yt', 'wherapon all the house was sylent'.[22]

Cecil's summaries of Elizabeth's presentation were not only aides-mémoire for his speech to the Commons on 6 November; they became the reason for a petition to the Queen which Cecil worked on just over a week later. The Commons' petition was a problem for Neale. He argued that early November 1566 was a 'moment of crisis' and it was not surprising that leadership in the House 'swung over to the moderates'.[23] But if the chronology and the personnel of mid- to late October are accurate, with the Comptroller, his colleagues in the Privy Council, and the Lords all pressing Elizabeth, Neale's analysis is revealed for what it is: an attempt to explain away the fact that Cecil and the Clerk of the Privy Council, Hampton, were responsible for the Commons' petition and not his radical MPs. There are three versions of the text of the petition. The first is undated, but the second was drafted on 15 November and the third a day later.[24]

But it is not only the chronology of the petitions which demonstrates that the Commons was determined to pursue the issues of marriage and succession. Cecil's summaries of Elizabeth's speech on 5 November reveal that he understood fully the Queen's mind. She had argued that a settlement of the succession was 'doutfull to trye' and 'perilloss' to herself and 'the People', mainly 'for the nombre of Competitors having so manny frendes'. The 'decision wold make devision'.[25] In effect, the Privy Council believed that a settlement could only heal existing wounds; Elizabeth thought that it would open them. So the petition, in this sense, was not a misunderstanding of the Queen's position – it was based on a different interpretation of cause and effect. The petition also had a clear campaigning intention: Cecil endorsed the first draft as 'The thankes gyven by the Commens' but the second became a 'sute' and the third 'a forme of a petition to the Quenes Majesty by the Comens'. And it was not an independent political exercise. The second version was 'a draught shewed to the 30 committe in the Comen howss'.[26] So the group committed to pushing the issues of the Queen's marriage and the kingdom's succession was not a victim of a group of radical MPs: it included the privy councillors sitting in the Commons, the Master of the Rolls, Sir Thomas Wroth, and other senior

---

[22] For Cecil's notes of the speech, 5 November 1566, see SP 12/41, fo. 12r; and SP 12/41, fos. 14r–v, 15v; 6 November 1566, Journals, Commons, fo. 266r (*CJ*, I, p. 76).

[23] Neale, *Elizabeth I and her parliaments*, I, p. 154.

[24] SP 12/41, fos. 38r–40v; 15 November 1566, SP 12/41, fos. 41r–44v; 16 November 1566, SP 12/41, fos. 45r–48v.

[25] SP 12/41, fo. 12r.   [26] SP 12/41, fo. 44v.

men like Sir Nicholas Throckmorton, Sir Maurice Berkeley, Sir John Chichester, Sir Thomas Gargrave, Sir Thomas Gerard, and Sir John Sellinger.[27] These were mainstream and senior MPs, law officers, and privy councillors using Cecil as their draughtsman, the Clerk of the Privy Council as his assistant, and prepared, even after Elizabeth's clear prohibition on 5 November and the order to silence debate a day later, to press sensitive political issues.

Cecil's drafts are important in themselves. Taken as three parts of a single text, there are subtle changes of language, emphasis, and political meaning. Neale noticed these differences and called them 'verbal corrections', but he did not fit a technical examination into his narrative.[28] The alterations and additions are also difficult to pick up from printed transcripts. In the third version, for example, Hampton copied a line which had developed over the first two drafts. Before the final version, corrected by Cecil on 16 November, it dealt with 'the renewing of a former sute made in the last session to your Majesty, which being obteyned we were fully persuaded shuld tend to the glory of God'. But because the 'being obteyned' suggested that the suit had already been successful in 1563, Cecil altered it to 'the renewing of a former sute made in the last session to your Majesty, which we were fully persuaded *being obteyned* shuld tend to the glory of God'.[29] This was a fairly minor textual point, but it does help to put Cecil's powers of close reading and attention to detail into clearer focus. Language mattered to Cecil – an aspect of his work which even a very good transcript can obscure.[30]

The petition had a strong political purpose and Cecil reinforced this by detailed editing. There is a sense of cumulative and conscious development in the language and structure of the drafts. Near the end of the first version, Cecil recounted the Queen's command to silence the House and balanced it against the Commons' rights and duties. Before Cecil went through the text for the first time, Hampton's original read:

And because we your most loving subjectes, have sence your Majesties answer herin given to us, receaved some messages and commandementes importing some dowtes not only that your Majesty might conceave of us lack of duty in receaving of this your answer, but by the manner of the wordes expressed in your commandement that we shuld therby be as it were deprived or at the least sequestred from an ancient laudable custome always from the beginning annexed to our assembly, and by your Majesty most gratiously confirmed, that is, a suffrance and lefull liberty to treate and devise of matters honorable for your Majesty and profitable for your realme . . .

---

[27] Cambridge University Library, Gg.3.34, fo. 209; Hartley, pp. 145–6.
[28] Neale, *Elizabeth I and her parliaments*, I, p. 155.   [29] SP 12/41, fo. 45r.
[30] Although Hartley, p. 155, prints Cecil's insertion, Bernard Hampton's first 'being obteyned' is not shown.

But even from Cecil's first set of corrections, it is clear that he wanted more effectively to emphasize the power he claimed for the Commons. He altered the 'ancient laudable custome' which was 'from the beginning annexed' to parliament to '*necessarely* annexed'; this had, of course, been 'gratiously confirmed', but it was now 'gratiously *allweiss* confirmed' as a '*leefull* suffrance'.[31] The second draft on 15 November was even stronger and more determined. Not only had the House been 'deprived or at the least sequestred from an ancient laudable custome always from the beginning necessarely annexed to our assembly', but the MPs had been 'sequestred *much to our discomfort and infamy*'. Even Elizabeth's 'leefull suffrance', which had been 'most gratiously always confirmed' in the first draft, lost its 'most gratiously'.[32] These changes over two drafts – from an ancient custom with annexed powers graciously confirmed by the Queen to necessary powers, always and lawfully confirmed, which had been withdrawn to the Commons' discomfort and infamy – stood without correction in the third and final version.[33] Although the second draft was 'not made nor presented', it was shown to senior MPs and councillors in 'the 30 committe'.[34] In other words, the representatives of the Commons read Cecil's second version on 15 November, presumably understood its importance, and allowed Cecil to leave it unaltered on 16 November. It was a subtle process, impossible to follow in any other form than in the original drafts, but one with profound implications for the relationship between parliament and monarch in November 1566.

II

The session of 1566 was an important part of an interpretation of parliamentary history which made a connection between Elizabethan tensions and political crisis in the seventeenth century, 'a premonition', according to Neale in 1921, 'one of the first and one of the clearest of which we have knowledge, of the great contest that was to follow in Stuart times'. 'Here was something fundamental', he added thirty-two years later, commenting on Paul Wentworth: 'an innovation in parliamentary tactics; dawn of a new age; harbinger of Stuart conflicts. How rapidly we are moving away from the days of Sir Thomas More!'[35] But if the sensitive issues of marriage and succession were being pressed in 1566 by senior MPs in the Commons, after a co-ordinated campaign organized at first by Sir Edward Rogers, why were these men trying to put pressure on Elizabeth? Neale's radicals had the luxury of constitutional action in the

---

[31] SP 12/41, fo. 39v.   [32] SP 12/41, fos. 42v–43r.   [33] SP 12/41, fo. 46v.
[34] SP 12/41, fo. 44v.
[35] Neale, 'Succession question', 497; Neale, *Elizabeth I and her parliaments*, I, p. 152–3.

Commons' bid for 'corporate' development; socially conservative council-lors did not. From the shape of the campaign, its personnel, and its political language, the events of October and November were probably attempts to emphasize the part parliament could and should play in the decisions on the Queen's marriage and the kingdom's succession. This had been an important theme in the first session in 1563 and it was again three years later.[36]

Elizabeth tried personally to silence the debate in parliament in No-vember 1566. Sir Robert Catlyn (Chief Justice of the Queen's Bench), Sir James Dyer (Chief Justice of the Common Pleas), and Sir Edward Saunders (Chief Baron of the Exchequer) argued that if the Queen sent a 'prohibition unto the nether house of the parliament by her privy counsell . . . that no further treatie or speech should be used touching the petition made by both the houses' on the succession.[37] The justices possibly reached this legal conclusion between 6 November, when Rogers and Cecil explained Eliza-beth's position to the Commons, and 9 November, when Sir Francis Knollys repeated her 'expresse comandement' to the House 'that they shulde no furder procede in ther sute'; the memorandum may also explain why Knollys prepared a list of three questions on the right of the Queen, through the Council, to prohibit debate.[38] If these dates are correct, then Cecil's drafts of the Commons' petition are put into a clearer and more radical perspective. Elizabeth had a legal judgement before 9 November; six days later, Cecil was prepared to call this a sequestration of parliament's ancient right of free discussion and counsel.

There were strong echoes of the debate in 1563: parliament had a duty to counsel the prince, to 'hearken out', as the speaker identified as 'Master Lambert' argued, the 'benefittes or inconveniences that might growe to the head, bodie, or any member' of the kingdom, and to 'prevent the evills of trayterous fflattery & divellish dissimulacion & many other inconven-iences'.[39] Freedom of speech lay not in constitutional liberty or the institutional independence of radical politics but in counsel and advice to the monarch.[40] This was the freedom of speech which Cecil emphasized in

---

[36] See above, pp. 103–9.

[37] *Reports from the lost notebooks of Sir James Dyer*, ed. J.H. Baker, 2 vols. (Selden Society, 109, 110; London, 1993–4), I, p. 125.

[38] 9 November 1566, Journals, Commons, fo. 267r (*CJ*, I, p. 76); for Knollys' notes, SP 12/41, fo. 33r.

[39] 8 November 1566, Journals, Commons, fo. 266v (*CJ*, I, p. 76); for a text, preserved by William Petyt, see SP 46/166, fos. 3r–11v, and printed in Hartley, pp. 129–39; for a discussion of the speaker and the text, see Elton, *Parliament of England*, pp. 370–1 and n. 64; and cf. *Descriptive list of state papers supplementary (SP 46), private papers, series I, 1535–1705* (List and Index Society; London, 1968).

[40] Sir Thomas Smith, *De republica Anglorum*, ed. Mary Dewar (Cambridge, 1982), Book II, chapter 2, pp. 80–1.

his drafts for the committee of thirty MPs and councillors on 15 and 16 November 1566. The Queen's position was different. On 24 November, she met eight privy councillors, Catlyn, Dyer, Saunders, and another man whose name is illegible in the minutes, to draft 'The report of the Quenes Majestes messadg to the Comen howss, for delyveryng of the same from a Command'. The text was uncompromising: there had to be an end to debates on the succession, a prohibition enforced by the Speaker. Cecil had drafted his own version of the Queen's message to parliament on 6 November. Just over two weeks later, Elizabeth was determined not to allow her subjects the luxury of a misunderstanding: using Cecil as her clerk, she corrected the draft which was given to Speaker Onslow and read to the Commons the next day.[41]

The Queen's interpretation of parliament's role in 1566 was very different from the importance Cecil placed on the competence of the three estates to deal with marriage and succession. In November Cecil began a holograph note on 'Parlement matters' with two statements: first, 'That the mariadg may procede effectually'; and second, 'That it may be declared how necessary also it is to have the succession stablished' for the 'suerty and quietnes of the Quenes Majesty' and 'for the comfort of all good subjectes'. These were not drafted as rhetorical civil questions to be debated; in fact, they may have been summaries of the type of argument used by parliament in the first two months of the session. But Cecil wanted more. Because 'it semeth very uncomfortable' for Elizabeth 'to here of this at this tyme, and that it is hoped, that God will direct hir hart to thynk more comfortably herof', he thought 'for the satisfaction of hir people' she should prorogue parliament until she considered marriage. Only then should the Queen 'begyn hir Parlement ageyn, and to procede in such sort, as shall seme metest then for the matter of succession'.[42]

The politics of Cecil in 1566 can be measured on two levels: on the first, he was determined to tie Elizabeth to the vague promises she had made in the first and second sessions of the parliament; on the second, he was prepared to argue that the 'three estates' in parliament had a duty to counsel the Queen. In March 1565 Sir Thomas Smith had argued that parliament 'giveth formes of succession to the crowne'. Cecil too maintained that parliament could and should contribute to the debate.[43] By November 1566 he was prepared even to sacrifice the security of the subsidy to the cause of a settled succession. This connection between

---

[41] Drafted by Cecil, 24 November 1566, SP 12/41, fos. 61r–v, 62v, and printed in Hartley, pp. 160–1; 25 November 1566, Journals, Commons, fo. 272v (*CJ*, I, p. 78).

[42] SP 12/40, fo. 225r, printed in Hartley, p. 164.

[43] Smith, *De republica Anglorum*, ed. Dewar, Book II, chapter 1, p. 78; see above, pp. 35–7.

money and succession in 1566 has traditionally been a controversial one. A committee met to discuss the subsidy on 18 October, but the Molyneux speech on the same day seemed to link the 'sute for Succession' to the Commons' consideration of money for Elizabeth. The issue reappeared on 27 November 1566 when Cecil declared that the Queen 'for the good wyll she beareth to her Subjectes that her hignes doth remytte the iijde payment of the Subsidye before rated'. The bill became 'An acte of the graunte of one xvth and xth' in late December, but not before what Elton interpreted as 'a ludicrous and abortive' attempt to tie Elizabeth's promises to the preamble of the Act. Dr Alsop went further: taxation would not have been refused and pressure on Elizabeth was a bluff. Cecil was a key player but he did not mastermind the main events.[44]

Alsop was partly right. There is no evidence to suggest that the Commons seriously considered withholding money from the Queen in 1566 and Cecil did not plant speeches. But the politics of the session are more subtle than Alsop admitted. Parliament did try to link the Queen's promises to the preamble. Elizabeth saw a copy of one of the drafts of the preface and she was furious. But it was *not* Neale's radicals who were responsible for working on the preamble as 'a vehicle of propaganda'.[45] Cecil was the principal draughtsman. He used Bernard Hampton as his clerk and he collaborated with the group of six MPs responsible for drafting the main clauses of the bill. After the issue of supply was raised in the Commons, a committee had to be appointed to consider the 'articles' for the rates and dates of payment. Once these were agreed, the details were turned into a bill either by the same MPs or by other legal specialists.[46] The men working on the bill in 1566 were listed on the last folio of a draft of the clauses as 'master Sekford, master Gargrave, master norton, master ffletewood, master Barram, master Chyverton'. Thomas Seckford read the bill for the grant of one fifteenth and tenth and the subsidy immediately after Cecil addressed the Commons on 27 November and so, presumably, the MPs produced drafts of the clauses before this date.[47]

The sensitive task for the historian of 1566 is to separate parliamentary

[44] 27 November 1566, *Journals, Commons*, fo. 273v (*CJ*, I, p. 78); 8 Elizabeth I, c. 18, printed in *Statutes of the realm*, ed. A. Luders, T.E. Tomlins, J. Raithby *et al.*, 11 vols. (London, 1810–28), IV, pp. 505–19; Elton, *Parliament of England*, p. 373; Alsop, 'Parliament and taxation', in D.M. Dean and N.L. Jones (eds.), *The parliaments of Elizabethan England* (Oxford, 1990), p. 98; Alsop, 'Parliamentary session of 1566', 223, 225–6, 239.

[45] Lansdowne 1236, fo. 42r–v, printed in Neale, 'Succession question', 519–20; Neale, *Elizabeth I and her parliaments*, I, pp. 161–2.

[46] Elton, *Parliament of England*, p. 158.

[47] House of Lords Record Office, Main Papers (17 May 1499–2 March 1581), fo. 42v; 27 November 1566, *Journals, Commons*, fo. 273v (*CJ*, I, p. 78).

procedure from expressions of political purpose. Nicholas Barham, Henry
Chiverton, William Fleetwood, Sir Thomas Gargrave, Thomas Norton,
and Seckford worked on the bill. All of them had a legal background.
Barham, Seckford, and perhaps Gargrave had been at Gray's Inn between
the 1520s and 1540s; Seckford and Barham were Cecil's contemporaries at
Gray's. Chiverton had studied at Lincoln's Inn in the 1530s, Fleetwood at
the Middle Temple in the 1550s, and Norton at the Inner Temple from
1555. Only Gargrave had sat on the committee to deal with the subsidy
back in October 1566 but the other MPs had different qualifications.
Fleetwood was competent enough to become the Recorder of London and
Barham the Queen's Serjeant; Norton was a parliamentary workhorse who
had been involved in the Commons' petition to the Queen in 1563. But
although this committee helps to rescue Barham and Chiverton from the
parliamentary obscurity of Norah Fuidge's short biographies for the
History of Parliament Trust, its existence is not in itself important: the
political significance of the MPs and their drafts lies in the relationship they
had with Cecil's papers.[48]

The drafts of the preamble to the Subsidy Bill were detailed exercises in
the development, use, and application of political language. They were
written in a very controlled way and Cecil kept his own copies of the
different versions. All of them were written by Bernard Hampton and
corrected by Cecil. These were Cecil's copies in the Principal Secretary's
archive, with no other contributions or corrections in other hands.
Hampton also acted as the clerk for the versions now in the custody of the
House of Lords Record Office but these two texts were corrected by Cecil
and at least two others. Fleetwood and Norton seem to have been the
editors. But the significant point is this: Elizabeth read a fairly late text of
the preamble and she was angry then, and this was more conciliatory than
Cecil's earlier versions had been. Fleetwood, Norton, Hampton, and Cecil
were independently and collaboratively working on a text with which the
Queen was extremely unhappy.[49]

These preambles – especially Cecil's – were co-ordinated, planned, and
carefully edited. Every attempt was made, as Elizabeth perceptively pointed
out, to use her 'privat answers to the realme' as moral and political
leverage. After one draft, Elizabeth's 'assent with determination to marry'
became, after Cecil's corrections, her '*gratiooss & resolute* assent'. A few
lines later, he tried to apply moral pressure by emphasizing the Queen's

---

[48] Hasler, I, pp. 392 (Barham), 603 (Chiverton); II, pp. 133 (Fleetwood), 167 (Gargrave); III,
pp. 145 (Norton), 362 (Seckford). Barham, like Cecil, was admitted to Gray's Inn in 1540,
Harley 1912, fo. 176v. On Norton, see Michael A.R. Graves, *Thomas Norton. The
parliament man* (Oxford and Cambridge, Massachusetts, 1994).
[49] For the textual details, see Alford, 'British succession crisis', pp. 180–1.

duty to marry and settle the succession, based, of course, on the rather vague promises she had made to sixty lords and commons at the beginning of November. Hampton's original was fairly clear on its own: 'yet considering your Majestes answer that yow will not faile but in convenient tyme have due regard therto for our profitt', but Cecil's addition made it even stronger. Elizabeth's 'answer given to us' became 'your Majestes *manifest and assured declaration expressed to us in princely wordes* that yow will not faile but in convenient tyme have *good and* due regard therto for our *suerty and* profitt'.[50] By the second draft even Cecil's own 'expressed to us' was too vague. Hampton incorporated the corrections to the first draft, but Cecil made sure that the Queen's 'manifest and assured declaration' was delivered '*publickly to a select nombre of your three estates of parlement in very* Princely wordes *expressed*'.[51]

Developments from the first draft to Cecil's third and final version are important. The central section from Hampton's draft is a good example:

And though your Majesty hath not to this your graunt of mariage joyned as this tyme for sundry great consideracions and respectes as your Majesty hath declared to be best knowen to your Majesty, the present prosequution of the stablishing of the succession of the Crowne after your self and your children, which thing also we your subjectes for furder suerty have most humbly desired and so do continew . . .[52]

In his first set of corrections, Cecil made a couple of fairly cosmetic changes. 'Your children' became '*the Issew of your body*' and he added a '*therin*' between the 'so' and 'do' of 'so do continew'.[53] The second draft escaped with five small changes to this short section, but the 'have most humbly desired' of the Queen's subjects became '*have most ernestly of long tyme* desired'.[54] This perhaps played the part of the humble subject too subtly; the changes Cecil made to the third version of the preamble were significantly more forceful. The 'present prosequution of the furder establishing of the succession of the Crowne after your self, and the issue of your body' by 'we your subjectes' became the 'present *deliberation and* prosequution *by authorite of parlement*', which the MPs '*humbly required and ernestly* desired, and so therin do *still* continew'.[55] Even a fairly small editorial correction, like the change from 'in our hartes hitherto continewed' to 'in our hartes *and in this parlement re*continewed', was calculated to have an effect.[56]

In each one of these four examples Cecil tried to make a political point. He manipulated Elizabeth's promise eventually to marry and to settle the succession. She used the humanist-classical model of counsel to hear advice

[50] See below, pp. 229–31.   [51] SP 12/41, fo. 88v.   [52] See below, p. 230.
[53] See below, p. 230.   [54] SP 12/41, fo. 87r.   [55] SP 12/41, fo. 95r.
[56] SP 12/41, fo. 93r.

and reject it as a political way of disarming opposition;[57] her Principal Secretary was equally prepared to deploy Elizabeth's words against her. In Cecil's preamble it was the duty of parliament to press the Queen. In the draft corrected by Norton, 'your Realme agreable' was changed to '*Realme in parlyament* agreable'.[58] If Elizabeth had made it clear that she was going to marry, Fleetwood wanted to make sure that she remembered the fact by reinforcing the original draft with 'the most comefortable *Assurancis & promysse* by your Majesty made and declared unto us'.[59]

III

When Elizabeth read a copied draft of the third paragraph of the preamble to the Subsidy Bill, she blamed 'thes felowes' for turning her words against her.[60] Just over a month later, on 2 January 1567, she ended parliament with a clear message to her MPs: the prince's 'opinion and good wyll ought in good ordar have bine felt in other sort than in so publik a place', spoken from 'a zelous princes consideration' and not from 'so lippe labored orations out of suche subjects mouthes'. In her first draft she had called them 'rangling subjects', but her temper subsided with editing.[61] Elizabeth and her councillors and MPs accepted the physical metaphor of the English body politic, but for the Queen the head had to command the feet not to stray; for her subjects, the monarch was the head of the commonwealth, ordained by God, and bound by duty 'carefully to devise & put in execucion all things most commodious for the body & every member therof'. It was Caesar's 'dutie to yeald protection & defence unto his people' and 'wisely to foresee & prevent the eville that may come unto any part' of the body. The same speaker reminded the Commons of the duties of a shepherd.[62] Cecil added a short prayer to one of the drafts of the preamble to the Subsidy Bill: 'The Lord God of the spirittes of all flesh, set on over this great multitude, which maye goo out and In before them, and leade them out and in, that the Lords people be not as shepe without a shephard.'[63]

Elizabeth, her parliament, and her Council held a wide disparity of views of the nature of their polity. The Queen expected her subjects to accept her word without debate, and she openly criticized 'others whos eares wer deluded by pleasing perswations of comen good'. But whereas Elizabeth reassured the Lords and Commons that she was 'a remembrancer for your

---

[57] John Guy, 'The rhetoric of counsel in early modern England', in Dale Hoak (ed.), *Tudor political culture* (Cambridge, 1995), p. 294.
[58] House of Lords Record Office, Main Papers (17 May 1499–2 March 1581), fo. 46r.
[59] See below, p. 231.   [60] Lansdowne 1236, fo. 42v.   [61] Cotton Charter 4.38 (2)r.
[62] SP 46/166, fo. 6v; Hartley, pp. 133–4.   [63] SP 12/41, fo. 97r.

wele', everything in her relationship with parliament over two sessions had eroded MPs' and councillors' confidence in her determination to marry and to settle the succession.[64] Constitutional change was not the issue in 1566. Cecil, Rogers, and the committees worked to hold Elizabeth to her duties as Queen. The irony of the second session is that the 'monarchical republicanism' of Cecil and the Privy Council was a conservative reaction to the proprietary political instincts of Elizabeth. Abstract theory was not applied to the political problem of England's unsettled succession in the 1560s: the actions of men like Cecil, even if they look radical, were encouraged by a Queen who emphasized the independence of the head of the body politic rather than the duties of the head to the body when the body tried to counsel it.

The two sessions of the second parliament concentrated and exercised the minds of MPs and privy councillors. This is one of the connections between the politics of parliament in the 1560s – particularly the part Cecil played in it – and the succession as a political issue: the presence of Mary Stuart in Scotland, her tacit role as heir apparent to the English crown, and Elizabeth's refusal even to allow the Lords and Commons to debate the future of the kingdom encouraged MPs and councillors to consider alternatives, to plan independent action, and to disobey the Queen. Elizabeth believed that her *imperium* was ordained by God, unlimited by counsel; succession was the issue which encouraged the Queen to retreat back into her prerogative, although she needed little excuse.[65] It allowed Cecil to argue that as the three estates of the kingdom, parliament had a part to play in the polity – not as an independent or corporate institution, but as Smith's 'whole universall and generall consent and authoritie aswell of the prince as of the nobilitie and commons' and 'the whole head and bodie of the realme of England'.[66]

---

[64] Cotton Charter 4.38 (2)r–v; Hartley, pp. 174–5.
[65] John Guy, 'The 1590s: the second reign of Elizabeth?', in John Guy (ed.), *The reign of Elizabeth I. Court and culture in the last decade* (Cambridge, 1995), p. 13.
[66] Smith, *De republica Anglorum*, ed. Dewar, Book II, chapter 4, p. 88.

Cecil's proposal for the settlement of Britain 1567–1568

By 1567 the situation in England and Scotland, influenced by wider European concerns, defied simple definitions. In 1565 and 1566 Mary Stuart successfully alienated a large section of her nobility; England considered a military expedition, but drew back. In April 1567 Cecil told Sir Henry Sidney in Ireland that Scotland was 'in a qua[g]myre; no body semeth to stand still; the most honest desyre to goo away; the worst tremble with the shakyng of ther conscience'. England wanted to reclaim Calais with 'trompettes and shott' but there was not enough money. 'The poore protestantes in Flaunders', he added, 'ar brought to wor[l]dly desperation, and must trust only to myracles'.[1] There were other problems. Although the minds of MPs were concentrated by the birth of a Scottish heir in June 1566, the future James VI, Elizabeth suffocated debate and refused to consider a domestic parliamentary settlement of the succession. So when civil war broke out in Scotland in 1567 and Mary crossed the border into Cumbria in May 1568, her claim to the throne and her presence in England were still crucial issues. But the solution, as well as the implication, was Anglo-British. Diplomacy between 1560 and 1563 had been marked by gestures of amity and perpetual friendship but these were stifled by religious war in Europe and the chaos of 1565 and 1566. In effect, 1568 was a return to the pattern of politics influenced by Cecil in 1559 and at the Treaty of Edinburgh. His solution was remarkably similar: a settlement based on a British treaty and a political declaration of his Queen's status as an imperial and superior monarch, designed to control and restrict Mary. The protective custody of the Queen of Scots in England from 1568 was an important political opportunity.

---

[1] 23 April 1567, SP 63/20, fo. 144r.

I

Elizabeth's political conservatism meant that she found it extremely difficult to cope with the dangerous reality of 1567. Her reaction was silent indecision. This hardly suited the seriousness of the problem: 1567 and 1568 saw the British succession crisis at its worst before 1584 and 1585, an untidy and dangerous mix of Mary's interest in the English throne, rebellion in Scotland, and threats from Europe. But the immediate result of Darnley's death looked positive. In February 1567 the Queen of Scots, 'now an unfortunat wydow', assured Elizabeth that she had 'prohibited the commyng of any moo scottes into Irland, and will spedely revoke those that be ther'.[2] After the military rigours of 1566 and the connections between Mary and Shane O'Neill, the prospect must have seemed promising. Still, this was only one of the defining moments in a process of gradual disintegration in Scotland. By spring 1567 the earl of Bothwell was a main player and Mary was 'presumynge of the Poopes dyspensacion, of her furyous Love' for Hepburn.[3] These were not simply domestic concerns. As two of five 'matters to be considered' in Scotland, Cecil noted 'that if uppon inquisition it may be found that the Quene there is disposed to marry with the Erle of Bothwell that all meanes be used to interrupt it' and, as an extension of problems with Mary, 'that the lyke be used to interrupt any leage with france, or the alteration of relligion'.[4] Once again, English Protestants were starting to make a disturbing connection between political problems in Scotland, events in Europe, and their own domestic security.

By the summer of 1567 there had once again been a strange reversal of interests: men like Maitland of Lethington had taken an open stand against Mary and were prepared to take radical action. The English – perhaps even ironically – were desperate to anaesthetize the Scots' dangerous impulses. Scottish noblemen met together at Stirling in May and put their grievances in writing a month later. English privy councillors knew that their counterparts were not prepared to hand the young Prince James back to his mother.[5] Throckmorton was sent to Scotland in July 1567 with a message of peace and reconciliation, but he found a very serious problem when he arrived in Edinburgh. The political situation was chaotic – 'I dyd never se greater confusion emongst men', Throckmorton told Cecil, 'for they chainge theyr opinions very often' – but Mary's opponents were determined to prosecute, condemn, and imprison the Queen and crown James. This

[2] Cecil to Sidney, 25 February 1567, SP 63/20, fo. 78r.
[3] Throckmorton to Leicester, 9 May 1567, SP 12/42, fo. 143r; cf. Cecil to Sidney, 13 May 1567, SP 63/20, fo. 183r.
[4] SP 52/13, fo. 75r.
[5] Leicester to Cecil, 16 June 1567, SP 12/43, fo. 23r.

was the third and one of the more moderate proposals. The earl of Atholl and his supporters wanted Mary to leave the kingdom and resign the crown to her son, 'And to appoynte under hys aucthorytye a Counsell of the Nobylytie and others to governe thys Realme'. But 'The last and worste degree of all is', Throckmorton noted, 'not onelye to have the Quenes Proces made, and her condemnacion publycke, but also the depryvacyon of her estate and lyffe to Insue'. This course of action was supported by a 'gret nomber'. Throckmorton pushed for the first option – a restoration, with a divorce between Mary and Bothwell, conditions for the preservation of James, and a secure religious settlement – and he stood against trial and deposition; but the Scots argued that the extraordinary and monstrous circumstances warranted 'extraordynarye procedinges'. This was a counter to Throckmorton's first argument: 'there was no ordynarye Magistrate, No Competent Judge nor Judges: No suffycyent assemblye nor Tryle before whom theyre Quene and Soveraigne should have her proces made and her cause adjudged'.[6] So what was going to happen to Mary? Should she keep her throne or lose it? And if the deposition of the Queen of Scots was a tempting prospect, after nearly ten years of pushing her claim to the English crown, who should execute the plan? Subjects or a reigning monarch? An English commission or a great council? A Protestant queen or an imperial and superior monarch with powers over Scotland?

The English regime had a clear idea of the sort of settlement it wanted for Scotland even in the summer of 1567. One of the reasons for Throckmorton's concern may well have been that he already knew England wanted a moderate and balanced solution to the problem. Cecil had personally drafted Throckmorton's diplomatic instructions at the beginning of July, and these were based on the liberty of Mary 'with theis provisions followyng'. Most of them rested on a balance between the position of Mary and the rights of the nobility. There was also a strong element of conciliar involvement. The Queen of Scots would govern the realm 'with advise of the Parlement'; but more significant than this was the emphasis on the supervisory power of a Scottish great council, with power over Marcher wardens, principal officers of the kingdom, and ecclesiastical promotions. Replacements for deceased council members would be nominated by the Queen 'with the Consent of the rest'. Membership would have to be kept to the level where 'allweiss ther may be attendant monthly at the lest iiij or vj'; this, combined with formal orders for 'ther sittyng in Counsells and sollicityng of causees to the Quene', the supervision of a political settlement by the Scottish parliament, and the final note that Elizabeth 'may be moved

---

[6] Throckmorton to Cecil, 18 July 1567, SP 52/14, fo. 51r; Throckmorton to Elizabeth, 19 July 1567, Cotton Caligula C. 1, fos. 28r–29r.

to become a mayntenor of the same parlement', were not only possible solutions: they became part of Cecil's preferred approach to the British succession crisis.[7] And Cecil was not alone in thinking that this was the best way to tackle such an intricate and persistently thorny problem. Throckmorton showed his instructions to Sir Nicholas Bacon, and Bacon was a supporter: 'I fynd hys opinion to concurre with yours for the necessary havyng off the prynce off scottland the beynge same growndyd uppon grett reason.'[8]

The proposal seemed to fit the political circumstances, although in late July 1567 the earl of Bedford told the earl of Shrewsbury that there were rumours of Mary's abdication: 'that is to saye to renounce her title, and committ the Governement of the Prince to the lordes, and she her selfe to go abrode into a fforayne Realme'. After his visit to Mary and her court earlier in the year, Bedford was slightly sceptical.[9] But less than a year later, Mary was forced to take Atholl's option of abandoning Scotland, leaving her kingdom and her child in the hands of the nobility. This was the most important political event of the decade and it was a completely new situation. In 1559, when Cecil had sponsored the military campaign in Scotland, Mary had been in France; six years later, during the Darnley crisis, she was in a relatively solid political position in Scotland; and finally, after ten years of chipping away at Elizabeth's crown, she was in English hands. Cecil followed the whole process very carefully. He annotated Throckmorton's report on the groups in Scotland from 19 July 1567. He also corrected a detailed account of her escape. The earl of Moray ordered a search for the Queen and Mary's supporters signed a formal band soon after her escape. Her flight from Lochleven merely reinforced the party divisions in Scotland.[10]

But the fall of the Queen of Scots held two benefits for the English. First, she was in their hands; and second, a Moray regency in Scotland meant – or was perceived to mean – Protestantism and British friendship. In the providential scheme of things, the disintegration of Mary's power in Scotland was, in the words of Sir Walter Mildmay, a 'mervaylous tragedy'; but it happened to 'such as lyve not in the feare of god'. More important for Mildmay were the possibilities. 'If the governement rest onely in the Erle of Murray, it wilbe well as I thinke for stablishing of Religion, and

---

[7] SP 52/14, fo. 1v, printed below, pp. 233–4.
[8] Throckmorton to Cecil, 1 July 1567, SP 52/14, fo. 3r.
[9] 22 July 1567, Lambeth Palace Library, 3196, fo. 213, printed in Edmund Lodge (ed.), *Illustrations of British history, biography, and manners* . . ., 3 vols. (London, 1791), I, pp. 363–4.
[10] For Throckmorton's report, Cotton Caligula C. 1, fo. 28r–v; and the account of Mary's escape, 17 July 1568, Cotton Caligula C. 1, fos. 168r–173v; SP 52/15, fos. 18r–v, 19r, 20r, 21r; for the band, 8 May 1568, SP 52/15, fo. 22r–v.

contynuaunce of amytie here.' He also personally liked the Regent.[11] Two things had to stand: religion and amity, and Mildmay never looked 'for the latter to hold long, except the first be surelie stablisshed'.[12] Moray appeared willing to assume control of Scotland and promoted himself as the reluctant, godly, and virtuous representative of the kingdom, 'compellit and conwict in conscience to yeild to the manyfald preassinges of Many noble men heirabout, and to accept upon me this chardge wechtye . . . [which] . . . can bring to me nothyer proffeytt nor commodite'.[13] England and Scotland seemed to have become, on a new level, part of an integrated British Protestant culture.

Cecil realized that this change in the relationship between England and Scotland was disliked in Catholic Europe. Moray, for his part, sensed 'frenche practises' against the two kingdoms as soon as Mary had escaped.[14] Cecil wanted Protestant, friendly, and stable government in Scotland, but it was hard to escape the fact that (in foreign eyes) Elizabeth had effectively sanctioned the *de facto* deposition of Mary and had endorsed the earl of Moray's regency. This was made all the more worrying for Elizabethans by the fact that, from 1565, there had been persistent reports of an organized European conspiracy against Protestant England. By 1568 this seemed to have taken a more solid form in the duke of Alva's army. In March of the same year, Cecil told Sir Ralph Sadler that the palsgrave had seized some of Alva's campaign money from Genoa; he complained that the palsgrave was 'the only prince of Almayn that sheweth hym self a playn mayntenor of the Prynce of Condé, and Godes cause'.[15]

So the Queen of Scots' detention in England was an important event of major European significance. In May 1568 Cecil worked through some of the implications of her stay. The French presented the main threat, and he thought that an attempted restoration of Mary was one possibility. This would be engineered by the Guise, with two effects: first, it could trap England between a Franco-Scottish alliance; and second, it would encourage 'all papistes and discontented persons' in England, 'wherof the consequence is overdaungerooss to be mentioned'. Cecil proposed a clear course of action. England had to try to persuade the French not to intervene; just in case this failed, the navy had to be put 'in redyness' and the border reinforced. But justice for the Queen of Scots was one of his main themes: above all, England had to be *seen* to be treating Mary fairly

---

[11] Mildmay to Cecil, 4 August 1567, SP 12/43, fo. 89r.

[12] Mildmay to Cecil, 15 August 1567, SP 12/43, fo. 117r.

[13] *c.* 24 August 1567, Darnaway Castle, Forres, Moray TD 94/56, no. 58r.

[14] Moray to Leicester, 3 May 1568, National Library of Scotland, 3657, fo. 37r; P.J. Holmes, 'Mary Stewart in England', *Innes Review*, 38 (1987), 195.

[15] 14 March 1568, SP 12/46, fo. 113r.

and properly. For what they were worth, these two proposals were the first line of defence against European action.[16]

The regime had to face the serious issue of dealing with a monarch who, on the one hand, had been a persistent problem but, on the other, was apparently the focus of sympathetic European Catholic attention. Cecil knew that her part in the murder of Darnley was crucial: if Mary was innocent she could be restored with conditions; if guilty, her fate would depend on Elizabeth. England's options were limited and they all carried risks. It was dangerous for Mary to be allowed to return to Scotland, too risky to endorse a Stuart restoration in the kingdom, and a threat for her to remain in England. For Cecil the first meant a renewal of 'the old leage betwixt the Crowns of fraunce and scotland', the second would involve the collapse of the 'frendes of england' in government, and the third risked agitation over the succession and 'the boldnes of all evill subjectes'. But it was still 'necessary & proffitable' for Elizabeth to take action. Mary had persistently claimed a right to her cousin's throne. Only an alliance of England, Scotland, and Ireland could resist 'the malice of france, and the rest of Christendom'. By uniting England and Scotland 'in band ageynst the usurped power of Roome, the cause of Relligion' would 'also be furdered'. By 'these ij being frendly and peacibly Joyned with Irland quieted', the two kingdoms 'may preserve them selves with good government, from the malice of france and the rest of Christendom'.[17] So in 1568 the regime had to ask two related questions. How should Mary be dealt with in England and on what justification? And how could a Protestant Britain be defined and shaped to England's advantage?

II

Cecil's sense of how Britain could be ordered began to develop in May 1568. For Cecil, England was the natural imperial and superior power in Britain. In 1559 he had accepted and employed for political purposes the imperial origins of the English crown; and so near the end of the decade he developed arguments he had used at its beginning. In 1568, as in 1559, Cecil claimed that Elizabeth's superiority was the key to the comprehension of Mary and the political supervision of Britain.[18] His notes in 1568 were part of two discussions on the future of Mary, on the principle that 'it

[16] Cotton Caligula C. 1, fo. 76r–v, printed in Joseph Stevenson (ed.), *Selections from unpublished manuscripts in the College of Arms and the British Museum illustrating the reign of Mary Queen of Scotland 1543–1568* (Maitland Club, 41; Glasgow, 1837), pp. 308–9; Cotton Caligula C. 1, fos. 97r–98v, 99v–100v.

[17] Cotton Caligula C. 1, fos. 97v–100r.

[18] See above, pp. 59–60.

belongeth of very right to the Crown of england to gyve ordre to dissensions moved for the Crown of scotland'. This was written as a statement of fact and justification and not as a point for debate. Elizabeth was an arbiter in British affairs who could 'take uppon hir, the hearyng, decydyng and determyning of any controversy moved for the Crown of Scotland', based on the evidence he had used nearly ten years earlier of 'recordes, examples, and presidentes'.[19]

Cecil developed a more rounded sense of a settlement in August 1568, but the principles of the proposal had formed the foundation of the instructions given to Sir Nicholas Throckmorton in July 1567 for 'provisions' for a 'Graund Counsell' to advise Mary, the parliamentary supervision of Scotland, Protestantism, the end of the Franco-Scottish alliance, and the safety of Prince James.[20] In 1567 the focus was on a domestic settlement between the Queen of Scots and her nobility; in May and August 1568 Cecil concentrated more on Mary's position from an English perspective. He restated and reinforced the principle of the external control of Scotland by England so that Elizabeth could act as the 'defender of the accord betwixt the Quene and hir subjectes'.[21] The settlement had to be secured by the Scottish parliament and 'tripartited betwixt the Quene of England, the Quene of scotland, and hir sonne the Prynce and all them that have adhered to hym'. In this way, the agreement would be based on 'condition if the Quene of Scottes do violat hir part, that uppon the Judgment of the Quene of england the child may succede'.[22]

So there were two principles behind the early drafts of Cecil's proposal: first, that Scotland could be operated from within by council and parliament; and second, that Scotland's place in Britain should be supervised by Elizabeth as a superior monarch. The plan also carried the baggage of nearly a decade of argument and debate. The Treaty of Edinburgh had to be ratified and the security of Protestantism was crucial: the 'formular of england' could be used to settle Scotland. Cecil was equally keen to calm the Scots' fears of French officeholders and the sensitive issue of Mary's marriage to Bothwell. Moreover, he was not writing in a political vacuum. There was a strong relationship between Cecil's notes from May and August 1568, the reports he was receiving from Sir Francis Knollys on Mary, her representatives, and the situation in Scotland, and the conference held at York that autumn. Cecil acknowledged and endorsed Moray's

[19] See above, pp. 59–60; Cotton Caligula C. 1, fos. 76v, 98r; Stevenson (ed.), *Selections*, p. 309.
[20] See below, pp. 233–4.
[21] Cotton Caligula C. 1, fo. 100v.
[22] 'Memoriall Generall', 17 August 1568, SP 12/47, fo. 76r, with some punctuation added; see below, pp. 236–7.

position in Scotland. In this way, he was able to balance the demand of the Queen of Scots for a settlement and the clear benefit of having a sympathetic Protestant regime in Scotland.[23]

But there was still the difficulty of countering Mary's call for an audience with Elizabeth because of the Queen's determination not to have contact with a woman, monarch or not, alleged to have had a hand in the murder of her husband. Knollys raised the general issue with Mary at the end of May 1568. 'I objected unto hyr', he told Elizabeth, 'that in some cases prynces myght be deposed from theyr government by theyr subjects lawfully'. Madness was the example he used. 'And (sayd I) what dyfference is there betwene lunecye, and civell murderyng?'[24] Although on that occasion Knollys had to cope with the Queen of Scots' tears, Mary was resolutely determined to play on Elizabeth's sisterly duty to hear her case in person. Henry Middlemore, Throckmorton's secretary in France in the early 1560s, was sent into Scotland at the beginning of June with a threefold mission: to establish the earl of Moray's position, to air the idea of leaving Elizabeth to deal with the 'Inward Controversyes' of the problem and, more ominously, to tell Mary that she had not been received in London because 'the Quenes Majesty doth nother condem hir of the same, nor yet can acquit hir untill she shall heare what may be sayd therin'. This was the diplomatic problem: Elizabeth had to do her best to convince Mary that her intentions were fair; the Queen of Scots, on the other hand, wanted an interview and Elizabeth's full support. Even the relationship between London and Moray was a strange mix of the practically political and the monarchically virtuous. Elizabeth told Moray that the news of Mary's effective deposition 'can not but sounde very strange in the eares of us being a Prince Sovverayn having dominione and Subjectes committed to our Powre as she had', and yet the influence of the new regent was exactly what privy councillors like Cecil and Mildmay wanted.[25]

After receiving reports by Middlemore and Knollys in mid-June 1568, Cecil prepared two short discussions *in utramque partem*. On the same day, 20 June, eleven members of the Privy Council met to discuss the future of the Queen of Scots.[26] In sections 'Pro Regina scotorum' and 'Contra

---

[23] Cotton Caligula C. 1, fo. 100v; SP 12/47, fo. 76r; see below, p. 236.

[24] Knollys to Elizabeth, 30 May 1568, Cotton Caligula C. 1, fo. 114r.

[25] *c.* 8 June 1568, SP 52/15, fo. 58r; 8 June 1568, Cotton Caligula C. 1, fos. 122r, 123r.

[26] Middlemore [to Cecil], 14 June 1568, Cotton Caligula C. 1, fos. 130r–132v; Knollys [to Cecil], 13 June 1568; for Cecil's notes *in utramque partem*, Cotton Caligula C. 1, fos. 139r–140r; and for Bernard Hampton's copy of the minutes from Council, Cotton Caligula C. 1, fos. 137r–138r. The councillors were Arundel, Bacon, Bedford, Cecil, Clinton, Howard of Effingham, Leicester, Mildmay, Norfolk, Sadler, and a 'Lord Marquess', so either Northampton or Winchester; perhaps Northampton, because Winchester was usually referred to by his office of lord treasurer.

Reginam scotorum' Cecil worked through the arguments for the Queen of
Scots' innocence, but he also accepted the alleged evidence of her guilt. She
had arrived in England as a Queen unlawfully condemned and imprisoned
in Scotland. Mary was 'a Quene and monarch, subject to none, nor yet
bound by hir lawes to answer to hir subjectes'; she had charged some of her
subjects with equally serious crimes. The notes *contra* were just as compelling. Mary was alleged to have taken part in the murder of Darnley and to
have been 'ledd' and 'trayned' to 'placees dishonorable' by the earl of
Bothwell. She later had him acquitted, ended up as his wife, and 'gave also
to the partyes that executed the murdre, landes and officees'. In Scotland
her enemies gathered 'to consult how to procede in punishyng of the
murdre'.[27]

The meeting of the Privy Council supplied a corollary for Cecil notes.
Mary Stuart could not be allowed either to leave the realm or to be restored
to her throne 'before hir cause be honorably tryed'. Bernard Hampton's
first draft read 'honorably hard', but the euphemism was probably pointless. There were no marks of disagreement or dissension in the Council. It
was aware, like Cecil had been in May, of the interest of the French and
Spanish in the affair. The two kings had to understand Elizabeth's 'honorable intention and manner of dealing'. But a trial was still the only way of
proving English justice: a restoration without a proceeding could suggest
that Mary had been acquitted. This would encourage the French and could
mean that her heart would 'be more kindeled with ire and desire of revenge
against the Quenes Majesty'. Mary was a Catholic Queen; she had a
consistent record of challenging Elizabeth's right to the throne and she had
been prepared to 'trouble' her cousin. In this sense, the Queen of Scots was
a dangerous woman.[28]

The regime began to prepare the case against Mary in summer 1568. For
the sake of accurate reporting, the Council agreed on 20 June that the
proceedings should be observed by 'Princes Ambassadors to be named by
the Quene of Scottes'. But the main justification for the trial still lay in
Elizabeth's British authority, 'saving always the superiority that of ancient
right belongeth to the Crowne of England in causes of Scotland'. Just over
a week later, Matthew Parker wrote to tell Cecil that Henry III had ordered
a search of chronicle histories in 1246 or 1247 'concernyng the superiorytie
in scotland'. Parker's agents had found an interesting (and linguistically
very dubious) reference to the king of England as 'rex hibernie'. Three days
later, on 7 July, the Privy Council ordered a search of all private, state,
ecclesiastical, and civil archives; the circular was signed by the group of six
councillors who had all attended the meeting on 20 June. On 30 June Cecil

---

[27] Cotton Caligula C. 1, fos. 139r–140r.   [28] Cotton Caligula C. 1, fos. 137v–138r.

prepared a set of more concrete legal justifications for the trial of Mary. He had seen copies of the incriminating 'casket' documents, but even if the originals matched the duplicates, 'No proves can be taken for sufficient without hearyng of both partyes'. From Cecil's notes, the main aim of the process was Elizabeth's 'desyre to compound all differencees' between Mary and her subjects. England wanted a trial based on criminal evidence and Elizabeth's British superiority. The regime also wanted a 'good end' before the first day of August 1568.[29]

III

Cecil's timetable was optimistic. He made a note to 'nominat Commission-ars to heare the Lordes of scotlandes answer, and to treate with the Quene of scottes' at the beginning of August. It took nearly a week to name the candidates. Cecil mentioned the duke of Norfolk, the earl of Sussex, and Lord Hunsdon, but Hunsdon's commission was for the governorship of Berwick. Three men were eventually named: Norfolk, Sussex, and Sir Ralph Sadler. Sadler had had years of Anglo-Scottish diplomatic experi-ence. Norfolk was the most senior nobleman in England. Sussex had been in Ireland as lord lieutenant and he had been privy to the intricacies of British planning in the early 1560s and the strategic impact of Scotland's connections with Ulster. Like Norfolk he was also a member of the generally conservative Howard family.[30]

Cecil corrected Norfolk's, Sussex's, and Sadler's instructions, which established the method for dealing with the rival claims of Mary and the party of Prince James. The parties' individual 'requestes or complayntes' had to be heard separately, 'apart by them selves', and put down in writing. These individual charges had to be answered, again on paper. After this stage and a series of oaths for each group, the commissioners could 'treate with both parties together'. If the evidence against Mary seemed good, Norfolk, Sussex, and Sadler had to write to Elizabeth; if she was innocent, then the Scots had to consider 'in what sort the said Quene may be restored to hir Crowne according to hir estate without danger of a relaps to fall into misgovernment or without the danger of hir subjectes'.[31]

The second half of the 'memoriall' moves away from the mechanics of the conference to the nature of a proposed British settlement. In this sense,

---

[29] 20 June 1568, Cotton Caligula C. 1, fo. 137r; Parker to Cecil, 4 July 1568, SP 12/47, fo. 3r; for the Council's circular letter, 7 July 1568, Additional 35831, fo. 279r–v, and printed as *STC* 7754.6; and for Cecil's notes, 30 June 1568, Cotton Caligula C. 1, fo. 152r.

[30] 'Memoriall Generall', 8 and 17 August 1568, SP 12/47, fos. 75r–76r; see below, pp. 235–7.

[31] 'A memoriall for the order and proceding' of Norfolk, Sussex, and Sadler, drafted by Bernard Hampton and corrected by Cecil, Cotton Caligula C. 1, fos. 227r–232v.

it is a crucial document which makes an important connection between notes for a settlement prepared by Cecil in 1567, May 1568, and even 1570. Some of its main themes are a regency and council for Scotland, implemented by a British tripartite treaty, supervised by England as part of a settlement conscious of the need to break the connection between Scotland and France and to secure Ireland. It was Cecil who edited the instructions, possibly as a member of a group working on the Anglo-Scottish question and definitely supported by the Clerk of the Privy Council, Bernard Hampton.[32] The 'memoriall' was not an exercise in altruism. It underlined and used Elizabeth's 'power to be as umpere and principall arbitrer' in British affairs. According to the settlement it outlined, Mary's actions would be assessed by Elizabeth and a quorum of a 'graund Counsell' of Scotland, which was set at a third. So, in effect, the 'memoriall' dealt with the connected issues of the nature of the proceedings against Mary, the internal government of Scotland, and the practical justifications for the supervision of the political affairs of the kingdom. The main task of the Scottish council was to supervise the Queen, and its effectiveness depended on its permanence and its size. The 'memoriall' maintained that a 'convenient nomber' of men established at the 'time of this treaty' should govern the kingdom, the 'same to be allways renewed by the more parte, or two third partes, of the said Counsell' if there were any losses through death or incapacity. For the most part, the council's membership would be made up by 'the principall officers of the Realme': the chancellor, the archbishops and bishops, the lord justice, the comptroller, the treasurer, the admiral, the chamberlain, and the president and lords of session. Cecil also added the captains of castles, the provosts of burghs, all financial officers, and 'ambassadors or messengers to any forrayn princees'.[33]

This Scottish grand council was planned as a mixed, comprehensive, and large group of the important men of the kingdom, brought together 'for the good observation' of the treaty. It made Cecil's 1585 plan for a council to sit in the event of the death of Elizabeth look limited in its personnel.[34] But part of the responsibility for policing the settlement outlined in the 'memoriall' would lie with the Scottish parliament. This was a consistent theme in diplomatic instructions and Cecil's private notes between 1567 and 1568. According to the 'memoriall', Mary's rule had to be supervised

[32] The second and third parts of 'A memoriall for the order and proceding' of the English commissioners, Cotton Caligula C. 1, fos. 229r–232v, is printed below, pp. 238–43. On 17 August 1568 Cecil listed seven councillors – Norfolk, Arundel, Sussex, Bedford, Leicester, Sadler, and Mildmay – and Throckmorton; all of them, except perhaps Arundel, had either had direct diplomatic experience in Scotland or been in close contact with Scottish councillors; see below, p. 236.

[33] See below, pp. 238–9.

[34] See above, pp. 114–15.

by what Cecil was perfectly happy to call 'the .3. estates in parliament'. With the grand council and Elizabeth, parliament would be able to hear complaints against the Queen of Scots; in an extreme case, and supported by at least a third of the grand councillors or six lords of Scotland, it would be able to transfer Mary's crown to the next heir. The Queen of Scots would not be able to 'marry nor contract mariage with any parson without the assent of hir .3. estates or the more part therof'. Also, the settlement planned in the English commissioners' instructions endorsed the religious measures discussed and implemented in the parliament of December 1567, held in the name of James, and used to justify 'the caus of the detentioun of the quenis grace in the hous of Lochlevin'. In the 'memoriall' religious laws 'for the help and sustentation of the ministers of the Chirch, and for advancement of true relligion and abrogating of Idolatry and superstition' had to remain in force. This was a commitment to the protection of the reformed church and an endorsement of the Protestant parliamentary settlement in Scotland of 1560.[35]

Each part of this proposal was designed to limit and bind the Queen of Scots, secure the interests of England, and appease Catholic Europe: Mary back in Scotland, effectively supervised by council and parliament, reinforced by a settlement based on the protection of Protestantism, the safety of Prince James and his inheritance, and the imperial superiority of Elizabeth. The regime could preserve Moray's government of Scotland without having to take the risk of deposing Mary. But the 'memoriall' was also a statement of British security. At the end of the main text, Cecil prepared a separate list of clauses to make absolutely sure that England's position and Elizabeth's crown were secure. The Treaty of Edinburgh had to be ratified, something the Queen of Scots had refused to do in 1561. But the commissioners could make 'a Proviso': no part of the Edinburgh agreement would bind Mary or her children after the life of Elizabeth and her heirs. Among 'Certen other things necessary' was a new relationship with England in which the Scottish regime would reject the 'old league of Fraunce and Scotland' and agree not 'to receave or ayde any rebell or fugitive of the other'. Again, this was a long-standing aim. In 1562 Cecil calculated that the 'auncient leage' between France and Scotland had 'contynued these 478 yeres, and cold never be dissolved by no marriadg nor treaty with scotland, untill this daye'. Negotiations with Mary and Darnley

---

[35] See below, p. 239; cf. *Acts of the parliament of Scotland*, ed. Thomas Thomson and Cosmo Innes, 12 vols. (Edinburgh, 1814–75), II, pp. 548–9, for the security of the 'professouris of the said Religioun', April 1567; III, p. 14, 'Anent the abolissing of the Pape, and his usurpit authoritie' and 'Anent the annulling of the actis of Parliament, maid aganis Goddis word, and mantenance of Idolatrie in ony tymes bypast', 20 December 1567; and III, pp. 35–8, 'Ratificatioun of certane actis pronuncit in the parliament haldin in 1560', 20 December 1567.

in 1565 had included a principle that 'their Majesties shall nott enter into anye league or federation with anye forayne Prince to the hurte, damminge, or displeasure of the Queen and Realme of England'. For Cecil, the 'memoriall' was an expression of the strategic priorities the regime had had since the early 1560s.[36]

A crucial issue was Ireland and the strategic danger of contact between the west of Scotland and Ulster. The Treaty of Berwick had been the cornerstone of a policy which understood the intimate relationship between interests in Scotland and Ireland, but the earl of Argyle had not been used to support English forces, Sussex had failed spectacularly to counter Shane O'Neill, and Elizabeth and the Privy Council knew from 1565 that the Queen of Scots was funding O'Neill. In 1562 Shane had seemed willing to play the faithful servant of the English crown; by 1566 Ireland was (Cecil told Sir Thomas Smith) 'out of joynt' and 'out of Tune'.[37] The only domestic options seemed to be defensive military force and a policy of plantation. Externally, the English had to break the connection between Ireland and Scotland and prevent Scots crossing the Irish Sea. The Queen of Scots promised as much in February 1567, when Cecil told Sir Henry Sidney that Mary had 'prohibited the commyng of any moo scottes into Irland, and will spedely revoke those that be ther'. Argyle had promised 'to execut hir commandment'.[38] In May 1568 Cecil argued that one of the reasons for not allowing Mary's return to Scotland 'to rule as she did' was the danger to Ireland: 'Irland shall be molested with the scottes more than it hath bene'.[39] And so, again, the politics of 1568 provided the perfect opportunity to settle the issue once and for all. As part of the settlement Cecil sketched in August 1568, it was important to establish the principle that 'no subject of scotland' should 'resort into Irland' and 'no straungers men of warr to be reteyned in scotland'.[40] This was repeated in the instructions for Norfolk, Sussex, and Sadler. Any help for a foreign ruler to invade 'England or Irland or any Iles or membres of ether of the said Kingdomes' meant that Mary would lose whatever title she had or claimed to have to the English throne.[41] The 'memoriall' established the model for later negotiations. In May 1570, for example, one article presented to Mary maintained that she would 'suffer no scottishman or any other of the owt Iles of Scotland to enter into any part of Irland, Without licens of the

[36] See below, pp. 242–3; 20 June 1562, Cotton Caligula B. 10, fo. 211r; 13 August 1565, SP 52/11, fo. 26r.
[37] Cecil to Smith, 26 March 1566, Lansdowne 102, fo. 132r; Cecil to Smith, 11 April 1566, Harley 6990, fo. 72r.
[38] Cecil to Sidney, 25 February 1567, SP 63/20, fo. 78r.
[39] Cotton Caligula C. 1, fo. 98r.
[40] See below, p. 236.
[41] See below, pp. 242–3.

Depute there; nether shall [she] receave any rebell or fugytyve of Irland, or suffer any such to be maynteaned in scotland or in any part of the Iles'.[42]

The internal settlement of Scotland and the protection of England in a British context: these are the two key themes of the 'memoriall'. Its proposed Scottish grand council was an interesting extension of the model provided by Sir James Balfour of Pittendreich. According to Balfour's *Practicks*, the king's 'secreit', or privy, council should consist of two bishops, an abbot or prior, six barons, the chancellor, the master of the household, the chamberlain, the privy seal, the secretary, and the clerk of the register. In fact, as Lord President of the court of session in 1568, Balfour would have sat on the grand council of the 'memoriall'. What is more, some of the main councillors in 1568 were supporters of Moray's regime: Morton as Chancellor and Comptroller Sir William Murray from the commissioners' 'memoriall', and Secretary Maitland of Lethington and Clerk Register James McGill (both of whom were colleagues of Moray at the conference in York) in the privy council. Cecil understood the nature and personnel of power in Scotland; he was prepared also to endorse Moray's monopoly of it. From August 1567 privy seal writs in Scotland were issued in the name of the regent. Warrants under the great seal were witnessed by Morton after September 1567, with Moray acting as *avunculus regis*. The 'memoriall' tacitly endorsed Moray's *de facto* power in Scotland but it seemed also to support the Queen of Scots' *de jure* rights. The main issue facing Elizabeth's commissioners in autumn 1568 was the diplomatic resolution of this difficult problem.[43]

IV

The conference at York – termed by Gordon Donaldson Mary Stuart's 'first trial' – began as it went on: slowly and with a painfully limited sense of progress. At the beginning of October 1568, after some long and detailed debates over the accuracy of Mary's commission to her representatives – which maintained that Elizabeth had taken it upon herself to restore the Queen of Scots to her throne – the negotiations began too carefully. Moray was supported by the earl of Morton, Adam Bothwell (bishop of Orkney), Robert Pitcairn (archdeacon of St Andrews and commendator of Dunferm-

---

[42] 7 May 1570, Cotton Caligula C. 2, fo. 23v.
[43] Sir James Balfour, *Practicks*, ed. Peter G.B. McNeill, 2 vols. (Stair Society, 21, 22; Edinburgh, 1962–3), I, p. 14; *Registrum secreti sigilli regum scotorum: the register of the privy seal of Scotland*, ed. M. Livingstone *et al.*, 8 vols. (Edinburgh, 1908–82), VI, p. vi, from August 1567; *Registrum magni sigilli regum scotorum: the register of the great seal of Scotland*, ed. James Balfour Paul, 11 vols. (Edinburgh, London, and Melbourne, 1984), IV, p. 455 and n. 1; cf. CP 138, fo. 44v, 5 October 1568, where the great seal of Scotland was used in Moray's commission at York.

line), and Patrick, Lord Lindsay. But the team which advised Moray and Prince James' other commissioners was perhaps even more impressive, a fact which makes Norfolk's, Sussex's, and Sadler's lack of support surprising: Maitland of Lethington, Clerk Register James McGill, the lawyer Henry Balnaves of Halhill, and George Buchanan, academic and (very probably at this point) author of *De jure regni apud Scotos*. Mary's representatives were the earl of Cassillis, the bishop of Galloway, lords Herries and Boyd, Sir John Gordon of Lochinvar, Sir James Cockburn of Skirling, and John Leslie, bishop of Ross, probably the only commissioner to write an account of the early proceedings against the Queen of Scots and work some of the material into printed form.[44]

Moray was worried from the beginning. Herries and his colleagues had apparently said that, even with a guilty verdict, Elizabeth intended to support and restore Mary. James' party may have been calmed by the 'frendlye talke of sundrie mattirs' between Moray, Morton, Norfolk, Sussex, and Sadler, but the talks took four days to get going. From a very early stage, it was clear that the treaty proposals in the English commissioners' instructions were not going to be settled quickly. Gordon Donaldson has argued that the rival commissioners, as old friends, got on very well together, but this should not hide the fact that Mary's and James' representatives were taking irreconcilable positions. Leslie, Herries, and their colleagues presented a set of grievances against Moray; they maintained that he had taken 'upon him the name of Regent, usurpinge thereby the supreame aucthoritie of that Realme, in the name of that Infant'. That afternoon, Moray's party countered with the claim that Mary was 'the devisour and procurer of that murder, or otherwise was giltie thereof'.[45]

The conference was flawed for two main reasons. The positions of Moray and of Mary's representatives were virtually impossible to comprehend and, perhaps more significantly, the issue was just too big for three groups of men effectively to deal with. Elizabeth's commissioners followed their instructions. They met the other representatives separately and took written statements of their respective positions. But if they were expected to negotiate a full settlement of the problem – and the proposed treaty clauses of their 'memoriall' seem clear enough on this point – then there seems to have been a return to the old diplomatic problem of expecting more than is entirely reasonable. Not only were Norfolk, Sadler, and

---

[44] Gordon Donaldson, *The first trial of Mary, Queen of Scots* (London, 1969), especially pp. 106–21. For Leslie's manuscript account of proceedings between September 1568 and March 1572, Lansdowne 231, fos. 244r–322v; cf. *A defence of the honour of the right highe, mightye and noble princesse Marie quene of Scotlande* . . . (*STC* 15505; [Rheims,] 1569).

[45] For the claims and counter-claims of 8 October 1568, see Cotton Caligula C. 1, fo. 259r; and CP 138, fos. 49v, 50r.

Sussex slowly disappearing under the small mountain of paper being created by Mary's commissioners but their commission was challenged by Moray, who asked whether Elizabeth's representatives had 'sufficient aucthoritie from the Quenes Majestie of England, to pronounce in the Cause of the murder, giltie, or not giltie'.[46]

Norfolk, Sussex, Sadler, and the Privy Council took the issue very seriously. Moray had his legal team in York; the English commissioners relied on support from London, with Cecil as the principal bridge between them and the Council. Cecil dealt with Moray's questions on 9 October 1568, and Bernard Hampton acted as his clerk. The core group – in effect a subcommittee of the Council – consisted of the earls of Arundel and Leicester, lords Clinton and Howard of Effingham, and (according to the record but hard to reconcile with his presence in York) Sadler. Moray wanted to know four things. Did the English commissioners have the power to pass judgement on Mary? If Norfolk, Sussex, and Sadler had authority, then was London prepared to pronounce 'Immediatly and without ony further delay'? If Mary was found guilty, would she be sent back into Scotland or kept in England for the safety of James? And if Mary was guilty, would England endorse the 'procedinges in tymes past' of Moray and his colleagues, and maintain the authority of James, established in the regency and according to an act of parliament?[47]

In reply, the Privy Council maintained that the commissions were secure. The draft text of their answer promised to pronounce a verdict 'without any unnecessary delay'. The reply to Moray's third question, on the future of Mary in the event of a guilty verdict, was suitably vague; but it still established that she would either be returned to Scotland with assurances and conditions or be kept in England. The answer to the fourth was the most important, carefully worded and refined by Cecil from the basic notes to Bernard Hampton's copy. It stated that if Mary should 'be proved and found gilty of the murder', Elizabeth would 'allow' their proceedings against the Queen of Scots if they had been lawful at the time. In other words, if Moray could prove that Mary was guilty then Elizabeth, even under pressure from the Catholic powers of Europe, was prepared to bless the regency.[48]

Mary's part in the murder of Darnley has traditionally been the territory of antiquarians, amateur historians, and romantic biographers, but it is actually a good deal more politically important than it seems. England wanted a settlement based on a Moray regency, strict conciliar and

---

[46] Cotton Caligula C. 1, fo. 310r; CP 138, fo. 51v.
[47] For the minutes of the Privy Council's meeting, 9 October 1568, CP 155, fo. 130r; Cotton Caligula C. 1, fo. 310r; CP 138, fos. 51v–52r.
[48] Cotton Caligula C. 1, fo. 311r–v; CP 155, fo. 130r.

parliamentary supervision, and imperial control. But the regime needed solid evidence. In European terms, Elizabeth and her Privy Council were skating on rapidly thinning ice. Only a few days before the York conference began, Sir Nicholas Throckmorton warned Cecil that the 'generall deseygne' of the Catholic powers 'ys to extermynate all nations dyssentyng with them yn relygion'; he thought that after the military campaigns in France and the Netherlands, England was next. In April 1567 Cecil had lamented the 'poore protestantes in Flaunders'. He also wanted to take back Calais – and fight in France – 'if we had monny ynought'. So Cecil, for one, wanted to challenge European Catholic aggression with a counter-offensive. The situation was at least as serious a year later. London's plan for a trial for Mary and a settlement of Scotland and Britain was radical in itself, but the dangerous ideological and military situation in Europe put it in an even more urgent context. The Privy Council's answers, according to Cecil, were sensitive enough 'secretly to be imparted to the sayd Erle of Murray and to be secretly kept to hym self untill the Quenes Majesty shall have hard the cause and notefyed hir mynd therin'.[49]

The suspicion of Mary's guilt was confirmed at York on 10 October 1568, when Moray presented the English commissioners with his evidence. This included, according to their report back to Elizabeth, 'one horrible and longe Lettre of her owne hand, as they saye, conteyninge foule matteir and abhominable, to be either thowght of, or to be written by a Prince', a reference which warranted a marginal mark by Cecil. The commissioners' report was so detailed and damning that Cecil used it in the prosecution case against Norfolk in 1572, although he tinkered with it to emphasize the duke's belief in 1568 that Mary was guilty.[50] Copies of the evidence were sent down to London, but Sadler kept his own note of the Queen of Scots' 'speciall wordes'.[51] The earl of Sussex confirmed that the conference was going to be a trial of Mary *in absentia* when he told Cecil of 'an abstract to be presently made of all thecawses depending in this cowrt'. But Moray's evidence caused more problems for the conference than it solved. As early as 10 October, Sussex gave a 'warninge by proclamacion' that the next sitting was going to begin on 22 November because he thought that 'proceding by order of lawe bredeth in these partes a grownded hatred betwene the parties'. The complexity of the proceedings, the explosive potential of the evidence, and fear of sympathy for Mary in Yorkshire

---

[49] Throckmorton to Cecil, 18 September 1568, CP 155, fo. 117r; Cecil to Sidney, 23 April 1567, SP 63/20, fo. 144r; Privy Council, 9 October 1568, CP 155, fo. 130r.
[50] Commissioners to Elizabeth, 11 October 1568, Cotton Caligula C. 1, fo. 260v.
[51] For Sadler's notes, Additional 33593, fos. 11r–12v. For copies of the evidence sent down to London, Cotton Caligula C. 1, fos. 260v–261r; CP 352, nos. 1–4; and Harley 787, fos. 44r–45v.

meant that Professor Donaldson's collegial good humour had given way to something darker and more political.[52]

The conference did begin again in late November, but it reappeared as a trial by council at Westminster. Something had clearly changed in the English approach: from a small commission in constant touch with Elizabeth, briefed and backed by the Privy Council at a distance, the conference reinvented itself. Religion and geography played their part. Councillors of the north and JPs occasionally expressed their concern for the Queen of Scots in an area so obviously sympathetic to her cause. But there was more to the issue than physical security. In October 1568 the regime reconsidered its strategy. On the sixteenth Cecil wondered 'Whyther it shall not be found resonable that the Quenes Majesty being Quene of england, and therby superior lady and Judg over the realm of Scotland, shall here and determyn this case betwixt the Quene of Scottes and hir sonne and subjectes adhearyng to hym'.[53] This implied a meeting in London. Two months later, Sussex thought that there should be a full settlement based on the proof of Mary's guilt. By the imperial power of the English crown, this would include a judicial sentence, detention, the crowning of Prince James, and a confirmation of Moray's regency. He argued that even if the Queen of Scots denied the evidence it would be 'beste to procede by a composycyon' and for Elizabeth to force her to surrender.[54]

The Privy Council met at Hampton Court on 30 and 31 October 1568 and it had two principal aims: to meet Mary's and Moray's representatives and to plan the institutional structure of the next phase of the Queen of Scots' trial. Elizabeth and seven councillors – Arundel, Bacon, Cecil, Clinton, Howard of Effingham, Leicester, and Sadler – met the bishop of Ross and Herries early on 30 October; the Queen and all but Bacon interviewed Maitland of Lethington and James McGill later that day. The Council's tactics are intriguing. From the start, it worked out the way to interview the two groups of Scots. It had to be emphasized to Mary's commissioners 'how desyrooss' Elizabeth was 'to have some good end'. Cecil noted that this 'generall manner of talk' was best, in case the two men 'shuld perceave . . . the matters wherwith ther Quene might be charged for the murdre of hir husband', which was of course the intention. Maitland of Lethington and McGill had to be treated very differently. If they were prepared to back their own argument that Mary was guilty, 'than hir Majesty will never restore hir to the Crown of Scotland, nor permitt hir to be restored, without such assurancees, as they shall alow to be good for

[52] Sussex to Cecil, 10 October 1568, SP 15/14, fo. 72r.
[53] Draft of Cecil to Norfolk, 16 October 1568, CP 155, fo. 124r.
[54] Sussex to Cecil, 22 December 1568, CP 4, fo. 50v.

them, but will make it manifest to the world what she thynketh of the cause'. And this is exactly what the Privy Council did. Three weeks after Moray's questions about English powers and intentions, the six councillors committed England to the effective deposition of Mary, the crowning of James, and the regency of Moray on proof that the Queen of Scots was a guilty woman. Cecil's minutes ended with a sentence on Elizabeth's concern for Mary, wishing 'that hir honor and estate might be preserved and found whole, sound and firme'. He crossed it out: it was practically pointless, because on 30 October the Council worked through a proposal for a larger political body of the realm to hear the Queen of Scots' case.[55]

This wider consultative and political exercise was discussed in private session at Hampton Court before the meetings with Leslie, Herries, Maitland of Lethington, and McGill: one of Cecil's paragraphs had Elizabeth finding a 'probabilite' in the evidence 'after that the messyngers of scotland shall have shewed ther prooves'.[56] So on the morning of Saturday 30 October seven privy councillors proposed that, because 'it hath bene alweiss thought mete that the kynges of this Realme shuld use the advise of the principall states of the Realme, wherby the end and determination therof have bene allowed by them, and so accepted by the Realme', the Queen of Scots should be tried by a great council. Medieval great councils were afforced sessions of the monarch's Council, attended by temporal and clerical lords and perhaps specialists, summoned less formally than a parliament. They had sometimes been called to resolve a difficult point of law, which was appropriate for 1568; Edward II had referred a legal question either to parliament or to a *convocatio prelatorum et magnatum de regno*. The Council's proposal in October 1568 was planned as a three-stage process. First, privy councillors and earls 'shuld be called to heare and gyve ther advise in the same'. Then, after the presentation of Moray's proof, the rest of the 'Counsell absent' would be sent for. And finally, the Privy Council in London planned to summon 'the other peres of the realme' and the archbishop of Canterbury and the bishop of London.[57]

Cecil's notes are in some ways haphazard: the consultation of earls, for example, is mentioned in the first part of the process but senior men like the earls of Shrewsbury, Sussex, and Huntingdon are listed later on. But

---

[55] For Cecil's minutes, 30 October 1568, CP 155, fos. 128r–129r; 30 October 1568, Cotton Caligula B. 9, fo. 359r–v; [30 October 1568,] CP 155, fo. 130r; 31 October 1568, CP 155, fo. 129v.

[56] CP 155, fo. 129r.

[57] CP 155, fo. 128v; H.G. Richardson and G.O. Sayles, *Parliaments and great councils in medieval England* (London, 1961), pp. 12–13, 19; John Guy, 'The rhetoric of counsel in early modern England', in Dale Hoak (ed.), *Tudor political culture* (Cambridge, 1995), p. 298; G.O. Sayles, *The functions of the medieval parliament of England* (London and Ronceverte, 1988), p. 32.

there is still an institutional shape to the proposal. There were fifteen privy councillors in October 1568. Sir Ambrose Cave and Sir Edward Rogers had died that year and Sir William Petre was in conciliar retirement. Petre's importance to the plan for a great council is an interesting measure of the seriousness of the proceedings. Cecil made a marginal note to call Petre to London on 30 October. Arundel, Bacon, Cecil, Clinton, Howard of Effingham, Leicester, and Sadler were at Hampton Court on 30 October 1568. Knollys, Mildmay, Norfolk, Northampton, and Winchester were absent. Edward, third earl of Derby was also a privy councillor, but he had a poor record of around fifteen early Elizabethan attendances and none of them beyond 1565. The earl of Bedford was not mentioned, but he was an experienced Anglo-Scottish diplomat and had a good attendance record in the 1560s. So seven councillors could look at the proof of Mary's guilt submitted by McGill and Maitland of Lethington and evaluate the evidence; they would then send for their eight absent colleagues. And this process was important enough to call Petre and Derby to London.

The first stage of the planned consultation included the presentation of advice by the kingdom's earls. Cecil listed Huntingdon, Northumberland, Shrewsbury, Sussex, Westmorland, and Worcester. In part, this was an expression of magnates' traditional ability to advise the monarch on key political issues, but it also suggests that they would have been involved in the technical sifting of proof and evidence before a full trial. So if Cecil's notes were definitive, six men would have been able to reinforce the seven privy councillors. The 'Counsell absent' would make a subtotal of twenty-one, and the 'very consonant' addition of Matthew Parker as archbishop of Canterbury and Edmund Grindal as bishop of London put the projected council at twenty-three. But the choice of whom to consult was Elizabeth's. Cecil wrote that 'no manner of opinion concerning' Mary could be 'uttered or pronounced' until the Queen had had the advice and opinion of the Privy Council and 'such other of hir states as she shall please to conferr with all'.[58]

These councillors, earls, and senior clergymen were barely a tenth of the political elite of 1568 and 1569. There was a large reserve of men in the counties and Cecil knew exactly who they were. As Principal Secretary, he could refer to an accurate and impressive breakdown of the kingdom's privy councillors, nobility, clergy, and gentlemen prepared (in all prob-

---

[58] CP 155, fo. 129r; Thomas Starkey included 'ij byschoppys as of london & canterbury' in his council of fourteen, *A dialogue between Pole and Lupset*, ed. T.F. Mayer (Camden Society, fourth series, 37; London, 1989), pp. 12–13; cf. John Guy, 'The Henrician age', in J.G.A. Pocock (ed.), *The varieties of British political thought, 1500–1800* (Cambridge, 1993), pp. 19–20; and John Guy, 'The king's council and political participation', in Alistair Fox and John Guy, *Reassessing the Henrician age. Humanism, politics and reform 1550–1550* (Oxford and New York, 1986), p. 140.

ability) just after April 1568. This was a joint exercise. Bernard Hampton prepared lists of men by county and Cecil corrected this document and added his own introductory sections of 'Counsellors', 'Nobilite', and 'Clergy'. At the end of the 1560s the regime could rely on just over thirty peers, fifty-two archbishops, bishops, and deans, and gentlemen at court and in the shires. Even if the physical and military power of the early Elizabethan polity was limited, its potential for national consultation was not.[59]

The Queen of Scots was not tried by this great council, and the evidence is not strong enough to connect the meeting on 30 October to Cecil's and Hampton's lists. But the general principle is more significant. In 1568 the Elizabethan regime was willing to employ a traditional great council to hear the case; it planned the stages of consultation and agreed on personnel; and if the Queen decided to receive advice from the kingdom's gentlemen, their names and counties were held by the Principal Secretary and the Clerk of the Privy Council – as they had been consistently in commissions of the peace edited by Cecil since the beginning of the reign. The plan was taken seriously five days after the meeting of the Privy Council, when Cecil drafted letters calling Norfolk and Sussex back to London. But why did the Privy Council – small, compact, efficient, and executive – decide that councillors, lords temporal and spiritual, and gentlemen were in a better position to judge Mary in 1568, when it is generally agreed that great councils were redundant by Elizabeth's reign? Part of the answer lies in 'A Treatise of the Office of a councellor and Principall Secretarie to her Majestie', prepared by Robert Beale in 1592. The 'Treatise' describes how Henry VII's mother-in-law had been disinherited by a great council, and how other kingdoms used this form of council 'upon extraordinarie occasions'. Late Elizabethan England was different: 'now in our State there is no competicion, as the cases differ, so the reasons varie'. But 1592 was not 1568, and Beale did not have to consider the possibility of trying a reigning monarch.[60]

In part, the proposed great council was a response to the religious and political situation in Europe in autumn 1568. England had to be seen to be treating the Queen of Scots fairly and responsibly. A day after the main meeting, Cecil noted three 'Questions' on the back of the minutes from

---

[59] SP 12/59, fos. 95r–96v. This set of notes seems to have been the model for a list of JPs by county prepared by Cecil in October 1569, SP 12/59, fos. 90r–93v.

[60] For the drafts of letters to Norfolk and Sussex, CP 155, fo. 131r; Guy, 'King's council', p. 146; P.J. Holmes, 'The great council in the reign of Henry VII', *English Historical Review*, 101 (1986), 840–62; P.J. Holmes, 'The last Tudor great councils', *Historical Journal*, 33 (1990), 1–22; for 'A Treatise of the Office of a councellor and Principall Secretarie', see Conyers Read, *Mr Secretary Walsingham and the policy of Queen Elizabeth*, 3 vols. (Oxford, 1925), I, pp. 423–43

Council. 'It wer mete in this cause', he added as the third point, 'to have some forme observed of the procedyng by some expert person in the Cyvill law'. The trial had to be put on a solid and international legal footing; proceedings under civil law would also avoid the sort of claim made by Mary in 1586 that she was not subject to English common law. Even the involvement of members of the conservative nobility like Northumberland and Westmorland perhaps had as much to do with religion as it did with the traditional right of magnates to advise and counsel. Also, Cecil's sense of religious conflict in Europe was as sharp as ever in autumn 1568. In September he argued on paper that the 'quarrell' involved Elizabeth for four reasons: religion; 'hir special ennemy', the cardinal of Lorraine; the advancement of Mary; and the interference of Rome. Sir Nicholas Throckmorton offered an equally conspiratorial reading of European politics.[61]

The plan for Mary was based on the medieval model of a great council summoned to give advice to the monarch on an important issue. The development of Privy Council and parliament meant the effective extinction of Tudor *magna consilia*, but a traditional great council in 1568 could offer a wide base of consultation and a show of concern for justice. It was perhaps also a way of making sure that potentially dangerous members of the nobility were at Westminster during this tense and difficult period: if Northumberland, Westmorland, and Norfolk had been in London exactly a year later, the decade may well have ended very differently. A great council could be more inclusive than a small privy council, less formal (and, after 1563 and 1566, probably less troublesome for Elizabeth) than a parliament, and more judicial than Mary's preferred option of a private audience at court. This proposal was unique in the 1560s. It was different from three related conciliar plans – Cecil's 'council of estate' in 1563, which would have been temporary and small; the grand or great council for Scotland in 1568, which on paper was large, staffed by officers of the kingdom, and supervisory; and the drafts from 1585, which envisaged a large group of royal officers operating in an interregnum.[62]

v

The first stage of the project began at Westminster on 23 November 1568, when Arundel, Bacon, Cecil, Clinton, Leicester, Norfolk, Sadler, and Sussex

---

[61] CP 155, fo. 129v; John Guy, *Tudor England* (Oxford and New York, 1988), p. 334; for Cecil's notes on military support for Rochelle and the French, *c.* September 1568, SP 12/47, fo. 195r, probably dated by Arthur Champernowne to Cecil, 10 September 1568, SP 12/47, fo. 131r; Throckmorton to Cecil, 2 September 1568, SP 12/47, fos. 106r–107r; Throckmorton to Cecil, 18 September 1568, CP 155, fos. 117r–118r.

[62] See above, pp. 112–15, 168.

sat as 'a table of Counsell', 'in Commission', Cecil wrote to Sir Henry Sidney, 'to heare the scottish great cause'. They met in the Painted Chamber at Westminster, 'aunciently called Camera depicta', just north of St Stephen's Chapel in the Old Palace, and connected to the Commons' lobby by the Long Gallery. John Leslie later recorded in an account of the conference that Mary's representatives refused to convene in any room 'deputed for any court or Judgement'. The proceedings were still being held in London, but the 'eight Comissioners of the principalls of the Queenes councell' (in Leslie's words) combined councillors resident at Hampton Court in October 1568 and members of the 'Counsell absent'. In York, Mary's cause had been heard by an extremely small group of commissioners. Later in the month, the Privy Council planned a great council to act as judge and jury, but by November its senior officers – without the earls, archbishop, and bishop – were still sifting through the Scottish commissioners' evidence.[63]

So the Privy Council in 1568 barely reached the first of the planned three stages of national consultation. It took the regime nearly twenty years to try Mary fully; the final phase of the affair began when Cecil annotated a seating plan for her trial in October 1586. But in November and December 1568 the earl of Sussex and a subcommittee of the Privy Council had to work their way through the rival commissioners' submissions. The complexities of the legal case against Mary, based as it was on controversial documentary evidence and the delicate political history of the decade, meant that Westminster, like York, began to stagger under the weight of paper. The Painted Chamber in December 1568 saw the exchange of claims, counter-claims, and submissions; in principle the regime wanted to support Moray, but in practice Elizabeth had to live up to a language of friendship and amity which had marked early diplomatic exchanges between the two queens. On 15 December Cecil told Sir Henry Sidney that he was dealing with the Queen of Scots' cause to the exclusion of all other business. Seven days later, he privately explored the political ideal: that Mary should be persuaded to stay in England; that Scotland should be governed by Moray; and that James should be 'brought into england and kept here under the rule of some of Scotland'.[64]

Exhaustion and diplomatic deadlock got the better of the settlement for Scotland, Ireland, and England. But the insights of this period – the light it sheds on the nature of the English polity, the relationship between the three

---

[63] 23 November 1568, Cotton Caligula C. 1, fo. 297v; 25 November, Cotton Caligula C. 1, fo. 294r; Cecil to Sidney, 29 November 1568, SP 63/26, fo. 101r; for Leslie's description, Lansdowne 231, fo. 252r.

[64] Cecil to Sidney, 15 December 1568, SP 63/26, fos. 120r–121r; Cecil's notes, 22 December 1568, Cotton Caligula C. 1, fo. 368r.

kingdoms, and the implications for Cecil's historical reputation – nevertheless outweigh for historians the diplomatic difficulties of Elizabethans. These three themes are related. Cecil's vision of Britain in the late 1560s – Protestant, imperial, supervised in Scotland by parliament and council, and part of a settlement which recognized strong strategic connections between Ireland, Scotland, and England – was the main alternative to the union of dynasties proposed by Elizabeth in 1564. In 1568 this meant the direct control of a *de jure* monarch, the management of her kingdom, and power over her choice of husband. Cecil pressed the benefits of a godly British union against the combined powers of Catholic Europe and used the same arguments for English superiority in Britain he had deployed in August 1559. It was also an extension of his domestic political creed in a British context and an expression of his faith in a 'mixed' constitution of crown, council, and parliament.

Cecil's British political convictions were a curious mix of radical and conservative: radical in implication but not in method. The proposed great council was part of a tradition of feudal-baronial counsel which had its roots in medieval concepts of royal accountability; but in 1568 it was part of a controversial and dangerous attempt to try and convict a reigning monarch. Cecil's belief in the reality of English imperial superiority over Scotland can be traced back to chronicle histories and the political theories of the Henrician reformation; nevertheless, it helped to underpin and bond his model of a Protestant Britain. Similarly, Cecil's British Protestantism had far more in common with the fighting ideology of John Ponet in 1556 and Edmund Guest in 1565 than it did with a mediocre conformism. But the radical thrust of the British solution to Mary had an important effect both on the domestic politics of England and on the kingdom's relationship with Europe. Mary's fate was still an open issue at the end of 1568 and at the beginning of 1569 England's tolerable relationship with Spain deteriorated to a dangerous degree. The truly conservative elements in the English polity – men like the earls of Northumberland and Westmorland – found it exceptionally difficult to stomach the consequences. Over the next year, Cecil's British settlement had to come to terms with a more dynastic solution to the Queen of Scots and the English succession.

The crisis of 1569 and an alternative remedy

Most studies of the early part of Elizabeth's reign divide the period, perhaps even unconsciously, into chronological phases. In *The reign of Elizabeth*, J.B. Black dealt with the crisis between 1568 and 1575, separately from Mary Stuart and the succession.[1] Professor Wallace MacCaffrey maintained that, as a unit, 1558 to 1572 represented 'the last phase of a grave political disturbance' which had begun with Henry VIII in the 1530s.[2] But whatever the degree or type of periodization used by a single historian, one thing is usually clear at the end of the 1560s: there is a disproportionate amount of attention paid to the planned Howard–Stuart marriage as a conspiracy (rather than as a political proposal), the northern rising in isolation from the polity it challenged, and the later uncertainties of the Ridolfi plot. The main themes of Elizabeth's first full decade – the domestic impact of the succession on the politics of the reign, Anglo-British negotiations, and the search for a political settlement of Mary Stuart and Britain – seem to end even before the revolt of the northern earls. But did the 1560s effectively end in 1568? Was the regime interested in anything more than putting troops against some Catholic noblemen and decoding secret correspondence? With the apparent guilt of the duke of Norfolk and the appearance of Ridolfi, did the Privy Council in general and Cecil in particular abandon the proposals they discussed in 1568 to work out a new form of Protestant Britain?

I

In June and July 1569 Cecil wrote two political assessments of England's internal condition and the kingdom's relationship with Scotland, Ireland, and the powers of Catholic Europe.[3] The situation looked remarkably

---

[1] J.B. Black, *The reign of Elizabeth 1558–1603* (Oxford, 1959 edn), pp. xii–xiii.
[2] Wallace MacCaffrey, *The shaping of the Elizabethan regime* (London, 1969), p. 17.
[3] 'A necessary consideration of the perillous state of this tyme comprised in two propositions,

grim. The fragile understanding between Philip II and Elizabeth had been challenged and apparently broken by the seizure of Spanish treasure ships in December 1568. Spanish military forces under the duke of Alva were in the process of crushing Dutch Protestantism and the Privy Council thought that England was next.[4] For Cecil, this was part of a Spanish strategic realignment. After the death of Suleyman the Magnificent in 1566 and the succession of his son, Selim II, a man 'nowise gyven to any warr nor feared', Philip was free to 'withdraw his forcees from Italy to serve his purpooses ether to england or Irland'.[5] The 'new rebellion in Irland' was 'mixt with a spanish practise'. This was one element in the 'weaknes of the Quenes Majesty['s] estate'.[6] For Irish matters, Cecil wrote to Nicholas White in August 1569, 'I can wryte nothyng, but seing all your affayres ar in a maze, God be the Guide to yow all, and so I trust yow will all call uppon hym for asistance'.[7]

'A necessary consideration' and the extracts 'out of the booke of the state of the Realme' represent Cecil's intellectual key to the decade in general and 1569 in particular. Cecil's method in the 'booke' was rhetorically precise and structured. He began with short summary points and general statements of fact often split into two or three sections of supporting evidence, usually followed by more detailed and consistent prose restating and explaining the basic assertions. Conceptually, the extracts deal with the European political scene, Scotland, and internal problems in England as three separate, but definitely interconnecting, issues; they are the synthesis of intelligence Cecil had received and assessed over a period of ten years, sometimes from fact but generally based on the instincts of an embattled English Protestant. The extracts can be treated as a sophisticated exercise in trying to balance theory against known fact, first, to make sense of British and Continental affairs and, second, to decide and to explain future policy.

The structure of the 'booke' was peculiarly suited to the political situation as Cecil understood it in 1569. 'A short memoryall' and 'a

---

and their explanations, with some Provisions for the [same] conteyned in two degrees', 7 June 1569, drafted by Bernard Hampton and heavily corrected by Cecil, SP 12/51, fos. 9r–13v. July or August 1569 are the best dates for 'A short memoryall' and 'a memoryall of Remedyes', two discussions written by Cecil and taken 'out of the booke of the state of the Realme', CP 157, fos. 2r–8v, printed in Haynes, pp. 579–88. The 'booke' mentions Mary Stuart's detention in England (so it was written after May 1568) and the earl of Moray as a political player (so before his assassination in January 1570). A reference to 'the new rebellion in Irland' (fo. 2v) probably refers to the revolt led by James Fitzmaurice Fitzgerald and the brothers of the earl of Ormond in July 1569.
[4] See above, pp. 174, 178–9.
[5] CP 157, fo. 3v.
[6] CP 157, fo. 2v.
[7] 9 August 1569, Lansdowne 102, fo. 148r.

memoryall of Remedyes' cover the main themes of the year, summarize the regime's concerns over a decade, and demonstrate the influence of dynastic politics in Britain and Europe set in a providential context. In effect, Cecil's notes are the intellectual key to the practical politics of 1569: the break-down of England's relationship with Spain, the continuing search for a political settlement for Britain and Mary Stuart, and the later push by men like the earl of Moray, the duke of Norfolk, and the earl of Leicester for a dynastic settlement.

Cecil began his 'short memoryall' with one of the most significant political metaphors of the decade. The perils facing England were great, many, and imminent because of 'persons' and 'Matters'. Elizabeth was the victim or, as Cecil put it, the 'pacient'. The Pope, the Kings of Spain and France, and their associates were 'authors and workars', and Mary Stuart 'the Instrument, wherby the matters shall be attempted ageynst the Quenes Majesty'. The 'Matters' were 'for recovery of the Tiranny to the Pope', which meant the 'enforcyng of all christian realmes to receave the Counsell of Trent', and 'eviction' of the crown of England from Elizabeth to Mary. These two aims were connected. The re-establishment of Catholicism meant war in France 'ageynst the protestantes' and 'chaungyng the state of england to popery', which included, as a matter of course, putting the Queen of Scots on the English throne. So, the argument ran, the 'exaltyng of the Quene of Scottes' would please the Pope, all the Catholics in christendom, England, and Scotland, and 'the 2. monarchees'.[8]

Cecil's 'twoo monarquees the next neighbors' of England is a common phrase and an important theme in the 'booke'. His account of the part France and Spain played in acting against England and Elizabeth's throne ranged from the general to the specifically detailed. He argued that their aim was 'to subvert not only ther own subjectes but also all others refusyng the tyranny of Roome'.[9] Cecil had been charting the relationship between the Guise, the Queen of Scots, Elizabeth's crown, and England's safety for ten years; the language of Protestant England set against Catholic Europe had found its voice. But the significant point in late 1568 and 1569 was that, both on paper and politically, there was a move to translate the anti-Spanish language of a decade into practical policy. This happened in November 1568, when five Spanish ships carrying gold to Antwerp were forced into English ports on the south coast and the cargo seized. But why, when the relationship between England and Europe was 'as ticklish as it was',[10] did the regime take such provocative action?

[8] CP 157, fo. 2r.
[9] CP 157, fo. 6r.
[10] Conyers Read, 'Queen Elizabeth's seizure of the duke of Alva's pay-ships', *Journal of Modern History*, 5 (1933), 447.

Commentators on Elizabethan politics in the 1560s have spotted in the seizure of the ships one of the great factional moments of the early part of the reign, with Cecil as the intended victim. According to some secondary accounts, Cecil was targeted by a 'reactionary camp' for pushing bold and forward policy, presumably against Spain and for the European Protestant interest.[11] John Clapham named the earl of Pembroke as leader of a group which brought charges against Cecil – this included (according to William Camden) the duke of Norfolk, the marquess of Winchester, and the earls of Arundel and Leicester.[12] Antonio de Guadras, who acted as Spain's diplomatic representative in London after the expulsion of Guerau de Spes, added Lord Howard of Effingham to the collection of privy councillors, and named Sir Nicholas Throckmorton, Lord Lumley, and the earls of Derby, Northumberland, Westmorland, and Shrewsbury as members of the anti-Cecil group.[13] But there are inconsistencies in the evidence, generally supported by weak analysis. First of all, it is clear that a distinction can be made between the seized money from Spain and the supposed reason why Cecil's colleagues took action (Camden has 'once or twice before') against the Principal Secretary, which was money sent to French Protestants.[14] Support for the French was an issue (from Cecil's correspondence and his own notes on policy) in autumn 1568 and not February and early March 1569.[15] If Spanish money was going to be sent across the Channel in spring of that year, the part it played in English calculations could only have been the continuation of a principle of help for coreligionists discussed in September 1568. Action by Cecil's colleagues in February and March, three months after the Spanish ships were first held in English ports, does seem rather late.

Most commentators have made two basic mistakes. First, they have not tested sources like Camden and Clapham, writing years after the event and using evidence which is at best questionable. And second, they have been too willing to subscribe to a factional model of early Elizabethan politics. For example, the quality of de Guadras' intelligence should be tested against Throckmorton's letter to Cecil on 2 September 1568, in which he told Cecil that 'yn my symple opinion the cowrse you have takyn ys to

[11] E.I. Kouri, *England and the attempts to form a Protestant alliance in the late 1560s: a case study in European diplomacy* (Helsinki, 1981), p. 71.

[12] John Clapham, *Elizabeth of England. Certain observations concerning the life and reign of Queen Elizabeth*, ed. Evelyn Plummer Read and Conyers Read (Philadelphia and London, 1951), pp. 75–6; William Camden, *Annals, or, the historie of the most renowned and victorious Princesse Elizabeth, late Queen of England*, ed. R. Norton (STC 4501; London, 1635), p. 104.

[13] Kouri, *Protestant alliance*, pp. 71–2.

[14] Camden, *Annals*, ed. Norton, p. 104.

[15] See above, pp. 174, 178–9; Conyers Read, *Mr Secretary Cecil and Queen Elizabeth* (London, 1955), pp. 441–2.

good porpose for sondry respectes'. This 'cowrse' was in Elizabeth's dealings with the French 'yn favor off hyr well wyllers', and 'the releffe off those off the relygion yn Fraunce'; the policy involved support for the Prince of Orange against Alva and it meant also that the 'prynces off germany be assystant yn thys cause'. Throckmorton asked Cecil to give his 'humble commendations' to Arundel and Leicester, who, according to de Guadras, were Cecil's factional enemies and Throckmorton's allies. Camden even maintained that Throckmorton was Cecil's 'emulating adversary', which is hard to balance against any sort of evidence in the 1560s.[16] Just over two weeks later, Throckmorton wrote again with his fears for European Protestantism. It was clear to Throckmorton, and must have been even more familiar to men who worked inside the charmed circle of the Privy Council, that assistance to the French meant some action for La Rochelle, 'a marityme towne and off grett importance'. Cecil noted down details of merchants and money for the town, ships and support for the French, and a loan.[17] If the factional model is accurate, then why did Throckmorton support Cecil? This was surely the policy and the opportunity to stop Cecil in his tracks. Guadras' evidence is a classic case of the report of a 'merchant-*cum*-diplomat' written at a distance from good intelligence.[18] The same is true for Clapham's history of Elizabeth's reign, written in 1603. Clapham even admitted in September 1598 that he was not acquainted with Cecil's papers, and so unless he had done five years of good archival research his sources were less than satisfactory.[19] It is also clear that in Clapham's version the attempted coup could have happened at any time between 1561 and 1572: he did not make the point clear, but the standard secondary accounts of the early part of the reign have assumed that it must be the 1568–9 attempt and they have not explained Clapham's unclear chronology to their readers.[20]

The factional interpretation of late 1568 and 1569 finds it difficult to distinguish between political disagreements and virulent disputes. The first were inevitable but the second were extremely rare in the first decade. It also underestimates the power of a providential interpretation of European politics which was as relevant in 1569 as it had been ten years earlier. The Privy Council divided itself in December 1559 on the application of practical policy and not over the basic interpretation of how the Catholic

[16] 2 September 1568, SP 12/47, fos. 106r–107r; Camden, *Annals*, ed. Norton, p. 104.
[17] Throckmorton to Cecil, 18 September 1568, CP 155, fo. 117r, printed in Haynes, pp. 471–2; Throckmorton to Cecil, 2 September 1568, SP 12/47, fo. 106v; for Cecil's notes, SP 12/47, fos. 194r–195r.
[18] Kouri, *Protestant alliance*, p. 71.
[19] Hasler, I, p. 609.
[20] Clapham, *Elizabeth of England*, ed. Read and Read, pp. 75–6; Read, *Cecil*, p. 441; Kouri, *Protestant alliance*, p. 71.

powers wanted to challenge England and Elizabeth's throne. Less than a year later Lord John Grey of Pirgo screamed faction, but Sir John Mason and Sir William Petre were clearly not Cecil's enemies.[21] In fact, the strength of what can be too easily dismissed as paranoia is demonstrated by the content and tone of Throckmorton's letters to Cecil in September 1568: the immediacy of the Continental threat, persecution in Flanders and France, and the sense of England's imminent fate. It is probably fair to say that this interpretation of England in Europe was shared by Cecil's colleagues on the Privy Council who, if they disagreed at all, were divided on the application of policy.

The great shift in Anglo-Spanish relations had as much to do with the remorseless logic of Protestant privy councillors in 1568 and 1569. The pillars of Cecil's European political assessment were generally accepted principles, described and explained in 1559 and accepted by his colleagues over ten years. Condé was the victim of the cardinal of Lorraine, and the situation in France concerned Elizabeth 'for relligion', because Lorraine was her 'special ennemy' and Mary Stuart was the cardinal's niece.[22] The motive of money, after the closure of the Antwerp markets, was significant. But Spain's actions made sense because they fitted into an accepted pattern of international affairs. The intellectual preoccupations of men like Cecil had a rather self-fulfilling quality. In a long letter to Elizabeth, Sir Francis Knollys realized that the 'stay of the Traffike' with the Low Countries was a significant point in the relationship between Philip II and Elizabeth, but he was more concerned to condemn the 'Audawcious boldnes of the Duke of Alva' – a phrase Knollys repeated five times – who was determined 'in this unseasonable tyme for him to spit owte his poysonid malice'.[23]

Without the firm evidence of an order for the seizure, and no explanation by Cecil, the whole relationship between the interpretation of policy and the final English decision to act is not only unclear but circumstantial. But why, when it had seemed likely all along that Spain would join the other Continental powers and that some attempt on England was basically inevitable, was preemptive action so unreasonable? After all, Cecil had used the same sort of argument for intervention in Scotland in 1559. Cecil admired the actions of the German palsgrave in March 1568, after he had seized Genoese gold on its way to Alva and so proved himself a 'playn mayntenor of the Prynce of Conde, and Godes cause'.[24] Condé was the focus of English Protestant attention in autumn 1568; in the 'booke of the state of the Realme', Cecil proved 'The Immynency and neare approchyng'

[21] See above, pp. 77–8.
[22] SP 12/47, fo. 195r.
[23] 17 January 1569, SP 12/49, fos. 57r–58v.
[24] Cecil to Sir Ralph Sadler, 4 March 1568, SP 12/46, fo. 113r.

of crisis by appealing to 'the persequutions made' by the Kings of France and Spain in their own countries, arguing that Condé was under pressure from a French regime supported by Philip's money, the Pope's men, and the dukes of Florence, Savoy, and Feria.[25] Arthur Champernowne and his colleagues told the Privy Council that some of the captured Spanish sailors said that the money was 'apointed from the king of spaine' for Alva, but others told him that it was 'gathered by order of the Bushop of Rome, upon the clerge, for reliefe of the saide duke, against the protestants'.[26] This was not a justification for action, but it was a very solid piece of *ex post facto* reasoning.

This not only made sense in the political climate of the late 1560s, with Alva's military campaign in the Low Countries after 1566, but confirmed for early Elizabethans the trend of a decade and (although there is no documentary evidence to prove this) what must have been the rationale behind the seizure. By 1569 Cecil thought he had good evidence to prove specific offences by Spain. John Man had been 'dishonorably used' by the Spanish and exiled from the court in April 1568, 'specially by the arrogant mallice' of the duke of Feria. Some 'slanderooss bookes and historyes' had been published against Elizabeth, 'over manifest a token of mallyce'. And the attempt to stay English 'traffick of merchandise' with the Low Countries 'audacioossly was attempted in the plage tyme'.[27] The combination of this sort of evidence, an intellectual approach to Spain which put Philip II in the same camp as the other aggressive powers, and an absolute certainty that England was going to be Alva's next target does make some sense of the seizure of the ships.

But more important, in a sense, are the implications for Cecil's view of England, Britain, and Europe in 1569. Both the actual seizure and the mental processes behind it demonstrate the importance of what should not be dismissed as English Protestant paranoid delusion; this is clear in the approach to policy-making and probably in policy itself. Cecil blended the skills of practical planning – on potential support for French Protestants in September 1568, for example – with a providential and immensely structured idea of how European politics either worked against England or could work to the kingdom's advantage. E.I. Kouri has very usefully looked at the attempts to form a Protestant alliance between England and some of the Continental powers in the late 1560s as a 'case study in European diplomacy'. Although Kouri's argument draws a false distinction between 'true faith' (or Protestant commitment) and 'national interest' (political advantage) in Elizabethan policy and sits on the questionable premise of

<hr/>

[25] CP 157, fo. 3r.
[26] 1 January 1569, SP 12/49, fo. 1r.
[27] CP 157, fo. 5r.

political faction, it does at least raise an important issue.[28] At times, early Elizabethans had a problem reconciling religious sympathy and intervention. But this was the result of the practical difficulty of opposing the Catholic powers of Europe coupled with the danger of military overextension; it was not cynical diplomacy intended to manipulate European Protestantism.[29] Cecil, for example, mentioned the 'solliciting of the Pryncess protestantes in Germany' in a note to Elizabeth in March 1560.[30] By 1569 he had developed a more sophisticated idea of the part potential alliances with Protestant powers could play in balancing Continental politics – 'A conjunction with all princes protestantes for defence' against 'the conspyration of the Pope and the monarchees', 'some leage of the princes protestantes of the Empire'.[31] But this was only part of a comprehensive plan to counter the Catholic powers of Europe.

II

Cecil's analysis of the European situation in 1569 was neither cynical nor paranoid. It was the perfect complement to his assessment of Mary Stuart and the part she played, first, in challenging Elizabeth's throne and, second, as the 'Instrument' of the '2. monarchees' in the 'booke of the state of the Realme'. The Queen of Scots was strong because by the 'unyversall opinion of the world' her case seemed just, she had the support of the 'strongest monarchees of Christendom', and 'the probable opinion of a great multitud both in scotland and england' had a 'naturall instynction' to join the two realms with one king or under Mary.[32] Although Cecil understood the political and religious dangers of Mary to England, he was prepared also to admit that 'the more the cause of Relligion be furdred and the tyranny and practises of Roome ar abassed, the less is the daunger of the Quene of Scottes'.[33]

There was no basic difference between the debate over Mary's future in 1568 and Cecil's private notes and the regime's policy a year later. Just as Cecil had understood that Elizabeth could defuse and solve the British succession crisis by acting as an 'umpere' in Mary's and Moray's cause in 1568,[34] so he realized in 1569 that if his Queen 'may have commodite to

---

[28] E.I. Kouri, 'For true faith or national interest? Queen Elizabeth I and the Protestant powers', in E.I. Kouri and Tom Scott (eds.), *Politics and society in reformation Europe* (Basingstoke and London, 1987), p. 412.
[29] Kouri, 'True faith or national interest?', pp. 426–8.
[30] 25 March 1560, SP 12/11, fo. 84r.
[31] CP 157, fo. 8r; SP 12/51, fo. 10v.
[32] CP 157, fo. 2r–v.
[33] CP 157, fo. 7v.
[34] Cotton Caligula C. 1, fo. 230v; see below, p. 240.

determyn' the issue between Mary and her opponents, she could 'therwith provide for the pretence of hir title to the prejudyce of the Quenes Majesty & hir Issew, the daunger may be of less moment'.[35] There was a strong sense of the sort of British settlement Elizabeth and Anglo-Scottish Protestantism needed. According to 'a memoryall of Remedyes', the earl of Moray had to 'be regarded not to be overthrowen' and Mary Stuart 'compounded & hir pretended tytle relesed by hir self and by parlement of Scotland'.[36] For the benefit of form and for the Continental powers, Cecil argued in January 1569 that 'Generally what so ever shall be determyned' should be agreed to by the Queen of Scots 'without any oppen note of compulsion'. But the first of these 'endes' was clearly controversial: that, for the political settlement of Scotland, Mary should stay in England, James 'hir sonne may remayn kyng and be brought upp' in England (safe from the 'cyvill troobles' in Scotland), and 'the Government to be in the Erle of Murray'.[37]

This proposal for the settlement of the problem of Mary had to be kept from her, but explained to John Leslie, bishop of Ross, in the hope that he would 'counsell the Quene of Scottes to the same', and 'lyke wise the Erle of Murray wold be very secretly informed' of the proposal 'and yet oppenly answered with comfort to contynew the state wherin he is'.[38] This recognized need for secrecy (which had been one of the central features of the negotiations with Moray's party in autumn 1568) was starting to change, and over the late winter and early spring of 1569 England began to identify more openly with the Protestant interests of Mary's enemies. In January 1569 Cecil drafted a proclamation to defend Elizabeth and the Regent against 'sundry matters lately in Scotland contrary to all trueth & meanyng of the said Quene as it appereth maliciously devised to blemisshe the honour & sucoritie of hir majestie and to bring therle of Murrey in hatred with his own freendes'.[39] The general aim, as Cecil made very clear in an alteration to a draft of the proclamation, was to dismiss rumours which encouraged 'factions & discordes and hating the good quietnes and concorde betwixte the two realmes of England & Scotland'. In a cancelled paragraph, the regime promised to have Mary 'demaunded' if she had been responsible for the attack on the Regent's motives.[40] As a mark of the seriousness of the issue and the importance of the investment England had made in Moray's Protestant regency, Cecil questioned the earl of Lennox's

[35] CP 157, fo. 7v.
[36] CP 157, fo. 8r.
[37] 7 January 1569, Cotton Caligula C. 1, fo. 373r.
[38] Cotton Caligula C. 1, fo. 373v.
[39] 22 January 1569, Cotton Caligula C. 1, fo. 392r; for a draft corrected by Cecil, CP 155, fo. 75r, printed in Haynes, p. 500; for a secretarial copy, SP 52/16, fo. 11r.
[40] CP 155, fo. 75v; Cotton Caligula C. 1, fo. 392r.

servant, Thomas Bishop, to find out who had produced a book against Moray and how many people had read it.[41] The Regent countered in Scotland in early March by publicly proclaiming Mary's connection with the murder of Darnley, a copy of which the Queen of Scots sent south probably in protest.[42]

Even if the principles of the proposed political settlement of Britain were accepted (and acceptable), their translation into practice was a more difficult business. This was made more sensitive by competing claims of sovereignty in Scotland. In 1568 England's relationship with Moray and his government had been sympathetic, but still fairly formal; by 1569 there was a changing sense of priority which included an exchange of proposals between England and the regency. Henry Middlemore was chosen to 'explore the state of the Erle of Murrays part' in March 1569, but he seems not to have gone.[43] Nevertheless, the regime was still prepared, as Cecil put it in his 'booke of the state of the Realme', to send a representative to Moray 'to understand the estate of his affayres'.[44] The intention of Middlemore's mission, more specifically, was to assess the strength of the regency, and, if it was doubtful, to let London know immediately. The regime was in the process of a county assessment of light horsemen in March, and instructions were issued to Bacon as Lord Keeper of the Great Seal to increase the number of commissioners in some counties for maintaining horses and weapons, and to take general musters.[45] This was part of an increasing awareness that 'the decay of the martiall state' had to be repaired, and quickly.[46] For Cecil, the internal condition of England and the strengthening of the kingdom's military reserves were part of a comprehensive package of measures designed to counter the pretensions of the Queen of Scots.

The Privy Council explained to John Leslie that because the issue of Mary 'concerneth them which ar now in scotland, it is necessary to have some conference with them'.[47] It was becoming clear that unless the Queen of Scots made some sort of amends for her claim to Elizabeth's throne, progress was unlikely. The Council played its best cards for all they were worth: in 1559 Mary had publicly challenged the 'present title to the Crown of england', and she had 'at sondry tymes refused to confir[m]' the

[41] March 1569, Cotton Caligula C. 1, fo. 398r.
[42] 'Certane heidis contenit in ane proclamatioun maid in Scotland be the erle of Murrayes command', endorsed in England and dated 13 March 1569, SP 52/15, fo. 27r.
[43] 'A memoryall for Henry Middlemore being sent into scotland', 17 March 1569, Cotton Caligula C. 1, fo. 400r.
[44] CP 157, fo. 8r.
[45] March 1569, SP 12/49, fos. 175r–182v; 12 April 1569, SP 12/49, fo. 183r–v.
[46] CP 157, fo. 8r.
[47] April 1569, Cotton Caligula C. 1, fo. 411r.

Treaty of Edinburgh. The commissioners at Edinburgh had been acting under the great seals of France and Scotland and the earl of Bedford had pressed for ratification at the christening of James in 1566. There was no excuse.[48] Privately, Cecil was still committed to a negotiated, political settlement. In a 'Consideration of the matters betwixt the Quene of Scottes and hir sonne and subjectes', he argued that there were two ways to establish a 'concord betwixt both the realmes': to support James' (and, by implication, Moray's) position and to maintain that he could 'be accepted as a kyng in name & possession joyntly' with his mother. If these points could not be accepted, then 'in respect of avoydyng inward quarrells betwixt hir subjectes' a 'perpetuall good amyty' had to be agreed between England and Scotland.[49]

Cecil's proposal for a treaty in spring 1569 rested on five familiar principles. Religion had to be established and 'unyversally receaved and observed', separate 'from the forrayn Jurisdiction of Roome as the Crown of england is', and based on the English model. It was obvious that 'for avancement of Justice, and quietnes both in [that] realme, and with England', a 'speciall noble man' had to be established as regent, supported by some members of the Scottish nobility 'and other wise persons', and 'elected' – the original clause had 'appoynted' – by parliament to assist Mary. If the Queen wanted to remove men from any of the 'Pryncipall officees' of the kingdom she would have to have the 'consent' (rather than the more neutral approval) of the Regent and 'the Gretar part of hir Counsell'. Restoration of properties and offices was the third principle of the proposed settlement, and the exclusion of foreigners from offices the fourth. The fifth, more generally, was an agreement to secure the relationship between Mary and England, 'because the gretest felicite that can be devised for scotland is to have a perpetuall peace and love stablished betwixt it and England'.[50]

This was remarkably similar, in both sentiment and expression, to the sort of settlement Cecil and the Privy Council had proposed in 1568. It was also close to the language of 'A memoriall of certain pointes meete for restoring the Realme of Scotland to the Auncient Weale', which had 'noted that the best worldly felicitie that Scotland can have is . . . to contynew in a perpetuall peace with the kingdom of Ingland', and had pushed for a religious settlement on the model of England's freedom from idolatry.[51] Familiar too were the other provisions necessary for a settlement with Mary in Scotland: regency control backed by an effective conciliar

---

[48] Cotton Caligula C. 1, fo. 410r.
[49] Cotton Caligula C. 1, fo. 413r.
[50] Cotton Caligula C. 1, fos. 413v–414r.
[51] See below, pp. 223–4.

mechanism, the return to the principles established by the Scottish parliament 'held whan the Prynce was Crowned' (which was a radical proposal in itself, given the question of the legitimacy of the 1567 session), and the argument that for the security of the settlement 'it is necessary that this accord be made tripartyte' between Elizabeth, Mary, and James. If the Queen of Scots violated the agreement, Elizabeth reserved the right to take Mary's crown, which would 'immediatly pass and be invested in hir sonn the Prynce' without the need for 'any other actuall coronation or inauguration'. Cecil's choice of political language was crucial to what would be a settlement based on Mary's effective powerlessness. The tripartite agreement was designed 'for assured performance' of the agreed articles. The Queen of Scots would 'yeld to hir sonne and hir subjectes'. And in a term which prefigured his plan for an association of Elizabeth's subjects in June 1569, Cecil maintained that the agreement would be confirmed in 'the bond' between Mary and Elizabeth.[52]

The 'Consideration' was not written in a political vacuum. Cecil made it clear that 'befor any of these articlees' could be 'treated and concluded uppon, it is necessary that some speciall person be chosen by the Quenes Majesty to be sent to the Erle of Murraye, to communicat with hym secretly'. Moray had to send men down to negotiate in England, and William Maitland of Lethington was named as a good candidate.[53] More informally, John Wood, Moray's servant, was sent to the English court in very late March, 'in charge to do sum service convenient' for his master.[54] Wood collected a prepared set of notes from English debates on Mary's future written at some point in May. These notes were clearly modelled on his 'Consideration'.[55] The proposals were taken by Wood, with Elizabeth's blessing and in hope of a favourable reception by Moray, on or about 16 May 1569, so it seems likely that the Council debated matters for the first two weeks of the month or perhaps, if the issues were discussed at length before Cecil wrote the 'Consideration', for even longer.[56]

The 'degrees' had significant implications for the position of Elizabeth, the Privy Council, and Britain. In May 1569 London committed itself to a Protestant Scotland with Mary in the kingdom, a regency in the name of Moray, the kingship of James VI established at a parliament held – according to the Queen of Scots – by questionable right, and a British treaty between the two realms' three monarchs. It was a critical success for

---

[52] Cotton Caligula C. 1, fo. 414v–415r; see below, pp. 195–8.
[53] Cotton Caligula C. 1, fo. 415v.
[54] Moray to Valentine Brown, 23 March 1569, Darnaway Castle, Forres, TD 94/56, no. 81.
[55] SP 52/16, fos. 45r–v; CP 156, fo. 31r–v, printed in Haynes, pp. 516–17; Cotton Caligula B. 5, fo. 327r–v.
[56] Elizabeth to Moray, 16 May 1569, SP 52/16, fo. 44r.

Cecil because these were themes and principles of action he had privately
written about exactly a year before; although the proposals were filtered
into the instructions for the York commissioners, they had been suffocated
by the proceedings in autumn and winter 1568.[57] But even more than this,
the distilled version of the 'Consideration' was a statement of British
Protestant imperialism. It was a remarkably comprehensive document, but
not dynastic. The proposal did not rest on marriage as an act of union – it
worked on the principle of the control of a monarch by a regent and a
council, with set penalties and an agreed mechanism in the case of what
amounted to a contractual default.

Cecil wanted some form of close political settlement with Scotland. In
June 1569, just over three weeks after Wood had returned to Moray with
the 'degrees', Bernard Hampton acted as clerk to Cecil in the composition
of 'A necessary consideration of the perillous state of this tyme'. It was
'comprised', as Hampton put it, 'in two propositions and their explanations, with some provisions for the same conteyned in two degrees'.[58] 'A
necessary consideration' was both enthusiastically British and fiercely
critical of Europe. In a similar exercise to the 'booke of the state of the
Realme', Cecil's 'necessary consideration' not only provides a glimpse of
the state of European politics in summer 1569 from the angle of a privy
councillor; it is another snapshot of Cecil's political creed – and especially
his sense of England in Britain and Europe – at a crucial point in the
decade. England's isolation is a persistent theme. The kingdom was 'most
offensive both to the King of Spayne and the french King for sundry
considerations and specially for succoring of the persequuted'. It was
without allies and 'so standeth alone upon the gard of it self, as never it did
at any tyme before by the memory of any recordes or storyes'. At this point,
Hampton's original fair copy moved on to the fourth point of the section
on the 'secret practises and mislikings of sundry people of every estate', but
Cecil made an editorial insertion. The 'recordes and storyes' remained, but
the sentence continues with Cecil's holograph: 'in which matter is to be
noted that ther is no contrey with which it may be more proffitably knitt
than with scotland and next to it with some leage of the princes protestantes of the Empire'.[59]

Cecil wanted British peace and co-operation and some form of Continental Protestant alliance. These were two ways of defending England
against the 'violent procedinges' of the Pope and his 'tyrannous bloody and
poysoning persequutors'.[60] But there was more to England's protection

---

[57] See above, pp. 167–71; and below, pp. 238–43.
[58] SP 12/51, fo. 9r.
[59] SP 12/51, fo. 10v.
[60] SP 12/51, fos. 9r, 10v.

than action in Europe. 'A necessary consideration' pressed for a national renewal and the strengthening of England's institutions. It was the political equivalent of the prayer Cecil had corrected during one of Elizabeth's illnesses in 1568, when God had punished England with her 'sicknes for our synnes'; it even paralleled his daughter's 'dooble bastard tertian' fever in April 1569, which Cecil interpreted as a way for God to avenge her father's sins.[61] In the same way, weaknesses in the Elizabethan polity only strengthened the hand of the kingdom's enemies in 'the quarrell to be made for the delyvery of [the] Quene of Scottes now remayning in England'.[62] Some 'imperfections' were 'very daungerooss, some others ar rather lackes and so to be supplied with care and dilligence'. There was 'a dissolution of Government'. This included the decay of the service of God and the sincere profession of Christian religion, 'and in place therof, partly papacy and partly paganism and irreligion ar crept in'; it also meant weaknesses in the 'administration of the Cyvill Pollycy', with a loss of reverence for magistrates.[63] The strange irony of Cecil's analysis was that the ecclesiastical corruption of the Pope and his church only added to the dangerous power of Catholicism, but military weakness and 'the unskilfulnes, or the imperfectnes of the nation to make warr offensive or defensive' in England was linked intellectually and practically to 'the dyvision of the people in every shyre by dyversite of opinions in the matter of relligion'.[64] The only way to defend the kingdom against the horrors in France, the Low Countries, Spain, 'and their appendantes' was by the 'mayntenance of Relligion, suerty of the Quenes person, Mayntenance and Contynuance of the Monarchy, conservation of the subjects in peace'.[65]

Although 'A necessary consideration' is central to understanding Cecil's intellectual approach to succession crisis in 1569, it was copied by Bernard Hampton and edited by Cecil for a more important and practical reason. The text explored the kingdom's weaknesses but it also outlined a response to a military attack by the Continental powers. 'A necessary consideration' was an early form of the instrument of association.[66] Conyers Read made the basic connection, but he argued, rather strangely, that it 'revealed Cecil's distrust of the competence of the ordinary machinery of administra-

---

[61] Lansdowne 116, fo. 75r; see above, pp. 26–8; Cecil to Nicholas White, 15 April 1569, Lansdowne 102, fo. 141r.

[62] SP 12/51, fo. 10v.

[63] CP 157, fo. 4r.

[64] SP 12/51, fo. 10v.

[65] SP 12/51, fo. 11v.

[66] 'The Instrument of an association for the preservation of her Majesties Royall person', SP 12/174, fo. 10r; for drafts, SP 12/173, fos. 128r–v, 129r–v, 130r–131r; cf. David Cressy, 'Binding the nation: the bonds of association, 1584 and 1696', in Delloyd J. Guth and John W. McKenna (eds.), *Tudor rule and revolution* (Cambridge, 1982), pp. 217–34.

tion to cope with internal disorders, particularly if they sprang from religious differences'. Read, who had no time for the nature or language of political proposals, dismissed 'A necessary consideration' as impractical.[67] But the text is a crucial political and intellectual link between the first decade and the later part of the reign. In 1569 the first stage of the fight against 'any foreyn or domesticall attempt against hir Majesty for the chaung of hir estate, or alteration of the lawes established for relligion' was going to be a secret consultation led by the Privy Council and expanded to include 'speciall noblemen, Bishops, Knights and others head gentlemen in every shire within the Realme'. From this, a secret 'booke' would be made of 'their *severall* names', and they would be told 'the substance of all the premisses' of the project: how 'beside the commen band which every subject by nature oweth to hir Majesty', they would be expected '*also* to profess and by othe to promise to associat them selves with all estates of their degrees at all tymes and places to defend the Quenes Majesties most royall parson, and the comen peace of the Realme' without 'suffring any parson *english or stranger* to the uttermost of their power, to attempt *by practise or force* any thing to the contrary'. This included the defence of the ecclesiastical establishment.[68] If the 1584 'Instrument of an association for the preservation of her Majesties Royall person' was a proposal 'which served to bind the country to the Crown, to combat disorder, to focus the concerns of the political elite, and to achieve a dramatic and public attestation of loyalty' to Elizabeth,[69] then 'A necessary consideration' had the same sort of intention. It was not as 'spontaneous' as the 'Instrument' in its organization, but its principal aim – to bind the Queen's subjects by oath – was almost identical.

The proposal for an association in 'A necessary consideration' combined the aim of the 1584 'Instrument' – with its commitment to preserving the subjects of the crown in 'the profession and observation of the tru Christian Religion' – and its method: expressed in the privy councillors' determination 'voluntarily and moost willingly [to] bynd ourselves every one of us to the other Joicntly and severally in the bond of one firme and Loyall societie'.[70] Cecil's project in 1569 established the language of 1584, with its oath, a call for association, the use of the term 'instrument', and the idea of a subscription campaign organized by shire. A parliamentary diarist in 1585 recorded how 'A Bill for the Queenes saiftie' was compared to the 'othe of assocya-

<hr />

[67] Conyers Read, 'William Cecil and Elizabethan public relations', in S.T. Bindoff, J. Hurstfield, and C.H. Williams (eds.), *Elizabethan government and society* (London, 1961), p. 33; Read, *Cecil*, pp. 452–3.
[68] SP 12/51, fo. 12r. Cecil's corrections and additions are in *italics*.
[69] Cressy, 'Binding the nation', p. 218.
[70] SP 12/174, fo. 10r.

tion'. One MP argued that the two were incompatible: the 'othe of assocyation did so greatlye Disagree withe the Bill alreadie drawne'.[71] But the principles and practice of both the 'Instrument' (for the theory behind the project) and the 'bill for the Quenes savety' (for the administrative detail) had already merged in the proposal of 1569.[72] To show 'for more evident proofe' the constancy of Elizabeth's leading subjects in 1569, these men would *'by promiss and othe to performe the same* to subscribe *also* such an Instrument as may be devised for *this purpooss in* every shire' in the kingdom. 'A necessary consideration' set out a clear mechanism for action: in an emergency, the subscribers would contribute 'such a some of money . . . to be payed to the handes of one principall parson of creditt' in the shire, after a warning from the Queen or the Privy Council.[73]

The 1569 proposal was more socially comprehensive than the 'Instrument' of 1584. Although the 'speciall secret booke' would be compiled by the Privy Council after the return of certificates from the shires, organized by 'noble men, Bishops and head gentlemen', Cecil argued for the inclusion of 'an other *second* choyse' of 'other inferior gentlemen, *ecclesiasticall persons,* merchantes, clothyers, farmors, howsholders *and such lyke'*.[74] Men of all classes enthusiastically signed the 'Instrument' of 1584, but the original intention was rather more limited.[75] But 'A necessary consideration' is perhaps more useful as an interesting case study in the nature of the relationship between the centre of government and the shires and in methods of administrative organization. In an emergency, the Privy Council would deal with noblemen who were near London or the court. Matthew Parker and Edmund Grindal would co-ordinate the bishops. For the rest of 'the head gentlemen' of England, the Privy Council would *'by the bookes of the subsidy* peruse the names of them', and call two or three from each county to London.[76] Cecil generally knew his men: two months before 'A necessary consideration', he worked through a copy of the names of men in the counties who could provide light horsemen and lances and corrected the names of fathers and sons. Probably by late 1568 he had a list by county of England's privy councillors, noblemen, senior clergymen, and gentlemen.[77] 'A necessary consideration' was inclusive. In 1584 Cecil

---

[71] Northamptonshire Record Office, Fitzwilliam (Milton) Political 2, fo. 27r.
[72] SP 12/176, fos. 40r–47v; Huntington Library, San Marino, California, Ellesmere 1192, fos. 1r–4r; Patrick Collinson, 'The monarchical republic of Queen Elizabeth I', in his *Elizabethan essays* (London and Rio Grande, 1994), pp. 48–52.
[73] SP 12/51, fo. 12r–v. Cecil's insertions are in *italics*.
[74] SP 12/51, fo. 12v, with some punctuation added. Again, Cecil's corrections are in *italics*.
[75] Cressy, 'Binding the nation', p. 223; SP 12/174, fo. 10r.
[76] SP 12/51, fo. 13r. Cecil's additions are in *italics*.
[77] April 1569, SP 12/49, fos. 175r–181r, 182v; SP 12/59, fos. 95r–96v; see above, pp. 177–8.

emphasized in private that 'this Association' would include different 'partyes in the societe'.[78] A man was a 'recusant' in 1569 if he refused 'to associat him self *in comen cause* by oth and subscription'. Even if he took the oath but 'yet shall refuse to contribute any some of money', then his loyalty was measured by the same standard, 'for therof is the gretest difference to be made'.[79] This was an opportunity to pledge one's loyalty to the kingdom; once it was rejected, the oath was absolutely exclusive.

The whole exercise was an astounding example of Cecil's holistic approach to the crisis of succession and its wider implications and causes. It demonstrates the influence of the political and military situation in Europe and establishes a close connection between the 1560s and the later crises over Mary in the early 1570s and mid-1580s. It shows Cecil's ability to link the grand theory of 'the booke of the state of the Realme' and the earlier parts of 'A necessary consideration' – with their providential sense of conflict over succession, the influence of Mary Stuart, the opposition of the Continental powers, and the fight for a common Protestant Britain – to practical details of policy, organization, and 'points of contact' between the regime in London and gentlemen in the localities. But above all, the association was the last piece in Cecil's British political jigsaw. Along with the resettlement of Mary in Scotland and the guarantees for her control, 'A necessary consideration' proposed four things: to defend England against Continental attack; to develop an efficient mechanism for finding money and holding the counties; to bind the kingdom's subjects; and to identify and mark dissenters.

III

The 'provisions' of 'A necessary consideration of the perillous state of this tyme' were part of a Cecil project. But did they express the fears and priorities of other privy councillors in the same way that 'the booke of the state of the Realme' and 'A necessary consideration' explained those of Cecil himself? This is a difficult question: part of Cecil's interest as a politician and a writer lies in the fact that he wrote things down and saved them. But his political priorities were remarkably consistent, defined by the importance he gave to Britain as a Protestant island and to a settled Mary, and by his sense of the (usually dangerous) influence of Europe. As the focus of intelligence reports sent in by the representatives of the regime, Cecil was near to European diplomatic and political source material and its implications – perhaps closer than his colleagues. So were there any

---

[78] Cecil to Walsingham, 19 October 1584, SP 12/173, fo. 134r.
[79] SP 12/51, fo. 12v. Cecil's additions are in *italics*.

effective differences between the way Cecil mapped and interpreted England, Britain, and Europe at the end of the 1560s and the interests and priorities of other privy councillors?

The 'degrees' taken back to Scotland by John Wood in May 1569 were approved by Elizabeth and the Privy Council. But some of the councillors were nearly seven months into planning a settlement of the British problem very different to the one Cecil had been working on for over a year. This was not 'faction'. It did not involve conspiracy – at least in a dangerous sense – and most of the sources agree that Cecil knew about the proposal. The alternative plan involved the duke of Norfolk, Mary Stuart, the earls of Leicester, Pembroke, and Arundel, Lord Lumley, and Sir Nicholas Throckmorton. Throckmorton is a problem, because he had agreed so enthusiastically with Cecil's assessment of the European scene in September 1568.[80] Other men acted as messengers, including the bishop of Ross who was used quite openly to negotiate informally between Elizabeth, the Privy Council, and Mary. The planned Howard-Stuart match was not pure conspiracy; although Cecil later pieced together the agents, the ciphered correspondence, and the shadowy cash payments, the reasons for Norfolk's marriage were more solid. Cecil preferred a political settlement of the British succession problem. Norfolk favoured the more traditional dynastic option.[81]

But was the duke of Norfolk that selfless? Or was he, as Dr Jenny Wormald has suggested, more prepared to lead a Catholic uprising to remove Elizabeth from the throne to benefit himself and Mary?[82] In 'A discoorse touchinge the pretended mach betweene the Duke of Norfolke and the Queene of Scotes' – written after the marriage plan was uncovered and usually attributed to Francis Walsingham – the author identified the duke with the Catholic cause and wondered whether it was 'likelie that anie man that professeth true religion' could marry Mary.[83] Norfolk was a conservative and yet probably not a Catholic; he fiercely denied this accusation in two letters to Cecil in November 1567.[84] But what was his plan in 1569? Cecil wanted a Protestant Britain and an England bound, for the sake of security, by an oath, by money, and by soldiers. Was Norfolk prepared to aim for a Protestant settlement, but willing to conciliate and to appease the kingdom's conservatives rather than exclude or isolate them? Mary Stuart's personal life looked particularly murky in late 1568 and

[80] See above, pp. 174, 178–9.

[81] For Cecil's examination of the Norfolk plan in January 1572, see SP 12/85, fos. 35r–38r.

[82] Jenny Wormald, *Mary Queen of Scots. A study in failure* (London, 1991 edn), p. 182.

[83] Northamptonshire Record Office, Fitzwilliam (Milton) Political 224; Harley 290, fos. 117r–119r, printed in Conyers Read, *Mr Secretary Walsingham and the policy of Queen Elizabeth*, 3 vols. (Oxford, 1925), I, pp. 68–74.

[84] 15 November 1567, SP 12/44, fos. 90r–91v; 24 November 1567, SP 12/44, fos. 98r–99v.

1569, but her Catholicism was less of an issue with English privy councillors than her reputation might lead one to expect. Even a hardened and experienced observer like Knollys was impressed that by July 1568 Mary had 'recevyd an ynglyshe chaplyn' and had 'herd hym in hys sermons invaye agaynst faresaicall Justification of Workes and all kyndes of papistrie, & that to the advancement of the gospell, with attentyve & contented ears'.[85] This was taken seriously: for all the guarantees of Scottish religion in Cecil's 'Consideration of the matters betwixt the Quene of Scottes and hir sonne and subjectes', the proposal argued that if Mary could not accept the Scottish 'articlees of relligion', she could perhaps adopt and 'oppenly profess the forme of the Relligion as it is established in the Chirch of england, accordyng as she hath semed to allow hir being in england'.[86] Marriage to Mary as a political and religious strategy was not, for Elizabethans, an unacceptable idea.

Piecing together the Howard–Stuart proposal as a political plan for the settlement of the British succession is a difficult business. The duke of Norfolk's late confession in November 1571 made a play on his own innocence. Norfolk maintained that he was put under considerable political pressure by William Maitland of Lethington and the earl of Moray at Hampton Court, presumably in October 1568.[87] A year later, the Regent told Elizabeth that 'the Duke of norffolke did first Directlie and in playn wordes, motioun the mater of the said mariage to me' at York in early October. According to Moray's version of events, Maitland of Lethington was involved, but the Regent conveniently distanced himself from the Scottish Secretary's conversations with Norfolk.[88] Sir James Melville of Halhill, writing years after the event, argued for an early discussion of the subject which involved Moray and Lethington; Melville also included Leicester, Pembroke, and Cecil as supporters, but his sense of political perspective should be tested and seriously questioned because of his treatment of Norfolk's influence in England at the time, ruling the Queen, the Privy Council, and two 'contrary factions' in the kingdom, 'baith protestantis and papistis'.[89] Norfolk maintained that Leicester was the prime mover, using Throckmorton as a go-between, in what must have been very late October and November 1568. Pembroke, Arundel, Lumley, and Cecil were told later.[90] The evidence is confusing, muddled, and contradictory.

[85] 28 July 1568, Cotton Caligula C. 1, fo. 178r.
[86] Cotton Caligula C. 1, fo. 413v.
[87] For Norfolk's confession, SP 12/83, fo. 23r.
[88] Moray to Elizabeth, 19 October 1569, SP 52/16, fo. 119r.
[89] *Memoirs of his own life by Sir James Melville of Halhill. 1549–1593*, ed. Thomas Thomson (Bannatyne Club, 18; Edinburgh, 1827), pp. 208–9, 214.
[90] SP 12/83, fos. 23r, 24r–v, 26r.

So what was going on? If it can be accepted that these men were not fighting some sort of factional war and that they were all (perhaps with the exception of Arundel) firm Protestants, what were they trying to do? Both Norfolk and Melville hinted at it in their late accounts. Throckmorton had an impact on Melville; he was a man, in the *Memoirs*, 'wha had ever travelit to the union of this yll'.[91] Norfolk maintained that Leicester pressed the case for a Howard–Stuart marriage on two grounds, 'the one for Religion, the other for that thereby she [Mary] should be made wholy to depend upon the Queens Majesty'.[92] Melville described a more active Norfolk who, in the presence of Maitland of Lethington, wanted to be sworn the Regent's brother, 'of a religion, schutting continowally at a mark, with the mutuel intelligence of others myndis; the ane to ruell Scotland, and the other to reull England, to the glory of God and weall of baith the princes and ther contrees; sa that the posterite suld reput them the happyest twa instrumentis that ever was bred in Britany'.[93] Even if Norfolk was taking a remarkably cynical and manipulative line, he tried to sell the marriage plan to Moray with the language of Protestant unity. Norfolk wanted Moray's support for 'thadvauncement of your commen weale, and the unytinge of this Ilande', and he wrote against enemies who were against 'the unytinge [of] this lande into one kyn[g]dome in tyme commynge and the mayntenaunce of gods true religion'. He shared his plans with Moray because he was convinced of the Regent's interest in the 'mayntenaunce of godes glory and the advauncement of the comen weale of this Ilande'.[94] This was not the language (even if it was the intention) of private gain, and it can only have been in Moray's political interest to support a plan for a Protestant Britain, a sympathetic England, and a controlled Mary.

Even with this confusing mass of evidence from sometimes conflicting commentators, Norfolk's marriage plan was a British succession project based (unlike Cecil's own notes and advice) on dynastic union. Although the sources disagree on matters of detail, their interpretations of why the plan was conceived in the first place are remarkably similar. It is hardly likely that the earl of Moray, Maitland of Lethington, Throckmorton, and the earl of Leicester would have taken interest in any sort of project which could not have underpinned the stability of England, the Scottish regency, and the security of Protestantism. In other words, their goal was similar to Cecil's but their method was radically different. Even Melville's interpretation of Norfolk sounds authentic. Elizabeth's marriage and the English

[91] *Memoirs* , ed. Thomson, p. 214.
[92] SP 12/83, fo. 23v.
[93] *Memoirs*, ed. Thomson, p. 209.
[94] Norfolk to Moray, 1 July 1569, Harley 290, fo. 49r–v; CP 156, fo. 37r–v, printed in Haynes, p. 520.

succession, says Melville's Norfolk, were subjects 'meit the estaitis of England suld tak some ordour with, as they had essayed dyvers tymes to do at every parlement, to the Quenis gret discontentement' but, because they had not been dealt with, 'yet he and uther noblemen of England, as fathers of the contre, ar myndit to be cairfull'.[95]

Melville is too weak to use effectively, but there are other reasons to suggest that the Norfolk plan – before Ridolfi and without agents – was not a serious grievance for Elizabeth. On progress at Southampton in September 1569, Cecil told William Drury that Moray had used John Wood to 'motion and ernestly labor' for the Howard–Stuart match, 'wherof nether he him self nor any of his did ever notify the same' to Elizabeth.[96] Even as late as 1572, Norfolk's main offences were his 'secret counsells gyven to lyddyngton ther at york' in October 1568.[97] The duke's charges in 1571 included 'Contynuall wrytyng' to Mary, his knowledge of the intention of the northern rebellion, and the sums of money paid to Mary and 'hir ministers', with the involvement of the duke of Alva. But these were the sixth, fourth, and third charges respectively: the first, quite simply, was 'The disclosyng of the Quenes Majestes Counsell whan he was in Commission at york in favor of the Quene of Scottes'.[98] At the bottom of a 1572 secretarial summary of Norfolk's offences in 1568 and 1569, Cecil added in his own hand that 'contrary to that othe and duty of a Counsellor he did behave hym self'.[99] That was precisely the point. As a privy councillor, Norfolk had sworn to 'furder kepe secrett, all maner of counselles and Conferencees without disclosing any part thereof to any manner of person'.[100] This is exactly what he did not do at York when he discussed the future of Mary and his own interest in it beyond the limit of his instructions.[101] In 1568 and 1569 he broke his faith and his oath to Elizabeth, explicitly as a privy councillor and implicitly as England's leading peer.

In what almost seems like Norfolk's inevitable progress from the

---

[95] *Memoirs*, ed. Thomson, p. 207.

[96] 9 September 1569, CP 156, fo. 51r, printed in Haynes, p. 521.

[97] 16 January 1572, SP 12/85, fo. 33r.

[98] SP 12/83, fo. 57r; cf. Cecil's note of Norfolk as 'the principall of degree and trust' at York, 20 January 1570, CP 156, fo. 11r.

[99] SP 12/85, fo. 33r.

[100] For 'The othe of a Co[u]nsellor', 17 November 1558, SP 12/1, fo. 3v. As a late entrant *c.* 1563 Norfolk may well have taken a slightly different version, but his oath would have been substantially the same; cf. the oath taken by the earl of Shrewsbury in 1571, with a promise to 'keepe secret all maters committid and revealid to yow as her majestes counsell or that shalbe treatid of secretly in Counsell', SP 12/83, fo. 72r, and printed in J.R. Tanner (ed.), *Tudor constitutional documents A.D. 1485–1603 with an historical commentary* (Cambridge, 1940 edn), p. 225.

[101] Cotton Caligula C. 1, fos. 227r–232v.

marriage plan to Westminster Hall and the block, it is too easy to forget that he was forgiven by the Queen for his first offences. The Howard–Stuart marriage was not outrageous as a political proposal: even Mary, in contemporaries' eyes, could conform to a Protestant settlement of religion, and this had been the rationale behind Elizabeth's aim to marry the Queen of Scots to the earl of Leicester in 1564.[102] Norfolk made the connection between his own plans and the Dudley–Stuart proposal either (if his testimony is accurate) in October or November 1568, when he spoke to Leicester, or certainly by November 1571, in his confession.[103] This was planned as a dynastic solution to the British problem: even if Norfolk's motives are read extremely critically, it is still clear that he sold the project to Moray, and justified it to his initiated colleagues and later to Elizabeth, on its dynastic benefits as a union of marriage and religion. Political settlement by marriage was an essential element in Norfolk's intellectual approach to the whole issue of the Queen of Scots and her pretensions to the succession. It was a strange mixture of the language of Henry VIII's plan for the future Edward VI's union with Mary and Norfolk's own view of himself, in the office of Earl Marshal, as the powerful political and conciliar figure of the *Modus tenendi parliamentum*.[104] If Cecil's ideal for Britain was Protestant, bound by treaty, and ultimately imperial, then perhaps Norfolk's was equally reformed, united by dynasty, and medieval in principle.

But whatever the aims and intentions of the Howard–Stuart marriage plan, its disclosure left the regime shocked and shaken. In September 1569 the earls of Shrewsbury and Huntingdon were instructed to move Mary to more secure accommodation.[105] Cecil was extremely busy at the beginning of the month, probably planning the questioning of Arundel, Pembroke, Lumley, John Leslie, Throckmorton, and some other men involved in the proposed match.[106] The examinations were carried out, usually in teams of three or four, over October, and Cecil and Bacon were the most prominent

---

[102] See above, pp. 122–4, 140.

[103] SP 12/83, fo. 23r.

[104] David Starkey, 'Stewart serendipity: a missing text of the *Modus tenendi parliamentum*', *Fenway Court*, (1986), 38–51; Linda Levy Peck, 'Peers, patronage and the politics of history', in John Guy (ed.), *The reign of Elizabeth I. Court and culture in the last decade* (Cambridge, 1995), p. 99; Nicholas Pronay and John Taylor (eds.), *Parliamentary texts of the later middle ages* (Oxford, 1980), pp. 75, 87.

[105] Leicester and Cecil to Shrewsbury, 29 August 1569, Lambeth Palace Library, 3206, fo. 543, printed in Edmund Lodge (ed.), *Illustrations of British history, biography, and manners, in the reigns of Henry VIII, Edward VI, Mary, Elizabeth, and James I, exhibited in a series of original papers . . .*, 3 vols. (London, 1791), II, p. 20; Lambeth Palace Library, 3196, fo. 229, Elizabeth to the earl of Huntingdon, 22 September 1569, printed in Lodge (ed.), *Illustrations*, II, pp. 21–2.

[106] Mildmay to Cecil, 8 September 1569, SP 12/58, fo. 169r.

interrogators. From the lists, it is clear that Winchester, Bacon, Howard of Effingham, Clinton, Bedford, Sadler, Mildmay, Knollys, and Cecil were untouched by accusations of involvement.[107] Questioning the marriage planners was a fairly straightforward business; piecing the Anglo-Scottish negotiations back together again was more difficult. There seem to have been rumours that the Norfolk plan had Elizabeth's support, which, because it can be read as an extension of the Dudley proposal, was not beyond belief. Cecil had to explain to Nicholas White in Ireland that 'how so ever' he heard 'plentefully of a marriadg intended', 'I can assure yow, the Quenes Majesty at this present so mislyketh it, as I know no body dare deale therin'.[108] Important wires had crossed. Although Throckmorton maintained that even Leicester and Pembroke understood the delicate situation in Europe, and Moray's precarious position in Scotland, he maintained that Elizabeth 'had in purpose' to restore Mary.[109] Elizabeth, on the other hand, wanted Moray to explain his involvement in the Norfolk plan. England now needed hostages: this had always been part of the agreement, from Cecil's draft 'Consideration' to documents carried to the Regent by John Wood, but there was a new and rather harsh insistence on guarantees by Moray.[110]

Cecil had to readjust the proposal for the political settlement of Mary Stuart, but the central themes of it remained unchanged. Mildmay told Cecil that nothing could be done 'without the Quenes Majestes good contentacion and savetye, and the preservation of the cause of Relligion uppon which twoo principall pillers, as you know, the hole state of our common wealth is fownded'; if these were neglected, there could only be 'ruine and desolation'. 'But', as Mildmay put it, 'whie this to you?'[111] Mary's restoration was taken for granted in the 'degrees', but the secret manoeuvres of Norfolk and Moray raised questions which the York and Westminster commissioners had been struggling with a year before: 'Whyther', wrote Cecil, 'the Quene of Scottes shall be restrayned, or putt to liberty'? 'Whyther she shall be kept in England or dely[vere]d into scotland'?[112] Cecil tackled Elizabeth directly. The Queen of Scots 'in dede is and shall allweise be a daungerooss person to your estate, yet ther be degrees wherby the daunger may be more or less'. Elizabeth's marriage would lessen the threat, 'and whylest yow doo not, it will incress'. If Mary was 'restrayned' either in England or in Scotland, 'it will be less', but the

[107] CP 157, fo. 1r.
[108] 8 September 1569, Lansdowne 102, fos. 149v, 150v.
[109] 10 October 1569, CP 156, fo. 88v.
[110] CP 156, fos. 56v–57r.
[111] SP 12/58, fo. 169r.
[112] Cotton Caligula C. 1, fo. 458r.

Queen of Scots at liberty was more dangerous. If she was allowed to have no other husband while Bothwell lived, it would help. Cecil pressed for an open declaration of Mary's guilt, because then 'she shall be less hable to be a person perillooss'. With Norfolk, Cecil thought that 'if he shall be charged with the cryme of treason' but not found guilty, it would 'not only save, but increass his creditt'.[113]

Cecil spent the next couple of weeks arguing for a restoration of Mary, probably for the Privy Council and certainly in collaboration with Mildmay. Cecil prepared two versions of a discussion of the 'Daungers to insew' if the Queen of Scots either stayed in England or returned back into Scotland,[114] and a third in which he concluded that Mary could go back to her kingdom, provided for by Elizabeth, 'that she may lyve the naturall courss of hir liff in suerty, and to that end is to have a sufficient nombre of hostages'.[115] Later in the month, Cecil and Mildmay both worked on the subject of whether it was safer for Elizabeth 'and the quyetnes of the Realme to retayne' the Queen of Scots 'or retourne hir home'.[116] The central themes of the British debate were included in both sets of notes: the security of religion in Scotland, the crucial role of Moray as guardian of the settlement north of the border (and the possible consequences of his death), the succession dimension, and the fears of foreign intervention. But the focus of attention had changed. The regime had been conscious of the risks of Mary's presence in England since summer 1568, but the Norfolk enterprise had redefined the problem. Even regency which hung on Moray's life and a plan 'to delyver hir into scotland to be kept there in savety' seemed more secure and more appropriate than custody in England.[117]

But Cecil was conscious above all that Mary, the Norfolk plans, and the perceived sympathy of England were a test of the legitimacy and nature of the regime – of the way it governed, and of its approach to the problem of the Queen of Scots. Internal subversion by 'ffactions of the Papistes and other ambitious folkes' was one of Cecil's favourite themes, but he realized that it had developed a new edge. Some favoured the marriage between Mary and Norfolk because of the Queen of Scots' 'owne person, others the Duke hym self', but there were some who did not regard 'the Quene or

---

[113] Drafted by Cecil as his 'advise to the Quenes Majesty in the Duke of Norfolkes case', 6 October 1569, Cotton Caligula C. 1, fo. 456r–v.

[114] For the first draft, Cotton Caligula C. 1, fos. 459r–460v, 461v; and the second, 17 October 1569, Cotton Caligula C. 1, fos. 462r–462v.

[115] 'Reasons to prove that in Justice & honor the Quenes Majesty may delyver the Quene of Scottes into scotland', Cotton Caligula C. 1, fos. 463r–464r.

[116] Cotton Caligula C. 1, fos. 276r–277r; Magdalene College, Cambridge, PL 2503, fos. 349–55, 356, printed in part in Stanford E. Lehmberg, *Sir Walter Mildmay and Tudor government* (Austin, Texas, 1964), pp. 80–2.

[117] Cotton Caligula C. 1, fo. 463r.

Duke, for them selves, but as persons so devoted to certenty of some succession to be capable of the Crowne both of england and scotland'. Cecil wanted an agreement between the two kingdoms based on a common religion, the policing of Mary, and a tripartite treaty underwritten by the power of the imperial crown of England. He admitted that others wanted 'an union perpetuall of the .2. kyngdoms', but through a dynastic match between the Queen of Scots and Norfolk.[118]

IV

The language and intentions of the northern earls expressed the tension between these two significantly different approaches to Mary and the nature of the early Elizabethan polity. Nominally, the earls of Westmorland and Northumberland were supporters of Norfolk. After the failure of the rebellion in November and December 1569, Northumberland later confessed the earls' commitment to the restoration of 'Catholick religion', triggered by Norfolk's decision to marry Mary Stuart.[119] Religion was the key to recruitment in the rising, and not feudal loyalty, but the reverse is true of the earls' general motives.[120] Northumberland and Westmorland had a different view of the way in which the Elizabethan polity should have worked in the 1560s: they were on the periphery of it, effectively excluded, and Mary was not only a focus for attention but a justification for action. The regime and its methods were, at least for the earls, novel. It is certainly significant that the only opportunity they had really been given in ten years to offer counsel on Mary Stuart's cause was in October 1568, when Cecil and the Privy Council planned a great council to judge the Queen of Scots' guilt, a method which accorded more with late medieval and early Tudor practice, bound up with the concept of a broad base of noble advice.[121] This was a matter of political culture and method of government. The duke of Norfolk could define his own political role in two ways, either as a privy councillor or in the office of Earl Marshal. Northumberland and Westmorland did not have the luxury of being able to express their own medieval and magnate identities in a polity which relied more on members of a service nobility and an exclusive and identifiable group of men linking the centre to the localities.

---

[118] Cotton Caligula C. 1, fo. 276r; Magdalene College, Cambridge, PL 2503, fo. 349; Cotton Caligula C. 1, fos. 462r, 463r.
[119] Cuthbert Sharp (ed.), *Memorials of the rebellion of 1569* (London, 1840), pp. 190, 201.
[120] Susan E. Taylor, 'The crown and the north of England, 1559–70: a study of the rebellion of the northern earls, 1569–70, and its causes', PhD thesis, University of Manchester (1981), pp. 270–1; cf. M.E. James, 'The concept of order and the northern rising 1569', *Past and Present*, no. 60 (1973), 49–83.
[121] See above, pp. 176–9.

Eight men had attended the first meeting of Elizabeth's Privy Council on 20 November 1558 and five of them were of fairly low birth, educated, and talented: Cecil, Sir Ambrose Cave, Sir Thomas Parry, Sir Richard Sackville, and Sir Ralph Sadler. In 1568 and 1569 noble privy councillors accounted for barely half of the total number of peers listed by Cecil and Bernard Hampton.[122] The early Elizabethan Privy Council was small, defined, efficient, and strongly bureaucratic, but its acceptance by some contemporaries should not be taken for granted. Mary Stuart generally, and the crisis of 1569 specifically, concentrated traditional and conservative minds. The objections of Northumberland and Westmorland were actually similar to the accusations levelled against men like Thomas Cromwell, Thomas Cranmer, Thomas Audley, and Sir Richard Riche in 1536. Henry VIII's councillors were 'subverters of the good laws of this realme and maynteners of the false sect of those heretiques and the first inventors and bryngands in of them';[123] in the same way, 'divers disordered, and evell disposed persons' near to Elizabeth had, 'by ther subtill and craftye dealinge', challenged Catholicism, 'disordered the realme, and now lastlie seke and procure the destruction of the nobilitye'.[124] One version of the northern earls' proclamation challenged the 'diverse newe set upp nobles about the Quenes Majestie', aimed perhaps at men like Leicester and Warwick. The rebels' aim was simple: to 'see redresse of those things amysse with restoringe of all auncyente customes and liberties to godes churche, and this noble Realme'.[125] These were the concerns of men who considered themselves *consiliarii nati*, excluded, like their counterparts in the 1530s, from a practice of politics which centred more on bureaucracy and professionalism. It was also the language of the 'feudal-baronial' right to bridle the monarch. The political world of the 1560s, exposed by the succession crisis, was very different.[126]

After the northern rebellion, Cecil and Bernard Hampton worked on two drafts of a proclamation to be read by curates to their parishioners.[127] The unpublished 'declaration' was a defence of the regime and an explanation of the theory behind it. In part, the two versions of the 'declaration' are

---

[122] SP 12/59, fo. 95r. This list does not include Northumberland or Westmorland.

[123] John Guy, 'The king's council and political participation', in Alistair Fox and John Guy, *Reassessing the Henrician age. Humanism, politics and reform 1500–1550* (Oxford and New York, 1986), p. 144; Anthony Fletcher, *Tudor rebellions* (London, 1973 edn), pp. 128–30.

[124] Lansdowne 11, fo. 120r.

[125] Sharp (ed.), *Memorials*, p. 42; Fletcher, *Tudor rebellions*, p. 150; Lansdowne 11, fo. 120r.

[126] Guy, 'King's council', p. 143; John Guy, 'The rhetoric of counsel in early modern England', in Dale Hoak (ed.), *Tudor political culture* (Cambridge, 1995), pp. 297–8.

[127] For the first draft, written by Hampton and heavily corrected by Cecil, CP 157, fos. 9r–12r, printed in Haynes, pp. 589–93; for the second – again prepared by Hampton and edited by Cecil – SP 12/66, fos. 147r–152v.

very standard expressions of Elizabeth's intentions, past and future: 'the obedience of all our subjectes *of all sortes, both hygh and low* by love and not by compulsion, by their owne yielding and not by our exacting', *'which was well sayd'*, Cecil added to the first draft, *'by a wise prince of the Grekes that kyng to be in most suerty that so ruled over his subjectes, as a naturall father'*; and the 'conservation of commen peace and lawe'. In some ways, 'the Ecclesiasticall externall pollicy of our Realme by lawes differreth from somme other Contreys'. The reason for this was simple: not only was authority exercised by Elizabeth 'as Quene and Governor of this realme' according to 'the Lawe of God & this Realme always due to our progenitors, soverayns and Kinges of the same', but these laws had been 'always *annexed to the Crown of this realme and* due to our progenitors, Soveraignes and Kinges of the same, *as by good sufficient and auncient authoritees is to be proved'*. This was a thoroughly sound expression of Tudor imperial power, but Cecil included a crucial distinction. In the first draft of the 'declaration', the ecclesiastical and imperial settlements of Henry VIII and Edward VI had been 'clerely recognised to all the estates of the Realme'. In the second they were 'clerely recognized *to the Imperiall Crown of this realme* by all the estates of the *same in parlementes* as the like hath ben in our tyme'. The rebellion and the succession crisis, British in theme and European in perspective, had at last forced the regime publicly to define itself.[128]

The last year of the decade encouraged the Privy Council to question the sort of settlement of the succession it wanted. It also persuaded some noblemen outside the charmed circle to challenge a polity which had excluded them. As a focus of political attention, Mary Stuart allowed men like Northumberland and Westmorland to dispute the terms on which the polity was based, and forced a councillor like Cecil to defend and explain them. One of the reasons why men like Northumberland and Westmorland felt excluded was because of the nature of the Privy Council: it was an effective political body which, by even the middle part of the decade, was starting to take a political line on policy and felt that its voice ought to be heard. Cecil believed that parliament also had a part in the crucial decisions of the decade, reinforcing and recognizing the sort of imperial power he used to underpin and underwrite the political settlement of Britain. After all, in October 1569, he considered a prohibition of 'all persons to treate upp[on] the title of a successor' except by Elizabeth's licence or 'by parlement'.[129] At the end of the decade, this was a perfectly accurate summary of one of its central themes.

---

[128] CP 157, fos. 10r–11r; SP 12/66, fos. 149r–150r. Cecil's corrections are in *italics*.
[129] Cotton Caligula C. 1, fo. 458r.

Conclusion: the early
Elizabethan polity

One of the main themes of this book has been the radicalization of British and domestic politics in the 1560s and the distinctive political culture of the 'first reign' of Elizabeth I. But the first decade was not an isolated period and there are crucial connections – and central differences – between early and late Elizabethan politics and political culture. From the start of the reign, for example, Cecil established the vocabulary of Catholic conspiracy and political emergency which allowed him and his colleagues to understand the nature of European politics – and the relationship between Mary Stuart, Elizabeth's crown, and the domestic crisis – well into the 1580s. To understand fully the bond of association of 1584 and the plan for conciliar interregnum in an emergency in 1584 and 1585 it is important first to explore the language of (and the solutions offered by) Cecil and the Privy Council in the first decade. In other ways, the political culture of the 1560s, 1570s, and early 1580s was substantially different to that of the late 1580s and the 1590s. Cecil developed a rounded domestic and British political creed in the 1560s and it is worth considering how his ideas, preoccupations, and priorities influenced later debate on the nature of the Elizabethan polity.

I

There were profound differences between the Privy Council of the 1560s and its late Elizabethan successor. The first was political experience. The Council in the 1590s was purely Elizabethan, but early councillors were generally Edwardian and – in the case of Sir Ralph Sadler – Henrician. Commoners in the Privy Council shared the experience of training at the universities, the Inns of Court, or the royal court; their noble colleagues often combined the same sort of educational background and overt Protestantism. There were no clerics in the early Elizabethan Privy Council. Matthew Parker, unlike John Whitgift, did not play a part in Council as archbishop of Canterbury and Archbishop Heath of York had only a marginal role before 1559. The first generation of early privy councillors had died by the 1580s and early 1590s: the earl of Bedford (1585), Lord Admiral Edward Clinton (1585), the earl of Leicester (1588), and Sir Walter Mildmay (1589). There were some familiar names in the intermediate Privy Council of the 1570s and 1580s – Sir Henry Sidney and Sir Francis Walsingham in the council of 1586, for example – but they were dead by 1590.[1]

The late 1580s and 1590s belonged to new men. Lords Buckhurst and Cobham, Whitgift, Richard Cosin, and Richard Bancroft were central to the nature of the late Elizabethan regime – and the ideological differences showed. Robert Beale, the Clerk of the Council, challenged Whitgift in the parliament of 1584. Cecil refused to involve himself in Christopher Hatton's and Whitgift's move to hammer puritanism and was not part of the caucus in Star Chamber which discussed the prosecution of presbyterian leaders. He complained to Whitgift in 1584 about the methods being used in the campaign and the severity of the articles of subscription which employed the *ex officio* oath. In 1590, 1593, and 1596 he protected one of the principal thorns in the archbishop's side, the puritan lawyer James Morice. Whitgift understandably accepted that it was Buckhurst, and not Cecil, who could provide the key to his security in Council.[2] But this was not merely an issue of political control or influence. The late 1580s and early 1590s were culturally distinct from the 1560s. Men like Morice – and Cecil – had something to say about the nature of their polity.

Cecil was an instinctive conciliarist. He was part of a political tradition which emphasized the role of parliament and Council in the governance of a realm, even in a British context. A native constitutional tradition, the impact on the English polity of two female monarchs, and the experience of governing the kingdom during the reign of a minor between 1547 and 1553 were reinforced by a literature of European conciliarism. This had become part of English political and ecclesiastical debate in the 1530s. *The boke named the governor* made a strong connection between training in the common law and governorship, a discipline in which training was carried out intensively, coherently, and in the small communities of the Inns of Court. Cecil was a common lawyer; so too were Nicholas Bacon and Francis Walsingham. The six men who worked on the Subsidy Bill in 1566 were all common lawyers. This was, in part, a question of training and legal expertise; but their background may also have made them more

[1] Penry Williams, *The Tudor regime* (Oxford, 1979), pp. 453–5.

[2] John Guy, 'The Elizabethan establishment and the ecclesiastical polity', in John Guy (ed.), *The reign of Elizabeth I. Court and culture in the last decade* (Cambridge, 1995), p. 129 and n. 8; James E. Hampson, 'Richard Cosin and the rehabilitation of the clerical estate in late Elizabethan England', PhD thesis, University of St Andrews (1997), pp. 20, 31–2.

willing to draft a preamble to the Bill in which they thanked Elizabeth for her help 'to establish that which with assent of your Realme in parliament maye be agreable and consonant to lawe and Justice' – the English succession.[3]

There was an intellectual thread running through European conciliarism, the writings of Christopher St German, and some late Elizabethan interpretations of the relationship between royal authority, law, and counsel in parliament. Even in the 1560s, some common lawyers began to examine the origin of power and authority in their commonwealth. Around 1562 Chief Justice James Dyer – who, like Cecil, had to bend to Elizabeth's desire in 1566 to silence parliament legally – began to collect precedents of *habeas corpus*. Dyer was one man who even from the beginning of the reign began to question the authority of the High Commission to imprison offenders at its discretion.[4] In a draft of a lecture to the Middle Temple in 1578–9 James Morice argued that the laws of the realm 'ordayned and enriched the Royall Throne'. He explored the source of the monarch's prerogative and found it in the 'Lawes, Lybertie, Goodes, or Landes' of his or her subjects and – with echoes of St German in the early 1530s – 'the High and Stately Courte of Parlyament'.[5] Cecil, interestingly, asked for a copy of the text.

The importance of common law should not be overstated, but these arguments were part of a wider debate in the 1560s and 1570s. Philip Sidney had studied Venice and republican Rome, read Machiavelli, and visited Florence; he was extremely conscious of the impact of European (and particularly Dutch) politics on the English polity, the threat of democracy, the dangers of aristocratic oligarchy, and the flaws of the monarchical system – especially during a period when royal interregnum would have meant the dissolution of government. The response of Sidney's friend, Daniel Rogers, to George Buchanan's *De jure regni apud Scotos* was startlingly frank: it would be rejected by flatterers but appreciated by men who had the welfare of the kingdom at heart.[6] Perhaps one of the surprising facts of the 1560s and 1570s is that Cecil, the Privy Council, John Aylmer, and Thomas Cartwright shared this emphasis on the 'mixed polity' as a common constitutional position. England was a polity in which parliament could be interpreted as the democratic element; it was Elizabeth and her estates who debated and decided and not the Queen in isolation – or at least that was the ideal. This was central to the relationship between

---

[3] See above, pp. 153–6; and below, p. 232.
[4] Hampson, 'Cosin', p. 36; see above, pp. 151–2.
[5] Hampson, 'Cosin', pp. 31–2, 37–9; see above, p. 36.
[6] Blair Worden, *The sound of virtue. Philip Sidney's* Arcadia *and Elizabethan politics* (New Haven and London, 1996), pp. 227–52, especially 226, 239.

politics and political culture in the first three Elizabethan decades. Aylmer maintained that England was 'a rule mixte' of monarchy, oligarchy, and democracy, and on that point he was supported by the writer who explored the structure of the early Elizabethan polity, Sir Thomas Smith.[7] Cartwright found an 'image' of mixed government 'in the policy of this realm; for as, in respect of the queen her majesty, it is a monarchy, so, in respect of the most honourable council, it is an aristocracy, and, having regard to parliament, which is assembled of all estates, it is a democracy'.[8]

The political implications of this reading of the locus of power in the polity were profound. Council and parliament could be – and by Cecil were – turned into institutions which actively participated in the running of the polity and contributed to decisions which affected the future of the realm. This was the position of Cecil, the Privy Council, and MPs in the 1560s. Even Richard Hooker was seduced. In *Of the law of ecclesiastical polity*, he argued that the law limited the power of the king and that the ability to make law 'should belong to the whole, not to any certain part of a political body'. In England the body of the whole realm was parliament.[9] Hooker wrote the first book in retirement in Wiltshire in 1593; the eighth was available only in manuscript until publication in 1648, and probably for good reason. He dedicated the fifth book *Of the laws of ecclesiastical polity* to John Whitgift, but Hooker pushed his argument beyond the boundaries of what Whitgift would have found acceptable. For Whitgift – and Elizabeth – a 'mixed' polity was anathema. Representation could be separated, but 'judgement, confirmation, and determination' rested in the prince; 'therefore the state is neither "aristocracy" nor "democracy" but a "monarchy"'. 'The government of this kingdom is a right and true monarchy.'[10] So in the final part of Elizabeth's reign, the language of mixed government became (in Professor John Guy's words) 'politically incorrect', part of the conformist push for order in the church and royal power in the polity.[11] In the 1560s ideas of mixed polity were current and natural, accessible to the Privy Council and men in its orbit and wholly inaccessible to the Queen. Both Cecil and Elizabeth were remarkably consistent but in radically different ways.

[7] John Aylmer, *An harborowe for faithfull and trewe subjectes, agaynst the late blowne blaste, concerninge the government of wemen . . .* (STC 1005; London, 1559), sig. H2v–H3r; Sir Thomas Smith, *De republica Anglorum*, ed. Mary Dewar (Cambridge, 1982), Book I, chapter 6, p. 52; see above, pp. 34–7.
[8] Guy, 'Ecclesiastical polity', p. 127; John Guy, *Tudor England* (Oxford, 1988), p. 375 and n. 56.
[9] Richard Hooker, *Of the laws of ecclesiastical polity*, ed. Arthur Stephen McGrade (Cambridge, 1989), pp. 92–4; Howell A. Lloyd, 'Constitutionalism', in J.H. Burns and Mark Goldie (eds.), *The Cambridge history of political thought 1450–1700* (Cambridge, 1991), pp. 279–83.
[10] Guy, 'Ecclesiastical polity', p. 127.   [11] Guy, 'Ecclesiastical polity', p. 130.

A number of shared experiences bound and united the early Elizabethan Privy Council: European and British pressures, Cambridge in the 1530s and 1540s, the Inns of Court, political positions under Edward VI, and ties of family and dynasty. There *were* disagreements and debates within the regime in the 1560s – surely an inevitable part of any political process – but these were rare and (more importantly) strategic rather than ideological. Even in the divided advice presented to Elizabeth over intervention in Scotland in December 1559, the Council as a whole accepted the evidence for French Catholic conspiracy; the issue was how to deal with it.[12] The work of the Council in the 1560s was fairly smooth and much of it went on unnoticed and uncommented on. It was only when the system occasionally broke down – in July 1563, for example, when Cecil wrote a letter of complaint to his brother-in-law Nicholas Bacon – that the conciliar process revealed itself.

The court was at Richmond in mid-summer 1563 and the Council met on 20 July. At this meeting, according to Cecil, Bacon treated him extremely badly. Bacon had disagreed with 'resolutions' in some letters prepared by his brother-in-law. Cecil pointed out that 'that which I had written was so also ordered by the Quenes majestie'; also, 'Others there of the Councell did not disallowe the lettres'. This was not the issue: it was Bacon's rudeness in the Council chamber – worse than the treatment of his clerks in chancery – which had infuriated him. But this letter reveals even more. Cecil's part in the active process of Council, his relationship with other councillors, and the way in which the Privy Council debated incoming information and formed replies are all important themes. It discussed the outgoing letters on 20 July, and a day later Cecil prepared the final copies to be signed. He went to Bacon's room that morning, 'as became me', to 'shew yow both master [Thomas] Smithes lettres out of Fraunce, and others to be newely signed'. Bacon was out 'to take the ayre', and so because 'the matter required hast' and because Cecil had to return to his 'busynes' for the rest of the morning, the letters were despatched without Bacon's signature.[13]

The incident between Bacon and Cecil was not a factional episode: it was a hiccup in an otherwise extremely smooth conciliar operation. Although Cecil maintained in his letter to Bacon that he was 'no clerke to write your resolutions, nor lettres for yow or the Councell, there be Clerkes for that purpose', he clearly acted as the central focus of early Elizabethan conciliar

---

[12] See above, pp. 66–70.
[13] Cecil to Bacon, 21 July 1563, Lansdowne 102, fos. 69v–70v.

government. He liaised with the Queen and the Council and prepared drafts which his colleagues could discuss and comment on. He circulated final copies, which were signed by a quorum of councillors. The Council was part of a complex web of communication in which it acted as a contact with other councils in Ireland, the north of England, and continental Europe, reinforced by personal letters directed to councillors like Cecil and Leicester and to the Queen. Incoming information and outgoing instructions were part of a highly integrated, political, and conciliar process. Cecil received intelligence, read and synthesized it, and presented reports to the Privy Council. The Clerk of the Council, Bernard Hampton, was an important part of this system. He was trusted enough to have access to material from sensitive meetings and could act as a bridge between the Council and individual representatives of the crown; it was Hampton who drafted the Council's 'instruments' and maintained contact with the earl of Sussex in Ireland in June 1560.[14]

This was not a factional system, paralyzed by internal division or ideological conflict. Sometimes the Council informally divided itself into 'subcommittees' or appointed small commissions of councillors, reinforced by local experts like Thomas Randolph, Sir Ralph Sadler, and Sir Nicholas Throckmorton. These men wrote to the Council, to Elizabeth, and to senior colleagues. Written intelligence or counsel was often filtered through Cecil and the Privy Council. Throckmorton advised Leicester and Cecil in 1565.[15] Leicester and Cecil co-ordinated their efforts to counsel the Queen to action over political crisis in Scotland in 1567.[16] Elizabeth also met representatives and agents and relied on audiences with Cecil. In 1561 he was annoyed that the earl of Sussex had not sent him the latest news with which to brief the Queen.[17] On his return from Ireland in June 1566, Sir Francis Knollys spent time 'in debat' with Elizabeth.[18] But the Council could also become part of this process. In 1562 Sir Nicholas Bacon, the marquess of Northampton, the earl of Pembroke, Knollys, and Cecil met Shane O'Neill before his audience with the Queen. He 'submitted' himself and received 'some sharp rehersall . . . of his generall fawltes' in a meeting called to establish whether the councillors could act as 'meanes' for Shane's reconciliation to Elizabeth.[19]

Conciliar government in the 1560s may seem fairly ordinary and uninspiring. The Privy Council worked in the same way in the 1570s and in the early 1580s because it was, in part, a bureaucratically and administra-

---

[14] See above, pp. 49–50.   [15] See above, pp. 126–7.
[16] Cecil to Leicester, 15 May 1567, Magdalene College, Cambridge, PL 2502, fo. 737; Leicester to Cecil, 16 June 1567, SP 12/43, fo. 23r–v.
[17] See above, p. 49.   [18] See above, p. 142.
[19] Cecil to Sussex, 7 January 1562, Cotton Titus B. 13, fo. 75r; see above, p. 90.

tively established system. There are strong (and, considering the experience of early Elizabethan councillors, probably significant) similarities to the Edwardian method.[20] But the whole process was turned into a serious political issue in 1587 when the Council signed and despatched the warrant authorizing the execution of Mary Stuart 'for [the Queen's] special service tending to the safety of her royal person and universal quietness of her whole Realm'. Elizabeth's reaction to what she perceived as a challenge to her prerogative was simple: royal pressure to hang William Davison, her Principal Secretary, and extremely bad relations between the Queen and her privy councillors.[21] More generally, conciliar efficiency was not the key to the politics of the very late 1580s and 1590s. In his disagreements with Whitgift, Cecil routinely absented himself from Council meetings. Gaps in attendance were filled by the Clerk of the Privy Council, Robert Beale. And as Lord Treasurer, Cecil alone authorized warrants for payment.[22] He had (potentially) massive powers in the 1560s – the ability to guide the Privy Council and edit written communications with the Queen, personal access to Elizabeth as Principal Secretary, the stamp of Elizabeth's sign manual – but the importance of counsel, debate, and conciliar process in the 1560s was emphasized by the Bacon incident and by occasional breakdowns in the system.

Parliament was an important part of this conciliar network. The connections between the Privy Council and the Commons in the 1560s were more subtle than Professor G.R. Elton and Professor Michael Graves have admitted. There *were* 'men of business' in the early Elizabethan Commons; after 1572, with Cecil out of the Commons, there was a role for trustworthy and capable men able to deal with affairs in the Lower House and keep independent records of its proceedings; MPs were supported and sustained by councillors and courtiers in their areas of regional influence. But it is a mistake for historians to make even tentative connections between clients, patrons, and debates when individual allegiances or larger 'networks' cannot be worked out in detail and parliamentary records for the 1560s are so incomplete. The Privy Council did not 'plant' debates in 1563 and 1566; but it *did* act with senior MPs, the Speaker of the Commons, and the Lords to put pressure on Elizabeth to act in what they

[20] Dale Hoak, *The King's Council in the reign of Edward VI* (Cambridge, 1976), pp. 145–64. Cf. two letters sent out by the Edwardian council in March 1548 and July 1553, the first to the bishops and the second to Lord Rich in Essex 'from the Counsell named Quenes Janes Counsell'; both bear the signatures of councillors written (like their Elizabethan counterparts) in strict order of rank. 15 March 1548, SP 10/4, fo. 3r–v; 19 July 1553, Lansdowne 3, fo. 50r.

[21] John Guy, 'Tudor monarchy and its critiques', in John Guy (ed.), *The Tudor monarchy* (London, 1997), pp. 98–9.

[22] John Guy, 'The 1590s: the second reign of Elizabeth I?', in Guy (ed.), *Reign of Elizabeth I*, p. 14.

thought was a central issue of counsel. Although they were technically restatements of the Queen's promises to parliament, the Commons' and Lords' petitions and preambles to the Subsidy Bill of 1566 are examples of early Elizabethan counsel offered as compelling political advice – they were clearly not innocent declarations. What is more, there were strong conciliar connections. Bernard Hampton – whose job, at least in theory, was to supervise junior clerks and support the administrative activities of the Privy Council – acted as draughtsman for Cecil and a wider committee of senior MPs and councillors. He was involved in extremely controversial business – or at least controversial for Elizabeth. Also, there is considerable overlap between the group of men who attempted to press the Queen in parliament in 1566 and Cecil's and Bernard Hampton's list of the political elite prepared at the end of the decade.[23] There is a sense in which early Elizabethan privy councillors, gentlemen in the counties, law officers, and administrators were, as MPs, attempting to counsel Elizabeth.

III

In the 1980s E.I. Kouri argued that Cecil was one of a group of 'anti-interventionists' in the Elizabethan Privy Council, opposed by councillors who favoured 'the identification of English interest' with Protestantism and Protestant alliance policy in continental Europe.[24] Although more recent research has helped to establish the importance of Cecil in the making of forward, Protestant policy, it is still a challenge to move away from standard interpretations which have been ingrained since the early twentieth century.[25] Put simply, councillors like Walsingham and Leicester were 'hot gospellers'; Cecil was a *politique*.[26] The implications of this position are twofold. First, the argument ran, the early Elizabethan Privy Council must have been factionalized, but this was simply not the case. And second, it appeared that Cecil and some of his colleagues interpreted wider affairs in radically different ways. I hope this book has demonstrated that this is an equally misguided reading of politics in the first decade.

Elizabethan historians have often been too willing to pigeonhole and

---

[23] See above, pp. 153–7.

[24] E.I. Kouri, 'For true faith or national interest? Queen Elizabeth I and the Protestant powers', in Kouri and Tom Scott (eds.), *Politics and society in reformation Europe* (Basingstoke and London, 1987), pp. 413–14; Kouri, *England and the attempts to form a Protestant alliance in the late 1560s: a case study in European diplomacy* (Helsinki, 1981), pp. 41–2.

[25] Jane E.A. Dawson, 'William Cecil and the British dimension of early Elizabethan foreign policy', *History*, 74 (1989), 196–216.

[26] Principally Conyers Read, 'Factions in the English Privy Council under Elizabeth', *Annual Report of the American Historical Association*, 1 (1911), 115; Read, 'Walsingham and Burghley in Queen Elizabeth's Privy Council', *English Historical Review*, 28 (1913), 37.

categorize. The regime in the 1560s did not pursue separate 'policies': affairs in England and decisions on issues in Ireland, Scotland, France, and Spain simply cannot be written off as 'domestic' or 'foreign'. This problem was a confusing one for Victorian archivists: they attempted to separate and categorize Elizabethan state papers but found that there was substantial overlap between, for example, 'Scottish' and 'foreign' documents. Kouri made the same sort of mistake when he drew a false and misleading distinction between 'true faith' – Protestantism – and 'national interest'. The central point is that Cecil and the Elizabethan Privy Council did not think that simply. They considered the ecclesiastical structure of their polity, wider events in Europe, the position of the English crown, and Scotland and Ireland, two kingdoms which (in their minds) were strategically linked.

For Cecil, the key to British and European policy-making was the preservation of the (Protestant) state of the realm – the condition of the kingdom and, in embryonic form, the maintenance of government and polity even without the monarch. This was at once British *and* domestic. Policy-making in the 1560s rested on privy councillors' ability to connect the English to the Scottish and Irish and the religious and ecclesiastical to the politically secular. It has been too easy to underestimate the part providence could play in the formulation of Elizabethan policy. In 1565 the Privy Council debated the intricate relationship between 'truth and pollycy': strengthening the link between the centre and the localities, countering subversion, and securing Elizabeth's marriage were some of the ways the regime could deal with the union between the Queen of Scots and Lord Darnley, but political action at a national level was clearly underscored and complemented by the true worship of God.[27]

If Cecil was conscious of the influence of providence in politics and determined to preserve the health of the ecclesiastical polity, then what did he believe? Cecil was aware of the heritage of the post-Reformation English church. In 1563 he wrote to Cranmer's physician, John Herd, because he understood that 'yow have very fortunatly, and studioosly preserved certen collections or comen placees gathred and wrytten by the late most reverent and godly father Thomas archibishopp of Canterbury'. This archive was 'such a Jewell', and it should not 'be kept in secrett oblivion, as a candle under a busshell, but rather ought to be sett abroade, to the publique use of the church of Christ'. Cecil wanted to commission transcripts of the papers.[28] Cranmer had been such an important part of the European Protestant movement and one of the keys to the evangelical environment Cecil had experienced in Cambridge and encouraged in

[27] See above, p. 129.   [28] 14 April 1563, SP 12/28, fo. 118r.

government.[29] Two members of the 'Cambridge connection' were responsible for commissioning and translating *An apology of the Church of England*, written in Latin by John Jewel in 1562. Cecil sponsored the book and Matthew Parker translated it into English in 1564; the English edition was dedicated to Cecil's sister-in-law Ann Bacon, the wife of Nicholas. In June 1564 Parker commented on the 'reverent mediocritie' of the 'ministracion of our common prayer and sacramentes'. He maintained, in an argument similar to Jewel's, that the English church grounded itself 'upon thapostolicall doctrine and pure tyme of the primityve churche'. But England had clearly and completely rejected the pope, 'not in wordes as in Edward the thirdes dayes'.[30]

But there was a different side to Cecil's religious and ecclesiastical position: labelling him a conformist is too limited. He was a Calvinist and had been since the 1550s. He married into the Cooke dynasty and maintained a reformed household. His servants and secretaries were Protestant; some of them had been trained in the common law at the Inns of Court or been educated at Cambridge.[31] Cecil was responsible for the Elizabethan religious settlement of the 1560s: if Professor Norman Jones succeeded in demolishing the notion of a 'puritan choir' agitating for change in the first parliament, he also underestimated the religious conservatism of Elizabeth and the influence of Cecil in pushing the settlement as far as it could go.[32] In his position as the Queen's minister – and a man conscious of the need for order and discipline in the face of subversion and conspiracy – he was open to criticism. Still, Cecil was quite capable of defending himself against some puritan criticism in the 1570s. In fact, he clearly protected puritans like James Morice against Whitgift and the High Commission in the 1580s. Cecil's priorities were clear, subtle, and multi-layered. His concern right from the beginning of Elizabeth's reign was for active, reforming bishops. He thought that an effective ecclesiastical settlement meant a secure polity but there is no sense in which he supported the power of bishops – or ecclesiastical power – for its own sake. In 1559 Cecil argued that the internal dangers facing the kingdom were 'for lack of good government Ecclesiasticall, wherby people ar not duly tought to lyve in obedience to the laws established for matters of Relligion'. This was a perfect opportunity for 'papistes, Jesuittes and seminary prestes' to take advantage of the situation. The key was pastoral and moral reform, with

[29] Winthrop Hudson, *The Cambridge connection and the Elizabethan settlement of 1559* (Durham, North Carolina, 1980).
[30] Parker to Cecil, 3 June 1564, SP 12/34, fo. 40r–v.
[31] Richard C. Barnett, *Place, profit, and power. A study of the servants of William Cecil, Elizabethan statesman* (Chapel Hill, 1969), pp. 159–69.
[32] Norman Jones, *Faith by statute. Parliament and the settlement of religion 1559* (London, 1982).

archbishops and bishops 'charged to have more regard to ther charges' and prepared to remedy 'there own evill examples in Covetosnes, loosnes of lyff and with manny other defaltes'.[33]

But there are even more clues. In 1559 Cecil suggested the Danish *Ordinatio ecclesiastica* (1537) as a model for the Scottish church. There are strong links between the *Ordinatio* and the *The first book of discipline*, drafted by John Knox and his colleagues in 1560. The model was a presbyterian one. Cecil's priorities in reformation were an end to papal jurisdiction, the enrichment of the crown, help for the youth of the nobility, the maintenance of ministry in the church, education, and the relief of the poor. In 'some poyntes' there had been oversight during England's first, Henrician reformation, notably help for the ministry and care of the poor.[34] In June 1569 Cecil compared the 'authority of this pompe of the Chirch of Roome' to 'the forme of the primitive Chirch, which was in wordly shew and substance in formar tyme meane and poore, and yet had sufficiency, but in hollynes, vertue, humblynes, prayer, preaching, and such like divine servyces abundant'.[35] This commitment to ministry had been the concern of John Hooper and Cecil in the 1550s. It is hardly coincidental that Cecil's priorities in the 1560s in England and Scotland echo an anonymous Edwardian paper of 1552 on the use of church property for the public use of the whole ministry and the reconstruction of education.[36]

Cecil believed in an ecclesiastical polity in which parliament had a role, reinforced by effective ministry. He reacted to Whitgift's attempts to under-score the imperial power of the monarch Elizabeth had been so determined to press in the debate over clerical vestments, the first clash with Cartwright and puritanism, and the problems over Edmund Grindal in the 1570s. But although historians have tidy minds, their Elizabethan subjects often did not. Perhaps one of the best examples of this was the ability of a career cleric like Edmund Guest to echo the arguments of John Ponet in 1565 in the debate over military intervention in Scotland.[37] Cecil, on the other hand, was consistent. In his providential pattern of European politics, England's religion mattered. Antichrist, Satan, and the anger of God transmitted through human agents were as real to Cecil as they were to men conventionally considered more radical: John Knox, Walsingham, and Throckmorton. But Cecil not only accepted their reading of national and

---

[33] 'A Memoryall of thynges to be reported to hir Majesty', SP 12/4, fo. 135r.
[34] Cecil to the lords of the congregation, 28 July 1559, SP 52/1, fo. 147v; Gordon Donaldson, '"The example of Denmark" in the Scottish reformation', in his *Scottish church history* (Edinburgh, 1985), p.67.
[35] 'A necessary consideration of the perillous state of this tyme', SP 12/51, fo. 9v.
[36] SP 10/15, fos. 158r–161r.   [37] See above, pp. 133–6.

international politics; he also developed a political, constitutional, and ecclesiastical response.

IV

The best examples of Cecil's deep analysis of the European and British crisis in the first decade are 'A necessary consideration of the perillous state of this tyme' and 'the booke of the state of the Realme'. But these documents – and papal issue of the bull *Regnans in excelsis* in February 1570 – only confirmed what Cecil had thought for over a decade: a fear of encirclement by the forces of the pope, France, Spain, the Netherlands, and hostile groups in Scotland, armed against an England internally divided over the succession and religion, and aggravated by 'Imperfection in the Government of Irland'.[38] The solutions were connected. In 'the booke' he looked to an alliance with Protestant princes, an international declaration of Elizabeth's position, the remedy of 'defectes' in English religion, civil and legal obedience, and the restoration of the kingdom's decayed 'martiall state'. 'A necessary consideration' offered a plan for comprehensive association.[39]

Two crucial elements of this wider plan were Anglo-Scottish solidarity and peace in a settled Ireland. One of the most interesting developments in recent Elizabethan scholarship has been the exploration of Cecil's strategic mentality. He understood that policy on Scotland and security in Ireland were connected. A main principle of action was the support of the earl of Argyle in return for English military help for the lords of the congregation in 1560. The reluctance of Cecil and the Privy Council to fight Mary Stuart in 1565 was, in part, based on the realization that war in Scotland meant a campaign in Ireland. So the appointment of Sir Henry Sidney as Lord Deputy in the same year and the mission of Sir Francis Knollys in spring 1566 were not only responses to internal political crisis in Ireland. The joint policy of military security and plantation was a response to a growing realization that there *were* strong links between Stuart government in Scotland, rebellion in Ireland, and a combined threat to Elizabeth's crown.[40]

Strategy was only one element of Cecil's sense of the relationship between England, Scotland, and Ireland. His Anglo-Scottish ideal was that 'these ij being frendly and peacibly Joyned with Irland quieted, may savely preserve them selves with good government, from the malice of france, and

---

[38] SP 12/60, fo. 226r.   [39] CP 157, fo. 8r–v; see above, pp. 195–8.

[40] Principally Jane E.A. Dawson, 'Two kingdoms or three? Ireland in Anglo-Scottish relations in the middle of the sixteenth century', in Roger A. Mason (ed.), *Scotland and England 1286–1815* (Edinburgh, 1987), pp. 113–38; also see above, pp. 140–1.

the rest of Christendom'.[41] England and Scotland shared a past which could be defined or conceptualized in two very different ways. Union through Protestantism *and* English rights over Scotland were principles which were accepted and deployed by Cecil. The arguments for superiority became part of a long and continuing tradition. The English Whig lawyer William Atwood argued even in 1704 that the Scottish church was under the archiepiscopal jurisdiction of York and that England's 'imperial crown' exercised 'direct dominion' over Scotland.[42] The interesting point for Elizabethan historians is that these traditions could be woven into an interpretation of the relationship between England and Scotland: united by Protestant common interest in the face of European Catholicism, conscious of the need to limit Stuart power, and prepared to press for an authentically British treaty underwritten by the superiority of the English crown.

v

One specific aspect of Cecil's response to perceived political crisis in the 1560s – the proposal for association in 'A necessary consideration of the perillous state of this tyme' – found a place in the political philosophy of the eighteenth-century writer James Burgh. Burgh argued that the power of government and governors was delegated and limited and that 'All lawful authority, legislative and executive, originates from the people.' This was a reaction to the moderate Whig position that sovereignty rested in monarch, Lords, and Commons in parliament. Burgh's alternative was the association, which had its origin in the Elizabethan bonds. The association was an expression of the sovereignty of the people, and it could be used to limit their representatives in parliament.[43] This was a travesty of Cecil's political creed – his emphasis on the mixed polity was radical enough in the first Elizabethan decade – but it underlines an important point. Willing or unwilling, aware or unaware, the British succession crisis of the 1560s forced Cecil to consider and reconsider the relationship between subjects and their monarch. And this applied to Scotland as well as England. When the central premise of a treaty is the control of a monarch by grand council and parliament, affecting a queen's power to choose a husband, the religion of her kingdom, the quality of her rule, and the nationality of royal officers and soldiers, the implications are profound.

[41] May 1568, Caligula C. 1, fo. 98r.
[42] Mark Goldie, 'Divergence and union: Scotland and England, 1660–1707', in Brendan Bradshaw (eds.), *The British problem, c. 1534–1707. State formation in the Atlantic archipelago* (Basingstoke and London, 1996), pp. 240–1.
[43] Martha K. Zebrowski, 'The corruption of politics and the dignity of human nature: the critical and constructive radicalism of James Burgh', *Enlightenment and Dissent*, 10 (1991), 78–103. I owe this reference to Dr Mark Goldie.

In 1955 Conyers Read was unaware that William Cecil was part of an important change in the nature and language of English political culture, encouraged by European thought and printing, and given a radical edge by the British crisis of the 1560s. Read used the size of the Cecil archive to demonstrate, empirically, that the Principal Secretary was an efficient and conservative administrator, and that his 'patience and his diligence were alike indefatigable'.[44] Cecil's archive is impressive and it does demonstrate his amazing capacity for work. But there is more. Almost everything he wrote – from detailed examinations of political crisis like 'the booke of the state of the Realme' to occasional notes, written discussions *in utramque partem*, and letters – was influenced by the European, English, Scottish, and Irish situations. Other writers in the sixteenth century analyzed and discussed contemporary political affairs; Cecil actually responded to them and could influence action at the highest level. This is one of the most exciting challenges for historians of the sixteenth century: to use a rich archive to reconstruct the practical politics of Elizabeth's reign, demonstrate a sensitivity to thought and language, and use the two to explore the nature and the complexity of the polity.

[44] Conyers Read, *Mr Secretary Cecil and Queen Elizabeth* (London, 1955), p. 10.

APPENDIX 1

'A memoriall of certain pointes meete for restoring the Realme of Scotland to the Auncient Weale', 31 August 1559[1]

In primis it is to be noted that the best worldly felicitie that Scotland can have is either to contynew in a perpetuall peace with the kingdom of Ingland or to be made one Monarchie with England as they both make but one Ile devided from the rest of the world.

If the first be sought, that is to be in perpetuall peace with England then must it necessarily be provided that Scotland be not so subjecte to the appointmentes of fraunce, as it is presently, which being an Auncient Ennemy to England seketh allways to make Scotland an Instrument to Exercise therby theyr malice upon England and to make a footestoole therof to looke over Ingland as they may.

Therfore when Scotland shall com to the handes of a meete Scottish man in blud, then may there be hope of som such accord. But as long as it is at the commandement of the french, there is no hope to have accord long betwext these two Realmes.

Therfore seing it is at the french King his commandement by reason of his wife, it is to be considered for the weale of Scotland, that untill she have children, and during her absence out of the Realme, the nex heyres to the Croune which be the house of Hameltons shuld have regard herto, and to see that nether the croune be empayred nor Wasted, and on the other syde the nobilitie and commonaltie ought to forsee that the lawes and old customs of the land be not altered, nether that the Countrie be empover-ished by taxes, emprest or new Imposts, after the manner of fraunce, for provision wherof both by the law of god and man the french King and his wife may be moved to refourme there misgovvernance of that land.

And for this pourpose it wear good, that the nobilitie and Commens joyned with the next heyre of the Croune to seeke due reformation of such

---

[1] Endorsed by Cecil 'Art. pro conjunctione Anglie. Scotie', 31 August 1559, Lansdowne 4, fos. 26r–27r. There are at least two later copies: Cotton Caligula B. 10, fos. 22r–24r; and National Library of Scotland, Advocates 31.2.19. For a printed version, see Arthur Clifford (ed.), *The state papers and letters of Sir Ralph Sadler*, 2 vols. (Edinburgh, 1809), I, pp. 375-7.

great abuses as tend to the ruine of theyr Countrie, which must be don befor the french grow to strong and Insolent.

Fyrst that it may be provided by consent of the thre Estates of the land, that the land may be free from all Idolatry like as England is, for justification wherof, yf any free generall counsell may be had wher the Pape of Rome have not the seate of Judgement they may offre to shew theyr cause to be most agreable to Christes Religion.

Next to provide that Scotland might be govverned in all rules and offices by the auncient blud of that Realme without eyther Captens, lieutenaunts or souldiours, as all other Princes govverne theyr Countries, and specially that the forts might be in the handes of meete Scottish men.

Thirdly, that they might never be oce occasioned to enter into warres against England, except England shuld give the Cause to Scotland.

Fourthly that no noble man of Scotland shuld receave pension of fraunce except it weare whilest he did service in fraunce. for otherwise the french wold shortly corrupte many to betray theyr owne Country.

Fyftly, that no office abbey living or Commoditie be gyven to any but meete Scottish man.

syxtly, that ther be a Counsell in Scotland appointed in the Queenes absence to governe the hole Realme, and in those cases not to be directed by the french.

Seventhly, that it be by the saide thre Estates appointed how the revenue of the Croune shalbe expended, how much the Queene shall have for her portion and estate during her absence, how much shall be lymited to the govvernance and defense of the Realme, how much yeerly appointed to be kept in Tresure.

In these and such lyke pointes yf the french King and the Queene be found unwilling, and will withstand this provision for the weale of that Land, Then hath the thre Estates of the Realme autoritie fourthwith to intimate to the saide King and Queene theyr humble requestes, and yf the same be not effectually graunted then finally they may committ the Govvernaunce therof to the next heyre of that croune binding the same also to observe the Lawes and Auncient rights of the Realme

Fynally yf the Queene shalbe unwilling to this as it is likely she will in respecte of the greedy and Tyrannouse affection of fraunce, then is it apparant that Almightie god is pleased to transferr from her the Rule of that Kingdom for the weale of it, and in this tyme must be used greate Circumspection to avoide the deceits and tromperies of the french. And then may the Realme of Scotland considre being once made free what meanes may be devised through godds goodnes to accord the two realmes to endure for ever at the pleasure of the Almighty, in whose handes the hartes of all Princes be.

APPENDIX 2
'A clause to have bene inserted in an act ment for the succession but not passed', 1563[1]

And because it shall be very necessary ~~that~~ beside the ordynary government of the Realme by the Pryncipall ^or ordynary^ officers ^above mentioned^ having authorite to ~~administer Justice betwixt subject and subject, that~~ ^conserv peace within the realme that^ there shuld remayne a Counsell of estate ^usually named a privee Counsell^, to consider and direct the ^publick^ affayres of the realme ^as well^ towardes other ~~Pryncess~~ forrayn princess ~~and people for mayntenance of all manner leages intelligencees entercoursees and mutuall amytyes by all commendable meanes~~ ^and Contreys^ ^for mayntenance of amytye, and defence of the realme upon any accident that shall ~~chan~~ or maye chaunce^ as ^also^ to the avancement of Justice ^and ~~mayntenance of~~ peace within the realme^ by aydyng and supportyng of all ordynary officers ~~in~~ ^and ministers^ as well ^spirituall as temporall in^ there Jurisdictions as nede shuld requyre, Be it ~~also~~ enacted ^by authorite of this present parlement^ that if ~~it so shuld please God^ ^which we trust^ to call to his mercy ^that^~~ the Quenes Majesty ^our soverayn lady^ ~~whose liffe we trust the same God will long with~~ shuld decess (which ^almighty^ God forbydd) without issew of hir body ~~and~~ ^or^ before ^the tyme^ that any ~~lawfull her~~ person ~~shuld~~ ^shall^ be declared by ^authorite of^ parlement to be the leefull ^heyre or^ successor ^to hir Majesty^ of ~~this~~e Imperiall crowne of this realme, that then ^and from thenc forth^ all such persons which ~~shuld~~ ^shall^ be knowen to be ~~sworne~~ of the privee Counsell to hir Majesty ~~shuld~~ ^shall^ remayne and contynew counsellors with lyke ^interest^authorite place and degree, as at the tyme of hir Majestes dethe, (which God long ~~prolong~~ ^di prolong from hir^) they or any of them ^did^ hold or ~~did~~ exercise, and that such other persons ^or persons^ spirituall or temporall whom ^so ever^ hir Majesty by hir last will ~~shuld~~ signed with hir hand and sealed with the great seale of

[1] SP 12/28, fos. 68r–69v, in Cecil's holograph. The last section seems to have been an alternative introduction. A later copy of the clause, SP 12/28, fos. 70r–71v, 72v, was made before tears and creases obscured some parts of the original and readings are supplied from this text.

england, ~~shuld~~ ^shall^ apoynt or name to be ^~~ether president of the sayd~~ ~~privee Counsell or otherwise of the same Counsell~~^ sworen to be of ~~the~~ the same privee Counsell, ~~shuld~~ ^shall^ also after ^his or^ there ^a^ othe taken, be accepted and reputed of the same privee Counsell all which counsellors ~~shuld~~ ^shall also^ contynew as Counsellors of estate ^onely^ untill the daye ~~of the~~ ^that by^ proclamation ~~shuld~~ ^shall to^ be made ~~of~~ ~~the~~ by authorite of Parlement ~~who~~ ^it shall be declared to whom^ of right ~~ought to enjoye~~ the Imperiall crowne of this realme of England ^ought to belong^./. And for that the variete of accidentes ^of matters to be ordred by a privee Counsell of estate^ aswell from the partes without the realme, as within maye happen ~~and~~ ^as^ by experience ~~doo chance~~ ^is dayly seene^ to be such, as no ^such^ certenty of direction or order can be by wrytyng prescribed or lymitted ^sufficiently^ in particularety, be it therfor ^[also]^ en[ac]ted that the sayd counsellors of the estate, ^which^ otherwise ^hath bene^ comenly hertofore called the Pryvee Counsell shall kepe there assemblees and sittynges ~~within the ho~~ at such placees and tymes, as in the liffe of hir Majesty which God long preserve they wer ^usually^ accustomed, and that no assemblee ^of counsell^ shall be kept to here ~~or d~~ and determyne any thyng by authorite of the ~~Privee Counsell~~ ^same assemble^, ~~w~~ but where ^~~vj~~ ~~viij~~ x^ at the lest shall be present and asistyng, wherof the Chancellor or kepar of the ~~Priv~~ great seale ^of england^, the Treasoror of england ^the president of the Counsell if any than shall be^ the Marshall of england the stuard of the howshold ^the Lord admyrall the Chamberlayn ~~and the president of the Counsell if the Quenes Majesty shall name any by~~ ~~hir last will to be made as above is mentioned~~^ with ^a Marquass an erle ~~one Marquass erle vicont baron and~~^ ~~one secretary of the state~~ shall be ~~one~~ ~~twoo~~ ^one^. And that the sayd Counsellors ^or ~~vj~~ x of them at the lest as above is expressed^ shall ~~treate~~ ~~consult~~ ^by awthorite of this parlement^ consult ~~and~~ determyne and putt in execution all manner of orders ^&^ commandmentes that ~~shall~~ shall properly belong and appertayne to be ordred and Commanded ^and that usually hath bene ordred and Commanded^ by a counsell of estate, ~~usyng therin the lyke and no gretar~~ ~~authorite than hertofore hath bene usuall for Counsellors of the estate to~~ ~~use and exercise~~ and that ~~no manner~~ no commandment order or execution shall be by them ~~determyned~~ ^or put in ure^ ~~and~~ as Counsellors of the estate ^determyned or put in ure^, to ~~dissese any manner of person~~ punish of this realme^ in his body goodes landes or liberty contrary to the lawes statutes or ^laudable^ customes of this realme.

And Be it also ^furder^ enacted that for the preservation of the townes fortressees bulwarkes and other placees ^of this realme of england wales ~~or~~ Irland^ ~~where~~ or in ^of sol^ any other part without the~~y~~ realme where^ any garrison ^or company of horsemen or footemen ~~or~~ gunnors or any other soldiors^ shall be ~~stablished~~, and for the savety of the Navy, ^belongyng to the crowne of this realme^ with all manner of ordonnance, armur and stoore of habillymentes of warr therto belongyng, and lykewise ^for the suerty and gard^ of the tower of London, and of all ~~armu~~ treasur, ~~armur, n~~ ^~~plate~~^ Jewells, ^in monny bullion ~~or~~ plate or & of all manner of wardrobes of robes ~~or~~ sylkes beddes ~~or~~ hangynges or other stuff or ~~and~~ or of any habillymentes^ armur ordonnancee, ~~and all~~ or other provisions ^of warr or for warr ether^ ~~apperte both~~ in the sayd tower ~~and~~ ^or^ els where ^~~in the sayd realmes of England Irland wales or of~~^ in any wise belonging to the ~~mayntenance~~ Crowne of this realme, and also for the withstandyng and resis[tance] of any forrayn ^attempt ~~by any~~ directly or indirectly intended by anny ^ennemy ageynst this realme, and for the suppression of any tumult or rebellion within this realme or any other the Quenes Majestes dominions or for enterteynment of any ^messengers or^ embassadors serving without the realme, or for reward of any messengor or embassador that shall come into this realme, the sayd Counsellors of estate or ~~vj~~ ^viij x^ of them ~~whe~~ in manner above expressed shall ~~have~~ ^by ~~ordre~~ have^ authorite by warrant ~~to~~ ^signed with there hand to command^ any treasorors ^chamberlayns^ receavors tellors or ~~to~~ any other officer ^or officers^ of what name ^or quallite^ so ever he or they be or shall be that hath chardg or ^or rule^ of any such tresor, in monny or plate, or of any ~~armur, ordonance~~ ^wardrobes of any sort or of any^ shippes ~~or~~ ^vessell or any other thyng or thynges^ belongyng to ~~the sea~~ navy ^or the seas,^ or of any armur ordonnance or ~~any~~ other provision belongyng to the warr ether for defence ~~of~~ or offence to ~~delyver~~ paye ~~or~~ delyver ^use send^ or employe any such ^manner of^ thyng or thynges ^bryng^ in there Custody ^or under there chardg^ in such sort and manner and to such purposees and intentes as the sayd Counsellors by there wrytyng shall lymitt and appoynt, and that such treasorors and other the above named officers having charge of any the premisees, shall accordyng to the sayd [warrants] ^obey follow and execute^ ^orders and commandmentes^ as above is mentioned, and so doyng ^by vertue of those warrantes^ shall ~~be~~ ^uppon there accomptes^ be saved harmeless ageynst all manner of Persons, and specially ageynst ~~the successor~~ ^kyng or Quenes^ of this imperiall crowne of england, and his ^or there^ heyres or successors ~~Provyded a nevertheless, that no manner of reward enterteynment nor wages so to be ordred or gyven shall excede the usuall manner and sort used in lyke casees used~~ Provyded nevertheless that

And because it ~~is~~ shall be most necessary that besyde the ordynary government of the r

1563 [A] clause to have bene inserted in an act ment for the succession but not passed

Item it shall be nedefull for the ^such manner of^ affayres of the realme ~~which ar r~~ as ar ~~and~~ usually governed and directed by the authorite of a privee Counsell, ~~aswell~~ ~~or~~ and cannot conveniently be directed by any other ordynary officers of the realme, that by authorite of Parlement ~~it ther b~~ it be enacted that there shall be a Pryvee Counsell established to contynew untill the tyme that a successor to the Crowne shall be ^by^ parlement declared and that ~~it~~ the same Counsell, may have authorite to govern command and direct the publick affayres of the realme, in lyke manner, as they have usually doone in the lyves of the kynges or Quenes of the realme, so as no act nor order by them shall ~~te empee deminish any man~~ be contrary ^or repugnant^ to the lawes statutes and Customs of this realme And that it be ordred how manny ^of the sayd Consellors^ at the lest, shall have authorite, and how they shall kepe there assemblees.

APPENDIX 3
Two preambles to the Subsidy Bill, 1566

A [1]

We your Majestes most humble subjectes well considering and certenly understanding how your Majesty could not hitherto in such honorable and good sorte have so long and quietly governed your Realmes and Dominions to the honor of Almighty God & the surety of us your subjectes in so long and assured peace ^*within our selves, having so manny* ~~and sondry~~ *dangerooss enterpricees* ~~intended and~~ *wrought ageynst this realme*^ without great expences extraordinary ^*necessarely spent to withstand the same*^ were ^*heruppon*^ ~~necessarely~~ provoked and consequently after good deliberation determined to have offred unto your Majesty some such ^*~~lyke~~*^ portion of our substance by waye of subsedy, as might have made declaration of our good wills and some relief towards your Majestes great excessive charges which we see dayly like to encrease only for the ~~defence and~~ honor ^*and suerty*^ of your dominions. which gift whilest we were about to have in our accustomed manner perfected and made redy to have ben presented to your Majesty, we receaved from the same a most gratious and princely answer, that it ^*though your Majestes affayres* ~~did~~ *might require as much as we intended yet*^ it did more content yow to here of our faithfull mindes expressed in our conferences and intentions, than in the substance of the gift, And therfore your Majesty too declare the same ~~more~~ playnly ^*and evydently*^ towards us, ~~willed~~ ^*moved*^ us to forbeare at this tyme the extending of our gift to that ~~greatenes, which your Majesty had heard~~ ^*largeness your Majesty*^ by reporte~~d~~ ^*~~as your~~ had hard*^ we intended, and that we ~~shuld~~ ^*might*^ with your Majestes assured favor ^*and contentation* ~~notwithstandyng~~^ retayne a ~~great~~ part therof to remayn with our selves, judging ^*accomptyng us* ~~at~~ *your best* ~~treasor~~^ ~~us the best kepers~~ ^*kepars*^ therof ~~as~~ ^*being*^ ~~a sure~~ ^*the*^ treasure, wherof your

[1] SP 12/41, fos. 82r–83v, drafted by the Clerk of the Privy Council, Bernard Hampton, and corrected by Cecil. Cecil's holograph is in *italics*.

Majesty ~~sawe~~ by good experience ~~yow~~ might make accompt of to be your owne at all tymes, as in dede the same is with all the rest that we have to defend and preserve your royall person estate and dignity for the honor and suerty of your Realmes and Dominions.

This most princely gracious and bountefull dealing with us, your most humble and lowly subjectes yea most happy of such a soveraigne, provoketh us to acknowledg our unwordines and unhability to give worthy thankes to yow our dreed and deare Soveraigne, And so for lack of sufficiency to express the intention of our hartes, we wholly give and render our selves in all manner of obedience that any wise can be by subjectes toward yow our Soveraigne Lady, conceaved or expressed. Secondly we can not forbeare also most humbly to thank Almighty God, that at this present tyme of this assembly hath to our most comefort, moved your Majesty in hart to graunt to us ~~the~~ a peticion begonn ~~a~~ long tyme past, continued in our hartes without intermission, and now ^at the length^ most comfortably embraced, that is, your Majestes ^gratiooss & resolute^ ~~assent with~~ determination to marry for ^the^ ~~our~~ comefort ^of all your faythfull subjectes^, wherin we also now to the more perfection of our joy, ^humbly^ beseche your Majesty having therto as we perceave the assistance of Godds grace, to be pleased to accelerat all your ^honorable^ actions that we that now lyve may see the ^joyfull^ dayes of that mariadg and ~~also cause~~ ^consequently^ ~~to~~ recommend to our ~~posterity~~ ^children^ the ~~assurance of the joyfull~~ ^assured hope of a happy^ regiment ~~of your most happy children~~ ^by sight of some noble fruct of ~~the~~ your most royall person to contynew^ without interruption ~~of~~ ^the^ lineall succession of ~~your royall person~~ ^the most victorioss prince our late soverayn your noble father Kyng Henry the eight^

And though your Majesty hath not to this your graunt of mariage joyned at this ^~~present~~^ tyme for sundry great consideracions and respectes as your Majesty hath declared to be best knowen to your Majesty, the present prosequution of the stablishing of the succession of the Crowne after your self and ~~your children~~ ^the Issew of your body^, which thing also we your subjectes for furder suerty have most humbly desired and so ^therin^ do continew: yet considering your Majestes ~~answer~~ ^~~signification and pryncely promise~~ manifest ~~declar and~~ and assured declaration expressed to us in princely wordes^ that yow will not faile but in convenient tyme have ^good and^ due regard therto for our ^suerty ~~mo~~ and^ profitt, ^~~and suerty~~^ and knowing how acceptable the same shalbe also to ^all^ us your Majestes ~~subjectes~~ ^~~humble an~~ faythfull subjectes^ that seke ^nor desyre any thyng more but^ ~~by all meanes~~ to be directed by order ^truth^ and suerty to continue ~~the loyall obedience~~ ^the loyall obedience^ of us and our posterity to this emperiall Crowne, we do most humbly submitt our selves ^herin^ to the will of Almighty God, in whose ~~hand~~ ^*hand*^ we know all powers ~~are inclosed~~ ^*ar conteyned*^, beseching him to give your Majesty ^*~~his spiritt of~~*^ wisdome to forsee, ^*~~without delaye~~*^ oportunity to consult, ^*in season*^ and power to fulfill ^*~~with~~ without unnecessary delaye*^ all that shalbe nedefull for us your humble subjectes and our posterity in the stablishing of the succession of this Crowne, principally in your royall person and progeny, and next therto in such ^*onely*^ as Justice shall direct limitt and maintayne. with which assured hope ^*of ~~sue~~ good success*^ we do present to your Majesty not so much as we intended, ^*~~and wer mete~~ ~~was nedefull~~*^ but such a portion as your highnes is ^*for this tyme*^ pleased to accept. And for the more effectuall manner ~~of~~ ^*to*^ bringe~~ing~~ the same to ~~be in redines for~~ your Majestyes, ^*use*^ we desire as followeth . *Be it enacted*

B²

We your Majestes most humble subjectes meaning according to our most bounden dutyes to present unto your Majesty by way of Subsedy some relief for the great extraordinary charges susteyned in the defence of your Majestes Dominions and countreys against sundry dangerous attemptes, can not forbeare but with all humblenes most thankfully to sett before the same our most lowly thankes for three speciall matters proceding from your Majesty to our benefitt joye and comefort in this present assembly. First, for the most princely consideration had of us in the ~~declaration of your contentacion to~~ forbeare*yng*[3] at this tyme some portion of that which according to the greatenes and necessity of your affaires, we of duty ment ^*and intended*^[4] to have yelded unto your Majesty. secondly, for the most comefortable ^*Assurancis & promysse*^[5] by your Majesty made and declared unto us, that for our weale and suerty, your Majesty wold marry as sone as God shuld give yow oportunity to accomplish the same wherof we have receaved infinite comfort and shall pray to Almighty God to furder and prosper all your Majestes actions tending therunto, that we your most naturall subjectes may spedely see some noble issew of your body, to continew perpetually ~~in~~ ^*bi discent*^[6] the succession of this ^*Imperiall*^[7] Crowne/

Thirdly for the great hope and comefort we have conceaved by the meanes of your Majestes most honorable speche uttred and declared unto us of your most gratious and princely disposition and determination whan

[2] House of Lords Record Office, Main Papers (17 May 1499–2 March 1581), fos. 43r–44r, drafted by Bernard Hampton, with corrections in two other hands: first, Cecil's holograph; and second, perhaps the holograph of William Fleetwood; see above, pp. 153–6.
[3] The final 'yng' of 'forbeareyng' in Cecil's holograph.
[4] '*and intended*' in Cecil's holograph.   [5] '*Assurancis & promysse*' by Fleetwood.
[6] '*bi discent*' in Fleetwood's holograph.   [7] '*Imperiall*' by Fleetwood.

tyme shall therunto serve conveniently ^with the suerty of your Majestes
person and the weale and tranquillity of your realm^ to have due regard to
the furder stablishing of the succession of your Imperiall Crowne as lawe
and Justice shall require the same after the succession of the issew of your
body/ for <u>all which your Majestes benefittes</u> ~~offred to us~~ <u>though we can not
render unto your Majesty such worthy thankes as we know the same doth
deserve, yet we could not without condemnation of our selves, but in this
our simple manner recognise the same, and beside that according to our</u>
first meaning present to your Majesty/[8]

  In which your gratious disposition and care for us, we most humbly
beseche Almighty God to continew your Majesty and to prosper your
intentions and actions to establish that which ~~may be~~ with assent of your
Realme in parliament ^*maye be*^[9] agreable and consonant to lawe and
Justice, and to remain to all ages herafter inviolable, and to the praise
honor and memory of your Majesty and yours perpetually, And that
touching the graunt of our said subsedy, It may be enacted in manner and
forme following/

[8] Underlined by one of the editors.   [9] '*maye be*' in Fleetwood's holograph.

APPENDIX 4
Throckmorton's diplomatic instructions, July 1567[1]

The Quene to be at Liberty with theis provisions followyng.

The truth of Bodwells fact to be duly proved before hir, and that she may for hir satisfaction therin be induced to beleve the same by all Probable meanes.

That theruppon a dyvorce be effectually made.

That she gyve commission to certen noble men, to procede ageynst Bothwell. and his complicees.

That a parlement be assembled with spede.

That a generall Peace be proclaymed thrugh the realm./

That the Castlees at Dunbarr & Dumbrytton, be in the Custody of such of the Nobilite as be not partakers with bothwell as the Quene shall name, they gyving pledges to the Lordes which kepe the Prynce that nether bothwell nor any straunger be therin mayntened./

That for the Government of the realme and the Prynce, the Quene with advise of the Parlement doo constitut certen./

That all officees of wardens. chastellans provostshippes, Judicatures and the Principall officees of the realm, and all ecclesiasticall promotion be gyven by the Quene with advise and consent of the more part of the great Counsell.

wardens of the marchees/. Edenburgh./ sterlyng./. Dunbarr Dumbritton. Insskeyth./.[2]

That uppon the deth of any of the gret Counsell the Quene name others with the Consent of the rest.

That the stablishyng of the succession of the Crown be renovated and confirmed accordyng to the last actes of Parlement

That the cause of Relligion be stablished. exceptyng none but the Quenes Person, and some competent nombre for hir attendance, not excedyng

That

That a Generall Pardon be graunted by Parlement

---

[1] SP 52/14, fo. 1r–v, in Cecil's holograph, and endorsed 'at sir N. Throkmortons goyng into scotland Julij 1567'; undated but c. 1 July 1567.

[2] Marginal note.

That all bothwells landes be annexed to the Crown, and be employed uppon the education of the Prynce./

the armitage. to serve a warden./. admyrall duryng liff only. shyrriff weke of Lord[. . .][3]

That the Graund Counsell consist uppon such a nombre, as allweiss ther may be attendant monthly at the lest iiij or vj/.

That ordres be accorded uppon for ther sittyng in Counsells and sollicityng of causees to the Quene.

That no strangers born, beare any office in the Quenes howshold.

That all the articlees above sayd and all other theruppon dependyng be stablished by Parlement. and that it be made for the tyme punishable by loss of goodes & imprisonment the 2. tyme treson who so ever shall contraven./ and that it shall be lefull to all other persons to pursew hym that shall break the same as a traytor/

That the Quene of England may be moved to become a mayntenor of the same parlement/

[3] Marginal note.

APPENDIX 5
'Memorial Generall', 8 and 17 August 1568[1]

St Albons./. 8 Augusti 1568
To send the Erle of sussex to york as president
commission
Instructions.
warrant. Dormant. for dyett
To send the Lord. of Hunsdon to Barwyk.
commission.
barwyk
est marchees.
Instructions.
warrant monny emprest
To nominat Commissionars to heare the Lordes of scotlandes answer,
   and to treate with the Quene of scottes
To appoynt lieutenantes.
To make new musters in the realm
to appoynt also muster masters, and ledars and traynors of People
to increase harquebussery in the realme
To advertise the Quene of scottes of the disordres moved on the bordres
   by sondry of hir part./
To lett hir understand that if any french men shall land in scotland, or
   that any new troobles or levyes of men of warr shall be that the
   Quenes Majesty can not take hir cause into hir protection/
To devise how to make certenty of monny afore the next spryng.
To cause the officees of the Admiralte. ordonnance Armory to be
   sufficiently provyded
To renew the Commission. in wales. accordyng to my Lord. presidents.
   memoryall. a vicepresident. sir Hugh paulett

---

[1] SP 12/47, fos. 75r–76v, in Cecil's holograph. Drafted on 8 and 17 August 1568, but the second part of the memorandum is clearly a continuation of the first part written at St Albans; the endorsement for 8 August 1568 covers both sections.

17. August.

The Commission etc for the Duke of Norfolk etc

The Commission etc. for the erle of Sussex.

The Commission etc for the Lord. Hunsdon.

Lieutenants. in shyres with musters

Doutes. whyther the Commissioners. shall not first repayre to the Quene of Scottes.

Generall.

That all articlees by whych the Quene of scottes. shall graunt promiss or accord to any thyng shall be procede of hir voluntary good will and of hir clemency to hir subjectes.

Duke of Norfolk./.

Erle. Arundell.

Erle. sussex

Erle. bedford

Erle. Lecester.

Sir Raff. sadler

Sir Walter Mildmay.

Sir. Nicholas. Throgmorton.

Newcastle

Durham

Rychmont

The Ground of the matter is to heare the answer of the Regent. to the Complaint. of the Quene of scottes.

The treaty of leth to be confirmed

no leage to be made with france offensyve against: england

no subject of scotland to resort into Irland. no straungers men of warr to be reteyned in scotland

The Quene not to marry without any potentat being a prince in blood without the consent of the Quenes Majesty.

The relligion allredy stablished in scotland to contynew, and no other to be used except the same, and the formular of england.

To punish. the murdre of the kyng

The yong prince to be in savety

The murderors of the kyng and all accessoryes to be punished.

The Erle of Murray and his party to be admitted in to there former states wherin they wer whan the Quene: was [. . .]/

The mariadg of Bothwell to be undone by order of Law and parlemen[t]

The accord of all these thynges to be also confirmed by parlement, and in scotland. and the treaty to be tripartited. betwixt the Quene of

England the Quene of ~~fran~~ scotland, and hir sonne the Prynce and all them that have adhered to hym with condition if the Quene of Scottes do violat hir part, that uppon the Judgment of the Quene of england the child may succede

That ether the Quene remayn in england untill the Parlement be kept, or good hostages

The hammiltons tytle to the Crown to be ratefyed.

8. August: 1568
Memorial Generall.

APPENDIX 6
An extract from the instructions for the English commissioners at York, 1568[1]

First it semeth ^very^ mete that this treaty shuld be tripartite that is, betwixt the Quenes Majesty of England on the one party as principall author and mediator of the same. and the Quene of Scottes on the second. and the Prince hir son on the third. And that the wholl accord may be also spedely confirmed by act of parliament in Scotland, wherby both the Quene of Scottes and hir subjectes may be in justice bound to observe the same. And the Quene of England by hir great seale of England to maynteyne the same. And that also from the end of the treaty untill some convenient time to follow the end of the same parliament, there might remayne iij. or iiij good hostages of ether part in England for the more orde[?rly] holding of the parliament, and better observation of the treaty and herunto may well be added to be thought of, tha[?t] the said parliament might be kept and ended before the Quene of Scottes returne to hir Contrey.

Item, the first article in this accord wold be in this manner or such That all thinges (saving only the murder of the King) whic[?h] have ben attempted by the Quene or any of hir part against them which tooke the part of hir sonn the Prince as their King, And all thinges on the said Princes part and th[?em] which avowed their actions in his name as King from the dea[th] of the Quenes husband, shuld be committed after this treaty ended to a perpetuall oblivion, And that no action, dammage offence, calumniation or reproche shuld at any time to come be used or extended any manner of wise by one against the other upon some great paynes.

Secondly, It is most necessary to be provided, that by the said Quene of Scottes owne princely motion, upon good perswasion [?to] be made to hir in that behalf, It may be accorded that the Realme of Scotland may ^be^

---

[1] From 'A memoriall for the order and proceding of the Duke of Norffolk, the Erle of Sussex, and sir Raff Sadler the Quenes Majesties Commissioners appoynted and authorised by hir Majesties Commission to mete at ^the City of^ york', Cotton Caligula C. 1, fos. 229r–232v, drafted by Bernard Hampton and corrected by Cecil, late August or early September 1568; for the whole document, Cotton Caligula C. 1, fos. 227r–232v. Cecil's corrections are in *italics*.

governed under hir as ~~the~~ Quene ^*of the realme*^ by a graund Counsell of a convenient nomber to be ^*now*^ chosen and stablished at the time of this treaty, of the noble and wise men of ~~the~~ birth of that Realme, and the same to be allways renewed by the more parte, or two third partes of the said Counsell, whan any of the parsons of the said Counsell shall depart or become impotent to serve. For otherwise the quiett of the Quene ^*hir self*^ and the Realme ^*also*^ by privat government shalbe easely broken, and the ^*whole*^ fruct of this treaty, and the Quenes Majesties labors utterly frustrate. In which matter also is to be remembred in what sorte the principall officers of the Realme shalbe appoynted being at the Quenes disposition As the Chancellor, ^*ambassadors or messengers to any forrayn princees*^ the Archbushops, Bushops, the Lord Justice, the Comptroller, the Treasoror the Admirall, the Chamberlain the President and Lordes of Session, the Captens of Castles the Sheriffes, ^*the provostes of burghes*^ the wardens of the marches, ^*and all officers of fynancies*^ and such like as may be for the good observation of this treaty.

3. Thirdly, is to be remembred that the Quene in respect of hir undiscrete mariage with Bothwell may accord not to marry nor contract mariadg with any parson without the assent of hir .3. estates or the more part therof. Upon payne that the parson with whom she shall contract and all others counselling or furdering the same shalbe ipso facto adjudged Traytors, and shall suffer death and forfeyte as in cases of treason

4. Fourthly that all good meanes be devised and accorded how to procede severely against the said Bothwell and all other subjectes or servauntes to the Crowne of Scotland for the murder of the said King, or for mayntenaunce and comefort of the said murderors, and their landes confiscated to the Crowne of Scotland, with clause never to be graunted away from the Crowne without assent of parliament.

5. Item, that all lawes and orders accorded upon by parliament as well before the Quenes emprisonment as sence for the help and sustentation of the ministers of the Chirch, and ^*for the*^ adva[nce]ment of true relligion and abrogating of Idolatry and su[per]stition may remayne in full force, and continew withou[t] repealing of the same/ ^*otherwise than by a sufficient parlement.*^

6. Item, in particuler also it is mete to be remembred, that no stra[nger] borne be enterteyned in that Realme in the roome of a Capt[en] or of a soldior. Nor that any stranger borne have any office spirituall or temporall within the Realme, nor ^*that*^ any pens[ion] ^*be*^ granted to any stranger out of any office spirituall or temporall. Nor that any parson ~~shall~~ beare any office within that real[m] which openly by any act shall ^*hereafter*^ avow that the Bushop of Roome ~~ot~~ ought to have any other preeminence within that Realme, than such as the King or Quene of that Realme an[d]

their successors with the consent of the .3. estates in parliament shall allowe/

7. Item, it is also very necessary to provide for the safety of the life of the young Prince, considering all such as shal[l] live in Scotland having ben in dede privy to the murder [of] his father, though not therof convinced shall and may be suspected that thcy will desire the death of the Pr[ince] fearing his avenge when he shall come to age. And in this behalf, it is to be well considered, in wh[at] place, and with what parson he shall remayne, and w[ith] what allowance of the revenue of the Crowne he shalb[e] maynteyned. And if it may be indirectly procured to come of the Quene of Scotland hir self, It semeth good ^*and saffe for all partyes*^ that the Prince might be brought and nourished in England in the ^*chardg and*^ custody of persons of the birth of Scotland.

8. Item, it were also mete that the titles and challenges of the Crowne hertofore made as well by one party as an other were made parfectly clere and certenly stablished, therby to take away factions amongst the subjectes.

9. Item, it may be reasonably required of the Erle of Murray and others, that considering the many difficulties that may arise ^*uppon the understandyng of this treaty and specially*^ in choyse of the great officers of the Realme, by reason of many competitors amongst the Nobillity, that it may be at the request of the wholl nobillity of Scotland, and with the good consent of the Quene of Scottes accorded that the Quenes Majesty of England may have power to be as umpere and principall arbitrer, to determine upon all contraversies ^*arrisyng uppon this treaty, and specially*^ in choyse of any such officer, So as hir Majesty ^*make no other interpretation* ~~but~~ *nor*^ name none ^*to any office*^ but such ~~one~~ as shalbe ^*adjudged or*^ named by the Quene hir self, or by one third part of the graund Counsell of the Realme for the time being. And that whosoever shall intromitt him self ~~into any such office being in contra-versy~~ ^*to doo any thyng therin contrary and*^ without the judgment of the Quenes Majesty of England, ^*as above is lymitted*^ shalbe judged as a perturbator of the commen tranquillity of that Realme and shalbe incompatible of any maner of office for ever or otherwise punished with some sharper payne.

And that it shalbe leefull for any of the nobillity or ~~gentlemen~~ ^*subjectes*^ of Scotland being greved or injuried with any thing committed against this treaty, to resort to the Quenes Majesty of England ^*to make resonable complaynt*^ without any empeachement of the Quene of Scottes or any other. And that for so doing they shall incurr no forfeyture of life landes or goodes, nor be any wise dammaged in their body.

10. Item, it is also necessary for the more assurance of the obs[er]vation of this treaty in the behalf of the subjectes of Scotland, to be accorded, that

if the Quene of Scottes shall willingly breake or permitt to be broken any part of this treaty concerning the su[?rety] of any hir subjectes which have sence the death of hir husband and before this present treaty holden part against hir, and that such hir breaking or permission of the breaking be first notifie[d] to the Quene of Scottes and adjudged by the Quene of England against the Quene of Scottes, having therto the assent of the third part of the grand Counsell aforementioned, or of vj. Lordes of parliament of Scotland being not parties against the said Quene at the time of this treaty or of their heyres ^*succedyng them in there states*^ being above the age of xxj: In those cases without such refo[r]mation made by the Quene of Scottes as to the said Quene of England and the said third part of the said Counsell or the said nomber of vj. Lordes of Scotland as is aforesaid shall some m[e]ans be assigned and notified to the said Quene.

It shalbe leefull immediatly upon publick knowledg given [to] the Quene of England by open proclamation in the Townes of Barwick and Carlile conteyning the particuler breache of th[e] treaty, and the ^*manifest*^ refusall of the reformation, for the Prin[ce] of Scotland hir sonn, or any of the Nobillity of Scotland for him whilest he shalbe under the age of xiiij. (if he the Prince be than living) And if he shalbe dead, than for the next heyre to that Crowne to enter into the reall possession of the said Crowne and Kingdome ^*and every percell therof*^ in like mann[er] as the said Quene were departed from this life. And the said Quene shall by vertue of this treaty forbeare to hold the said state or title as Quene of that Realme, an[d] shall not enjoy any thing of the said Realme otherwise than such provision of the yerely revenues of the said Crowne, as hertofore hath ben at any time allowed to any wife of ~~a King~~ of a King of Scottes for a Dowery, if she so will accept and obey the foresaid Judgment of the Quene of England being made with the assent of the said third part of the said Counsell, or of the said .vj. Lordes of Scotland or their heyres being of the age of xxj./ And whosoever shall attempt any thing contrary to the said Prince or the next heyre to the Crowne, (fayling the Prince) after hir or their entry or clayme of the said Crowne, shalbe (ipso facto) taken and used to all intentes as a traytor adjudged and condemned.

Certen other things necessary to be remembred in this treaty for the behalf of the Quenes Majesty and hir Realme

1. Inprimis, that the treaty made at Edenburgh in July Anno Domini *1560* may be ratified and confirmed. In the treating wherof, if objectio[n] be made that there are certen clauses in the said treaty, (as namely the vth article) which do bring great prejudice to the Quene o[f] Scottes in that it is accorded that she shuld from the tyme of th[e] treaty forbeare to use the

stile title or armories of England,[2] wherby it may be indirectly gathered, that she shalbe exclude[d] not only during the lief of the Quenes Majesty & of the lives of the heyres of hir Majesties body (which in dede was expressly me[?nt] on both partes at the time of the treaty) but also afte[r] the determination of the life of the Quenes Majesty (which God Long pres[erve)] and also of the heyres of hir body, of which cause at the time of the treaty no mention was made: Therfore now at this treaty after the said confirmation to be made of the said Treaty made at Edenburg, there may be a Proviso. therto now of new devised that no part of the said treaty made at Edenburgh shall bind the said Quene of Scottes or hir children after the determination of the life of the Quenes Majesty (which God long preserve) and the heyres of hir body.

2 Item, it wold be also required ~~and attempted~~ ^*if it may be resonably obteyn[ed]*^ that a Leag[ue] shuld be made at this time betwixt both the Quenes of Englan[d] and Scotland for them selves, their Realmes and subjectes that ether of the Realmes shuld ayde the other in cases that any other Prince shuld first invade them or any percel[l] of them without notorious cause given by open warres to the invador, wherin if any difficulty be made because of the old league of Fraunce and Scotland, First theyr may be much sayd ~~that~~ ^*and can not be denyed of the Commission[ers] of Scotland*^ to prove that Scotland hath these many hundred yeres taken more harme than good by that treaty. And secondly though the treaty with Fraunce percase shalbe thought not mete to be utterly dissolved: yet in this particoler sort to contract as is expressed in this article ^*may be sayd*^ is not against the true intent of the league of France. For by that treaty the Kings of Scotland are ~~only~~ bound to ayde france if England shall move warr against Fraunce, but not if France shall first move warr against England.

3. Item, as it is well ~~remembred~~ covenaunted by ancient leagues betwixt England and Scotland that nether of them shuld receave or ayde any rebell

---

[2] Just after the negotiation of the treaty, Bernard Hampton (on the instructions of the Privy Council) wrote a summary of it for the earl of Sussex in Ireland: 'the ffrenche King and Quene doo not onely relinquishe the style, tytle, and armes of Englande and Irelande by speciall woordes in the treatie, but doo allso bynde them sellfes from hence forth to forbeare any more to use and beare the sayd title and armes, and shall forbyd theyr subjectes the using of the sayd title in what sorte so ever it be within any of theyr countries or dominions/ for bydding asmuche as in them shall lye the joyning or quartering any manner of wayes the armes of Englande with those of Scotland or france.' Harley 289, fo. 71r; also above, pp. 83–5. Sir Nicholas Throckmorton raised the issue of ratification with Mary in August 1561. According to his report back to Elizabeth, the Queen of Scots replied: 'To the 5[th article] you know monsieur ambassador that I do performe yt + have done ever synce the deathe off my late lord + husbond: For I do nether beare the armes nor use the style: and me thynkyth thys my doyngs shuld better please the Quene your mistres then yff I had ratified the treatie + donn as I had done before.' 11 August 1561, Additional 35830, fo. 176v.

or fugitive of the other: So the like accord wold be made at this time for Irland and Scotland.

4 Item, it wold be also accorded that if the Quene of Scottes during hir lief shall ayde or willingly permitt any of hirs to ayde any Prince or potentate to invade by hostillity the realmes of England or Irland or any Iles or membres of ether of the said Kingdomes, That therupoun immediatly the said Quene shall forfeyte and Leese all manner of title or challeng that she any wise hath or can ~~make or~~ pretend to be inheritable to the Crowne of England or Irland . . .

BIBLIOGRAPHY

MANUSCRIPT SOURCES

A specific description of a manuscript is given only if it contains a very clear and coherent set of documents from the 1560s; most of the volumes are miscellaneous collections of Elizabethan (but sometimes Edwardian or Jacobean) political papers.

BRITISH LIBRARY, LONDON

Additional:

4126
6128
12093 Sir John Mason's volume of Anglo-Scottish records
19401
23108
23109
32091
33591
33592
33593
35125
35830 Sir Nicholas Throckmorton's papers
35831 Sir Nicholas Throckmorton's papers
36081
48023
48027

Cotton:

Caligula B. 4
Caligula B. 5
Caligula B. 8
Caligula B. 9 Cecil's Anglo-Scottish papers
Caligula B. 10 Cecil's Anglo-Scottish papers
Caligula C. 1 Cecil's Anglo-Scottish papers
Caligula C. 2 Cecil's Anglo-Scottish papers

Charter 4.38.
Cleopatra E. 6
Julius F. 6
Titus B. 2
Titus B. 13 Cecil's letters to the earl of Sussex
Titus C. 7
Titus F. 1
Vespasian C. 7
Vitellius C. 16

Egerton:

1049
1818
1962
3376

Harley:

35
36
94
169
253
289
290
398
787
1300
1877
1912
2185
4111
4243
4314–21
4666
4667
5176
6990

Lansdowne (a Cecil archive):

1–12
94
95
102 Cecil's letters to Sir Thomas Smith
103
104
116
118

211
504
982
1218
1236

CAMBRIDGE UNIVERSITY LIBRARY

Dd.3.20
Dd.9.14
Gg.3.34
Ii.5.8

Additional :

40

DARNAWAY CASTLE, FORRES

TD 94/56

FOLGER SHAKESPEARE LIBRARY, WASHINGTON, D.C.

V.a.143
V.a.197
V.a.209
V.a.235
V.a.340
V.a.348
V.b.151
V.b.173
V.b.214
V.b.317
X.c.34
X.d.19

HATFIELD HOUSE LIBRARY, HERTFORDSHIRE

Cecil Papers (a Cecil archive):

2–5
133–4
138
140–1
144
147
152–7
170
198
201

205
210
214
229
230
232–5
352

Family papers:

2/93

Library catalogues:

1568

Maps:

II/14

HOUSE OF LORDS RECORD OFFICE

Braye:

4

Main papers:

17 May 1499–2 March 1581

Journals:

House of Commons 1
House of Lords 4

Original Acts:

8 Elizabeth I, c. 18.

HUNTINGTON LIBRARY, SAN MARINO, CALIFORNIA

Ellesmere:

1192
1862
1863

LAMBETH PALACE LIBRARY, LONDON

3196
3206

MAGDALENE COLLEGE, CAMBRIDGE

Pepys (earl of Leicester's papers):

PL 2502
PL 2503

NATIONAL LIBRARY OF SCOTLAND, EDINBURGH

1707
3278
3657
9931

Advocates:

1.2.2
6.1.13
22.2.18
31.2.19
33.1.1

NORTHAMPTONSHIRE RECORD OFFICE, NORTHAMPTON

Fitzwilliam (Milton) correspondence:

21
26
31

Fitzwilliam (Milton) miscellaneous:

36
541

Fitzwilliam (Milton) political (Sir Walter Mildmay's papers):

2
4
5
46
51
78
95
96
102
113
169
170
180

199
200
213
223
224

Westmorland (Apethorpe):

Box 1

Westmorland (Apethorpe) Miscellaneous:

28
35

PUBLIC RECORD OFFICE, LONDON

PC 2 Acts of the Privy Council, Elizabeth I.
SP 10 State Papers, Domestic, Edward VI.
SP 12 State Papers, Domestic, Elizabeth I.
SP 15 State Papers, Addenda, Elizabeth I.
SP 46 State Papers, Domestic, Supplementary.
SP 52 State Papers, Scotland, Elizabeth I.
SP 63 State Papers, Ireland, Elizabeth I.
SP 70 State Papers, Foreign, Elizabeth I.

SCOTTISH RECORD OFFICE, EDINBURGH

GD 1/371/3
GD 97/3/33
GD 124/10/26
GD 124/15/1
GD 124/17

PRIMARY AND REFERENCE SOURCES

Acts of the Parliament of Scotland, ed. Thomas Thomson and Cosmo Innes, 12 vols. (Edinburgh, 1814–75).

Acts of the Privy Council of England, ed. John Roche Dasent *et al.*, new series, 46 vols. (London, 1890–1964).

Adams, Simon (ed.), *Household accounts and disbursement books of Robert Dudley, earl of Leicester, 1558–1561, 1584–1586* (Camden Society, fifth series, 6; Cambridge, 1995).

Advertisments partly for due order in the publique administration of common prayers . . . (STC 10026; London, 1565).

Alumni Cantabrigienses. A biographical list of all known students, graduates and holders of office at the University of Cambridge, from the earliest times to 1900, ed. John Venn and J.A. Venn, 10 vols. (Cambridge, 1922–54).

Anderson, James (ed.), *Collections relating to the history of Mary Queen of Scotland*, 4 vols. (Edinburgh, 1727–28).

Aphthonius, *Aphthonii*, ed. Gentian Hervet (*STC* 699; London, *c.* 1520).

Aristotle, *The ethiques* . . . (*STC* 754; London, 1547).

The politics, ed. Stephen Everson (Cambridge, 1988).

Ascham, Roger, *The scholemaster* . . . (*STC* 832; London, 1570).

Disertissimi viri Rogeri Aschami angli . . . (*STC* 829; London, 1590).

English works, ed. William Aldis Wright (Cambridge, 1904).

The schoolmaster (1570), ed. Lawrence V. Ryan (Charlottesville, Virginia, 1974 edn).

Aylmer, John, *An harborowe for faithfull and trewe subjectes, agaynst the late blowne blaste, concerninge the government of wemen* . . . (*STC* 1005; London, 1559).

Balfour, Sir James, *Practicks*, ed. Peter G.B. McNeill, 2 vols. (Stair Society, 21, 22; Edinburgh, 1962–3).

Berthelet, *A declaration, conteynyng the just causes and consyderations, of this present warre with the Scottis, wherin alsoo appereth the trewe & right title, that the Kinges most royall majesty hath to the soverayntie of Scotlande* (*STC* 9179; London, 1542).

Bond, Ronald B. (ed.), *Certain sermons or homilies (1547) and a homily against disobedience and wilful rebellion (1570). A critical edition* (Toronto, Buffalo, and London, 1987).

Books in Cambridge inventories. Book-lists from vice-chancellor's court probate inventories in the Tudor and Stuart periods, ed. E.S. Leedham-Green, 2 vols. (Cambridge, 1986).

Broughton, Hugh, *A treatise of Melchisedek, proving him to be Sem* . . . (*STC* 3890; London, 1591).

Buchanan, George, *Vernacular writings*, ed. P. Hume Brown (Scottish Text Society, 26; Edinburgh and London, 1892).

Calendar of letters and state papers relating to English affairs, preserved principally in the archives of Simancas, ed. Martin A.S. Hume, 4 vols. (London, 1892–9).

Calendar of state papers, domestic series, of the reigns of Edward VI, Mary, Elizabeth 1547–1580, ed. Robert Lemon (London, 1856).

Calendar of state papers, foreign: Edward VI, Mary, Elizabeth I, ed. J. Stevenson *et al.*, 25 vols. (London, 1861–1950).

Calendar of the state papers, relating to Scotland . . . The Scottish series, of the reigns of Henry VIII. Edward VI. Mary. Elizabeth. 1509–1589, ed. Markham John Thorpe, 2 vols. (London, 1858).

Camden, William, *Annals, or, the historie of the most renowned and victorious princesse Elizabeth, late Queen of England*, ed. R. Norton (*STC* 4501; London, 1635).

Cameron, Annie I. (ed.), *The Warrender papers*, 2 vols. (Publications of the Scottish History Society, third series, 18–19; Edinburgh, 1931–2).

A catalogue of the Lansdowne manuscripts in the British Museum, ed. Henry Ellis, 2 vols. (London, 1812–19).

Caxton, William, *Booke of the cronicles of england* (*STC* 9991; London, 1480).

Cecil, William, *The execution of justice in England for maintenaunce of publique and Christian peace* . . . (*STC* 4902; London, 1583).

Certaine precepts, or directions, for the well ordering and carriage of a mans life . . . (*STC* 4897; London, 1617).

Chambers, E.K., and Greg, W.W. (eds.) 'Dramatic records from the Lansdowne manuscripts', *Malone Society Collections*, 1 (1911), 143–8.

Cicero, Marcus Tullius, *The thre bookes of Tullyes offyces/ bothe in latyne tonge & in englysshe*, trans. Robert Whittinton (*STC* 5278; London, 1534).

Marcus Tullius Ciceroes thre bokes of duties, to Marcus his sonne, turned oute of latine into english, by Nicolas Grimalde, ed. Gerald O'Gorman (Renaissance English Text Society, sixth series 12; Washington, D.C., 1990).

On duties, ed. M.T. Griffin and E.M. Atkins (Cambridge, 1991).

Clapham, John, *Elizabeth of England. Certain observations concerning the life and reign of Queen Elizabeth*, ed. Evelyn Plummer Read and Conyers Read (Philadelphia and London, 1951).

Clifford, Arthur (ed.), *The state papers and letters of Sir Ralph Sadler*, 2 vols. (Edinburgh, 1809).

Collins, Arthur (ed.), *Letters and memorials of state . . . written and collected by Sir Henry Sydney. . .*, 2 vols. (London, 1746).

The complete peerage of England, Scotland, and Ireland, Great Britain, and the United Kingdom, ed. Vicary Gibbs *et al*, 13 vols. (London, 1910–40).

The cronycles of Englonde with the dedes of popes and emperours and also the descripcyon of Englonde (*STC* 10002; London, 1528).

De Guevara, Antonio, *The golden boke of Marcus Aurelius emperour and eloquent oratour*, trans. J. Bourchier (*STC* 12436; London, 1535).

Descriptive list of state papers supplementary (SP 46), private papers, series I, 1535–1705 (List and Index Society; London, 1968).

D'Ewes, Sir Simonds, *The journals of all the parliaments during the reign of Queen Elizabeth, both of the House of Lords and House of Commons*, ed. Paul Bowes (London, 1682).

Dictionary of national biography, ed. Leslie Stephen and Sidney Lee, 63 vols. (London, 1885–1900).

Elton, G.R., *England 1200–1640* (London, 1969).

The Tudor constitution (Cambridge, 1982).

Elyot, Sir Thomas, *The boke named the governour . . .* (*STC* 7635; London, 1531).

The book named the governor, ed. S.E. Lehmberg (London and New York, 1962).

Foedera, conventiones, litterae . . ., ed. Thomas Rymer and Robert Sanderson, 20 vols. (London, 1704–35).

Foxe, Edward, *De vera differentia regiae potestatis & ecclesiasticae . . .* (*STC* 11219; London, 1538).

The true dyfferens betwen the regall power and the ecclesiasticall power . . ., trans. Henry, Lord Stafford (*STC* 11220; London, 1548).

Frescoln, Katharine P. (ed.), 'A letter from Thomas Randolph to the earl of Leicester', *Huntington Library Quarterly*, 37 (1973–74), 83–8.

Galloway, Bruce R., and Levack, Brian P. (eds.), *The Jacobean union. Six tracts of 1604* (Scottish History Society, fourth series, 21; Edinburgh and London, 1985).

Grafton, Richard, *An epistle or exhortacion, to unitie and peace . . .* (*STC* 9181; *STC2* 22268; London, 1548).

An epitome of the title that the kynges majestie of Englande, hath to the sovereigntie of Scotlande, continued upon the auncient writers . . . (*STC* 3196; London, 1548).

An abridgement of the chronicles of England (*STC* 12148; London, 1563).

A chronicle at large and meere history of the affayres of Englande and kinges of the same . . . (*STC* 12147; London, 1569).

Guy, J.A., *Christopher St German on chancery and statute* (Selden Society Supplementary Series, 6; London, 1985).

Hartley, T.E. (ed.), *Proceedings in the parliaments of Elizabeth I*, Volume I *1558–1581* (Leicester, 1981).

Haynes, Samuel (ed.), *Collection of state papers . . . left by William Cecil, Lord Burghley* (London, 1740).

Hearne, Thomas (ed.), *A collection of curious discourses, written by eminent antiquaries upon several heads in our English antiquities* (Oxford, 1720).

A collection of curious discourses written by eminent antiquaries upon several heads in our English antiquities, 2 vols. (London, 1771).

The history of parliament. The House of Commons 1509–1558, ed. S.T. Bindoff, 3 vols. (London, 1982).

The history of parliament. The House of Commons 1558–1603, ed. P.W. Hasler, 3 vols. (London, 1981).

Hobbes, Thomas, *Leviathan*, ed. Richard Tuck (Cambridge, 1991).

Hooper, John, *A declaracion of Christe and of his offyce* (STC 13745; London, 1547).

Hughes, Paul L., and Larkin, James F. (eds.), *Tudor royal proclamations*, 3 vols. (New Haven and London, 1964–9).

Journals of the House of Commons.

Journals of the House of Lords.

Knox, John, *A sermon preached by John Knox minister of Christ Jesus in the publique audience of the church of Edenbrough . . .* (STC 15075; n.p., 1566).

The works of John Knox, ed. David Laing, 6 vols. (Wodrow Society; Edinburgh, 1846–64).

On rebellion, ed. Roger A. Mason (Cambridge, 1994).

[Leslie, John, bishop of Ross,] *A defence of the honour of the right highe, mightye and noble Princesse Marie Queene of Scotlande . . .* (STC 15505; [Rheims,] 1569).

Lodge, Edmund (ed.), *Illustrations of British history, biography, and manners . . .*, 3 vols. (London, 1791).

MacLure, Millar, *Register of sermons preached at Paul's Cross 1534–1642*, ed. Jackson Campbell Boswell and Peter Pauls (Ottawa, 1989).

Maitland, James, 'The apologie for William Maitland of Lidington', ed. Andrew Lang, *Publications of the Scottish History Society*, 44 (1904), 135–228.

Memoirs of his own life by Sir James Melville of Halhill. 1549–1593, ed. Thomas Thomson (Bannatyne Club, 18; Edinburgh, 1827).

The mirror for magistrates, ed. Lily B. Campbell (Cambridge, 1938).

Molyneux, J. More, 'Letters illustrating the reign of Queen Jane', *Archaeological Journal*, 30 (1873), 273–8.

Murdin, William (ed.), *Collection of state papers relating to affairs in the reign of Queen Elizabeth from the year 1571 to 1596 . . .* (London, 1759).

Naunton, Sir Robert, *Fragmenta regalia*, ed. Edward Arber (London, 1870).

Neale, J.E. (ed.), 'Sir Nicholas Throckmorton's advice to Queen Elizabeth on her accession to the throne', *English Historical Review*, 65 (1950), 91–8.

Nichols, John Gough (ed.), *The chronicle of Queen Jane, and of two years of Queen Mary, and especially of the rebellion of Sir Thomas Wyat* (Camden Society, 48; London, 1850).

'Some additions to the biographies of Sir John Cheke and Sir Thomas Smith', *Archaeologia*, 38 (1860), 98–127.

Norton, Thomas (ed.), *Orations, of Arsanes agaynst Philip the trecherous kyng of Macedone* . . . (*STC* 785; London, *c.* 1560).

Norton, Thomas, and Sackville, Thomas, *The tragedie of Gorboduc, whereof three actes were wrytten by Thomas Nortone, and the two laste by Thomas Sackvyle* . . . (*STC* 18684; London, 1565).

The tragidie of Ferrex and Porrex, set forth without addition or alteration . . . (*STC* 18685; London, 1570).

Nowell, Alexander, *A catechism written in Latin*, ed. G.E. Corrie (Parker Society; Cambridge, 1853).

Ó Laidhin, Tomás (ed.), *Sidney state papers 1565–70* (Irish Manuscripts Commission; Dublin, 1962).

Park, W. (ed.), 'Letter of Thomas Randolph to the earl of Leicester. 14 February 1566', *Scottish Historical Review*, 34 (1955), 135–39.

Patten, William, *The expedicion into Scotlande of the most woorthely fortunate prince Edward, duke of Soomerset* . . . (*STC* 19479; London, 1548).

Peacham, Henry, *The compleat gentleman. Fashioning him absolut, in the most necessary and commendable qualities concerning minde or body, that may be required in a noble gentleman* . . . (*STC* 19504; London, 1634).

Ponet, John, *A shorte treatise of politike power, and of the true obedience which subjectes owe to kynges and other civile governours, with an exhortacion to all true naturall Englishe men* . . . (*STC* 20178; Strasburg, 1556).

A proclamacion declaryng the quenes majesties purpose, to kepe peace with Fraunce and Scotlande, and to provyde for the suretie of hir kyngdomes (*STC* 7910; London, 1560).

A proclamation declaryng the untrueth of certaine malitious reportes devised and publisshed in the realme of Scotlande (*STC* 8010; London, 1569).

Pronay, Nicholas, and Taylor, John (eds.), *Parliamentary texts of the later middle ages* (Oxford, 1980).

Public Record Office, *Museum catalogue* (London, 1974).

Rainolde, Richard, *A booke called the foundacion of rhetorike* . . . (*STC* 20604; London, 1564).

Registrum magni sigilli regum scotorum: the register of the great seal of Scotland, ed. James Balfour Paul, 11 vols. (Edinburgh, London, and Melbourne, 1984).

Registrum secreti sigilli regum scotorum: the register of the privy seal of Scotland, ed. M. Livingstone *et al.*, 8 vols. (Edinburgh, 1908–82).

Reports from the lost notebooks of Sir James Dyer, ed. J.H. Baker, 2 vols. (Selden Society, 109, 110; London, 1993–4).

Reports of Sir John Spelman, ed. J.H. Baker, 2 vols. (Selden Society, 93, 94; London, 1976–7).

Robertson, Joseph (ed.), *Inventaires de la royne Descosse douairiere de France. Catalogues of the jewels, dresses, furniture, books, and paintings of Mary Queen of Scots. 1556–1569* (Bannatyne Club, 111; Edinburgh, 1863).

St German's doctor and student, ed. T.F.T. Plucknett and J.L. Barton (Selden Society, 91; London, 1974).

Sharp, Cuthbert (ed.), *Memorials of the rebellion of 1569* (London, 1840).

Shirley, Rodney W. (ed.), *Early printed maps of the British Isles. A bibliography 1477–1650* (London and New York, 1980).

A short-title catalogue of books printed in England, Scotland, & Ireland and of English books printed abroad 1475–1640, ed. A.W. Pollard and G.R. Redgrave (London, 1926).

A short-title catalogue of books printed in England, Scotland, & Ireland and of English books printed abroad 1475–1640, ed. W.A. Jackson, F.S. Ferguson, and Katharine F. Pantzer, 3 vols. (London, 1986–91).

R.A. Skelton and John Summerson, *A description of maps and architectural drawings in the collection made by William Cecil first Baron Burghley now at Hatfield House* (Roxburghe Club; Oxford, 1971).

Smith, Alan G.R. (ed.), *The anonymous life of William Cecil, Lord Burghley* (Lewiston, Queenston, and Lampeter, 1990).

Smith, Sir Thomas, *De republica Anglorum*, ed. Mary Dewar (Cambridge, 1982).

Starkey, Thomas, *A dialogue between Pole and Lupset*, ed. T.F. Mayer (Camden Society, fourth series, 37; London, 1989).

Statutes of the realm, ed. A. Luders, T.E. Tomlins, J. Raithby *et al.*, 11 vols. (London, 1810–28).

Stern, Virginia F., *Gabriel Harvey. His life, marginalia and library* (Oxford, 1979).

Stevenson, Joseph (ed.), *Selections from unpublished manuscripts in the College of Arms and the British Museum illustrating the reign of Mary Queen of Scotland 1543–1568* (Maitland Club, 41; Glasgow, 1837).

Stones, E.L.G. (ed.), *Anglo-Scottish relations 1174–1328. Some selected documents* (London, 1965).

Strype, John, *The life of the learned Sir Thomas Smith, Kt. DCL Principal Secretary of State to King Edward the Sixth, and Queen Elizabeth* (Oxford, 1820).

The life of the learned Sir John Cheke, Kt. First instructor, afterwards Secretary of State, to King Edward VI . . . (Oxford, 1821).

(ed.), *Annals of the reformation and establishment of religion, and other various occurrences in the church of England . . .*, 3 vols. (London, 1725–7).

Tanner, J.R. (ed.), *Tudor constitutional documents A.D. 1485–1603 with an historical commentary* (Cambridge, 1940 edn).

Tytler, Patrick Fraser (ed.), *England under the reigns of Edward VI and Mary . . .*, 2 vols. (London, 1839).

Whetstone, George, *The English myrror. A regard wherein al estates may behold the conquests of envy . . .* (STC 25336; London, 1586).

Wilson, Thomas, *The arte of rhetorique, for the use of all suche as are studious of eloquence . . .* (STC 25799; London, 1554).

SECONDARY SOURCES

Adair, E.R., 'The Privy Council Registers', *English Historical Review*, 30 (1915), 698–704.

'The rough copies of the Privy Council Register', *English Historical Review*, 38 (1923), 410–22.

Adams, Simon, 'Faction, clientage and party: English politics, 1550–1603', *History Today*, 32 (1982), 33–9.

'Eliza enthroned? The court and its politics', in Haigh (ed.), *Reign of Elizabeth I*, pp. 55–77.

'The release of Lord Darnley and the failure of the amity', *Innes Review*, 38 (1987), 123–53.

'The Lauderdale papers 1561–1570: the Maitland of Lethington state papers and the Leicester correspondence', *Scottish Historical Review*, 67 (1988), 28–55.

'The Dudley clientele and the House of Commons, 1559–1586', *Parliamentary History*, 8 (1989), 216–39.

'Favourites and factions at the Elizabethan court', in Asch and Birke (eds.), *Princes, patronage, and the nobility*, pp. 265–87.
'The Dudley clientele, 1553–1563', in Bernard (ed.), *Tudor nobility*, pp. 241–65.
'The papers of Robert Dudley, earl of Leicester I. The Browne-Evelyn collection', *Archives*, 20 (1992), 63–85.
'The papers of Robert Dudley, earl of Leicester II. The Atye-Cotton collection', *Archives*, 20 (1993), 131–44.
'The patronage of the crown in Elizabethan politics: the 1590s in perspective', in Guy (ed.), *Reign of Elizabeth I*, pp. 20–45.
Adamson, J.S.A., 'The baronial context of the English civil war', *Transactions of the Royal Historical Society*, fifth series, 40 (1990), 93–120.
Alford, Stephen, 'Reassessing William Cecil in the 1560s', in Guy (ed.), *Tudor monarchy*, pp. 233–53.
Alsop, J.D., 'Parliament and taxation', in Dean and Jones (eds.), *Parliaments of Elizabethan England*, pp. 91–116.
'Reinterpreting the Elizabethan Commons: the parliamentary session of 1566', *Journal of British Studies*, 29 (1990), 216–40.
Asch, Ronald G., and Birke, Adolf M. (eds.), *Princes, patronage, and the nobility. The court at the beginning of the modern age c. 1450–1650* (Oxford, 1991).
Axton, Marie, 'Robert Dudley and the Inner Temple revels', *Historical Journal*, 13 (1970), 365–78.
The Queen's two bodies. Drama and the Elizabethan succession (London, 1977).
'The Tudor mask and Elizabethan court drama', in Axton and Williams (eds.), *English drama*, pp. 24–47.
Axton, Marie, and Williams, Raymond (eds.), *English drama: forms and development* (Cambridge, 1977).
Ball, Terence, Farr, James, and Hanson, Russell L. (eds.), *Political innovation and conceptual change* (Cambridge, 1989).
Barber, Peter, 'The minister puts his mind on the map', *British Museum Society Bulletin*, 43 (1983), 18–19.
'A Tudor mystery. Laurence Nowell's map of England and Ireland', *Map Collector*, 22 (1983), 16–21.
Barnett, Richard C., *Place, profit, and power. A study of the servants of William Cecil, Elizabethan statesman* (Chapel Hill, 1969).
Beddard, Robert, *A kingdom without a king. The journal of the provisional government in the revolution of 1688* (Oxford, 1988).
Bernard, G.W. (ed.), *The Tudor nobility* (Manchester and New York, 1992).
Bindoff, S.T., Hurstfield, J., and Williams, C.H. (eds.), *Elizabethan government and society* (London, 1961).
Black, J.B., *The reign of Elizabeth 1558–1603* (Oxford, 1959 edn.).
Bolgar, R.R. (ed.), *Classical influences on European culture A.D. 1500–1700* (Cambridge, 1976).
Bradshaw, Brendan, 'The Tudor reformation and revolution in Wales and Ireland: the origins of the British problem', in Bradshaw and Morrill (eds.), *British problem*, pp. 39–65.
Bradshaw, Brendan, and Morrill, John (eds.), *The British problem, c. 1534–1707. State formation in the Atlantic archipelago* (Basingstoke and London, 1996).
Brady, Ciaran, 'Court, castle and country: the framework of government in Tudor Ireland', in Brady and Gillespie (eds.), *Natives and newcomers*, pp. 22–49.

The chief governors. The rise and fall of reform government in Tudor Ireland 1536–1588 (Cambridge, 1994).

'England's defence and Ireland's reform: the dilemma of the Irish viceroys, 1541–1641', in Bradshaw and Morrill (eds.), *British problem*, pp. 89–117.

Brady, Ciaran, and Gillespie, Raymond (eds.), *Natives and newcomers. Essays on the making of Irish colonial society 1534–1641* (Dublin, 1986).

Bromley, J.S., and Kossmann, E.H. (eds.), *Britain and the Netherlands: V, Some political mythologies* (The Hague, 1975).

Burns, J.H. (ed.), *The Cambridge history of medieval political thought c. 350–c, 1450* (Cambridge, 1988)

The Cambridge history of political thought 1450–1700 (Cambridge, 1991).

Chambers, E.K., *The Elizabethan stage*, 4 vols. (Oxford, 1923).

Christian, Margaret, 'Elizabeth's preachers and the government of women. Defining and correcting a queen', *Sixteenth Century Journal*, 24 (1993), 561–76.

Coleman, Christopher, and Starkey, David (eds.), *Revolution reassessed. Revisions in the history of Tudor government and administration* (Oxford, 1986).

Collinson, Patrick, 'If Constantine, then also Theodosius: St Ambrose and the integrity of the Elizabethan *ecclesia anglicana*', *Journal of Ecclesiastical History*, 30 (1979), 205–29.

'Sir Nicholas Bacon and the Elizabethan *via media*', *Historical Journal*, 23 (1980), 255–73.

Elizabethan essays (London and Rio Grande, 1994).

'*De republica Anglorum*: or, history with the politics put back', in his *Elizabethan essays*, pp. 1–27.

'The monarchical republic of Queen Elizabeth I', in his *Elizabethan essays*, pp. 31–57.

'Puritans, men of business and Elizabethan parliaments', in his *Elizabethan essays*, pp. 59–86.

'Windows in a woman's soul: questions about the religion of Queen Elizabeth I', in his *Elizabethan essays*, pp. 87–118.

'The Elizabethan exclusion crisis and the Elizabethan polity', *Proceedings of the British Academy*, 84 (1995), 51–92.

Cressy, David, 'Binding the nation: the bonds of association, 1584 and 1696', in Guth and McKenna (eds.), *Tudor rule and revolution*, pp. 217–34.

Cross, Claire, Loades, David, and Scarisbrick, J.J. (eds.), *Law and government under the Tudors* (Cambridge, 1988).

Dawson, Jane E.A., 'Mary Queen of Scots, Lord Darnley, and Anglo-Scottish relations in 1565', *International History Review*, 8 (1986), 1–24.

'Two kingdoms or three? Ireland in Anglo-Scottish relations in the middle of the sixteenth century', in Mason (ed.), *Scotland and England*, pp. 113–38.

'William Cecil and the British dimension of early Elizabethan foreign policy', *History*, 74 (1989), 196–216.

'Revolutionary conclusions: the case of the Marian exiles', *History of Political Thought*, 11 (1990), 257–72.

'Resistance and revolution in sixteenth-century thought: the case of Christopher Goodman', in Van den Berg and Hoftijzer (eds.), *Church, change and revolution*, pp. 69–79.

'Anglo-Scottish Protestant culture and integration in sixteenth-century Britain', in Ellis and Barber (eds.), *Conquest and union*, pp. 87–114.

Dean, D.M., and Jones, N.L. (eds.), *The parliaments of Elizabethan England* (Oxford and Cambridge, Massachusetts, 1990).

Dewar, Mary, *Sir Thomas Smith. A Tudor intellectual in office* (London, 1964).

Donaldson, Gordon, *The first trial of Mary, Queen of Scots* (London, 1969).

All the Queen's men. Power and politics in Mary Stewart's Scotland (London, 1983).

Scottish church history (Edinburgh, 1985).

'"The example of Denmark" in the Scottish reformation', in his *Scottish church history*, pp. 60–70.

Doran, Susan, 'Religion and politics at the court of Elizabeth I: the Habsburg marriage negotiations of 1559–1567', *English Historical Review*, 104 (1989), 908–26.

'Juno versus Diana: the treatment of Elizabeth I's marriage in plays and entertainments, 1561–1581', *Historical Journal*, 38 (1995), 257–74.

Monarchy and matrimony. The courtships of Elizabeth I (London and New York, 1996).

Dwyer, John, Mason, Roger A., and Murdoch, Alexander (eds.), *New perspectives on the politics and culture of early modern Scotland* (Edinburgh, 1982).

Eire, Carlos M.N., 'Prelude to sedition? Calvin's attack on Nicodemism and religious compromise', *Archiv für Reformationsgeschichte*, 76 (1985), 120–45.

Ellis, Steven G., *Tudor Ireland. Crown, community and the conflict of cultures, 1470–1603* (London and New York, 1985).

Ellis, Steven G. and Barber, Sarah (eds.), *Conquest and union. Fashioning a British state, 1485–1725* (London and New York, 1995).

Elton, G.R., *The Tudor revolution in government* (London, 1953).

Studies in Tudor and Stuart politics and government, 4 vols. (Cambridge, 1974–92).

'The political creed of Thomas Cromwell', in his *Studies*, II, pp. 215–35.

'Tudor government: the points of contact I. Parliament', in his *Studies*, III, pp. 3–21.

'Tudor government: the points of contact II. The council', in his *Studies*, III, pp. 21–38.

'Tudor government: the points of contact III. The court', in his *Studies*, III, pp. 38–57.

'The state: government and politics under Elizabeth and James', in his *Studies*, IV, pp. 3–36.

'Parliament', in Haigh (ed.), *Reign of Elizabeth*, pp. 79–100.

The parliament of England 1559–1581 (Cambridge, 1986).

Emmison, F.G., *Tudor secretary. Sir William Petre at court and home* (London, 1961).

Evans, Florence M. Greir, *The Principal Secretary of State. A survey of the office from 1558 to 1680* (Manchester, London, and New York, 1923).

Fideler, Paul A., and Mayer, T.F. (eds.), *Political thought and the Tudor commonwealth. Deep structure, discourse and disguise* (London and New York, 1992).

Firth, C.H., '"The British empire"', *Scottish Historical Review*, 15 (1918), 185–9.

Fletcher, Anthony, *Tudor rebellions* (London, 1973 edn).

Fletcher, Anthony, and Roberts, Peter (eds.), *Religion, culture and society in early modern Britain* (Cambridge, 1994).

Ford, Philip J., *George Buchanan. Prince of poets* (Aberdeen, 1982).

Fox, Alistair, and Guy, John, *Reassessing the Henrician age. Humanism, politics and reform 1500–1550* (Oxford and New York, 1986).

Froude, James Anthony, *History of England from the fall of Wolsey to the death of Elizabeth*, 12 vols. (London, 1856–70).

Fryde, E.B., and Miller, Edward (eds.), *Historical studies of the English parliament*, 2 vols. (Cambridge, 1970).

Galloway, Bruce, *The union of England and Scotland 1603–1608* (Edinburgh, 1986).

Gleason, J.H., *The justices of the peace in England 1558 to 1640. A later eirenarcha* (Oxford, 1969).

Grant, Alexander, and Stringer, Keith J. (eds.), *Uniting the kingdom? The making of British history* (London and New York, 1995).

Graves, M.A.R., 'Thomas Norton the parliament man: an Elizabethan MP, 1559–1581', *Historical Journal*, 23 (1980), 17–35.

'The management of the Elizabethan House of Commons: the Council's "men-of-business"', *Parliamentary History*, 2 (1983), 11–38.

Thomas Norton. The parliament man (Oxford and Cambridge, Massachusetts, 1994).

Griffiths, Ralph A., *The reign of King Henry VI. The exercise of royal authority, 1422–1461* (London and Tonbridge, 1981).

Griffiths, Ralph A., and Sherborne, James (eds.), *Kings and nobles in the later middle ages* (Gloucester and New York, 1986).

Guth, Delloyd J., and McKenna, John W. (eds.), *Tudor rule and revolution* (Cambridge, 1982).

Guy, J.A., *The public career of Sir Thomas More* (New Haven and London, 1980).

'Law, faction, and parliament in the sixteenth century', *Historical Journal*, 28 (1985), 441–53.

'The French king's council, 1483–1526', in Griffiths and Sherborne (eds.), *Kings and nobles*, pp. 274–94.

'The king's council and political participation', in Fox and Guy, *Henrician age*, pp. 121–47.

'The Privy Council: revolution or evolution?', in Coleman and Starkey (eds.), *Revolution reassessed*, pp. 59–85.

'Thomas Cromwell and the intellectual origins of the Henrician revolution', in Fox and Guy, *Henrician age*, pp. 151–78.

Tudor England (Oxford, 1988).

'The "imperial crown" and the liberty of the subject: the English constitution from Magna Carta to the Bill of Rights', in Kunze and Brautigam (eds.), *Court, country and culture*, pp. 65–87.

'The Henrician age', in Pocock (ed.), *British political thought*, pp. 13–46.

'The Tudor theory of "imperial" kingship', *History Review*, 17 (1993), 12–16.

'The 1590s: the second reign of Elizabeth I?', in Guy (ed.), *Reign of Elizabeth I*, pp. 1–19.

'The Elizabethan establishment and the ecclesiastical polity', in Guy (ed.), *Reign of Elizabeth I*, pp. 126–49.

'The rhetoric of counsel in early modern England', in Hoak (ed.), *Tudor political culture*, pp. 292–310.

'Thomas Wolsey, Thomas Cromwell and the reform of Henrician government', in MacCulloch (ed.), *Reign of Henry VIII*, pp. 35–57.

'Tudor monarchy and its critiques', in Guy (ed.), *Tudor monarchy*, pp. 79–109.

(ed.), *The reign of Elizabeth I. Court and culture in the last decade* (Cambridge, 1995).

(ed.), *The Tudor monarchy* (London, 1997).

Haigh, Christopher, *Elizabeth I* (Harlow, 1988).

Haigh, Christopher (ed.), *The reign of Elizabeth I* (London, 1984).

Harcourt, L.W. Vernon, *His Grace the Steward and trial of peers. A novel inquiry into a special branch of constitutional government* (London, 1907).

Hartley, T.E., *Elizabeth's parliaments. Queen, Lords and Commons 1559–1601* (Manchester and New York, 1992).

Harvey, P.D.A., *Maps in Tudor England* (London, 1993).

Head, David M., 'Henry VIII's Scottish policy: a reassessment', *Scottish Historical Review*, 61 (1982), 1–24.

Hoak, Dale, *The King's Council in the reign of Edward VI* (Cambridge, 1976).

'Rehabilitating the duke of Northumberland: politics and political control, 1549–53', in Loach and Tittler (eds.), *Mid-Tudor polity*, pp. 29–51.

'The King's privy chamber, 1547–1553', in Guth and McKenna (eds.), *Tudor rule and revolution*, pp. 87–108.

'The iconography of the crown imperial', in Hoak (ed.), *Tudor political culture*, pp. 54–103.

(ed.), *Tudor political culture* (Cambridge, 1995).

Holmes, P.J., 'The great council in the reign of Henry VII', *English Historical Review*, 101 (1986), 840–62.

'Mary Stewart in England', *Innes Review*, 38 (1987), 195–218.

'The last Tudor great councils', *Historical Journal*, 33 (1990), 1–22.

Hotle, C. Patrick, *Thorns and thistles. Diplomacy between Henry VIII and James V 1528–1542* (Lanham, New York, and London, 1996).

Houlbrooke, R.A., 'Henry VIII's wills: a comment', *Historical Journal*, 37 (1994), 891–9.

Howell, W.S., 'Poetics, rhetoric, and logic in Renaissance criticism', in Bolgar (ed.), *Classical influences*, pp. 155–62.

Hudson, Winthrop S., *The Cambridge connection and the Elizabethan settlement of 1559* (Durham, North Carolina, 1980).

Hume, Martin, *The great Lord Burghley. A study in Elizabethan statecraft* (London, 1898).

Hurstfield, Joel, 'William Cecil: minister to Elizabeth I', *History Today*, 6 (1956), 791–9.

'Queen and state: the emergence of an Elizabethan myth', in Bromley and Kossman (eds.), *Britain and the Netherlands*, pp. 58–77.

Freedom, corruption and government in Elizabethan England (London, 1973).

'Church and state, 1558–1612: the task of the Cecils', in his *Freedom, corruption and government*, pp. 79–103.

Ives, E.W., *Faction in Tudor England* (Historical Association Appreciations in History, 6; London, 1979).

'Henry VIII's will – a forensic conundrum', *Historical Journal*, 35 (1992), 779–804.

'Henry VIII's will: the protectorate provisions of 1546–7', *Historical Journal*, 37 (1994), 901–14.

Ives, E.W., Knecht, R.J., and Scarisbrick, J.J. (eds.), *Wealth and power in Tudor England* (London, 1978).

James, M.E., 'The concept of order and the northern rising 1569', *Past and Present*, no. 60 (1973), 49–83.

Jardine, L., 'Humanism and dialectic in sixteenth-century Cambridge: a preliminary investigation', in Bolgar (ed.), *Classical influences*, pp. 141–54.

Jardine, Lisa, and Grafton, Anthony, '"Studied for action": how Gabriel Harvey read his Livy', *Past and Present*, no. 129 (1990), 30–78.

Jones, Norman L., *Faith by statute. Parliament and the settlement of religion 1559* (London, 1982).

'Elizabeth's first year: the conception and birth of the Elizabethan political world', in Haigh (ed.), *Reign of Elizabeth I*, pp. 27–53.

'Parliament and the governance of Elizabethan England: a review', *Albion*, 19 (1987), 327–46.

'William Cecil and the making of economic policy in the 1560s and early 1570s', in Fideler and Mayer (eds.), *Tudor commonwealth*, pp. 169–93.

The birth of the Elizabethan age. England in the 1560s (Oxford and Cambridge, Massachusetts, 1993).

Jordan, Constance, 'Woman's rule in sixteenth-century British political thought', *Renaissance Quarterly*, 40 (1987), 421–51.

Kantorowicz, Ernst H., *The King's two bodies. A study in medieval political theology* (Princeton, 1957).

Kelley, Donald R., 'Civil science in the Renaissance: jurisprudence Italian style', *Historical Journal*, 22 (1979), 777–94.

'Ideas of resistance before Elizabeth', in Schochet (ed.), *Law, literature, and the settlement of regimes*, pp. 5–28.

'*Jurisconsultus perfectus*: the lawyer as Renaissance man', in Schochet (ed.), *Law, literature, and the settlement of regimes*, pp. 143–70.

'Elizabethan political thought', in Pocock (ed.), *British political thought*, pp. 47–79.

Kouri, E.I., *England and the attempts to form a Protestant alliance in the late 1560s: a case study in European diplomacy* (Helsinki, 1981).

'For true faith or national interest? Queen Elizabeth I and the Protestant powers', in Kouri and Scott (eds.), *Politics and society*, pp. 411–36.

Kouri, E.I., and Scott, Tom (eds.), *Politics and society in reformation Europe* (Basingstoke and London, 1987).

Kunze, Bonnelyn Young, and Brautigam, Dwight D. (eds.), *Court, country and culture* (New York, 1992).

Lake, Peter, 'The significance of the Elizabethan identification of the pope as antichrist', *Journal of Ecclesiastical History*, 31 (1980), 161–78.

Lee, Maurice, *James Stewart, earl of Moray. A political study of the reformation in Scotland* (New York, 1953).

Lehmberg, Stanford E., *Sir Walter Mildmay and Tudor government* (Austin, Texas, 1964).

'The role of parliament in early modern England – a reconsideration', in *The Swedish Riksdag in an international perspective* (Stockholm, 1989), pp. 75–87.

'Sir Geoffrey Elton as a parliamentary historian: an appreciation', *Parliamentary History*, 14 (1995), 257–61.

Levack, Brian P., *The formation of the British state* (Oxford, 1987).

Levine, Mortimer, *The early Elizabethan succession question 1558–1568* (Stanford, 1966).

Loach, Jennifer, *Parliament and the crown in the reign of Mary Tudor* (Oxford, 1986).

Parliament under the Tudors (Oxford, 1991).

Loach, Jennifer, and Tittler, Robert (eds.), *The mid-Tudor polity, c. 1540–1560* (London, 1980).

Lockie, D. McN., 'The political career of the bishop of Ross, 1568–80', *University of Birmingham Historical Journal*, 4 (1953–4), 98–145.

Lynch, Michael, 'Queen Mary's triumph: the baptismal celebrations at Stirling in December 1566', *Scottish Historical Review*, 69 (1990), 1–21.

[Macauley, Thomas Babington,] 'Nares' *Memoirs of Lord Burghley*', *Edinburgh Review*, 55 (1832), 271–96.

MacCaffrey, Wallace T., 'Place and patronage in Elizabethan politics', in Bindoff, Hurstfield, and Williams (ed.), *Elizabethan government and society*, pp. 95–126.

'Elizabethan politics: the first decade, 1558–1568', *Past and Present*, no. 24 (1963), 25–42.

The shaping of the Elizabethan regime (London, 1969).

'Parliament: the Elizabethan experience', in Guth and McKenna (eds.), *Tudor rule and revolution*, pp. 127–47.

'Patronage and politics under the Tudors', in Peck (ed.), *Jacobean court*, pp. 21–35.

Elizabeth I (London, 1993).

'The Newhaven expedition, 1562–3', *Historical Journal*, 40 (1997), 1–21.

MacCulloch, Diarmaid (ed.), *The reign of Henry VIII. Politics, policy and piety* (Basingstoke and London, 1995).

MacDougall, Norman (ed.), *Church, politics and society. Scotland 1408–1929* (Edinburgh, 1983).

McFarlane, I.D., 'George Buchanan and European humanism', *Yearbook of English Studies*, 15 (1985), 33–47.

Maitland, F.W., 'Elizabethan gleanings', *English Historical Review*, 15 (1900), 531.

Mason, Roger A., '*Rex stoicus*: George Buchanan, James VI and the Scottish polity', in Dwyer, Mason, and Murdoch (eds.), *New perspectives*, pp. 9–33.

'Covenant and commonweal: the language of politics in reformation Scotland', in MacDougall (ed.), *Church, politics and society*, pp. 97–126.

'Scotching the Brut: politics, history and national myth in sixteenth-century Britain', in Mason (ed.), *Scotland and England*, pp. 60–84.

'Imagining Scotland: Scottish political thought and the problem of Britain 1560–1650', in Mason (ed.), *Scots and Britons*, pp. 3–13.

'The Scottish reformation and the origins of Anglo-British imperialism', in Mason (ed.), *Scots and Britons*, pp. 161–86.

(ed.), *Scotland and England 1286–1815* (Edinburgh, 1987).

(ed.), *Scots and Britons. Scottish political thought and the union of 1603* (Cambridge, 1994).

Mendle, Michael, *Dangerous positions. Mixed government, the estates of the realm, and the making of the Answer to the xix propositions* (Alabama, 1985).

Merriman, M.H., 'The assured Scots. Scottish collaborators with England during the Rough Wooing', *Scottish Historical Review*, 47 (1968), 10–34.

'War and propaganda during the "Rough Wooing"', *Scottish Tradition*, 9–10 (1979–80), 20–30.

'Stewarts and Tudors in the mid-sixteenth century', in Grant and Stringer (eds.), *Uniting the kingdom?*, pp. 111–22.

Miller, Helen, 'Henry VIII's unwritten will: grants of land and honours in 1547', in Ives, Knecht, and Scarisbrick (eds.), *Wealth and power*, pp. 87–105.

Moore Smith, G.C. (ed.), *Gabriel Harvey's marginalia* (Stratford, 1913).

Morrill, John, 'A British patriarchy? Ecclesiastical imperialism under the early Stuarts', in Fletcher and Roberts (eds.), *Religion, culture and society*, pp. 209–37.

Murphy, John, 'The illusion of decline: the privy chamber, 1547–1558', in Starkey (ed.), *English court*, pp. 119–46.

Nares, Edward, *Memoirs of the life and administration of the Right Honourable William Cecil, Lord Burghley . . .*, 3 vols. (London, 1828–31).

Neale, J.E., 'The Commons' Journals of the Tudor period', *Transactions of the Royal Historical Society*, fourth series, 3 (1920), 136–70.

'Parliament and the succession question in 1562/3 and 1566', *English Historical Review*, 36 (1921), 497–520.

'The Commons' privilege of free speech in parliament', in Seton-Watson (ed.), *Tudor studies*, pp. 257–86.

Queen Elizabeth (London, 1938 edn).

Elizabeth I and her parliaments 1559–1601, 2 vols. (London, 1953, 1957).

Essays in Elizabethan history (London, 1958).

'The diplomatic envoy', in his *Essays in Elizabethan history*, pp. 125–45.

Nicholson, Graham, 'The act of appeals and the English reformation', in Cross, Loades, and Scarisbrick (eds.), *Law and government*, pp. 19–30.

Peck, Linda Levy, *Northampton. Patronage and policy at the court of James I* (London, Boston, and Sydney, 1982).

'Peers, patronage and the politics of history', in Guy (ed.), *Reign of Elizabeth I*, pp. 87–108.

(ed.), *The mental world of the Jacobean court* (Cambridge, 1991).

Peltonen, Markku, *Classical humanism and republicanism in English political thought 1570–1640* (Cambridge, 1995).

Pettegree, Andrew, 'Elizabethan foreign policy', *Historical Journal*, 31 (1988), 965–72.

Marian Protestantism. Six studies (Aldershot and Brookfield, Vermont, 1996).

Pocock, J.G.A., *The Machiavellian moment. Florentine political thought and the Atlantic republican tradition* (Princeton, 1975).

(ed.) *The varieties of British political thought, 1500–1800* (Cambridge, 1993).

Pollard, A.F., 'The authenticity of the "Lords' Journals" in the sixteenth century', *Transactions of the Royal Historical Society*, third series, 8 (1914), 17–39.

The evolution of parliament (London, 1920).

'Queen Elizabeth's under-clerks and their Commons' journals', *Bulletin of the Institute of Historical Research*, 17 (1939–40), 1–12.

'A protean clerk of the Commons', *Bulletin of the Institute of Historical Research*, 18 (1940–1), 49–51.

Pollitt, R., 'An "old practizer" at bay: Thomas Bishop and the northern rebellion', *Northern History*, 16 (1980), 59–84.

Procopé, John, 'Greek and Roman political theory', in Burns (ed.), *Medieval political thought*, pp. 21–36.

Pulman, Michael Barraclough, *The Elizabethan Privy Council in the fifteen-seventies* (Berkeley, Los Angeles, and London, 1971).

Read, Conyers, 'Factions in the English Privy Council under Elizabeth', *American Historical Association Report*, 1 (1911), 109–19.

'Walsingham and Burghley in Queen Elizabeth's Privy Council', *English Historical Review*, 28 (1913), 34–58.

Mr Secretary Walsingham and the policy of Queen Elizabeth, 3 vols. (Oxford, 1925).

'Queen Elizabeth's seizure of the duke of Alva's pay-ships', *Journal of Modern History*, 5 (1933), 443–64.

Mr Secretary Cecil and Queen Elizabeth (London, 1955).

'William Cecil and Elizabethan public relations', in Bindoff, Hurstfield, and Williams (eds.), *Elizabethan government and society*, pp. 21–55.

Reid, R.R., 'The Rebellion of the Earls, 1569', *Transactions of the Royal Historical Society*, new series, 10 (1906), 171–203.

The king's council in the north (London, 1921).

Richardson, H.G., and Sayles, G.O., *Parliaments and great councils in medieval England* (London, 1961).

Rodríguez-Salgado, M.J., *The changing face of empire. Charles V, Philip II and Habsburg authority, 1551–1559* (Cambridge, 1990 edn).

Rodríguez-Salgado, M.J., and Adams, Simon (eds.), 'The count of Feria's dispatch to Philip II of 14 November 1558', *Camden Miscellany XXVIII* (Camden Society, fourth series, 29; London, 1984), pp. 302–44.

Roskell, J.S., *Parliament and politics in late medieval England*, 3 vols. (London, 1981–3).

Ryan, Lawrence V., *Roger Ascham* (Stanford and London, 1963).

Sacks, David Harris, 'Private profit and public good: the problem of the state in Elizabethan theory and practice', in Schochet (ed.), *Law, literature, and the settlement of regimes*, pp. 121–42.

'The countervailing of benefits: monopoly, liberty, and benevolence in Elizabethan England', in Hoak (ed.), *Tudor political culture*, pp. 272–91.

Sayles, G.O., *The functions of the medieval parliament of England* (London and Ronceverte, 1988).

Schochet, Gordon J. (ed.), *Law, literature, and the settlement of regimes* (Folger Institute Center for the History of British Political Thought Proceedings, 2; Washington, D.C., 1990).

Schoeck, R.J., 'Rhetoric and law in sixteenth-century England', *Studies in Philology*, 50 (1953), 110–27.

Schreiber, Roy E., *The political career of Sir Robert Naunton 1589–1635* (London, 1981).

Seton-Watson, R.W. (ed.), *Tudor studies* (London, 1924).

Sharpe, Kevin, *Sir Robert Cotton 1586–1631. History and politics in early modern England* (Oxford, 1979).

Shaw, Barry, 'Thomas Norton's "devices" for a godly realm: an Elizabethan vision for the future', *Sixteenth Century Journal*, 22 (1991), 495–509.

Sherman, William H., *John Dee. The politics of reading and writing in the English Renaissance* (Amherst, Massachusetts, 1995).

Skinner, Quentin, *The foundations of modern political thought*, 2 vols. (Cambridge, 1978).

'The state', in Ball, Farr, and Hanson (eds.), *Political innovation*, pp. 90–131.

Reason and rhetoric in the philosophy of Hobbes (Cambridge, 1996).

Starkey, David, 'Stewart serendipity: a missing text of the *Modus tenendi parliamentum*', *Fenway Court* (1986), 38–51.

(ed.), *The English court: from the Wars of the Roses to the Civil War* (London and New York, 1987).

Stones, E.L.G., 'The appeal to history in Anglo-Scottish relations between 1291 and 1401', *Archives*, 9 (1969), 11–21, 79–83.

Thorp, Malcolm R., 'Catholic conspiracy in early Elizabethan foreign policy', *Sixteenth Century Journal*, 15 (1984), 431–48.

'William Cecil and the antichrist. A study in anti-Catholic ideology', in Thorp and Slavin (eds.), *Politics, religion, and diplomacy*, pp. 289–304.

Thorp, Malcolm R., and Slavin, Arthur J. (eds.), *Politics, religion, and diplomacy in early modern Europe* (Sixteenth Century Essays and Studies, 27; Missouri, 1994).

Tittler, Robert, *Nicholas Bacon. The making of a Tudor statesman* (London, 1976).

Ullmann, Walter, *Principles of government and politics in the middle ages* (London, 1961).

'"This realm of England is an empire"', *Journal of Ecclesiastical History*, 30 (1979), 175–203.

Van den Berg, J., and Hoftijzer, P.G. (eds.), *Church, change and revolution. Transactions of the fourth Anglo-Dutch church history colloquium* (Publications of the Sir Thomas Browne Institute, new series, 12; Leiden, 1991).

Viroli, Maurizio, *From politics to reason of state. The acquisition and transformation of the language of politics 1250–1600* (Cambridge, 1992).

Ward, Leslie, 'The Treason Act of 1563: a study of the enforcement of anti-Catholic legislation', *Parliamentary History*, 8 (1989), 289–308.

Watts, John, *Henry VI and the politics of kingship* (Cambridge, 1996).

Wernham, R.B., *The making of Elizabethan foreign policy, 1558–1603* (Berkeley, Los Angeles, and London, 1980).

Wiener, Carol Z., 'This beleaguered isle. A study of Elizabethan and early Jacobean anti-Catholicism', *Past and Present*, no. 51 (1971), 27–62.

Williams, C.H., 'In search of the Queen', in Bindoff, Hurstfield, and Williams (eds.), *Elizabethan government and society*, pp. 1–20.

Williams, Glanmor, *The Reformation in Wales* (Bangor, 1991).

Williams, Penry, *The Tudor regime* (Oxford, 1979).

'Court and polity under Elizabeth I', *Bulletin of the John Rylands University Library of Manchester*, 65 (1982–3), 259–86.

The later Tudors. England 1547–1603 (Oxford, 1995).

Worden, Blair, *The sound of virtue. Philip Sidney's* Arcadia *and Elizabethan politics* (New Haven and London, 1996).

Wormald, Jenny, *Mary Queen of Scots. A study in failure* (London, 1991 edn).

'The creation of Britain: multiple kingdoms or core and colonies?', *Transactions of the Royal Historical Society*, sixth series, 2 (1992), 175–94.

Wright, Pam, 'A change in direction: the ramifications of a female household, 1558–1603', in Starkey (ed.), *English court*, pp. 147–72.

Yates, Frances A., *Astraea. The imperial theme in the sixteenth century* (Harmondsworth, 1977).

Zebrowski, Martha K., 'The corruption of politics and the dignity of human nature: the critical and constructive radicalism of James Burgh', *Enlightenment and Dissent*, 10 (1991), 78–103.

UNPUBLISHED THESES

Alford, Stephen, 'William Cecil and the British succession crisis of the 1560s', PhD thesis, University of St Andrews (1996).

Cramsie, John R., 'Crown finance and governance under James I: projects, political culture, and policymaking 1603–1625', PhD thesis, University of St Andrews (1997).

Hampson, James E., 'Richard Cosin and the rehabilitation of the clerical estate in late Elizabethan England', PhD thesis, University of St Andrews (1997).

Lock, Julian, ' "Strange usurped potentates": Elizabeth I, the papacy and the Indian summer of the medieval deposing power', DPhil thesis, University of Oxford (1992).

Loughlin, Mark, 'The career of Maitland of Lethington *c.* 1526–1573', PhD thesis, University of Edinburgh (1991).

Morrison, G.R., 'The land, family, and domestic following of William Cecil, Lord Burghley *c.* 1550–1598', DPhil thesis, University of Oxford (1990).

Nicholson, G.D., 'The nature and function of historical argument in the Henrician reformation', PhD thesis, University of Cambridge (1977).

Retamal Favereau, Julio, 'Anglo-Spanish relations 1566–72: the mission of Don Guerau de Spes at London, with a preliminary consideration of that of Mr John Man at Madrid', DPhil thesis, University of Oxford (1972).

Swensen, Patricia Cole, 'Noble hunters of the romish fox: religious reform at the Tudor court, 1543–1564', PhD thesis, University of California Berkeley (1981).

Taylor, Susan E., 'The crown and the north of England, 1559–70: a study of the rebellion of the northern earls, 1569–70, and its causes', PhD thesis, University of Manchester (1981).

INDEX

anti-Catholicism of, 26–8, 53–5, 93–5,
188–9, 209
archive and memoranda, 5–8, 10–14,
18–20, 44, 145, 222
'The booke of the state of the realme',
182–4, 187–8, 198, 220
British political creed, 45–7, 59–63, 70,
181, 183–4, 188–94, 203, 205–6,
216–17
'Clause to have bene inserted in an act
ment for the succession but not passed,
A', 111–19
conciliarism of, 111–19, 210
correspondence of, 12–13
early career, 14, 21, 24–6
education and training, 7, 16–18, 22
Guise, fear of the, 54–5, 72, 94–5, 96, 127,
162, 179, 184, 187
imperial power of the English crown,
39–40, 47, 163–4, 166–7, 169, 207–8
and Ireland, 48–50, 75, 163, 170–1, 220
maps of Ireland and Scotland, 50–1
ministerial service, 6, 42, 69–70
'A necessary consideration of the perillous
state of this tyme', 182–3, 194–8, 220,
221
parliament, concept of, 36, 149–50, 152,
156–7, 208
political creed, 40–2
principal secretaryship, 9–11, 215
providence, sense of, 26–8, 77, 98, 183,
195, 198, 217
relationship with Elizabeth, 4, 37, 41, 145,
157, 212
relationship with the work of the Privy
Council, 32, 66, 145, 213–14
relationship with Robert Dudley, earl of
Leicester, 30, 31, 126, 214
religious views of, 24–6, 181, 216–20
Chaloner, Thomas, 64
Chamberlain, Thomas, 72, 73, 77, 79
Champernowne, Arthur, 188
Charles of Austria, Archduke, 77, 97
Châtelherault, James Hamilton, earl of Arran
and duke of, 74
see also Arran, James Hamilton, earl of
Cheke, John, 16, 21, 24, 25, 133
Cheyney, Thomas, 30
Chichester, John, 149
Chiverton, Henry, 153, 154
Cicero, 8, 16, 20, 21, 22, 41, 116
Clapham, John, 185, 186
Clinton, Lord Edward, 30, 66, 80, 83, 113,
125, 127, 173, 175, 177, 179, 204, 210
Cobham, William Brooke, Lord, 210
Cockburn, James, 172

Condé, prince, 95, 162, 187, 188
Cooke, Anthony, 24
Cordell, William, 143
Cosin, Richard, 38, 42, 210
council
see 'council of estate'; great council; Privy
Council
'council of estate', 33, 39, 112–15, 179
counsel, 7, 32–3, 69, 75, 100–3, 118, 151–2,
207–8
see also parliament; Privy Council
Cranmer, Thomas, 207, 217
Croft, James, 56, 64
Cromwell, Thomas, 42, 207
Cusake, Thomas, 130

Darnley, Henry Stuart, Lord, 120, 124, 131,
135, 140, 159, 163, 166, 169, 173, 191
Cecil's analysis of, 13, 18, 19, 120–1, 217
marriage to Mary Stuart, 120, 123, 126,
131, 142
Davison, William, 215
Day, John, 25, 100
De Guadras, Antonio, 185, 186
Denmark, 55
Protestant church settlement, 58, 219
Denny, Anthony, 118
De Quadra, Bishop, 110
Derby, Edward, earl of, 30, 113, 125, 127,
177, 185
De Spes, Guerau, 185
De Worde, Wynkyn, 100
Drury, William, 202
Dyer, James, 151, 152, 211

Edinburgh, Treaty of (1560), 79, 89, 95,
158
terms of, 83–5
failure to ratify, 86, 87
push for ratification of, 164, 169
Edward VI, 14, 24, 46, 58, 112, 118, 203,
208, 213
Elizabeth I
female rule, 34, 98
governor of the church, 38, 208
imperial monarchy, 38–9, 141, 207–8
indecision, 32, 120, 137
as *lex animata*, 31, 108–9
relationship with Cecil, 4, 37, 40–1, 212
relationship with parliament, 37–8,
143–57
refusal to marry, 31, 88, 98, 145, 148, 152,
158
refusal to settle the succession, 98, 103–4,
145, 148, 152, 158
role in daily government, 32

Cambridge Studies in Early Modern British History

Titles in the series

*Also published as a paperback